SOMETHING ABOUT THE AUTHOR®

Something about
the Author *was named
an "Outstanding
Reference Source,"
the highest honor given
by the American
Library Association
Reference and Adult
Services Division.*

ISSN 0276-816X

something ABOUT THE AUTHOR®

Facts and Pictures about Authors
and Illustrators of Books for Young People

EDITED BY
ALAN HEDBLAD

volume 90

GALE

DETROIT • NEW YORK • TORONTO • LONDON

STAFF

Editor: Alan Hedblad
Managing Editor: Joyce Nakamura
Publisher: Hal May
Contributing Editors: Kevin S. Hile, Thomas F. McMahon
Assistant Editor: Marilyn O'Connell Allen

Sketchwriters/Copyeditors: Linda R. Andres, Shelly Andrews, Joanna Brod,
Sheryl Ciccarelli, Ronie-Richele Garcia-Johnson, Mary Gillis, Janet L. Hile, Laurie Hillstrom,
Motoko Fujishiro Huthwaite, David Johnson, J. Sydney Jones, Susan Reicha,
Gerard J. Senick, Pamela L. Shelton, Diane Telgen, Michaela Swart Wilson, and Kathleen Witman

Research Manager: Victoria B. Cariappa
Project Coordinator: Cheryl L. Warnock
Research Specialist: Jennifer Lund
Research Associates: Tamara C. Nott and Norma Sawaya
Research Assistants: Alfred A. Gardner and Sean R. Smith

Permissions Manager: Marlene S. Hurst
Permissions Specialists: Margaret A. Chamberlain, Maria Franklin, and Kimberly F. Smilay
Permissions Associates: Diane Cooper, Edna Hedblad, Michele Lonoconus, Maureen Puhl,
and Shalice Shah
Permissions Assistants: Sarah Chesney and Jeffrey Hermann

Production Director: Mary Beth Trimper
Production Assistant: Deborah Milliken

Macintosh Artist: Sherrell Hobbs
Image Database Supervisor: Randy Bassett
Imaging Specialists: Mikal Ansari and Robert Duncan
Photography Coordinator: Pamela A. Reed

♾™ This book is printed on acid-free paper that meets the minimum requirements of American National Standard for Information Sciences—Permanence Paper for Printed Library Materials, ANSI Z39.48-1984.

Library of Congress Catalog Card Number 72-27107

ISBN 0-8103-9947-4 ISSN 0276-816X

Printed in the United States of America

10 9 8 7 6 5 4 3 2 1

Contents

Authors in Forthcoming Volumes viii
Introduction ix
Acknowledgments xi

A

Adams, Adrienne 1906- 1

Anderson, Poul (William) 1926- 4

Anderson, Susan 1952- 12

Ayres, Pam 1947- 13

B

Ballouhey, Pierre 1944- 15

Baltazzi, Evan S(erge) 1921- 16

Baron, Kathy 1954- 17

Barton, Byron 1930- 17

Bell, William 1945- 22

Bovaird, Anne E(lizabeth) 1960- 24

Bradley, Marion Zimmer 1930- 25

Bridgers, Sue Ellen 1942- 32

Browne, Vee F(rances) 1956- 36

Buckley, Helen E(lizabeth) 1918- 37

Butenko, Bohdan 1931- 39

C

Cabrera, Marcela 1966- 41

Campbell, Hugh 1930- 42

Carlson, Nancy L(ee) 1953- 43

Carrel, Annette Felder 1929- 46

Chang, Cindy 1968- 47

Chapman, Lee
  See Bradley, Marion Zimmer 25

Chekhonte, Antosha
  See Chekhov, Anton (Pavlovich) 48

Chekhov, Anton (Pavlovich) 1860-1904 48

Christelow, Eileen 1943- 55

Clem, Margaret H(ollingsworth) 1923- 59

Conrad, Pam 1947-1996
  Obituary Notice 60

Cousins, Linda 1946- 60

Cowley, (Cassia) Joy 1936- 61

Craig, A. A.

See Anderson, Poul (William) 4

Curry, Jane L(ouise) 1932- 65

Curtiss, A(rlene) B. 1934- 69

D

Dawson, Imogen (Zoe) 1948- 71

de Groat, Diane 1947- 71

Dexter, John
  See Bradley, Marion Zimmer 25

Driskill, J. Lawrence 1920- 74

Duke, Kate 1956- 76

DuQuette, Keith 1960- 83

E-F

Eller, Scott
  See Holinger, William (Jacques) 126
  and Shepard, Jim 212

El-Moslimany, Ann P(axton) 1937- 84

Forrester, Sandra 1949- 85

Fradin, Dennis Brindell 1945- 86

Fradin, Judith (Bernette) Bloom 1945- 90

Fraser, Wynnette (McFaddin) 1925- 91

Freedman, Jeff 1953- 92

G

Gardner, Miriam
  See Bradley, Marion Zimmer 25

Garfield, Leon 1921-1996
  Obituary Notice 94

George, Sally
  See Orr, Wendy 174

Gerrard, Roy 1935- 94

Gershator, Phillis 1942- 101

Gilbert, Roby Goodale 1966- 103

Glass, Andrew 103

Goldman, Elizabeth 1949- 106

Graves, Valerie
  See Bradley, Marion Zimmer 25

Gray, Luli 1945- 107

Greenwood, Barbara 1940- 108

H

Harrill, Ronald 1950- 111

Harris, Robie H. 1940- 112

Hatch, Lynda S. 1950- 114

Hausman, Gerald 1945- 116

Hausman, Gerry
   See Hausman, Gerald 116

Hazen, Barbara Shook 1930- 119

Heiligman, Deborah 1958- 125

Holinger, William (Jacques) 1944- 126

Hoon, Patricia Easterly 1954- 127

Howard, Norman Barry 1949- 128

Hudson, Margaret
   See Shuter, Jane Margaret 214

I-J

Imai, Miko 1963- 130

Isaacs, Anne 1949- 131

Ives, Morgan
   See Bradley, Marion Zimmer 25

Johns, Janetta
   See Quin-Harkin, Janet 188

Jones, Jennifer (Berry) 1947- 132

K

Kahn, Katherine Janus 1942- 134

Kent, Lisa 1942- 136

Kiesler, Kate (A.) 1971- 137

Kimball, Gayle 1943- 138

Kramer, Remi (Thomas) 1935- 138

L

Lee, Elizabeth Rogers 1940- 141

Lee, Liz
   See Lee, Elizabeth Rogers 141

LeMieux, A(nne) C(onnelly) 1954- 142

Lester, Alison 1952- 145

Lewin, Betsy 1937- 149

Loomans, Diane 1955- 152

Luccarelli, Vincent 1923- 152

Luther, Rebekah (Lyn) S(tiles) 1960- 153

M

Madsen, Susan A(rrington) 1954- 155

Marney, Dean 1952- 156

Marrin, Albert 1936- 157

McDonnell, Flora (Mary) 1963- 162

McLean, Virginia Overton 1946- 163

Mora, Francisco X(avier) 1952- 163

Morrison, Meighan 1966- 164

Moseng, Elisabeth 1967- 165

N

Nally, Susan W. 1947- 167

Newman, Shirlee P(etkin) 1924- 168

Numeroff, Laura Joffe 1953- 170

O

O'Connor, Francine M(arie) 1930- 173

Okomfo, Amasewa
   See Cousins, Linda 60

Orr, Wendy 1953- 174

Oxendine, Bess Holland 1933- 177

P

Packard, Edward 1931- 180

Pagnucci, Susan 1944- 185

Patience, John 1949- 186

Q-R

Quin-Harkin, Janet 1941- 188

Ragan-Reid, Gale 1956- 193

Ray, Mary Lyn 1946- 194

Rhoades, Diane 1952- 197

Rivers, Elfrida
   See Bradley, Marion Zimmer 25

Rosenblatt, Lily 1956- 198

Rowh, Mark 1952- 199

S

Sanders, Nancy I. 1960- 201

Sanders, Winston P.
   See Anderson, Poul (William) 4

Sawicki, Mary 1950- 202

Scarry, Richard (McClure) 1919-1994
   Obituary Notice 203

Schertle, Alice 1941- 203

Schrecker, Judie 1954- 207

Scott, Elaine 1940- 208

Sharma, Rashmi
  See Singh, Rashmi Sharma 215

Shepard, Jim 1956- 212

Shuter, Jane Margaret 1955- 214

Singh, Rashmi Sharma 1952- 215

Smith, Jenny 1963- 216

Stevens, Janet 1953- 219

Stoeke, Janet Morgan 1957- 223

Sun, Chyng Feng 1959- 225

T

Terada, Alice M. 1928- 228

Thomas, Jane Resh 1936- 229

Thomasma, Kenneth R. 1930- 232

Tichnor, Richard 1959- 233

Travers, P(amela) L(yndon) 1899-1996
  Obituary Notice 234

Tyler, Anne 1941- 234

V-W

V
  See Chekhov, Anton (Pavlovich) 48

Weber, Ken(neth J.) 1940- 238

Williams, Garth (Montgomery) 1912-1996
  Obituary Notice 239

Wilson, Darryl B(abe) 1939- 239

Woolman, Steven 1969- 241

Z

Zima, Gordon 1920- 243

Zubrowski, Bernard 1939- 244

Zubrowski, Bernie
  See Zubrowski, Bernard 244

Authors in Forthcoming Volumes

Below are some of the authors and illustrators that will be featured in upcoming volumes of *SATA*. These include new entries on the swiftly rising stars of the field, as well as completely revised and updated entries (indicated with *) on some of the most notable and best-loved creators of books for children.

Marcel Ayme: Among the most celebrated of modern French writers, Ayme wrote several books for children, two of which are regarded as international classics: *The Wonderful Farm,* illustrated by Maurice Sendak, and *The Magic Pictures.*

Truman Capote: A masterful stylist who took great pride in his work, Capote wrote several childhood reminiscences appropriate for young readers, including his classic stories *A Christmas Memory, The Thanksgiving Visitor,* and *I Remember Grandpa.*

*Allan W. Eckert: A respected author of documentary and historical fiction for young people, Eckert is perhaps best known for two tales of survival involving child protagonists: *Incident at Hawk's Hill,* a Newbery honor book, and *Savage Journey,* in which a thirteen-year-old girl must brave the Amazon jungle alone in attempts to return to civilization following the deaths of her archaeologist father and his colleagues.

*Eleanor Estes: Beloved American author and illustrator Estes wrote eighteen books for children, including her popular *Moffats* series and her Newbery Medal-winning *Ginger Pye.*

*Jamie Gilson: Gilson is the author of a number of humorous tales for middle graders, the most popular of which feature her trademark hero Hobie Hanson.

Anthony Hill: Australian author Hill has garnered favorable critical notice with his novel *The Burnt Stick,* which movingly describes the former practice of taking Aboriginal children of mixed parentage away from their mothers.

*Irene Hunt: Newbery Medal-winner Hunt is an acclaimed writer of historical fiction for young people whose novels, including such classics as *Across Five Aprils* and *Up a Road Slowly,* are praised for their credible and vividly drawn characters and settings.

*Beverly L. Keller: Keller is best known for her series of children's books based on her popular heroines Fiona and Desdemona.

Jane Kurtz: American author Kurtz's picture books *Fire on the Mountain* and *Pulling the Lion's Tale* are retellings drawn from her experience as a child growing up in Ethiopia.

Ron Lightburn: Acclaimed for his lively colored-pencil sketches, Canadian illustrator Lightburn created the award-winning pictures for Sheryl McFarlane's *Waiting for the Whales* and Nan Gregory's *How Smudge Came.*

*Bernard Most: Author and illustrator Most is best known for his colorfully illustrated and whimsical concept picture books that both entertain and teach young readers.

Nicholas Pine: A prolific and popular author of horror and suspense novels for adolescents, Pine is best known for his "Terror Academy" series.

*Hope Ryden: Ryden is a photographer, filmmaker, and author noted for her award-winning nature books for children and young adults.

Introduction

Something about the Author (*SATA*) is an ongoing reference series that deals with the lives and works of authors and illustrators of children's books. *SATA* includes not only well-known authors and illustrators whose books are widely read, but also less prominent individuals whose works are just coming to be recognized. This series is often the only readily available information source on emerging writers and artists. You'll find *SATA* informative and entertaining, whether you are a student, a librarian, an English teacher, a parent, or simply an adult who enjoys children's literature.

What's Inside SATA

SATA provides detailed information about authors and illustrators who span the full time range of children's literature, from early figures like John Newbery and L. Frank Baum to contemporary figures like Judy Blume and Richard Peck. Authors in the series represent primarily English-speaking countries, particularly the United States, Canada, and the United Kingdom. Also included, however, are authors from around the world whose works are available in English translation. The writings represented in *SATA* include those created intentionally for children and young adults as well as those written for a general audience and known to interest younger readers. These writings cover the entire spectrum of children's literature, including picture books, humor, folk and fairy tales, animal stories, mystery and adventure, science fiction and fantasy, historical fiction, poetry and nonsense verse, drama, biography, and nonfiction.

Obituaries are also included in *SATA* and are intended not only as death notices but also as concise overviews of people's lives and work. Additionally, each edition features newly revised and updated entries for a selection of *SATA* listees who remain of interest to today's readers and who have been active enough to require extensive revisions of their earlier biographies.

Two Convenient Indexes

In response to suggestions from librarians, *SATA* indexes no longer appear in every volume but are included in alternate (odd-numbered) volumes of the series, beginning with Volume 57.

SATA continues to include two indexes that cumulate with each alternate volume: the Illustrations Index, arranged by the name of the illustrator, gives the number of the volume and page where the illustrator's work appears in the current volume as well as all preceding volumes in the series; the Author Index gives the number of the volume in which a person's Biographical Sketch or Obituary appears in the current volume as well as all preceding volumes in the series.

These indexes also include references to authors and illustrators who appear in Gale's *Yesterday's Authors of Books for Children, Children's Literature Review,* and the *Something about the Author Autobiography Series.*

Easy-to-Use Entry Format

Whether you're already familiar with the *SATA* series or just getting acquainted, you will want to be aware of the kind of information that an entry provides. In every *SATA* entry the editors attempt to give as complete a picture of the person's life and work as possible. A typical entry in *SATA* includes the following clearly labeled information sections:

- *PERSONAL:* date and place of birth and death, parents' names and occupations, name of spouse, date of marriage, names of children, educational institutions attended, degrees received, religious and political affiliations, hobbies and other interests.

- *ADDRESSES:* complete home, office, electronic mail, and agent addresses, whenever available.

- *CAREER:* name of employer, position, and dates for each career post; art exhibitions; military service; memberships and offices held in professional and civic organizations.

- *AWARDS, HONORS:* literary and professional awards received.

- *WRITINGS:* title-by-title chronological bibliography of books written and/or illustrated, listed by genre when known; lists of other notable publications, such as plays, screenplays, and periodical contributions.

- *ADAPTATIONS:* a list of films, television programs, plays, CD-ROMs, recordings, and other media presentations that have been adapted from the author's work.

- *WORK IN PROGRESS:* description of projects in progress.

- *SIDELIGHTS:* a biographical portrait of the author or illustrator's development, either directly from the biographee—and often written specifically for the *SATA* entry—or gathered from diaries, letters, interviews, or other published sources.

- *FOR MORE INFORMATION SEE:* references for further reading.

- *EXTENSIVE ILLUSTRATIONS:* photographs, movie stills, book illustrations, and other interesting visual materials supplement the text.

How a SATA Entry Is Compiled

A *SATA* entry progresses through a series of steps. If the biographee is living, the *SATA* editors try to secure information directly from him or her through a questionnaire. From the information that the biographee supplies, the editors prepare an entry, filling in any essential missing details with research and/or telephone interviews. If possible, the author or illustrator is sent a copy of the entry to check for accuracy and completeness.

If the biographee is deceased or cannot be reached by questionnaire, the *SATA* editors examine a wide variety of published sources to gather information for an entry. Biographical and bibliographic sources are consulted, as are book reviews, feature articles, published interviews, and material sometimes obtained from the biographee's family, publishers, agent, or other associates.

Entries that have not been verified by the biographees or their representatives are marked with an asterisk (*).

Contact the Editor

We encourage our readers to examine the entire *SATA* series. Please write and tell us if we can make *SATA* even more helpful to you. Give your comments and suggestions to the editor:

BY MAIL: The Editor, *Something about the Author,* Gale Research, 835 Penobscot Bldg., 645 Griswold St., Detroit, MI 48226-4094.

BY TELEPHONE: (800) 347-GALE

BY FAX: (313) 961-6599

BY E-MAIL: CYA@Gale.com@Galesmtp

Acknowledgments

Grateful acknowledgment is made to the following publishers, authors, and artists whose works appear in this volume.

ADAMS, ADRIENNE. From an illustration in *The Christmas Party*. Copyright © 1978 by Adrienne Adams. Reprinted with the permission of Atheneum Books for Young Readers, an imprint of Simon & Schuster Children's Publishing Division. / From an illustration in *The Great Valentine's Day Balloon Race*. Copyright © 1980 by Adrienne Adams. All rights reserved. Reprinted with the permission of Atheneum Books for Young Readers, an imprint of Simon & Schuster Children's Publishing Division. / Adams, Adrienne, photograph. Reproduced by permission.

ANDERSON, POUL. Alexander, Paul. From a cover of *Orion Shall Rise* by Poul Anderson. Baen Books, 1991. Reproduced by permission. / From a cover of *The Boat of a Million Years* by Poul Anderson. TOR, 1991. Reproduced by permission. / Elmore, Larry. From a cover of *Operation Chaos* by Poul Anderson. Baen Books, 1992. Reproduced by permission. / Di Fate, Vincent. From a cover of *Harvest of Stars* by Poul Anderson. Copyright © 1993 Poul Anderson. Reproduced by permission of Tor Books. / Sweet, Darrell K. From a cover of *Three Hearts and Three Lions* by Poul Anderson. Baen Books, 1993. Reproduced by permission. / Whelan, Michael. From a cover of *The Enemy Star* by Poul Anderson. Reproduced by permission. / Anderson, Poul, photograph. Reproduced by permission.

ANDERSON, SUSAN. From an illustration in *Flowers for Mommy*. Africa World Press, 1995. Reproduced by permission.

AYRES, PAM. Ayres, Pam, photograph. Reproduced by permission.

BALLOUHEY, PIERRE. Ballouhey, Pierre, photograph. Reproduced by permission.

BALTAZZI, EVAN S. Baltazzi, Evan S., photograph. Reproduced by permission.

BARTON, BYRON. From an illustration in *Bones, Bones, Dinosaur Bones*. HarperCollins, 1990. Reproduced by permission of HarperCollins Publishers, Inc. / From an illustration in *Building A House*. Mulberry, 1981. Reproduced by permission. / From an illustration in *I Want to be an Astronaut*. HarperCollins, 1988. Reproduced by permission of HarperCollins Publishers, Inc. / From an illustration in *The Wee Little Woman*. HarperCollins Publishers, 1995. Reproduced by permission of HarperCollins Publishers, Inc.

BELL, WILLIAM. Martin, Marva. From a jacket of *Forbidden City: A Novel of Modern China* by William Bell. Bantam Books, 1990. Reproduced by permission of Bantam Books, a division of Bantam Doubleday Dell Publishing Group, Inc. / Bell, William, photograph. Reproduced by permission.

BOVAIRD, ANNE E. Bauer, Karyn. Photograph of Anne E. Bovaird. Reproduced by permission.

BRADLEY, MARION ZIMMER. Bralds, Braldt. From a cover of *The Mists of Avalon* by Marion Z. Bradley. Ballatine, 1982. Reproduced by permission. / Hescox, Richard. From a jacket of *The Heirs of Hammerfell* by Marion Z. Bradley. DAW Books, Inc., 1989. Reproduced by permission. / Kukalis, Romas. From a jacket of *Exile's Song* by Marion Zimmer Bradley. DAW Books, Inc., 1996. Reproduced by permission. / McLean, Wilson. From a jacket of *Firebrand* by Marion Zimmer Bradley. Copyright © 1987 by Marion Zimmer Bradley. Jacket design by Jackie Seow. Jacket painting by Wilson McLean. Copyright © 1987 by Simon & Schuster, Inc. Reprinted with the permission of Simon & Schuster. / Morris, Taub. From a jacket of *The Forest House* by Marion Zimmer Bradley. Viking, 1993. Reproduced by permission. / Bauer, Jerry. Photograph of Marion Zimmer Bradley. Reproduced by permission.

BRIDGERS, SUE ELLEN. Velasquez, Eric. From a cover of *Permanent Connections* by Sue Ellen Bridgers. Harper, 1987. Reproduced by permission of HarperCollins Publishers, Inc. / Bridgers, Sue Ellen, photograph. Reproduced by permission.

BROWNE, VEE F. Browne, Delilah. Photograph of Vee F. Browne. Reproduced by permission.

BUCKLEY, HELEN E. Ormerod, Jan. From an illustration in *Grandfather and I*. By Helen E. Buckley. Lothrop, Lee & Shepard Books, 1994. Illustrations copyright © 1994 by Jan Ormerod. All rights reserved. Reproduced by permission of Lothrop, Lee & Shepard Books, a division of William Morrow and Company, Inc. / Buckley, Helen E., photograph. Reproduced by permission.

BUTENKO, BOHDAN. Butenko, Bohdan, photograph. Reproduced by permission.

CABRERA, MARCELA. Cabrera, Marcela, photograph. Reproduced by permission.

CAMPBELL, HUGH. Campbell, Hugh, photograph. Reproduced by permission.

CARLSON, NANCY L. From an illustration in *What If It Never Stops Raining?* Viking, 1992. Copyright © 1992 by Nancy Carlson.

GLASS, ANDREW. From a jacket of *Folks Call Me Appleseed John*. Doubleday, 1995. Jacket illustration © 1995 Andrew Glass. Reproduced by permission of Doubleday, a division of Bantam Doubleday Dell Publishing Group, Inc. / From an illustration in *Spooky and the Wizard's Bats*. By Natalie Savage Carlson. Lothrop, Lee & Shepard Books, 1986. Illustration copyright © 1986 by Andrew Glass. All rights reserved. Reproduced by permission of Lothrop, Lee & Shepard Books, a division of William Morrow and Company, Inc.

GRAY, LULI. Gray, Luli, photograph. Reproduced by permission.

GREENWOOD, BARBARA. Collins, Heather. From a cover of *A Pioneer Story* by Barbara Greenwood. Kids Can Press, 1994, Ticknor and Fields, 1994. Text © 1994 by Barbara Greenwood and illustration © 1994 by Heather Collins. Reproduced by permission of Kids Can Press, Ltd., Toronto, Canada. In the U.S. by Houghton Mifflin Company. / Ronald Miller Photography Limited. Greenwood, Barbara, photograph. Reproduced by permission.

HARRILL, RONALD. Harrill, Ronald, photograph. Reproduced by permission.

HARRIS, ROBIE H. Harris, Robie H., photograph. Reproduced by permission.

HATCH, LYNDA S. Hatch, Lynda S., photograph. Reproduced by permission.

HAUSMAN, GERALD. Moser, Cara, and Barry Moser. From an illustration in *Turtle Island ABC: A Gathering of Native American Symbols*. By Gerald Hausman. HarperCollins Publishers, 1994. Text copyright © 1994 by Gerald Hausman. Illustrations copyright © 1994 by Cara Moser. All rights reserved. Reproduced by permission of HarperCollins Publishers, Inc. / Besold, Bobbe. Photograph of Gerald Hausman. Reproduced by permission.

HAZEN, BARBARA SHOOK. Goffe, Toni. From an illustration in *The Knight Who Was Afraid to Fight* by Barbara Shook Hazen. Dial Books for Young Readers, 1994. Reproduced by permission. / Morrill, Leslie Holt. From an illustration in *Fang* by Barbara Shook Hazen. Illustrations copyright © 1987 Leslie Holt Morrill. Reprinted with the permission of Atheneum Books for Young Readers, an imprint of Simon & Schuster Children's Publishing Division. / Ross, Tony. From an illustration in *The Knight Who Was Afraid of the Dark* by Barbara S. Hazen. Puffin, 1992. Reproduced by permission. / Soman, David. From an illustration in *Mommy's Office* by Barbara Shook Hazen. Illustrations copyright © 1992 by David Soman. All rights reserved. Reprinted with the permission of Atheneum Books for Young Readers, an imprint of Simon & Schuster Children's Publishing Division. / Hazen, Barbara Shook, photograph. Reproduced by permission.

HEILIGMAN, DEBORAH. Weissman, Bari. From an illustration in *From Caterpillar to Butterfly*. By Deborah Heiligman. HarperCollins Publishers, 1996. Illustrations copyright © 1996 by Bari Weissman. All rights reserved. Reproduced by permission of HarperCollins Publishers, Inc.

HOLINGER, WILLIAM. From a cover of *21st Century Fox* by Scott Eller (joint pseudonym of Holinger and Jim Shepard). Scholastic, 1989. Reproduced by permission.

HOON, PATRICIA EASTERLY. Hoon, Patricia E., photograph. Reproduced by permission.

IMAI, MIKO. Brais, Tom. Photograph of Miko Imai. Reproduced by permission.

ISAACS, ANNE. Isaacs, Anne, photograph. Reproduced by permission.

JONES, JENNIFER. Boettcher, Marvia. Photograph of Jennifer Berry Jones. Reproduced by permission.

KAHN, KATHERINE JANUS. From an illustration in *Sammy Spider's First Hanukkah*. Kar-Ben Copies, Inc., 1993. Illustration copyright © 1993 by Katherine Janus Kahn. Reproduced by permission. / Kahn, Katherine Janus, photograph. Kar-Ben Copies, Inc. Reproduced by permission of Katherine Janus Kahn.

KENT, LISA. Kent, Lisa, photograph. Reproduced by permission.

KIESLER, KATE. Kiesler, Gail. Photograph of Kate Kiesler. Reproduced by permission of Kate Kiesler.

KIMBALL, GAYLE. Teeter, Jeff. Photograph of Gayle Kimball. Reproduced by permission of Gayle Kimball.

KRAMER, REMI. Kramer, Remi, photograph. Reproduced by permission.

LEE, ELIZABETH ROGERS. Lee, Liz, photograph by Olan Mills. Reproduced by permission.

LeMIEUX, A. C. de Groat, Diane. From a cover of *Fruit Flies, Fish & Fortune Cookies* by Anne C. LeMieux. Tambourine Books, 1994. Reproduced by permission of Tambourine Books, a division of William Morrow & Co., Inc. / Velasquez, Eric. From an jacket in *Do Angels Sing the Blues?* by A. C. LeMieux. Jacket art copyright © 1994 by Eric Velasquez. Reproduced by permission of Tambourine Books, a division of William Morrow & Co., Inc. / Neafsey, Helen. LeMieux, Anne C., photograph. Reproduced by courtesy of the Westport News/Helen Neafsey, photographer.

LESTER, ALISON. From an illustration in *Imagine*. Houghton Mifflin, 1990. Reprinted by permission of Houghton Mifflin Company. / From an illustration in *The Journey Home*. Hodder Headline Australia. Copyright © 1989 by Alison Lester. All rights reserved.

something
about the
author®

ADAMS, Adrienne 1906-

■ Personal

Born February 8, 1906, in Fort Smith, AR; daughter of
Edwin Hunt (an accountant) and Sue (Broaddus)
Adams; married John Lonzo Anderson (a writer, under
name Lonzo Anderson), August 17, 1935. *Education:*
Stephens College, B.A., 1925; attended University of
Missouri, 1927, and American School of Design, New
York, 1929.

■ Addresses

Home—Florida.

■ Career

Artist, illustrator, and children's book author. Taught in
a rural school in Oklahoma, 1927-29; moved to New
York City in 1929, working as a freelance designer of
displays, murals, textiles, greeting cards, and other
materials, 1929-45; Staples-Smith Displays, New York
City, decorator of furniture and murals, and art director, 1945-52.

■ Awards, Honors

Spring Book Festival Award, *New York Herald Tribune,*
1953, for *Captain Ramsay's Daughter,* and 1960, for
Candy Floss; Honour List, International Board on
Books for Young People, 1958, for *The Fairy Doll;*
Runner-up, Caldecott Medal, 1960, for *Houses from the
Sea,* and 1962, for *The Day We Saw the Sun Come Up;*

ADRIENNE ADAMS

1

Lewis Carroll Shelf Award, 1962, for *Thumbelina;* Illustration Honor, *Boston Globe-Horn Book,* 1968, for *Jorinda and Joringel;* New Jersey Institute of Technology Award, New Jersey Institute of Technology, 1972, for *A Woggle of Witches,* and 1975, for *The Halloween Party;* Rutgers Award, Rutgers University College of Library Services, 1973, for contributions to children's literature; Irma Simonton Black Award, Bank Street College, 1976, for *The Easter Egg Artists;* University of Southern Mississippi Medallion, University of Southern Mississippi, 1977, for outstanding contributions to children's literature.

■ Writings

SELF-ILLUSTRATED; FOR CHILDREN

A Woggle of Witches, Scribners, 1971.
(Compiler) *Poetry of Earth,* Scribners, 1972.
The Easter Egg Artists, Scribners, 1976.
The Christmas Party, Scribners, 1978.
The Great Valentine's Day Balloon Race, Scribners, 1980.
A Halloween Happening, Scribners, 1981.

ILLUSTRATOR

Lonzo Anderson, *Bag of Smoke,* Viking, 1942, revised edition, Knopf, 1968.

Using his talents as an Easter egg artist, Orson Abbot enters his beautifully colored hot air balloon in the big Valentine's Day race. (From *The Great Valentine's Day Balloon Race,* written and illustrated by Adams.)

Patricia Gordon, *The 13th Is Magic,* Lothrop, 1950.
Patricia Gordon, *The Summer Is Magic,* Lothrop, 1952.
Elizabeth Fraser Torjesen, *Captain Ramsay's Daughter,* Lothrop, 1953.
Elizabeth Rogers, *Angela of Angel Court,* Crowell, 1954.
Rumer Godden, *Impunity Jane,* Viking, 1954.
Mary Kennedy, *Jenny,* Lothrop, 1954.
Norma Simon, *The Baby House,* Lippincott, 1955.
Beth Lipkin, *The Blue Mountain,* Knopf, 1956.
Rumer Godden, *The Fairy Doll,* Viking, 1956.
Priscilla Friedrich and Otto Friedrich, *The Easter Bunny That Overslept,* Lothrop, 1957.
Patricia Gordon, *The Light in the Tower,* Lothrop, 1957.
Margaret Glover Otto, *Great Aunt Victoria's House,* Holt, 1957.
Rumer Godden, *Mouse House,* Viking, 1957.
Rachel Lyman Field, *The Rachel Field Story Book,* Doubleday, 1958.
Rumer Godden, *Die Feenpuppe,* Boje Verlag, 1958.
Rumer Godden, *The Story of Holly and Ivy,* Viking, 1958.
Janice Udry, *Theodore's Parents,* Lothrop, 1958.
Alice E. Goudey, *Houses from the Sea,* Scribners, 1959.
Paula Hendrich, *Trudy's First Day at Camp,* Lothrop, 1959.
Jeanne Massey, *The Little Witch,* Knopf, 1959.
Aileen Lucia Fisher, *Going Barefoot,* Crowell, 1960.
Rumer Godden, *Candy Floss,* Viking, 1960.
Jakob Ludwig Karl Grimm, *The Shoemaker and the Elves,* Scribners, 1960.
Hans Christian Andersen, *Thumbelina,* Scribners, 1961.
Aileen Lucia Fisher, *Where Does Everyone Go?,* Crowell, 1961.
Alice E. Goudey, *The Day We Saw the Sun Come Up,* Scribners, 1961.
Mary Francis Shura, *Mary's Marvelous Mouse,* Knopf, 1962.
Clyde Robert Bulla, *What Makes a Shadow?,* Crowell, 1962.
John L. Anderson, compiler, *A Fifteenth Century Cookry Boke,* Scribners, 1962.
W. Saboly, *Bring a Torch, Jeannette, Isabella,* Scribners, 1963.
Virginia Haviland, *Favorite Fairy Tales Told in Scotland,* Little, Brown, 1963.
Mary Francis Shura, *The Nearsighted Knight,* Knopf, 1964.
Jakob Ludwig Karl Grimm, *Snow White and Rose Red,* Scribners, 1964.
Alice E. Goudey, *Butterfly Time,* Scribners, 1964.
Frances Carpenter, *The Mouse Palace,* McGraw, 1964.
Hans Christian Andersen, *The Ugly Duckling,* Scribners, 1965.
Aileen Lucia Fisher, *In the Middle of the Night,* Crowell, 1965.
Jan Wahl, *Cabbage Moon,* Holt, 1965.
Lonzo Anderson, *Ponies of Mykillengi,* Scribners, 1966.
Andrew Lang, *The Twelve Dancing Princesses,* Holt, 1966.
Barbara Schiller, *The White Rat's Tale,* Holt, 1967.
Jakob Ludwig Karl Grimm, *Jorinda and Joringel,* Scribners, 1968.

Lonzo Anderson, *Two Hundred Rabbits,* Viking, 1968.
Leclaire Alger, *The Laird of Cockpen,* Holt, 1969.
Natalia Belting, *Summer's Coming In,* Holt, 1970.
Carl Withers, *Painting the Moon,* Holt, 1970.
Lonzo Anderson, *Mr. Biddle and the Birds,* Scribners, 1971.
Lonzo Anderson, *Izzard,* Scribners, 1973.
Irwin Shapiro, *Twice upon a Time,* Scribners, 1973.
Lonzo Anderson, *The Halloween Party,* Scribners, 1974.
Jakob and Wilhelm Grimm, *Hansel and Gretel,* Scribners, 1975.
Kenneth Grahame, *The River Bank,* Scribners, 1977.
Lonzo Anderson, *Arion and the Dolphins,* Scribners, 1978.
Peter Barnhart, *The Wounded Duck,* Scribners, 1979.

■ Sidelights

Award-winning illustrator and author Adrienne Adams is known for creating vivid, colorful illustrations to complement simple stories for children. Having provided artwork for numerous other writers, Adams published her first effort as both an author and an illustrator in the 1971 work *A Woggle of Witches.* In this story, a group of young trick-or-treaters outsmart an old haven of witches on their broomsticks. Although she calls the story "thin and routine," *Horn Book* critic Ethel L. Heins applauds Adams's "expert drawing" and points out how Adams's strategic arrangement of witches creates "a graceful, fluid choreography."

This fluidness is also evident in *Poetry of Earth,* Adams's 1972 compilation of poems about nature. Accompanied by her illustrations, familiar American and British poems are brought together in this volume to introduce children to classic verses, including "Stopping by Woods on a Snowy Evening" by Robert Frost and "The Meadow Mouse" by Theodore Roethke. Describing the collection as "handsomely designed and beautifully illustrated," a *Bulletin of the Center for Children's Books* contributor suggests this book would be an excellent choice for young or independent readers. Georgess McHargue, writing in the *New York Times Book Review,* praises Adams's arrangement of the poems and their accompanying illustrations, saying the combination "asserts the quality of the selections."

Adams returns to her own fictional tales with the creation of the young rabbit Orson Abbot in *The Easter Egg Artists.* Despite the fact that his parents are artists who paint dozens of Easter eggs every year, Orson is at first not interested in this craft; he has his own methods of artistic expression, which include everything from painting the car like an Easter egg to doing the same to several other household items. When the season for egg painting finally arrives, Orson chooses a large ostrich egg and decorates it with his own humorous designs. Before they know it, the Abbots have found a new popular product. This creative story allows Adams to exercise "her strong sense of design" according to a *Bulletin of the Center for Children's Books* contributor. Merrie Lou Cohen, writing in *School Library Journal,* compliments Adams on her "delectable pastel illustra-

Orson Abbot and his neighborhood friends throw a surprise party for their parents in Adams's self-illustrated picture book *The Christmas Party.*

tions" which "enhance a good story about personal identity."

The spirited holiday adventures of Orson continue in two more stories—*The Christmas Party* and *The Great Valentine's Day Balloon Race.* In *The Christmas Party* he helps the other children in the neighborhood organize a surprise party for all their parents. A *Kirkus Reviews* contributor finds Orson's "fussing like a proper grown-up" entertaining. Writing in *Horn Book,* Ann A. Flowers calls Adams's illustrations for *The Christmas Party* "engaging elements in a colorful Christmas book."

In his third holiday adventure, *The Great Valentine's Day Balloon Race,* Orson makes a hot-air balloon with his parents and wins the Valentine's Day balloon race with the help of his friend Bonnie. In a review of *The Great Valentine's Day Balloon Race,* a contributor to *Bulletin of the Center for Children's Books* relates that "the story line is simple, but the text has a strong climax." *Horn Book* reviewer Virginia Haviland praises the combination of Adams's text and pictures, saying they "provide richness of pictorial embellishment."

Adams once explained to *SATA* the appeal of writing and illustrating such adventures for children: "I love children's books, and I feel very lucky to be involved in them. As I became involved, I discovered the satisfactions of a field which can be as sweetly innocent of the rank business-and-profit taint as any I can hope for, simply because a book cannot succeed unless little children love it and wear out its cover and pages so thoroughly that librarians must reorder it for the library shelves; you can not tell a child what to like."

■ Works Cited

Review of *The Christmas Party, Kirkus Reviews,* December 15, 1978, p. 1351.
Cohen, Merrie Lou, review of *The Easter Egg Artists, School Library Journal,* February, 1977, p. 53.
Review of *The Easter Egg Artists, Bulletin of the Center for Children's Books,* September, 1976, p. 1.
Flowers, Ann A., review of *The Christmas Party, Horn Book,* February, 1979, p. 50.
Review of *The Great Valentine's Day Balloon Race, Bulletin of the Center for Children's Books,* March, 1981, p. 125.
Haviland, Virginia, review of *The Great Valentine's Day Balloon Race, Horn Book,* February, 1981, p. 38.
Heins, Ethel L., review of *A Woggle of Witches, Horn Book,* December, 1971, p. 600.
McHargue, Georgess, "How Now, Poetry Lovers?," *New York Times Book Review,* November 5, 1972, p. 32.
Review of *Poetry of Earth, Bulletin of the Center for Children's Books,* January, 1973, p. 69.

■ For More Information See

PERIODICALS

Booklist, November 1, 1971, p. 244; November 15, 1972, p. 295; June 1, 1976, p. 1401; December 15, 1978, p. 681; January 15, 1981, p. 694.
Horn Book, February, 1973, p. 63; October, 1976, p. 488.
Kirkus Reviews, September 1, 1971, p. 933; September 15, 1972, p. 1096; April 15, 1976, p. 461; February 1, 1981, p. 137; February 1, 1982, p. 131.
New York Times Book Review, April 18, 1976, p. 24; November 13, 1977, p. 62; April 19, 1981, p. 27.
Publishers Weekly, October 4, 1971, p. 60; May 17, 1976, p. 56; November 13, 1978, p. 63; November 7, 1980, p. 61.
School Library Journal, February, 1981, p. 53; December, 1981, p. 48.*

* * *

ANDERSON, Poul (William) 1926-
(A. A. Craig, Winston P. Sanders)

■ Personal

Given name pronounced "pole"; born November 25, 1926, in Bristol, PA; son of Anton William (an engineer) and Astrid (a secretary; maiden name, Hertz) Anderson; married Karen J. M. Kruse (an editorial and research assistant and writer), December 12, 1953; children: Astrid May. *Education:* University of Minnesota, B.S. (with distinction), 1948.

POUL ANDERSON

■ Addresses

Home—3 Las Palomas, Orinda, CA 94563. *Agent*—c/o Ted Chichak, Chichak, Inc., 1040 1st Ave., New York, NY 10022.

■ Career

Freelance writer, except for occasional temporary jobs, 1948—. *Member:* Science Fiction Writers of America (president, 1972-73), American Association for the Advancement of Science, Mystery Writers of America (northern California regional vice-chairman, 1959). Society for Creative Anachronism, Scowrers (secretary, 1957-62), Elves, Gnomes, and Little Men's Science Fiction Chowder and Marching Society.

■ Awards, Honors

Morley-Montgomery Prize for Scholarship in Sherlock Holmes, 1955; first annual Cock Robin Mystery Award, 1959, for *Perish by the Sword;* Guest of Honor, World Science Fiction Convention, 1959; Hugo Awards, World Science Fiction Convention, 1961, for short fiction "The Longest Voyage," 1964, for short fiction "No Truce with Kings," 1969, for novelette "The Sharing of Flesh," 1972, for novella "The Queen of Air and Darkness," 1973, for novelette "Goat Song," 1979, for novelette "Hunter's Moon," and 1982, for novella "The Saturn Game;" Forry Award for achievement, Los Angeles Science Fantasy Society, 1968; Nebula Awards, Science Fiction Writers of America, 1971, for "The Queen of Air and Darkness," and 1972, for "Goat Song"; Hugo Award runner-up, World Science Fiction Convention, 1973, for *There Will Be Time;* August Derleth Award, British Fantasy Society, 1974, for *Hrolf Kraki's Saga;* Gandalf Award, Grand Master of Fantasy, World Science Fiction Convention, 1978.

■ Writings

SCIENCE FICTION NOVELS

Vault of the Ages (for children), Winston Press (Minneapolis, MN), 1952.

Brain Wave, Ballantine, 1954.

The Broken Sword, Abelard, 1954, revised edition, Ballantine, 1971.

No World of Their Own (bound with *The 1,000 Year Plan* by Isaac Asimov), Ace, 1955, published separately as *The Long Way Home*, Gregg (Rohnert Park, CA), 1978.

Star Ways, Avalon, 1956, published as *The Peregrine*, Ace, 1978.

Planet of No Return (bound with *Star Guard* by Andre Norton), Ace, 1957, published as *Question and Answer*, 1978.

War of the Wing-Men, Ace, 1958, published as *The Man Who Counts*, 1978.

The Snows of Ganymede, Ace, 1958.

Virgin Planet, Avalon, 1959.

The Enemy Stars, Lippincott, 1959.

The War of Two Worlds (bound with *Threshold of Eternity* by John Brunner), Ace, 1959.

We Claim These Stars! (bound with *The Planet Killers* by Robert Silverberg), Ace, 1959.

The High Crusade, Doubleday, 1960.

Earthman, Go Home! (bound with *To the Tombaugh Station* by Wilson Tucker), Ace, 1961.

Twilight World, Torquil, 1961.

Mayday Orbit (bound with *No Man's World* by Kenneth Bulmer), Ace, 1961.

Three Hearts and Three Lions, Doubleday, 1961.

The Makeshift Rocket (bound with the *Un-Man and Other Novellas*), Ace, 1962.

After Doomsday, Ballantine, 1962.

Shield, Berkley, 1963.

Let the Spacemen Beware! (bound with *The Wizard of Starship Poseidon* by K. Bulmer), Ace, 1963, published separately as *The Night Face*, 1978.

Three Worlds to Conquer, Pyramid, 1964.

The Star Fox, Doubleday, 1965.

The Corridors of Time, Doubleday, 1965.

Ensign Flandry, Chilton (Radnor, PA), 1966.

World without Stars, Ace, 1966.

Satan's World, Doubleday, 1969.

The Rebel Worlds, Signet, 1969, published as *Commander Flandry*, Severn House (London), 1978.

A Circus of Hells, Signet, 1970.

Tau Zero, Doubleday, 1970.

The Byworlder, Signet, 1971.

Operation Chaos, Doubleday, 1971.

The Dancer from Atlantis, Doubleday, 1971.

There Will Be Time, Doubleday, 1971.

Hrolf Kraki's Saga, Ballantine, 1973.

The People of the Wind, Signet, 1973.

The Day of Their Return, Doubleday, 1974.

Fire Time, Doubleday, 1974.

A Midsummer Tempest, Doubleday, 1974.

(With Gordon Ecklund) *Inheritors of Earth*, Chilton, 1974.

The Worlds of Poul Anderson (contains *Planet of No Return, The War of Two Worlds,* and *World without Stars*), Ace, 1974.

(With Gordon R. Dickson) *Star Prince Charlie* (for children), Putnam, 1975.

A Knight of Ghosts and Shadows, Doubleday, 1974, published as *Knight Flandry*, Severn House, 1980.

The Winter of the World, Doubleday, 1976.

Mirkheim, Berkley, 1977.

The Avatar, Putnam, 1978.

Two Worlds (contains *Question and Answer* and *World without Stars*), Gregg, 1978.

The Merman's Children, Putnam, 1979.

A Stone in Heaven, Ace, 1979.

Conan the Rebel, Bantam, 1980.

(With Mildred D. Broxon) *The Demon of Scattery*, Ace, 1980.

The Long Night, Pinnacle, 1983.

Orion Shall Rise, Pocket Books, 1983.

Agent of Vega, Ace, 1983.

The Game of Empire, Baen, 1985.

Time Wars, Tor, 1986.

The Year of the Ransom (for children), illustrated by Paul Rivoche, Walker & Co., 1988.

Conan the Rebel #17, Ace, 1989.

No Truce with Kings (bound with *Ship of Shadows* by Fritz Leiber), Tor, 1989.

The Boat of a Million Years, Tor, 1989.

The Shield of Time, Tor, 1990.

The Time Patrol, Tor, 1991.

Inconstant Star, Baen, 1991.

(With others) *Murasaki*, Bantam, 1992.

Harvest of Stars, Tor, 1993.

The Stars Are Also Fire, Tor, 1994.

Harvest the Fire, Tor, 1995.

"THE KING OF Ys" FANTASY SERIES; WITH WIFE, KAREN ANDERSON; PUBLISHED BY BAEN

Roma Mater, 1986.

Gallicinae, 1988.

Dahut, 1988.

The Dog and the Wolf, 1988.

SHORT STORY COLLECTIONS

(With Gordon R. Dickson) *Earthman's Burden*, Gnome Press, 1957.

Guardians of Time, Ballantine, 1960, revised edition, Pinnacle, 1981.

Strangers from the Earth: Eight Tales of Vaulting Imagination, Ballantine, 1961.

Orbit Unlimited, Pyramid, 1961.

Trader to the Stars, Doubleday, 1964.

Time and Stars, Doubleday, 1964.

Agent of the Terran Empire, Chilton, 1965.

Flandry of Terra, Chilton, 1965.

The Trouble Twisters, Doubleday, 1966.

The Horn of Time, Signet, 1968.

Beyond the Beyond, New American Library, 1969.

Seven Conquests: An Adventure in Science Fiction, Macmillan, 1969.

Tales of the Flying Mountains, Macmillan, 1970.

The Queen of Air and Darkness and Other Stories, Signet, 1973.

The Many Worlds of Poul Anderson, edited by Roger Elwood, Chilton, 1974, published as *The Book of Poul Anderson,* DAW Books, 1975.

Homeward and Beyond, Doubleday, 1975.

Homebrew, National Educational Field Service Association Press (Cambridge, MA), 1976.

The Best of Poul Anderson, Pocket Books, 1976.

The Earth Book of Stormgate, Putnam, 1978.

The Night Face and Other Stories, Gregg, 1978.

The Dark between the Stars, Berkley, 1980.

Explorations, Pinnacle, 1981.

Fantasy, Pinnacle, 1981.

Winners, Pinnacle, 1981.

Cold Victory, Pinnacle, 1981.

The Psychotechnic League, Tor, 1981.

The Gods Laughed, Pinnacle, 1982.

Maurai and Kith, Tor, 1982.

Starship, Pinnacle, 1982.

New America, Pinnacle, 1982.

Conflict, Pinnacle, 1983.

(With Gordon R. Dickson) *Hoka!* (for children), Simon & Schuster, 1983.

Time Patrolman, Pinnacle, 1983.

Annals of the Time Patrol (contains *Time Patrolman* and *Guardians of Time*), Doubleday, 1984.

(With K. Anderson) *The Unicorn Trade,* Tor, 1984.

Past Times, Tor, 1984.

Dialogue with Darkness, Tor, 1985.

(With others) *Berserker Base,* Tor, 1985.

Space Folk, Baen, 1989.

All One Universe, Tor, 1996.

OTHER NOVELS

Perish by the Sword, Macmillan, 1959.

Murder in Black Letter, Macmillan, 1960.

The Golden Slave, Avon, 1960.

Rogue Sword, Avon, 1960.

Murder Bound, Macmillan, 1962.

The Last Viking: The Golden Horn, Zebra, 1980.

The Devil's Game, Pocket Books, 1980.

The Road of the Sea Horse, Zebra, 1980.

The Sign of the Raven, Zebra, 1980.

NONFICTION

Is There Life on Other Worlds?, Crowell, 1963.

Thermonuclear Warfare, Monarch (Derby, CT), 1963.

The Infinite Voyage: Man's Future in Space (for young adults), Macmillan, 1969.

OTHER

(Adaptor) Christian Molbech, *The Fox, the Dog, and the Griffin,* Doubleday, 1966.

(Author of introduction) *The Best of L. Sprague de Camp,* Ballantine, 1978.

Contributor to books including *All about the Future,* edited by Martin Greenberg, Gnome Press, 1955; *The Day the Sun Stood Still: Three Original Novellas of Science Fiction,* Thomas Nelson (Nashville), 1972; *Science Fiction: Today and Tomorrow,* edited by Reginald Bretnor, Harper, 1974; *The Craft of Science Fiction,* edited by Reginald Bretnor, Harper, 1976; *Turning Points: Essays on the Art of Science Fiction,* edited by

Damon Knight, Harper, 1977; *Swords against Darkness,* edited by Andrew J. Offutt, Zebra, Volume 1, 1977, Volume 3, 1978, Volume 4, 1979; *The Blade of Conan,* edited by L. Sprague de Camp, Ace, 1979; *Space Wars* (short stories), edited by Charles Waugh and Martin H. Greenberg, Tor, 1988; *Modern Classic Short Novels of Science Fiction,* edited by Gardner Dozois, St. Martin's, 1994.

Also contributor to anthologies, including *Possible Worlds of Science Fiction,* edited by Groff Conklin, Vanguard, 1951; *A Treasury of Great Science Fiction,* edited by Anthony Boucher, Doubleday, 1959; *The Hugo Winners,* edited by Isaac Asimov, Doubleday, 1962; *Space, Time, and Crime,* edited by Miriam Allen de Ford, Paperback Library, 1964; *Monsters of Science Fiction,* Belmont Books, 1964; *The Hugo Winners,* edited by Isaac Asimov, Doubleday, 1971-72; *The Science Fiction Hall of Fame,* edited by Ben Bova, Doubleday, 1973; *The Future at War,* edited by Regi-

One of Anderson's early science fiction books, *Three Hearts and Three Lions* follows the journey of Holger Carlsen as he is transported to a mystical world which has long prepared for his coming. (Cover illustration by Darrell K. Sweet.)

nald Bretnor, Ace, 1979. Contributor of short stories and articles, some under pseudonyms A. A. Craig and Winston P. Sanders, to periodicals, including *Astounding Science Fiction, Analog Science Fiction/Science Fact, Boy's Life, Foundation: The Review of Science Fiction, Galaxy, Isaac Asimov's Science Fiction Magazine, Magazine of Fantasy and Science Fiction,* and *National Review.* Writer of a television documentary on the space program for the United States Information Agency, 1963-64. Anderson's books have been translated into eighteen foreign languages.

■ Adaptations

The High Crusade was adapted for a computer game by IRS Hobbies, 1983; "The Longest Voyage," "The Queen of Air and Darkness," "No Truce with Kings," and "The Man Who Came Early" were all adapted for an audio cassette, *Award-Winning Science Fiction by Poul Anderson,* by Listening Library; other stories by Anderson were recorded by Caedmon in 1986 under the title *Yonder—Seven Tales of the Space Age.*

■ Sidelights

The winner of several Nebula and Hugo awards, Poul Anderson is a prolific writer of science fiction and fantasy with well over one hundred novels and short story collections to his credit. Known for writing science fiction that is well-grounded in scientific knowledge, and for fantasy stories involving a heavy dose of Nordic mythology and libertarian values, Anderson is also a poet, translator, and writer of detective and historical novels. Science fiction is, perhaps, the one true cross-over genre; although only a handful of Anderson's works have been specifically written for a juvenile audience, his books and short stories are as popular with young readers as they are with adults. Anderson, who cut his teeth on magazine writing, is "one of the five or six most important writers to appear during the science-fiction publishing boom of the decade following the end of World War II," according to Michael W. McClintock in the *Dictionary of Literary Biography.*

Literary traditions with Anderson go back to Denmark on his mother's side, but his upbringing was not really a literary one. His early years were spent in Port Arthur, Texas, where he navigated a homemade kayak in the family's bayou-like backyard, and where "a neighbor boy made a pet of a small alligator he had found in his," as Anderson recalled in an essay for *Contemporary Authors Autobiography Series* (*CAAS*). The one negative in his youth was, according to Anderson, school: an "utter emptiness, a purgatory of boredom." Something of an introvert as a child, Anderson relied more on his wits than his athletic prowess to navigate the rough waters of the school yard. At the same time, he was raised with the "strict code of manners of the old South." The Danish influence on both sides of his family was strongly felt: Anderson's mother was born in Denmark, and though his father had been born in the United States, he was educated in Denmark.

When his father was killed in a car accident in 1937, Anderson's secure family life was turned on its head. At first his mother took him and his brother to Denmark in hopes of starting a new life. The war clouds of the late 1930s, however, drove them back to the safety of the United States, first to Maryland and then to Minnesota, where Anderson's mother joined her brother in investing what money the family had left in a farm, though the investment proved unwise. In the countryside around Northfield, Minnesota, Anderson completed junior high and then high school. "Those years are pretty bad in my memory," Anderson recalled in *CAAS.* "I was a total social misfit.... Anyway, I had my private world to retreat to, the world of books and, specifically of science fiction." A friend Anderson had earlier made in Maryland, Neil Waldrop, kept in touch with him and sent along copies of pulp magazines that introduced Anderson to the world of science fiction, magazines such as *Thrilling Wonder Stories, Amazing Stories,* and, of course, *Astounding Science Fiction.* He had read Jules Verne and H. G. Wells as a kid; now he was introduced

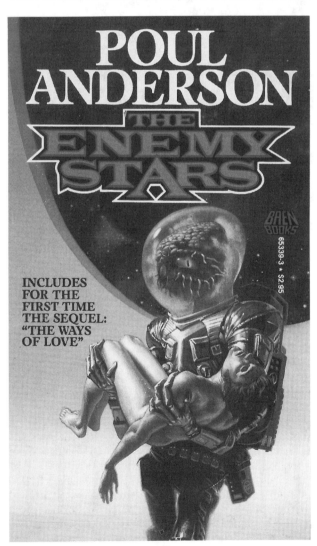

Sent to inspect a burned-out star, the crew of the spaceship *Southern Cross* must fight for their survival on a hostile planet.

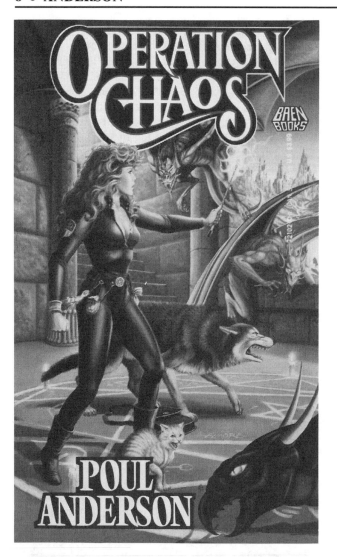

Fighting against the Caliphates in the American-Caliphate War, two secret agents, one a werewolf and the other a witch, must seek and destroy the enemy's deadliest weapon, a powerful demon. (Cover illustration by Larry Elmore.)

to contemporary practitioners such as Robert Heinlein and Isaac Asimov.

Turned down by the army because of a scarred eardrum resulting from a childhood illness, Anderson enrolled in the University of Minnesota in 1944. "Suddenly I was free," he wrote in *CAAS*. "The old maids and soft young faces of high school were behind me. I was among men, and men whose trade was knowledge. They regarded me as an adult." Initially, Anderson majored in physics, but when he realized how poor his math skills were, he moved into astronomy. He was reading science fiction as avidly as before and was writing his own stories to share with his friend, Waldrop. When Waldrop showed up as a student at the University of Minnesota, the two spent hours together in conversation. One of these midnight talks resulted in Anderson's first published story, "Tomorrow's Children," which dealt with the consequences of the atomic bomb. Anderson's favorite magazine, *Astounding Science Fiction,* took the story,

and this sale proved to be a deciding factor in a choice Anderson was then making. Graduating in 1948, he had to decide on a career. "I would never be more than a second-rate scientist," Anderson wrote in *CAAS*. And suddenly writing science fiction for a living seemed a possibility. Several more of his stories had been purchased by magazines; Anderson had also become a member of the Minneapolis Fantasy Society where he came into contact with other people in the writing trade, including Clifford D. Simak and Gordon R. Dickson. "This was when I settled into a writing career in earnest," he recalled. He sold stories to *Astounding Science Fiction* (which was later renamed *Analog*) and to *Planet Stories*. These early pieces were "blood-and-thunder adventure yarns," according to Anderson, and by 1952 he had published his first novel, *Vault of Ages,* an "apprentice" piece, as McClintock described it in *Dictionary of Literary Biography*. But by his second published science fiction novel, *Brain Wave,* Anderson had "followed the instruction of H. G. Wells to employ but a single 'marvel' in a story and work out the logical consequences of the innovation," McClintock noted. This logical processing of an innovation is a strong characteristic of Anderson's science fiction. Also, in early stories such as "Sam Hall," in which a bureaucratized government is battled by a computer-generated rebel, and in "Call Me Joe," in which a human escapes the constraints of his body by transferring his personality to a robot, Anderson established some of his most enduring themes. Here is the lone intellect, the individual battling society or other outside forces for freedom; here is the power of reason at work, as well as the use of technology for positive gain.

During the 1950s and '60s, Anderson wrote a score of novels based on a future history series documenting the Technic Civilization, beginning with *Star Ways*. Many of these short novels are constructed like mysteries or puzzles and also include Anderson's reliance on sound scientific extrapolation. But Anderson was also interested in mythology and Norse legend, and he soon adapted that interest to his writing in the form of fantasy novels. An early fantasy novel of Anderson's is *Three Hearts and Three Lions,* an examination "of the conflict between law and chaos," according to McClintock, which is set in a Carolingian-like world. In succeeding years these twin threads of science fiction and fantasy have occupied most of Anderson's writing output.

Meanwhile, Anderson married, had a child, and settled with his family in the San Francisco Bay area, where he still lives. He became involved in all aspects of the science fiction community, from attending conventions to sharing dinners with fellow writers. In 1958 Anderson published "the two most important novels of the first half" of his career, according to McClintock. *War of the Wing-Men* and *The Enemy Stars* "both feature vividly realized settings.... Both utilize to good effect elements of the most current scientific thought," McClintock commented. The political *War of the Wing-Men* introduced the self-indulgent and overweight Nicholas van Rijn, whom Anderson would return to often in his fiction as an unlikely entrepreneurial hero. With *The*

Enemy Stars, Anderson worked out the one "marvel"—involving constant and instantaneous gravity—in a story that takes on mythic and mystical proportions on the meaning of exploration. Not all reviewers found *The Enemy Stars* first rate, however. Roger Baker, writing in *Books and Bookmen,* commented that "the scientific mumbojumbo is just not good enough to blind us to the fact that [Anderson's] characters are more than usually weak stereotypes." *The High Crusade* also continues this literary exploration into the meaning of quest, a celebration of "human courage" and "intelligence," according to McClintock.

Fellow science fiction writer James Blish, writing in the *Magazine of Fantasy and Science Fiction,* labeled Anderson's 1970 work, *Tau Zero,* a watershed achievement. Blish called it "the ultimate 'hard science fiction' novel," and went on to note that "everybody else who has been trying to write this kind of thing can now fold up his tent and creep silently away." Here Anderson took the working out of an innovation to the maximum. He posited the question of what would happen to an interstellar vessel travelling at a steady acceleration of one gravity if it were damaged in such a way that its acceleration could not be stopped. Blish noted that Anderson worked out his problem thoroughly like a "born storyteller." This book was followed by *Operation Chaos,* a fantasy set on an alternate Earth where magic is part of everyday life and in which a witch and werewolf are the main protagonists. "The book is well populated and contains a great deal of humor," noted Blish in another *Magazine of Fantasy and Science Fiction* review. While noting that *Operation Chaos* is fundamentally about the contest between law and chaos, Sandra Miesel commented in her monograph *Against Time's Arrow: The High Crusade of Poul Anderson* that the book "celebrates ordinariness.... Homely values are soundest: domestic happiness is sweetest.... Law is not constraint but protection for these humble realities. Without Law, the very concept of normalcy would vanish. Chaos is ever its foe."

Such values are not simply empty speeches Anderson puts in the mouths of his characters, but are part of the author's belief system. "If I preach at all," Anderson once told Jeffrey M. Elliot in *Science Fiction Voices #2,* "it's probably in the direction of individual liberty, which is a theme that looms large in my work." Because of this insistence on individual freedom and libertarian values, Anderson is known in science fiction circles as "being fairly far to the right and has been called a reactionary," according to Charles Platt in *Dream Makers, Volume 2: The Uncommon Men and Women Who Write Science Fiction.* Anderson noted in his interview with Platt that if he had to call himself something, "it would be either a conservative libertarian or a libertarian conservative.... Basically, I feel that the concepts of liberty that were expressed ... by people like the Founding Fathers were actually the radically bold concepts from which people have been retreating ever since. And I don't believe that it's necessarily reactionary to say so."

Many years after a nuclear holocaust, a new war begins when the anti-industry Maurai battle with the pro-technology Northwest Union over the direction a new earth should take. (Cover illustration by Paul Alexander.)

But Anderson has also said that his first job as a writer is to entertain, and that is what he did with the award-winning novelette "The Queen of Air and Darkness" set in a "scientifically plausible Elfland," according to Miesel. Another important fantasy title is *The Merman's Children,* which is based on a Danish ballad depicting the ending of the world of the Faeries. Set in Denmark during the Middle Ages, it relates the battle between the mythic web-footed mermen and the Christian church. Gerald Jonas, writing in the *New York Times Book Review,* noted that the novel was a "hybrid" of fantasy, historical fiction, and science fiction. With 1974's *A Knight of Ghosts and Shadows,* Anderson returned to aspects of the Technic Empire (specifically its later phases, known as the Terran Empire), and put Dominic Flandry, who has inhabited the pages of much of Anderson's fiction, on center stage. The central conflict in the tale is characteristic of Anderson: the testing of rational judgement in a moral wilderness. A further book in that series includes *The Game of Empire.* Other popular series books by Anderson include his "Time Patrol" books, where time travel and science fiction are mixed neatly together. In the stories and novels of this series, the members of the Time Patrol are charged with the duty of keeping history unchanged by time travellers. *Annals of the Time Patrol, The Year of the Ransom,* and *The Shield of Time* are representative titles in the series. Reviewing *The Shield of Time,* Roland Green noted in *Booklist* that Anderson's "abiding love for history" carried the story's weight. And something of a turning point in Anderson's fiction was 1978's *The Avatar,* a book in which Anderson featured several women as leading characters and in which he attempted to "make sexual passion and an interstellar adventure somehow metaphoric," according to McClintock.

Anderson has never shied away from using his fiction as a way to proclaim his own views. Among the many issues that he has dealt with are those of the safe use of nuclear power and the benefits of space exploration,

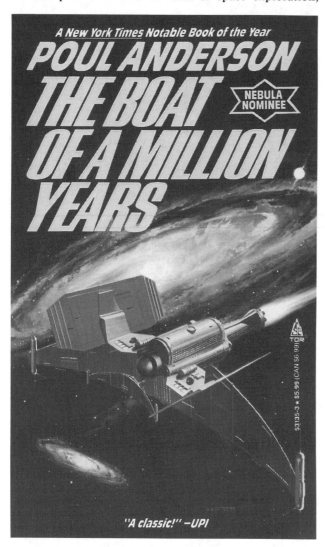

A New York Times Notable Book of the Year

POUL ANDERSON
THE BOAT OF A MILLION YEARS

NEBULA NOMINEE

"A classic!" —UPI

Anderson's first epic-length book follows the lives of eight humans who have been granted the gift of immortality.

both of which find a place in *Orion Shall Rise.* This story is an investigation of a world rebuilding itself many generations after a nuclear war. Two main powers—the non-industrial Maurai and the more technology-prone Northwest Union—are at odds about how their new world should progress. "This would be useful in classes discussing our current nuclear debate," concluded Nancy Choice in a *Voice of Youth Advocates* review of the novel. Anderson has also teamed up with his wife, Karen Anderson, on several projects, including the story collection, *The Unicorn Trade,* and the four-volume series, "The King of Ys."

More recently, Anderson has turned his hand to epic-length ventures, including *The Boat of a Million Years, The Stars Are Also Free,* and *Harvest of Stars. The Boat of a Million Years* tells the stories of eight immortals who trek through time. Blessed with eternal life, these special few range in time of birth from 310 B.C. to the present day. They slowly find each other on their journeys and band together to try to put meaning into their lives. "The novel is fascinating and masterfully done," noted a reviewer in *Kliatt,* adding that the book came "highly recommended." Jonas commented in another *New York Times Books Review* article that Anderson had been writing "solid, serviceable science fiction" for over four decades, but with *The Boat of a Million Years* "he aims higher and succeeds admirably."

Harvest of Stars was another long novel, detailing the future struggle between a North America that has been taken over by the Avantists, a techno-religious cult dictatorship, and Fireball, an interplanetary corporation and "the last bastion of free-enterprise," according to *Kirkus Reviews.* However, while noting that Anderson had written "wonderful short to medium-length stories," the *Kirkus Reviews* critic concluded that for Anderson to persist "in grinding out ponderous, somnolent, bloated offerings like this is one of science fiction's enduring mysteries." Jonas, in the *New York Times Book Review,* also criticized the book as "overwritten, underimagined and fatally flawed." Others disagreed. Howard G. Zaharoff, writing in *Kliatt,* found *Harvest of Stars* to be a "good, but rather lengthy, read," and *Booklist* contributor John Mort called it "a complex novel" and "a grand meditation."

The Stars Are Also Fire, a sequel to *Harvest of Stars,* covers five centuries and spans several worlds; it is another "epic novel," according to Vicky Burkholder in *Voice of Youth Advocates.* The future world of Earth is controlled by a giant mechanical mind called cybercosm, which rules peacefully over the population. But lost in this placid new world are individuality and the freedom of choice. The mechanical mind now pursues some rebels on distant outposts to bring them into line, especially the Lunar rebels. A *Kirkus Reviews* critic concluded that the book was proof of Anderson's "powerful storytelling talents," but that it also "betrays once again his tendency to hang far too much political, sociological, and technological baggage on the shining thread of the tale." Mort noted in another *Booklist* review that "Anderson's new epic owes clear allegiances

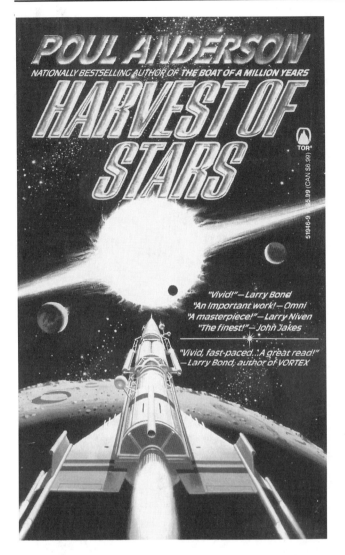

A young woman embarks on a dangerous space mission to rescue a captured rebel leader who she hopes can lead North America from the grips of a repressive dictatorship. (Cover illustration by Vincent Di Fate.)

to both Heinlein and Asimov and will appeal to their many fans." And a *Publishers Weekly* reviewer commented that Anderson got "back on track" with *The Stars Are Also Fire:* "Where its predecessor was disjointed, unbalanced and clogged with capitalist-libertarian preaching, this novel offers suspense, vivid writing and appealing characters." Third in the series, *Harvest the Fire* follows the adventures of the battle against cybercosm and the Lunarians, but John O. Christensen, writing in *Voice of Youth Advocates,* noted that the novel did not hold up on its own. "Background and plot are not well developed," Christensen commented, "and the characters are less than memorable."

"[There] is a basic attitude, I suppose, which underlies my writing," Anderson said in his interview with Elliot in *Science Fiction Voices #2.* "Namely, that this is a wonderful universe in which to live, that it's great to be alive, and that all it takes is the willingness to give ourselves a chance to experience what life has to offer." Through his science fiction and fantasy, Anderson has

attempted to make that attitude toward life manifest. Part of the post-war wave of writers who have helped to make science fiction "legitimate," Anderson employs such elements as humor, politics, puzzles, history, and science in his writing. "I have written quite a lot," Anderson once remarked, "and am proud to have done so, because science fiction is and always has been part of literature. Its long isolation ... is ending.... This is good, because the particular concerns of science fiction have never been parochial.... Not that I wish to make exaggerated claims. I merely set forth that science fiction is one human accomplishment, among countless others, which has something to offer the world. Lest even this sound too pompous let me say that at the very least it is often a lot of fun."

■ Works Cited

Anderson, Poul, essay in *Contemporary Authors Autobiography Series,* Volume 2, Gale, 1985, pp. 33-46.

Baker, Roger, "Into the Future," *Books and Bookmen,* August 1972, pp. xii-xiii.

Blish, James, "Books: 'Operation Chaos,'" *Magazine of Fantasy and Science Fiction,* December, 1971, p. 25.

Blish, James, "Books: 'Tau Zero,'" *Magazine of Fantasy and Science Fiction,* March, 1971, pp. 14-15.

Review of *The Boat of a Million Years, Kliatt,* April 1991, pp. 16-17.

Burkholder, Vicky, review of *The Stars Are Also Fire, Voice of Youth Advocates,* February, 1995, p. 343.

Choice, Nancy, review of *Orion Shall Rise, Voice of Youth Advocates,* December, 1983, p. 281.

Christensen, John O., review of *Harvest the Fire, Voice of Youth Advocates,* April, 1996, p. 34.

Elliot, Jeffrey M., "Poul Anderson: Seer of Far-Distant Futures," *Science Fiction Voices #2,* Borgo, 1979, pp. 41-50.

Green, Roland, review of *The Shield of Time, Booklist,* July, 1990, p. 2041.

Review of *Harvest of Stars, Kirkus Reviews,* June 15, 1993, p. 756.

Jonas, Gerald, review of *The Merman's Children, New York Times Book Review,* October 28, 1979, pp. 15-16.

Jonas, Gerald, review of *The Boat of a Million Years, New York Times Book Review,* November 19, 1989, p. 32.

Jonas, Gerald, review of *Harvest of Stars, New York Times Book Review,* September 12, 1993, p. 36.

McClintock, Michael W., "Poul Anderson," in *Dictionary of Literary Biography,* Volume 8: *Twentieth-Century Science-Fiction Writers,* Gale, 1981, pp. 3-12.

Miesel, Sandra, *Against Time's Arrow: The High Crusade of Poul Anderson,* Borgo, 1978.

Mort, John, review of *Harvest of Stars, Booklist,* June 15, 1993, pp. 1733-34.

Mort, John, review of *The Stars Are Also Fire, Booklist,* July 1994, pp. 1892-93.

Platt, Charles, *Dream Makers, Volume 2: The Uncommon Men and Women Who Write Science Fiction,* Berkley, 1983.

Review of *The Stars Are Also Fire, Kirkus Reviews,* June 15, 1994, p. 84.
Review of *The Stars Are Also Fire, Publishers Weekly,* July 18, 1994, p. 239.
Zaharoff, Howard G., review of *Harvest of Stars, Kliatt,* January 1995, p. 12.

■ For More Information See

BOOKS

Benson, Gordon, Jr., and Phil Stephenson-Payne, *Poul Anderson, Myth-Maker and Wonder-Weaver: A Working Bibliography,* 5th revised edition, Borgo, 1990.
Bretnor, Reginald, editor, *The Craft of Science Fiction,* Harper, 1974.
Contemporary Literary Criticism, Volume 15, Gale, 1980, pp. 10-15.
Tuck, Donald H., compiler, *The Encyclopedia of Science Fiction and Fantasy,* Volume 1, Advent, 1974.
Walker, Paul, *Speaking of Science Fiction: The Paul Walker Interviews,* Luna, 1978.

PERIODICALS

Analog, July, 1978, p. 175; January, 1979, p. 172; March, 1981, p. 164; September, 1983, p. 160; October, 1985, p. 179; December, 1993, p. 167.

Kliatt, fall, 1977, p. 10; spring, 1978, p. 11; winter, 1981, p. 11; winter, 1985, p. 16; September, 1991, p. 19; May, 1993, p. 12.
School Library Journal, March, 1977, p. 158; March, 1982, p. 162; August, 1988, p. 105; September, 1988, p. 122.
Times Literary Supplement, April 7, 1966, p. 281; June 29, 1967, p. 573; December 20, 1969, p. 1345; February 2, 1973, p. 129.
Wilson Library Bulletin, January, 1980, p. 323; January, 1995, p. 90.

—Sketch by J. Sydney Jones

* * *

ANDERSON, Susan 1952-

■ Personal

Born February 9, 1952, in Teaneck, NJ; daughter of Dudley (a stockbroker) and Bernice V. (a newspaper reporter; maiden name, DeLucia) Anderson; children: Aliya Anderson-Smith. *Education:* Cornell University, B.F.A., 1979; Syracuse University, M.F.A., 1990. *Politics:* "Elimination of poverty, racism (worldwide), human rights violations." *Religion:* "Respect and accep-

In her self-illustrated *Flowers for Mommy,* Susan Anderson shows the care a young girl takes when selecting the perfect flowers for her mother.

tance of personal differences; my own personal relationship with God."

Addresses

Home—220 Bundy Rd., Ithaca, NY 14850. *Office*—Goodhope Youth Home, Inc., 4010 McIntyre Rd., Trumansburg, NY 14886.

Career

Goodhope Youth Home, Inc., Trumansburg, NY, office manager, 1979—; GeNoa School of Furniture Design, Genoa, NY, instructor in design and drawing, 1991; Tompkins Cortland Community College, Cortland, NY, adjunct professor of design, drawing, figure drawing, and painting, 1992—. Freelance illustrator and portrait and landscape artist.

■ Writings

(Illustrator) Eddie Smith, *A Lullaby for Daddy,* Africa World Press, 1994.
(Self-illustrated) *Flowers for Mommy,* Africa World Press, 1995.

Work in Progress

A children's fairy tale entitled *Ravina the Woodnymph.*

Sidelights

Susan Anderson told *SATA:* "I come from a large, wonderful family of six girls and two boys. There were always many playmates when we were young. Now, in our adult years, we remain very close and have been blessed with many nieces and nephews to add to the fun."

*   *   *

AYRES, Pam 1947-

■ Personal

Born March 13, 1947, in Faringdon, Oxfordshire, England; daughter of Stanley William (an electrical linesman) and Phyllis Evelyn (a homemaker) Ayres; married Dudley Joseph Russell (a theater and concert producer), 1982; children: William, James. *Hobbies and other interests:* Music and song writing, painting, the cinema, creative work.

■ Addresses

Home—P.O. Box 64, Cirencester, Gloucestershire GL7 5YD, England. *Agent*—Richard Scott Simon Ltd., 43 Doughty St., London WC1N 2LF, England.

PAM AYRES

■ Career

Writer and performer in television, film, and radio, 1975—. Performs one-woman comedy show throughout Great Britain and internationally.

■ Writings

FOR CHILDREN

When Dad Cuts Down the Chestnut Tree, illustrated by Graham Percy, Knopf, 1988.
When Dad Fills in the Garden Pond, illustrated by Graham Percy, Knopf, 1988.
Guess What?, illustrated by Julie Lacome, Knopf, 1988.
Guess Who?, illustrated by Julie Lacome, Knopf, 1988.
Piggo and the Nosebag, illustrated by Andy Ellis, Parkwest, 1991.
The Bear Who Was Left Behind, illustrated by Nigel McMullen, BBC Books (London), 1991.
Piggo Has a Train Ride, illustrated by Andy Ellis, Parkwest, 1992.
The Works: Selected Poems (light verse), BBC Books, 1992.
Jack Crater, BBC Books, 1992.
Guess Where?, illustrated by Julie Lacome, Walker, 1994.
Guess Why?, illustrated by Julie Lacome, Walker, 1994.

■ Work in Progress

A book of verse and comedy sketches; a film script of a murder story with a background of the entertainment business; a film script about a young boy and his imaginary friend.

■ Sidelights

Pam Ayres is the author of several popular books for the pre-school set. From her rhyming "Guess" series for toddlers to *When Dad Fills in the Garden Pond* and other books for young readers, Ayres's work has been praised for its educational value as well as its playful, lighthearted approach. *Guess What?*, asks the title of the first of Ayres's four-part "Guess" books. Also including *Guess Who?, Guess Where?,* and *Guess Why?,* the "Guess" books provide rhyming clues on two-page illustrated spreads to a wide variety of intriguing picture-book puzzles that help youngsters up to ages three and four develop the observation skills that will aid them in understanding the logic of the world around them.

Our close link to the world of nature is examined in two other books by Ayres: *When Dad Fills in the Garden Pond* and *When Dad Cuts Down the Chestnut Tree.* When Dad is sent out into the backyard to begin a weekend home-improvement project—cutting down a tree to make wooden toys or filling in a small pond to allow Mom to start a flower bed—his young son begins to think about the repercussions. While life will be easier—fewer leaves to rake—he begins to take stock of the tree house he will loose, the small animals who will be left homeless, and the loss of the opportunity to sit and watch the bugs, frogs, snails, and fish that inhabit his family's small backyard pond. Critics have noted that these books can serve to introduce youngsters to environmental issues: "Discussions of this book would lead children to appreciate trees and nature," observed an *Appraisal* contributor in a review of *When Dad Cuts Down the Chestnut Tree,* for example.

"From the time I was at school, I had two strong feelings about what I wanted to do," Ayres told *SATA.* "First I wanted to write because I found it thrilling, and second I wanted to be on stage working with comedy. When I left school I found it was all right being on stage saying someone else's words, but it was much better saying my own, and I began to write songs and funny verse. I won a television talent show in 1975 and have worked as a writer and entertainer ever since. My books of verse have sold over two million copies."

Ayres didn't begin writing seriously for children until the early 1980s. "Before this time I never felt particularly maternal," she confessed, "and I was baffled about what to actually *say* to children when I was faced with them. I am glad to say all this changed when my two sons were born. In 1983 I was approached by the BBC to read some children's stories on the radio. Some of them seemed a bit stodgy to me, and I thought I could write something as good. I submitted one about a piglet called Piggo to a TV company, and was commissioned to write a further sixteen! I was really thrilled.

"As I read to my own babies and toddlers, I found that the books I enjoyed most were ones we could SHARE. There was limited appeal in pointing to a picture of a tree and saying 'There is a tree!' This is why I thought of my GUESS books, which would have an interesting picture and a simple question that rhymed. My book seemed to me to do three things: It encouraged the child to look carefully at the picture; it introduced rhymes and bouncy rhythms; it enabled me to congratulate my child on finding the correct answer. This exchange made us both feel very happy, and I am delighted that other families have enjoyed sharing my book, too."

Ayre's "Guess" books have been widely praised by critics as excellent sources of fun and learning for the very young. Writing in the *Long-Beach Press-Telegram,* David Ross called them "effective tools for teaching logic and comprehension skills." Praising Julie Lacome's double-page illustrations in the series for their bright colors and appealing patterns, *School Library Journal* reviewer Patricia Pearl predicted that pre-schoolers "will enjoy shouting out their answers and comments." Finally, a *Books for Keeps* writer considered the series "invaluable for developing observational skills."

■ Works Cited

Review of *Guess Where?* and *Guess Why?, Books for Keeps,* July, 1994, p. 6.

Pearl, Patricia, review of *Guess What?* and *Guess Who?, School Library Journal,* June-July, 1988, p. 83.

Ross, David, "Fun Reading for the Small Fry," *Long Beach Press-Telegram,* March 21, 1994.

Review of *When Dad Cuts Down the Chestnut Tree, Appraisal,* autumn, 1989, pp. 9-10.

■ For More Information See

PERIODICALS

Appraisal summer, 1989, pp. 10-11.

Booklist, June 1, 1988, p. 1671; November 15, 1988, p. 570.

Growing Point, January, 1992, p. 5624.

School Librarian, February, 1993, p. 19.

School Library Journal, December, 1988, p. 79.

B

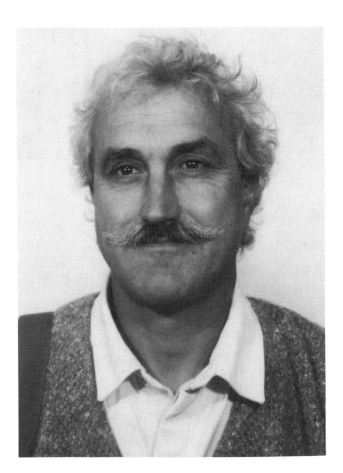

PIERRE BALLOUHEY

BALLOUHEY, Pierre 1944-

■ Personal

Born November 24, 1944, in St. Marcellin, France; son of Andre (a printer) and Germaine (Cluze) Ballouhey; married Denise Irles (a secretary), November 8, 1967; children: Stephane, Camille. *Education:* Graduated from Ecole Nationale Superieure des Beaux Arts de Paris, 1968.

■ Addresses

Home—Mas de Blagneux, 38160 Chevrieres, France.

■ Career

Illustrator. Also teaches drawing at Ecole Emile Cohl in Lyon, France. *Military service:* Served as a member of the "Chasseur Alpin" (French mountain infantry), 1969-70.

■ Writings

Velo, Glenat (Grenoble, France), 1985.

ILLUSTRATOR

A. De Graaf, reteller, *Oncle Tom's Cabin,* Scandinavia (Copenhagen, Denmark), 1986.
A. De Graaf, reteller, *Pinocchio,* Scandinavia, 1987.
Copain des villes, Milan (France), 1989.
R. Kayser, *Copain des bois,* Milan, 1991.
Simon, *Copain des champs,* Milan, 1993.
Anne Elizabeth Bovaird, *Goodbye U.S.A.—Bonjour la France: A Language Learning Adventure,* Barron's, 1993.
Anne Elizabeth Bovaird, *Goodbye U.S.A.—Bonjour la France: A Language Learning Adventure Volume II,* Barron's, 1994.

Also contributor of illustrations to various periodicals, including the *New Yorker.* Both volumes of *Goodbye U.S.A.—Bonjour la France* have been translated into an English/Spanish version by Harriet Barnett, Barron's, 1994.

■ Work in Progress

Copain des Pyrenees; Bon appetit Monsieur Bouffre.

BALTAZZI, Evan S(erge) 1921-

■ Personal

Born April 11, 1921, in Izmir, Turkey; son of Phocion Baltazzi (a civil engineer) and Agnes Varda (an author); married Nellie Biorlaro (a parliamentarian and civic activist), 1945; children: Vittoria, James, Maria. *Education:* Studied industrial chemistry at the University of Athens, Greece; Sorbonne, Paris, D.Sc., 1949; Oxford University, England, D.Phil. *Hobbies and other interests:* The American Self-Protection (A.S.P.) system, the combative arts, volunteering in national parks, fencing, history, dogs.

■ Addresses

Home and office—825 Greengate Oval, Greenwood Village, Sagamore Hills, OH 44967-2311.

■ Career

International Red Cross Committee, Thessaloniki (Salonika), Greece, chemist, 1941-45; chemist at the Institute Pasteur, Paris, the Dyson Perrins Laboratory, Oxford, and Nalco Chemical Company, Chicago, IL; IIT Research Institute, manager; the Bruning Company (later part of the Addressograph-Multigraph Corporation), director of exploratory research and the organic chemistry laboratory. Formed engineering consulting firm in 1978 and served as a consultant to American, European, and Japanese companies until 1988. Organized and chaired national and international symposia and conferences on chemistry. Served on the U.S. Olympic and A.A.U. Committees for Judo, 1964-72, and on the U.S. Currency Committee of the National Academy of Sciences, National Research Council, Washington, DC, 1984-86. Served as an official at the Panamerican Games, Winnipeg, and chaired the National YMCA Judo Committee, both 1967. Chaired the Health and Physical Education Research Methods conferences, Chicago, IL, 1969-70. *Military service:* Served in the Greek Army during World War II. *Member:* American Chemical Society (senior member), American Institute of Chemists (vice-president of the Chicago chapter), Society of Photographic Scientists and Engineers, Chicago Research Directors Society.

■ Awards, Honors

New Citizen of the Year Award, Citizenship Council of Metropolitan Chicago, 1964; Distinguished Service Award (Sciences), Immigrants' Service League, 1965; Best Program of the Year Award for developing the A.S.P. program, Metropolitan Chicago YMCA, 1967; fellow of the Royal Chemical Society, the American Institute of Chemists, and the French Chemical Society; fellowship to the Canadian National Research Center in Ottawa, Ontario, Canada.

EVAN S. BALTAZZI

■ Writings

FOR CHILDREN

Dog Gone West: A Western for Dog Lovers, illustrated by Gregory Kyziridis, Evanel, 1994.

FOR ADULTS; NONFICTION

Basic American Self-Protection: ASP, System of Mind-Body Self-Protection for Self-Defense, for Fitness, Evanel, 1972.
Kickboxing: A Safe Sport, a Deadly Defense, Tuttle, 1976.
Stickfighting: A Practical Guide for Self-Protection, Tuttle, 1983.
Self-Protection Complete, the A.S.P. System: A Complete System of Holistic Body-Mind Self-Protection, for Mental and Physical Fitness, for Self-Defense and Protection, for Sport, Evanel, 1992.

Also author of numerous scientific articles. Served as editor of electrophotography for the *Journal of Photographic Science and Engineering* for several years.

■ Work in Progress

Plato and Socrates' Trial, a free annotated translation of Plato's *Apology,* for the American Hellenistic Educational and Progressive Association, and *Africa My Love,* an autobiography based on Baltazzi's experiences as a young man in French Equatorial Africa before World War II.

■ Sidelights

Evan S. Baltazzi told *SATA:* "From my early teens to the present, I have been active in various combative arts and sports." As a student at the Sorbonne, he was a member of the Faculty of Sciences Fencing Team, and he is currently recognized as a fencing master. During his years at Oxford, Baltazzi was captain of the varsity Judo team, which remained unbeaten during his stay; he has achieved high black belt rankings in both Judo and Akido. In the early 1970s, Baltazzi decided to devote himself to developing the American Self-Protection (A.S.P.) method and system, and he began writing books about A.S.P. and related topics, such as *Basic American Self-Protection.* Baltazzi notes: "Several physical educators here and abroad, including the Administrators of the President's Council on Physical Fitness under Presidents Johnson and Bush, have recognized the outstanding qualities of A.S.P. A.S.P. is superior to all combative systems from the standpoint of yield for expended effort, degree of retention of the techniques learned over long periods, didactic value, and holistic approach. It is at least as effective as any other art."

Describing himself as a nature lover and history buff, Baltazzi has a special interest in dogs and is particularly attracted to the Conquest of the West. He notes that his children's book, *Dog Gone West,* "is the outcome of these two long-standing interests."

*   *   *

BARON, Kathy 1954-

■ Personal

Born April 10, 1954, in Torrance, CA; daughter of Walter (a stockbroker) and Irene (a homemaker) Ciejka; married Reinhold Baron (a financial analyst), July 15, 1978; children: Eric, Chris, Greg, Theresa. *Education:* California State University, Long Beach, B.F.A., 1979. *Religion:* Roman Catholic.

■ Addresses

Home and office—Eugene, OR.

■ Career

Author and illustrator. Freelance illustrator in California and Oregon, 1980—. *Member:* Society of Children's Book Writers and Illustrators, Sierra Club, National Wildlife Federation.

■ Awards, Honors

Museum Publications Design Award—Educational Resources, A.A.M., 1995.

■ Writings

(Self-illustrated) *The Tree of Time: A Story of a Special Sequoia* (children's nonfiction), Yosemite Association, 1994.

■ Work in Progress

Jigsaw puzzles on dogs and bugs; educational posters on the habitats of the desert and eastern forest as well as on fascinating animal facts; illustrations for the picture book *Erin's Zucchini;* writing and illustrating a nonfiction picture book about animals; a fictional story about a timid mole who overcomes his fears.

■ Sidelights

Kathy Baron told *SATA,* "I have loved to draw animals as far back as I can remember. In kindergarten, I was writing and illustrating stories on pieces of scratch paper stapled together. My greatest desire was to have a pet dog, and to illustrate a real book. And, at long last, both of these dreams have come true!

"Camping in the Sierra Nevada Mountains has always been central to my life, and I hope that my illustrations and stories will help bring a sense of wonder and appreciation of the natural world to others."*

*   *   *

BARTON, Byron 1930-

■ Personal

Surname originally Vartanian; name changed in 1953; born September 8, 1930, in Pawtucket, RI; son of Toros and Elizabeth (Krekorian) Vartanian; married Harriett Wyatt, December, 1967 (divorced, April, 1973). *Education:* Attended Los Angeles City College, 1948-50, and Chouinard Art Institute, 1953-56.

■ Addresses

Home—2 Washington Square Village, New York, NY 10012.

■ Career

Freelance writer, illustrator, and designer. Studio 7 Los Angeles, Los Angeles, CA, illustrator, 1956-57; Equitable Life Assurance Co., New York City, designer, 1957-60; Columbia Broadcasting System, Inc., New York City, designer, 1960-66. *Military service:* U.S. Army, 1950-52.

■ Awards, Honors

Spring Book Festival Middle Honor, *New York Herald Tribune,* 1969, for *A Girl Called Al; New York Times* Choice of Best Illustrated Children's Books of the Year, 1972, for *Where's Al?,* and 1988, for *I Want to Be an Astronaut;* Children's Book Showcase Title, Children's

With colorfully drawn construction workers, Byron Barton teaches children how a house is built, from laying the foundation to installing electrical wiring and plumbing. (From *Building a House,* written and illustrated by Barton.)

Book Council, 1972, for *The Paper Airplane Book,* and 1973, for *Where's Al?; Airport* was selected a *New York Times* Notable Book, 1982; Please Touch Award, Please Touch Museum for Children, 1990, for *Dinosaurs, Dinosaurs.*

■ Writings

FOR CHILDREN; SELF-ILLUSTRATED

Elephant, Seabury, 1971.
Where's Al?, Seabury, 1972.
Applebet Story, Viking, 1973.
Buzz Buzz Buzz, Macmillan, 1973.
Harry Is a Scaredy-Cat, Macmillan, 1974.
Jack and Fred, Macmillan, 1974.
Hester, Greenwillow, 1975.
Wheels, Crowell, 1979.
Building a House, Greenwillow, 1981.
Airport, Crowell, 1982.
Airplanes, Crowell, 1986.
Boats, Crowell, 1986.

Trains, Crowell, 1986.
Trucks, Crowell, 1986.
Machines at Work, Crowell, 1987.
I Want to Be an Astronaut, Crowell, 1988.
Dinosaurs, Dinosaurs, Crowell, 1989.
Bones, Bones, Dinosaur Bones, Crowell, 1990.
(Reteller) *The Three Bears,* HarperCollins, 1991.
Building a House: Big Book, Hampton-Brown, 1992.
Building a House: Small Book, Hampton-Brown, 1992.
(Reteller) *The Little Red Hen,* HarperCollins, 1993.
Dinosaurs, Dinosaurs Board Book, HarperCollins, 1994.
(Reteller) *Little Red Hen Big Book,* HarperCollins, 1994.
(Reteller) *Three Bears Big Book,* HarperCollins, 1994.
Planes, HarperCollins, 1994.
The Wee Little Woman, HarperCollins, 1995.
Big Machines, HarperCollins, 1996.
Dinosaurs, HarperCollins, 1996.
Tools, HarperCollins, 1996.
Zoo Animals, HarperCollins, 1996.

ILLUSTRATOR

Constance C. Greene, *A Girl Called Al,* Viking, 1969.

Alan Venable, *The Checker Players,* Lippincott, 1973.

Seymour Simon, *The Paper Airplane Book,* Viking, 1973.

Franklyn Branley, *How Little and How Much: A Book about Scales,* Crowell, 1976.

David A. Adler, *Roman Numerals,* HarperCollins, 1977.

Jack Prelutsky, *The Snopp on the Sidewalk and Other Poems,* Greenwillow, 1977.

Russell Hoban, *Arthur's New Power,* HarperCollins, 1978.

Marjorie Weinman Sharmat, *Gila Monsters Meet You at the Airport,* Simon & Schuster, 1980.

Mirra Ginsburg, *Good Morning, Chick,* Greenwillow, 1980.

Robert Kalan, *Jump, Frog, Jump!,* Greenwillow, 1981.

Charlotte Pomerantz, *Where's the Bear?,* Greenwillow, 1984.

Diane Siebert, *Truck Song,* Crowell, 1984.

Constance C. Greene, *Al's Blind Date,* Puffin Books, 1991.

Constance C. Greene, *Ask Anybody,* Puffin Books, 1991.

Charlotte Pomerantz, *The Tamarindo Puppy,* Greenwillow, 1993.

■ Sidelights

Through the use of simple text and bright, bold illustrations with thick black outlines, children's author and illustrator Byron Barton makes such activities as building a house, going on a space mission, and reassembling dinosaur bones accessible to young readers. With just a few rhythmic words running along the bottom of his illustrations, Barton tells his stories with pictures that give readers all the necessary details about his subject. Barton is "a master of simplicity," declares a reviewer in *Publishers Weekly.* Cathryn A. Camper, writing in

Five Owls, praises Barton's colorful, well-defined drawings which make "his books fun even for children too young to read."

Born in Pawtucket, Rhode Island, Barton's home was often his playground because of his father's job—he sold coal and wood during the winter and ice during the summer. "To a small boy, our home with its woodpiles, barns, and attics, made an ideal playground," Barton once told *SATA.* All this was left behind when Barton was in the fourth grade, though, when the family of seven moved to Los Angeles, California. It was in this new state that Barton's interest in drawing and art began, mostly because of the different teaching methods used in his new school. "In class, when subjects I had already learned came up, I was allowed to go to the back of the room to play with paints," Barton continued for *SATA.* "I remember making large paintings of Indians in their canoes, alongside their tepees, and hunting animals. My pictures were hanging all over the back walls of the class and cloakroom. I became known as 'the artist.'"

This early art interest continued as Barton received his formal art training at Los Angeles City College and Chouinard Art Institute. Having received a scholarship to Chouinard, Barton was forced to leave when he was drafted into the Army and sent to Korea; it was only after his discharge that he was able to complete his art training. A move to New York City brought Barton jobs as an illustrator for an advertising agency and as an animated film designer for CBS-TV. These experiences led to illustrating other author's works and eventually the writing and illustrating of his own children's books.

The author's first children's book contains no text. In *Elephant* Barton illustrates a young girl's journey through fantasy and reality by showing young readers all

and sleep in zero gravity.

For young readers who dream of space travel, Barton's self-illustrated *I Want to Be an Astronaut* offers a glimpse into the life of astronauts aboard the space shuttle.

We put the teeth in the head bones   and the head bones on the neck bones.

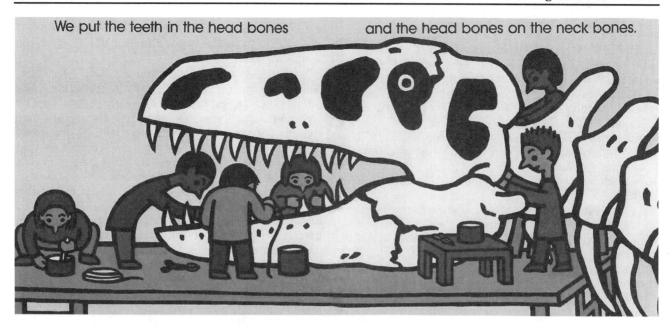

Children learn how paleontologists find, clean, and reassemble dinosaur bones by following the bold illustrations in *Bones, Bones, Dinosaur Bones.* (Written and illustrated by Byron Barton.)

the different shapes and sizes in which elephants may appear. A reviewer for *Publishers Weekly* asserts that no words are necessary to convey Barton's theme because the "bold, cheerful drawings ... send the imagination soaring." This first picture book has since been joined by several others, including *Where's Al?* and *Buzz Buzz Buzz,* all with Barton's trademark illustration style and simple text.

A very timid young boy is the focus of *Harry Is a Scaredy-Cat,* published in 1974. Afraid of everything, from other children to animals and cars, Harry is forced to face his fears during a trip to the circus with his father. Terrified of everything around him, Harry finds himself entangled in a bunch of balloons, lifted high into the air, and then dropped. Despite the hair-raising adventure, he discovers that the circus is not as scary as he thought. A critic writing in *Publishers Weekly* praises Barton's "dazzling, non-stop-action texts." *Horn Book* reviewer Ethel L. Heins compares Barton's illustrations to a "firmly drawn, concise, and spirited" comic strip but with much brighter colors.

Action plays a big part in most of Barton's stories, especially those that teach children about a certain activity, such as the construction of a house. *Building a House* starts with a plot of land being surveyed, moves on to laying the foundation, describes the electrical wiring and plumbing process, shows the walls being painted, and concludes with a family moving into the finished product. "In *Building a House* I wanted to show, with simple words and pictures, the different workers coming one after the other to do their part: digging the hole, making the floor, putting up the walls, putting in the plumbing," explains Barton in *Junior Literary Guild.* "Then, when all the work is done, the family comes to live inside the house."

With *Airport* Barton similarly shows his young audience the activities in an airport that surround the preparations for a flight before it takes off. Mary M. Burns showers praise on Barton in her *Horn Book* review for capturing all the "excitement and bustle of a major airport" while keeping the flow of events in a clear, well-focused order. A contributor to *Publishers Weekly* points out that the picture book is filled with Barton's hallmark "flashy primary colors and inspired character-izations" and goes on to say that *Airport* "is a wonder."

Airplanes are described again as part of Barton's series focusing on different forms of transportation. The books in this series, including *Trucks, Boats, Airplanes,* and *Trains,* feature illustrations of different vehicles that fall into these categories, as well as some of the activities surrounding them, such as a boat docking and a train stopping to pick up passengers. Linda Wicher, writing in *School Library Journal,* relates that all the books in the series feature "brightly colored illustrations" which present many "accurate details that preschoolers find so fascinating." A critic in *Publishers Weekly* applauds Barton's understandable concepts and illustrations, noting that "a little says a great deal here."

The details of a trip to outer space are the focus of Barton's *I Want to Be an Astronaut.* A crew of six children who want to be astronauts now, as opposed to waiting until they grow up, make up the crew of the space shuttle. Along with enjoying the new sensations of weightlessness and ready-to-eat space food, the young crew also fixes a satellite and builds a space factory before journeying back to earth. In *I Want to Be an Astronaut,* "Barton has provided an especially evocative early career book," according to Zena Sutherland in *Bulletin of the Center for Children's Books. Horn Book* contributor Nancy Vasilakis praises Barton's illustra-tions, stating that "astronauts, spaceships, and the earth

She got a wee little milk
from the wee little cow

in the wee little pail.

Barton retells the classic tale of a tiny woman and her devious little cat in his self-illustrated picture book *The Wee Little Woman*.

itself unite in dramatic visual harmonies." Writing in the *New York Times Book Review*, Roger Sutton describes Barton's vision of space as "downright giddy," going on to conclude: "*I Want to Be an Astronaut* has a sense of adventure that enlarges its context beyond space to the realm of imaginative journey."

Another profession is explored in *Bones, Bones, Dinosaur Bones*. In the beginning of the book, six young paleontologists methodically dig up dinosaur bones, carefully package their findings, and then travel with them to the natural history museum. The process of cleaning each bone and then assembling them into a recognizable dinosaur skeleton is detailed at the museum. And once the project is complete, the young workers leave in search of more bones, starting the cycle over again. *Horn Book* contributor Ellen Fader applauds Barton's "accuracy, simplicity, appropriateness, appeal for intended audience, and timeliness" in describing paleontological work. In *Five Owls* Camper calls *Bones, Bones, Dinosaur Bones* "a gentle rainbow procession of discovery, mixing a little magic into this search for bones."

In a departure from his more realistic stories, Barton tells the tale of a tiny woman in *The Wee Little Woman*. The daily activities of the wee little woman are the focus of this book. She starts her day by milking her wee little cow, placing the milk on her wee little table. Things go awry, though, when her wee little cat drinks the milk and runs away for a wee little time after being scolded. By the time the cat returns home, all is forgiven and a new bowl of milk is waiting for the petite feline. "This reassuring story is told in simple words with lots of repetition," observes Leone McDermott in *Booklist*. And Marcia Hupp, writing in *School Library Journal*, notices that the illustrations in *The Wee Little Woman*

"have a satisfying heft well suited to this most satisfying little tale."

■ Works Cited

Review of *Airport, Publishers Weekly*, January 29, 1982, p. 67.

Barton, Byron, comments in *Junior Literary Guild*, March, 1981.

Burns, Mary M., review of *Airport, Horn Book*, April, 1982, pp. 152-53.

Camper, Cathryn A., review of *Bones, Bones, Dinosaur Bones, Five Owls*, November/December, 1990, p. 28.

Review of *Elephant, Publishers Weekly*, October 4, 1971, p. 60.

Fader, Ellen, review of *Bones, Bones, Dinosaur Bones, Horn Book*, November/December, 1990, pp. 724-25.

Review of *Harry Is a Scaredy-Cat, Publishers Weekly*, February 25, 1974, p. 114.

Heins, Ethel L., review of *Harry Is a Scaredy-Cat, Horn Book*, June, 1974, p. 271.

Hupp, Marcia, review of *The Wee Little Woman, School Library Journal*, August, 1995, p. 114.

McDermott, Leone, review of *The Wee Little Woman, Booklist*, July, 1995, p. 1882.

Sutherland, Zena, review of *I Want to Be an Astronaut, Bulletin of the Center for Children's Books*, October, 1988, p. 26.

Sutton, Roger, "Don't Worry, Be Giddy," *New York Times Book Review*, November 13, 1988, p. 46.

Review of *Trucks, Boats, Airplanes*, and *Trains, Publishers Weekly*, May 30, 1986, p. 61.

Vasilakis, Nancy, review of *I Want to Be an Astronaut, Horn Book*, July/August, 1988, p. 476.

Wicher, Linda, review of *Airplanes, Boats, Trains,* and *Trucks, School Library Journal,* September, 1986, p. 116.

■ For More Information See

PERIODICALS

Bulletin of the Center for Children's Books, October, 1975, p. 21; September, 1979, p. 2; May, 1982, p. 162; October, 1988, p. 26; September, 1989, p. 3; January, 1992, p. 117.
Horn Book, June, 1979, pp. 290-91; August, 1981, p. 412; January/February, 1988, pp. 49-50; May/June, 1989.
Kirkus Reviews, July 15, 1973, p. 750; March 1, 1982, p. 269; June 15, 1986, p. 935; June 15, 1988, p. 896; July 15, 1991, p. 937.
New York Times Book Review, May 5, 1974, p. 46; October 26, 1975, p. 17; April 29, 1979, p. 45.
Publishers Weekly, October 4, 1971, p. 60; September 18, 1972, p. 73; January 29, 1982, p. 67; May 30, 1986, p. 61; August 10, 1990, p. 443; November 1, 1991, p. 79; May 3, 1993, pp. 304-305; May 8, 1995, p. 294.
School Library Journal, April, 1979, p. 39; April, 1981, p. 108; September, 1986, p. 116; May, 1988, p. 76; July, 1993, p. 80.

*   *   *

BELL, William 1945-

■ Personal

Born October 27, 1945, in Toronto, Ontario, Canada; son of William B. (a tool and die maker) and Irene (Spowart) Bell; children: Dylan, Megan, Brendan; companion to Ting-Xing Ye (a writer). *Education:* University of Toronto, M.A. (literature), 1969; Ontario Institute for Studies in Education, M.Ed., 1984.

■ Addresses

Home—Ontario, Canada.

■ Career

High school English teacher and department head in Ontario, Canada, 1970-82, 1984-85, 1987—; Harbin University of Science and Technology, English instructor, 1982-83; Foreign Affairs College of China, Beijing, English instructor, 1985-86. *Member:* Amnesty International, Greenpeace.

■ Awards, Honors

Ruth Schwartz Award for Excellence in Children's Literature, Belgium Award for Excellence in Children's Literature, and Ontario School Librarians' Award for Excellence, all 1990, all for *Forbidden City;* Manitoba Young Readers' Choice Award, for *Five Days of the Ghost.*

WILLIAM BELL

■ Writings

YOUNG ADULT NOVELS

Crabbe, Stoddart, 1986, published in the United States as *Crabbe's Journey,* Little, Brown, 1987.
Metal Head, Prentice-Hall, 1987.
The Cripples' Club, Stoddart, 1988, published as *Absolutely Invincible,* 1991.
Death Wind, Prentice-Hall, 1989.
Five Days of the Ghost, Stoddart, 1989.
Forbidden City, Bantam, 1990.
No Signature, Doubleday Canada, 1992.
Speak to the Earth, Doubleday Canada, 1994.

PICTURE BOOKS

The Golden Disk, illustrated by Don Kilby, Doubleday Canada, 1995.
River, My Friend, Orca Book Publishers (Victoria, British Columbia), 1996.

OTHER

Editor of *Contours,* an anthology of Canadian drama, Irwin (Toronto), 1993. Bell has also contributed two essays, "Selling Writing (Across the Curriculum)" and "Teaching Writing," to the periodical *Indirections,* published quarterly by the Ontario Council of Teachers of English.

Bell's books have also been published in Great Britain, Iceland, Norway, Sweden, Denmark, Finland, Belgium, Germany, and Spain.

■ Sidelights

Canadian young adult novelist William Bell is best known for his award-winning novel *Forbidden City*. An English teacher since 1970, Bell published his first book, *Crabbe* (also published as *Crabbe's Journey*) in 1986. The story of a teenage boy who runs away from home into the Canadian wilderness and learns some valuable lessons from another runaway named Mary, *Crabbe* received mixed reviews from critics, one of whom found the title character to be unlikable and uncompelling. "[It] is difficult to feel anything but contempt for this shallow fellow," remarked *Quill & Quire* critic Linda Granfield about Franklin Crabbe, the rich, lazy, and spoiled protagonist of the story. However, other reviewers saw Bell's debut book in a more positive light. For example, a *Kirkus Reviews* writer felt that the author writes about the wilderness "with a grace and perceptiveness often lacking in adolescent fiction."

In *Crabbe's Journey* Bell used the narrative technique of telling the story through journal entries. He would use the same device in some of his later novels, including *Forbidden City.* Set in 1989 and based on an actual incident, *Forbidden City* is about a young Canadian named Alex Jackson who journeys to China with his cameraman father to cover the unrest that will ultimately lead to the massacre of pro-democracy students by government soldiers. Recording his experiences in his journal, Alex writes about the people he meets, such as Lao Xu, an interpreter who is paid by the Communist government to spy on foreigners but who also has sympathies for the growing democratic movement. Just as Alex's father has finished his assignment and is preparing to leave the country, the conflict at Tian An Men Square reaches a head. In the confusion, Alex is separated from his father, but he is helped by some of the students and given a place to hide. One of the students, Xin-hua, proves herself particularly brave by offering to take Alex to the Canadian Embassy. In the attempt, she is killed by the People's Liberation Army. Alex, however, is reunited with his father and they return to Canada with the film and tapes that will show the tragic events to the rest of the world.

Many critics considered Bell's depiction of the turbulent time in China portrayed in *Forbidden City* to be masterful. "Well written, well paced, and all too believable, this is an impressive novel," asserted Zena Sutherland in the *Bulletin of the Center for Children's Books.* A *Growing Point* reviewer further praised the work, not only for its lucid depictions of "duplicity, intrigue and cruelty," but also for offering "strikingly individual views" of the massacre.

Bell returned to Canada as the setting for his young adult novels since *Forbidden City,* but the issues he tackles in these books are no less important than government treachery. *No Signature,* in fact, deals with

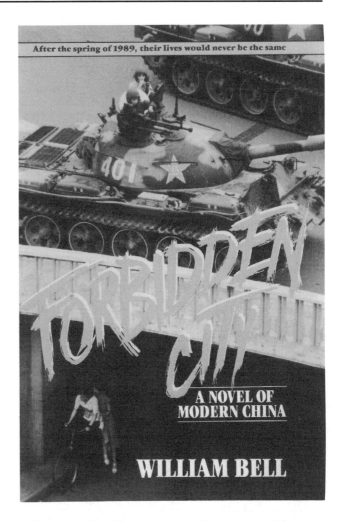

After the spring of 1989, their lives would never be the same

FORBIDDEN CITY

A NOVEL OF MODERN CHINA

WILLIAM BELL

Accompanying his cameraman father on a trip to China, seventeen-year-old Alex Jackson doesn't realize he will witness an important part of history as Communist authorities quell a student demonstration in Tian An Men Square.

many issues at once, including illiteracy, homosexuality, broken families, and prejudice. The story is centered on Wick Chandler, who learns that it was his mother's attempt to blackmail her husband that caused his father to abandon the family. But Wick learns some humility too, after he comes to realize that he similarly abandoned his friend after learning that his friend was gay. In his next work, *Speak to the Earth,* Bell's interest in the environment led him to write a fictional story based on the indiscriminate logging practices that continue to destroy much of the wilderness in British Columbia.

More recently, Bell has begun writing picture books for children. He returns to China, where he once spent two years as an English teacher, with *The Golden Disk,* the simple story of a little girl who sets out to discover what the moon is and learns of its connection to her name. He has continued along this vein with his next picture book, *River, My Friend.*

■ Works Cited

Review of *Crabbe's Journey, Kirkus Reviews,* May 15, 1987, pp. 790-91.
Review of *Forbidden City, Growing Point,* November 1990, p. 5435.
Granfield, Linda, "Coming of Age a Matter of Quality in Two New Young-Adult Novels," *Quill & Quire,* June 1986, p. 25.
Sutherland, Zena, review of *Forbidden City, Bulletin of the Center for Children's Books,* February 1991, p. 137.

■ For More Information See

PERIODICALS

Booklist, July 1987, p. 1671; November 15, 1987, p. 576; June 15, 1990, p. 2000; September 15, 1990, p. 178; January 15, 1991, p. 1054; February 1, 1991, p. 1122.
Bulletin of the Center for Children's Books, July-August, 1987.
Horn Book Guide, July, 1990, p. 87.
Junior Bookshelf, December, 1990, p. 304.
Kirkus Reviews, November 15, 1990, p. 1598.
Publishers Weekly, May 8, 1987, p. 73; November 16, 1990, p. 58.
Quill & Quire, June, 1990, p. 16; March, 1995, p. 78.
School Librarian, February, 1991, p. 29.
School Library Journal, May, 1987, p. 106; March, 1991, p. 211.

* * *

BOVAIRD, Anne E(lizabeth) 1960-

■ Personal

Born March 15, 1960, in New York, NY; daughter of James Alexander, III (an investor) and Elaine Francis Tobin Bovaird. *Education:* Denison University, B.A., 1982; attended University of Illinois Circle Campus, 1984-85.

■ Addresses

Home—521 Walnut St., Winnetka, IL 60093; and 63, rue des Vinaigriers, 75010 Paris, France.

■ Career

Grassroots Research, San Francisco, CA, journalist, 1989—; Universites de Paris X and XIII, Paris, teacher, 1991—. Journalist-on-staff for *Transatlantic,* a magazine for Americans living in Europe; freelancer in the fields of education, translation, and journalism for a number of clients both in France and the United States. *Member:* Association of American Residents Overseas, Amnesty International.

ANNE E. BOVAIRD

■ Writings

"GOODBYE U.S.A." SERIES

Goodbye U.S.A.—Bonjour la France: A Language Learning Adventure, illustrated by Pierre Ballouhey, Barron's, 1993.
Goodbye U.S.A.—Bonjour la France: A Language Learning Adventure Volume II, illustrated by Pierre Ballouhey, Barron's, 1994.

OTHER

(With L. Potier) *Dictionnaire anglais-francais,* Pierre Bordas et Fils, 1990.

Both volumes of *Goodbye U.S.A.—Bonjour la France* have been translated into an English/Spanish version by Harriet Barnett, Barron's, 1994.

■ Work in Progress

Continuation of the "Goodbye U.S.A." series.

■ Sidelights

"My inspiration for writing children's books came from several young members of my family who had a desire to learn some French words from their 'favorite aunt,'" Anne E. Bovaird told *SATA.* "After going through the bookstore shelves in search of teaching material, I discovered there was very little available. This fact motivated my creative juices and thus *Goodbye U.S.A.—Bonjour la France: A Language Learning Adventure* was born.

"I submitted the manuscript (without the aid of an agent) to several publishing houses and was very fortunate to have Barron's accept my story. Volume II followed, continuing the Tom and Pierre saga. In addition to the English/French version, my editors asked permission to translate the book into English/Spanish. Much to my dismay/surprise, the latter seems to be outselling the former.

"*Goodbye U.S.A.—Bonjour la France* was written not only to entertain, but to provide a subtle foreign language teaching tool, with many substantial references to cultural differences. It also includes phonetic pronunciation, and a bilingual glossary.

"Currently, my time is divided between teaching, journalism, creative writing, and enjoying Paris where I have been living since 1984. Another children's tale of Tom's adventures in Paris is underway."

■ For More Information See

PERIODICALS

Horn Book Guide, spring, 1995, p. 64.
Science Books & Films, August, 1994, p. 180.

* * *

BRADLEY, Marion Zimmer 1930-
(Lee Chapman, John Dexter, Miriam Gardner, Valeric Graves, Morgan Ives, Elfrida Rivers)

■ Personal

Born June 3, 1930, in Albany, NY; daughter of Leslie (a carpenter) and Evelyn (a historian; maiden name, Conklin) Zimmer; married Robert A. Bradley, October, 1949 (divorced, 1963); married Walter Henry Breen (a numismatist), June, 1964 (divorced); children: (first marriage) David Stephen Robert; (second marriage) Patrick Russell Donald, Moira Evelyn Dorothy. *Education:* Attended New York State College for Teachers (now State University of New York at Albany), 1946-48; Hardin-Simmons College, B.A., 1964; additional study at University of California, Berkeley. *Politics:* None. *Hobbies and other interests:* Supports Merola, an opera apprentice program.

■ Addresses

Home—Berkeley, CA. *Office*—P.O. Box 72, Berkeley, CA 94701. *Agent*—Scovil Chichak Galen Literary Agency, 381 Park Ave. S., #1020, New York, NY 10016.

MARION ZIMMER BRADLEY

■ Career

Writer, editor, and musician. *Member:* Authors Guild, Authors League of America, Science Fiction Writers of America, Alpha Chi.

■ Awards, Honors

Hugo Award nomination, 1963; Nebula Award nominations, 1964 and 1978; Invisible Little Man Award, 1977; Leigh Brackett Memorial Sense of Wonder Award, 1978, for *The Forbidden Tower;* Locus Award for best fantasy novel, 1984, for *The Mists of Avalon.*

■ Writings

SCIENCE FICTION/FANTASY

The Door through Space (bound with *Rendezvous on Lost Planet* by A. Bertram Chandler), Ace Books, 1961.
Seven from the Stars (bound with *Worlds of the Imperium* by Keith Laumer), Ace Books, 1962.
The Colors of Space, Monarch, 1963, revised edition, illustrated by Barbi Johnson, Donning (Norfolk, VA), 1983, illustrated by Lee Moyer, Donning, 1988.
Falcons of Narabedla [and] *The Dark Intruder and Other Stories,* Ace Books, 1964.
The Brass Dragon (bound with *Ipomoea* by John Rackham), Ace Books, 1969.
(With brother, Paul Edwin Zimmer) *Hunters of the Red Moon,* DAW Books, 1973.
The Parting of Arwen (short story), T-K Graphics, 1974.

The Endless Voyage, Ace Books, 1975, expanded edition published as *Endless Universe,* 1979.

The Ruins of Isis, illustrated by Polly and Kelly Freas, Donning, 1978.

(With P. E. Zimmer) *The Survivors,* DAW Books, 1979.

The House between the Worlds, Doubleday, 1980, revised edition, Del Rey, 1981.

Survey Ship, illustrated by Steve Fabian, Ace Books, 1980.

The Mists of Avalon, Knopf, 1982.

The Web of Darkness, illustrated by V. M. Wyman and C. Lee Healy, Donning, 1983.

Web of Light, illustrated by C. Lee Healy, Donning, 1983.

(Editor and contributor) *Greyhaven: An Anthology of Fantasy,* DAW Books, 1983.

Night's Daughter, Ballantine, 1985.

(With Vonda McIntyre) *Lythande* (anthology), DAW Books, 1986.

The Fall of Atlantis (includes *Web of Light* and *Web of Darkness*), Baen Books, 1987.

The Firebrand, Simon & Schuster, 1987.

Warrior Woman, DAW Books, 1988.

(With Andre Norton and Julian May) *The Black Trillium,* Doubleday, 1990.

The Forest House, Viking, 1994.

Lady of the Trillium, Bantam, 1995.

(With Andre Norton and Mercedes Lackey) *Tiger Burning Bright,* Morrow, 1995.

"DARKOVER" SCIENCE FICTION SERIES

The Sword of Aldones [and] *The Planet Savers,* Ace Books, 1962, *The Sword of Aldones* published separately with introduction by Richard A. Lupoff, Gregg Press (Boston), 1977, *The Planet Savers,* published separately with introduction by Bradley, Gregg Press, 1979, both volumes reprinted and bound together as *Planet Savers: The Sword of Aldones,* Ace Books, 1984.

The Bloody Sun, Ace Books, 1964, revised edition, Ace Books, 1979, with introduction by Bradley, Gregg Press, 1979.

Star of Danger, Ace Books, 1965, with introduction by Bradley, Gregg Press, 1979.

The Winds of Darkover (bound with *The Anything Tree* by John Rackham), Ace Books, 1970, with introduction by Bradley, Gregg Press, 1979.

The World Wreckers, Ace Books, 1971, with introduction by Bradley, Gregg Press, 1979.

Darkover Landfall, DAW Books, 1972, with introduction by Theodore Sturgeon, Gregg Press, 1978.

The Spell Sword, DAW Books, 1974, with introduction by Bradley, Gregg Press, 1979.

The Heritage of Hastur, DAW Books, 1975, with introduction by Susan Wood, Gregg Press, 1977.

The Shattered Chain, DAW Books, 1976, with introduction by Bradley, Gregg Press, 1979.

The Forbidden Tower, DAW Books, 1977, with introduction by Bradley, Gregg Press, 1979.

Stormqueen!, DAW Books, 1978, with introduction by Bradley, Gregg Press, 1979.

(Editor and contributor) *Legends of Hastur and Cassilda,* Thendara House Publications (Berkeley, CA), 1979.

(Editor and contributor) *Tales of the Free Amazons,* Thendara House Publications, 1980.

Two to Conquer, DAW Books, 1980.

(Editor and contributor) *The Keeper's Price and Other Stories,* DAW Books, 1980.

Sharra's Exile, DAW Books, 1981.

Children of Hastur (includes *The Heritage of Hastur* and *Sharra's Exile*), Doubleday, 1981.

Hawkmistress!, DAW Books, 1982.

(Editor and contributor) *Sword of Chaos,* DAW Books, 1982.

Thendara House, DAW Books, 1983.

Oath of the Renunciates (includes *The Shattered Chain* and *Thendara House*), Doubleday, 1983.

City of Sorcery, DAW Books, 1984.

(Editor, contributor, and author of introduction) *Free Amazons of Darkover: An Anthology,* DAW Books, 1985.

(Editor and contributor) *Red Sun of Darkover,* DAW Books, 1987.

(Editor and contributor) *The Other Side of the Mirror and Other Darkover Stories,* DAW Books, 1987.

(Editor and contributor) *Four Moons of Darkover,* DAW Books, 1988.

The Heirs of Hammerfell, DAW Books, 1989.

(Editor) *Domains of Darkover,* DAW Books, 1990.

(Editor) *Renunciates of Darkover,* DAW Books, 1991.

(Editor) *Leroni of Darkover,* DAW Books, 1991.

(Editor) *Towers of Darkover,* DAW Books, 1993.

(With Mercedes Lackey) *Rediscovery: A Novel of Darkover,* DAW Books, 1993.

Marion Zimmer Bradley's Darkover (short stories), DAW Books, 1993.

Exile's Song, DAW Books, 1996.

GOTHIC FICTION

(Under pseudonym Miriam Gardner) *The Strange Woman,* Monarch, 1962.

Castle Terror, Lancer (New York City), 1965.

Souvenir of Monique, Ace Books, 1967.

Bluebeard's Daughter, Lancer, 1968.

Dark Satanic, Berkley Publishing, 1972.

Drums of Darkness: An Astrological Gothic Novel, Ballantine, 1976.

The Inheritor, Tor Books, 1984.

Witch Hill, Tor Books, 1990.

Ghostlight, Tor Books, 1995.

NOVELS

(Under pseudonym Lee Chapman) *I Am a Lesbian,* Monarch, 1962.

(Under pseudonym Morgan Ives) *Spare Her Heaven,* Monarch, 1963.

(Under pseudonym Miriam Gardner) *My Sister, My Love,* Monarch, 1963.

(Under pseudonym Miriam Gardner) *Twilight Lovers,* Monarch, 1964.

(Under pseudonym Morgan Ives) *Knives of Desire,* Cornith (San Diego, CA), 1966.

(Under pseudonym John Dexter) *No Adam for Eve*, Cornith, 1966.
The Catch Trap, Ballantine, 1979.

Also author of novels as Valerie Graves and under other undisclosed pseudonyms.

CRITICISM

Men, Halflings, and Hero Worship, T-K Graphics, 1973.
The Necessity for Beauty: Robert W. Chamber and the Romantic Tradition, T-K Graphics, 1974.
The Jewel of Arwen, T-K Graphics, 1974.

OTHER

Songs from Rivendell, privately printed, 1959.
A Complete, Cumulative Checklist of Lesbian, Variant, and Homosexual Fiction, privately printed, 1960.
(Translator) Lope de Vega, *El Villano en su Rincon*, privately printed, 1971.
In the Steps of the Master (teleplay novelization), Tempo Books, 1973.
Can Ellen Be Saved? (teleplay novelization), Tempo Books, 1975.
(With Alfred Bester and Norman Spinrad) *Experiment Perilous: Three Essays in Science Fiction*, Algol Press, 1976.
The Ballad of Hastur and Cassilda (poem), Thendara House Publications, 1978.
(Editor) *Sword and Sorceress* (annual anthology), Volumes 1-14, DAW Books, 1984-97.
The Best of Marion Zimmer Bradley, edited by Martin H. Greenberg, Academy Chicago (Chicago, IL), 1986, revised edition published as *Jamie and Other Stories: The Best of Marion Zimmer Bradley*, 1991.

Contributor, sometimes under name Elfrida Rivers and other pseudonyms, to anthologies, books, and periodicals, including *Essays Lovecraftian*, edited by Darrell Schweitzer, T-K Graphics, 1976, *Magazine of Fantasy and Science Fiction*, *Amazing Stories*, and *Venture*. Editor of *Marion Zimmer Bradley's Fantasy Magazine*, 1988—.

■ Sidelights

Marion Zimmer Bradley is author of one of the best-loved series in science fiction and fantasy; her "Darkover" novels have not only inspired their own fan magazines, known as "fanzines," but also a series of story collections in which other authors set their tales in Bradley's universe. In addition, as the creator of the bestselling *The Mists of Avalon*, Bradley has become one of the genre's most widely known writers. Her retelling of the Arthurian legend from the female point of view has brought her insightful examinations of human psychology and her skill in plot and characterization to the attention of an appreciative new audience, including young adults. As Sister Avila Lamb states in *Kliatt Young Adult Paperback Book Guide*, "The name of Marion Zimmer Bradley is a guarantee of excellence. Creative imagination, strong, fleshed-out characters, compelling style, an uncanny ability to make all totally credible combine to involve readers from the first pages, never releasing them until long after the last page."

Bradley grew up in Albany, New York, and focused on reading and schoolwork to escape family troubles. She excelled in school, and recalled in *Contemporary Authors Autobiography Series* (*CAAS*) that while it wasn't popular for girls to show their smarts, "I thought most of the time that having brains was just fine, and I built my life on it, since I was stuck with it anyhow." Her academic achievements earned her a National Merit Scholarship, and at age sixteen Bradley graduated from high school. "I went to college and, almost at the same time, discovered pulp science fiction," the author continued in her essay. "I think I can honestly say this was the turning point of my life."

Bradley had always harbored a desire to write; "I'm told that I started dictating poems to my mother before I could print," she related in Daryl Lane, William Vernon, and David Carson's *The Sound of Wonder*. But when the author entered college, she wasn't sure which direction her ambition would take her. Bradley soon discovered the world of science fiction fandom, however, with its conventions, newsletters, and amateur

Returning to the planet she fled as a child, Margaret Alton discovers her long-buried memories painfully resurfacing. (Cover illustration by Romas Kukalis.)

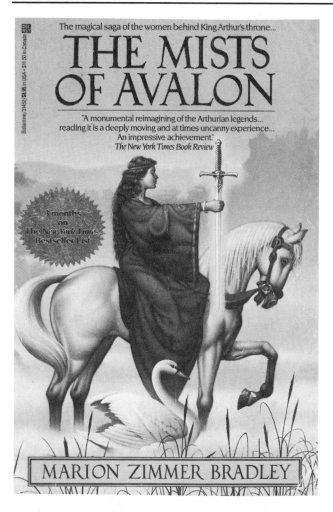

The magical saga of the women behind King Arthur's throne...

THE MISTS OF AVALON

"A monumental reimagining of the Arthurian legends...
reading it is a deeply moving and at times uncanny experience."
An impressive achievement."
The New York Times Book Review

3 months
on
The New York Times
Bestseller List

MARION ZIMMER BRADLEY

Bradley retells the magical legend of King Arthur and his half sister Morgaine's struggle to return Britain to its original Celtic religion. (Cover illustration by Braldt Bralds.)

magazines, or "fanzines." As she recalled in *The Sound of Wonder* interview: "When I discovered the new pulp magazines—*Astounding, Thrilling Wonder Stories,* that sort of thing—and I saw the fan magazines in the back, . . . it made me realize that there were other people who liked this sort of thing. All of a sudden, I realized that not only did I want to write for a living but that I wanted to write science fiction and fantasy." Through fandom the author saw her first story published—at age nineteen—and although she married young and was soon a mother, she continued writing while raising her children.

By the early 1960s, Bradley had published her first novels and was well on her way to establishing herself as a prominent figure in the genre. Although at that time science fiction was still dominated by male writers and editors, Bradley encountered no problems with discrimination. "I never knew an editor who cared whether I was a man or a woman or one of Aldous Huxley's fifty million apes as long as I could tell a good story," she recalled to Rosemary Herbert in *Publishers Weekly.* Bradley's first full-fledged Darkover works, *The Sword of Aldones* and *The Planet Savers,* appeared in a 1962

Ace double edition. By 1970 Bradley had written three more novels set on the forgotten Terran settlement of Darkover, and the series was gaining popularity among science fiction fans.

Bradley explained in *The Sound of Wonder* her rationale for returning to Darkover for material: "I realized that I'd had to cut out so much [from the first book] that what I had cut out would make a sizable new book." Because she was also busy caring for her husband and children, including two toddlers, using a familiar setting was easier than working out the details for an entirely new world. "I figured that since people would read lots of books about Tarzan, Perry Mason, or Nero Wolfe . . . that people evidently liked reading about stories with the same background; it was easier to write about [Darkover] than to invent a whole new universe for each book."

Despite her frequent trips to the Darkover universe, Bradley made it a point to keep the novels independent from each other. "I had a feeling, and other writers told me, rather cynically, that the life of a paperback book was about five or six months," Bradley stated in *The Sound of Wonder.* "I realized that it was not safe to assume that anyone who read any of my books had ever read a previous book or would ever read another book by me. So I work[ed] very hard to make each book stand on its own feet and not assume any knowledge of previous books." This strategy—and the intelligent, challenging novels that resulted from it—was rewarded with the loyalty and appreciation of readers; by the time Bradley thought people "must be getting tired of it," the series was well established and Bradley's fans demanded more novels of Darkover. As Margaret Miles asserts in *Voice of Youth Advocates,* Bradley's "tremendously popular network of writings" about Darkover "has long been notable for holding something for almost every taste."

Now consisting of over twenty books and spanning centuries of the world's history, Bradley's Darkover novels are less a "series" with a specific order than a network of individual stories linked by a common setting. Rediscovered after centuries of neglect by Earth's Terran Empire, the planet Darkover has now developed an independent society and a science based on powers of the mind. Darkover fascinates so many readers because it is a world of many contradictions; not only do the psychic abilities of the natives contrast with the traditional science of the Empire, but a basically repressive, male-dominated society coexists—however uneasily—with groups such as the Free Amazons, independent bands of women that govern themselves. The variety of internal and external conflicts produced by the collision of the Terran and Darkovan societies has provided Bradley with a wide range of story lines, told from the point of view of different people from different eras.

The constant culture clash on Darkover is one of the foremost conflicts in the series; the Empire is dependent on advanced technology—symbolized by the long-range blasters carried by the Terran Spaceforce—while the realms of Darkover have made a Compact that outlaws weapons that can kill from a distance. As a result, "the Darkover novels test various attitudes about the importance of technology," Rosemarie Arbur claims in *Twentieth-Century Science Fiction Writers,* "and more important, they study the very nature of human intimacy." The critic explains that by contrasting Darkover's technologically "backward" yet fiercely independent people with the bureaucratic Empire of the Terrans, "Bradley sets up a conflict to which there is no 'correct' resolution." The author never settles the issue herself; as she commented in *The Sound of Wonder,* "There are different universes for different mental sets.... The idea of leaving open options and choices for everybody so they can find the kind of life-style that suits them best instead of assuming that everybody has to belong to the same life-style [is] something that I felt very strongly about when I was a kid and I feel even more strongly about now than when I was fifteen." As a consequence, Bradley presents multiple viewpoints and "allows her readers almost complete freedom to decide which of the technologies, or which combination of the two, is the more humanely practical solution," Arbur concludes.

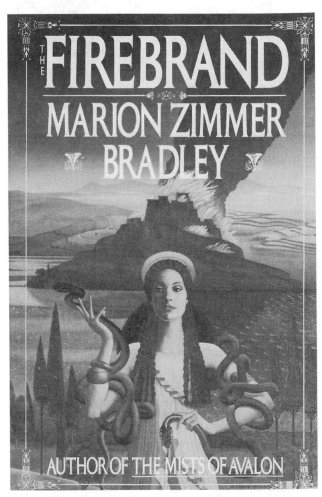

Through the words of Kassandra, the twin sister of Paris, Bradley retells the ancient story of the Trojan War. (Cover illustration by Wilson McLean.)

In *The Sword of Aldones,* for instance, a man of mixed Terran-Darkovan ancestry is called back to Darkover from self-imposed exile to oppose a renegade's illegal use of a destructive supernatural force known as "Sharra." Scarred by a previous encounter with Sharra's power, Lew Alton must use his Darkovan heritage in the service of a society that has never fully accepted him. "The most classically alienated of all Bradley heroes," as Laura Murphy describes him in the *Dictionary of Literary Biography,* Alton "is a metaphor for the uneasy union between the two cultures." In contrast to Alton, who remains outside both cultures, Terran Andrew Carr of *The Spell Sword* and *The Forbidden Tower* chooses Darkovan society over that of the Empire. Other books have followed the earlier exploits of Lew Alton, the friendship between a Terran boy and a youthful Kennard Alton (Lew's father), and a Terran scientist's efforts to cure a Darkovan plague; still others trace the long history of the planet prior to its discovery by the Empire, from the colony's founding to the forming of the Compact.

Despite the disparity in subjects, one theme in particular provides a foundation for the Darkover novels, Susan M. Shwartz observes in *The Feminine Eye: Science Fiction and the Women Who Write It:* "For every gain, there is a risk; choice involves a testing of will and courage." Unlike some fantasy worlds where struggles are easily or simply decided, "on Darkover any attempt at change or progress carries with it the need for pain-filled choice," Shwartz comments. While Bradley provides her characters with ample avenues of action "in the Darkover books, alternatives are predicated upon two things ... sincere choice and a willingness to pay the price choice demands." For example, Shwartz continues, "in *The Shattered Chain,* the payment for taking an oath is the payment for all such choices: pain, with a potential for achievement. In Bradley's other books, too, thc price of choice is of great importance."

The Shattered Chain is one of Bradley's most renowned Darkover novels and, as Arbur describes it in her study *Marion Zimmer Bradley,* the novel "is one of the most thorough and sensitive science-fiction explorations of the variety of options available to a self-actualizing woman." The novel begins as a traditional quest when Lady Rohana, a noblewoman of the ruling class, enlists the aid of a tribe of Free Amazons to rescue a kidnapped kinswoman from a settlement where women are chained to show that they are possessions. But while the rescue is eventually successful, it is only the beginning of a series of conflicts. Rohana's experiences force her to reevaluate her life, and both the daughter of the woman she rescues and a Terran agent who studies the Amazons find themselves examining the limits of their own situations. "In terms of its structure, plot, characterization, and context within the series," Shwartz argues, *The Shattered Chain* "is about all the choices of all women on Darkover and, through them, of all people, male and female, Darkovan and Terran."

Bradley also emphasizes two other themes, as Murphy states in the *Dictionary of Literary Biography:* "The first is the reconciliation of conflicting or opposing forces—whether such forces are represented by different cultures or by different facets of a single personality. The second," the critic continues, "closely related to the first, is alienation or exile from a dominant group." While these ideas are featured in Bradley's Darkover series, they also appear in the author's first mainstream best seller, *The Mists of Avalon.* "Colorfully detailed as a medieval tapestry, *The Mists of Avalon ...* is probably the most ambitious retelling of the Arthurian legend in the twentieth century," Charlotte Spivack maintains in *Merlin's Daughters: Contemporary Women Writers of Fantasy.* The critic adds that this novel "is much more than a retelling.... [It] is a profound revisioning. Imaginatively conceived, intricately structured, and richly peopled, it offers a brilliant reinterpretation of the traditional material from the point of view of the major female characters," such as Arthur's mother Igraine; the Lady of the Lake, Viviane; Arthur's half-sister, the enchantress Morgaine; and Arthur's wife, Gwenhwyfar.

In addition, Bradley presents the eventual downfall of Arthur's reign as the result of broken promises to the religious leaders of Avalon. While Arthur gained his crown with the aid of Viviane and the Goddess she represents, the influence of Christian priests and Gwenhwyfar led him to forsake his oath. Thus not only does Bradley present Arthur's story from a different viewpoint, she roots it "in the religious struggle between matriarchal worship of the goddess and the patriarchal institution of Christianity, between what [the author] calls 'the cauldron and the cross,'" writes Spivack. Despite critical praise for Bradley's fresh approach to Arthurian legend, *Washington Post* contributor Maude McDaniel finds *The Mists of Avalon* too motionless in its treatment of the Arthurian legend: "It all seems strangely static," the critic writes, "set pieces the reader watches rather than enters. Aside from a couple of lackluster jousts, everything is intrigue, jealousy and personal relationships, so that finally we are left with more bawling than brawling."

Maureen Quilligan, however, believes that Bradley's emphasis on Morgaine and the other female characters is both effective and appropriate; as she writes in the *New York Times Book Review,* by "looking at the Arthurian legend from the other side, as in one of Morgaine's magic weavings, we see all the interconnecting threads, not merely the artful pattern.... *The Mists of Avalon* rewrites Arthur's story so that we realize it has always also been the story of his sister, the Fairy Queen." By presenting another side, the critic adds, "this, the untold Arthurian story, is no less tragic, but it has gained a mythic coherence; reading it is a deeply moving and at times uncanny experience." "In short," concludes Beverly Deweese in a *Science Fiction Review* article, "Bradley's Arthurian world is intriguingly different. Undoubtedly, the brisk pace, the careful research and the provocative concept will attract and please many readers.... [But] overall, *Mists of Avalon* is one of the best and most ambitious of the Arthurian novels, and it should not be missed."

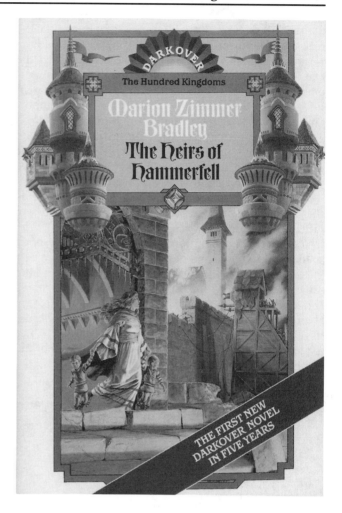

Part of the "Darkover" series, *The Heirs of Hammerfell* follows the lives of a special set of twins who must use magical powers to bring their people out of exile. (Cover illustration by Richard Hescox.)

Bradley employs similar themes and approaches in reworking another classic tale: *The Firebrand,* the story of the fall of ancient Troy and of Kassandra, royal daughter of Troy and onetime priestess and Amazon. As the author remarked in an interview with *Publishers Weekly's* Lisa See, in the story of Troy she saw another instance of male culture overtaking and obscuring female contributions: "During the Dorian invasion, when iron won out over bronze, the female cult died," Bradley explained. "The Minoan and Mycenaean cultures were dead overnight. But you could also look at [that period of history] and say, here were two cultures that should have been ruled by female twins—Helen and Klytemnestra. And what do you know? When they married Menelaus and Agamemnon, the men took over their cities. I just want to look at what history was really like before the women-haters got hold of it. I want to look at these people like any other people, as though no one had ever written about them before." The result of Bradley's reconstruction, as *New York Times Book Review* contributor Mary Lefkowitz describes it, is that Kassandra "becomes active, even aggressive; she determines the course of history, despite the efforts of her father, her brothers and other brutal male warriors to keep her in her place." "The dust of the war fairly rises off the page," notes a *Publishers Weekly* reviewer, "as Bradley animates this rich history and vivifies the conflicts between a culture that reveres the strength of women and one that makes them mere consorts of powerful men."

Bradley returns to ancient Britain with *The Forest House,* the story of the love between the erstwhile British priestess Eilan and the Roman officer Gaius Marcellius. The pair conceive a child before their respective families separate them, and Eilan in particular is caught between her feelings for Gaius, her position in the Forest House as High Priestess of the Great Goddess, and her problems with the competing influences of the Druids. After the two lovers are killed, Eilan's mentor takes their son Gawen to "Afallon." "With the sure touch of one at ease in sketching out mystic travels . . . ," explains a critic for *Kirkus Reviews,* "Bradley writes with an unhurried pace and uncluttered staging." "History and legend collide," declares Carolyn Cushman in *Locus,* "and though history dominates, by the end the mythic elements grow to hint satisfactorily at the Arthurian wonder to come."

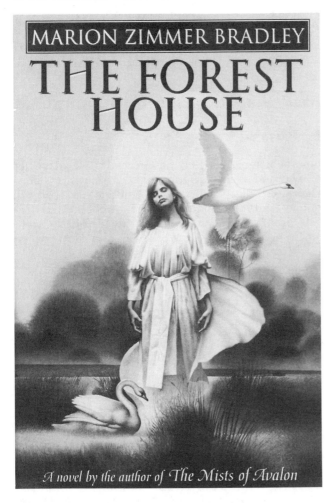

Knowing one day she will be High Priestess of the Oracle, Eilan must put aside her love for a young Roman intent on suppressing the Druidic religion of her British homeland.

Despite this emphasis on female viewpoints in *The Firebrand* and her other fiction, Bradley is not a "feminist" writer. "Though her interest in women's rights is strong," elaborates Murphy, "her works do not reduce to mere polemic." Arbur similarly states in her study that Bradley "refuses to allow her works to wander into politics unless true concerns of realistic characters bring them there. Her emphasis is on character, not political themes." "Bradley's writing openly with increasing sureness of the human psyche and the human being rendered whole prompted Theodore Sturgeon to call the former [science fiction] fan 'one of the Big ones' currently writing science fiction," Arbur relates in *Twentieth-Century Science Fiction Writers.* "That she has extended her range" beyond science fiction and into "mainstream" fiction, the critic concludes, "suggests that Sturgeon's phrase applies no longer only to the science-fiction writer Marion Zimmer Bradley continues to be, for she has transcended categories."

Although Bradley's reputation has spread beyond the science fiction and fantasy community, she has no intention of abandoning the genre. She enjoys it and appreciates both the new people and the new ideas she encounters through it. As she explains in *The Sound of Wonder,* "One thing that distinguishes the science fiction and fantasy fans [is that] they are thinking very seriously about the meaning of human life. Science fiction deals with the technological society in which we find ourselves and its various ramifications," the author continued. "Fantasy goes even deeper because it forces us to confront, you might say, the archetypal images in our own unconscious." She added that the science fiction and fantasy genre opens people's minds: "I think imagination is the one great thing that distinguishes us from the beasts, and science fiction is a very valuable corrective to modern education because it makes people think and it forces them to stretch their imaginations." Besides, she remarked in the introduction to *The Best of Marion Zimmer Bradley,* "I cannot imagine that the content of mainstream novels . . . can possibly compete with a fiction whose sole raison d'etre is to think about the future of the human race."

Although she has diabetes and has suffered two strokes, Bradley continues working from her office in Berkeley, California. There, with the assistance of a cousin, Bradley deals with the business end of being a writer: responding to mail, producing booklets of writing tips, editing original anthologies that introduce the work of new writers—in addition to working on original fiction. "God knows where I will go from here," the author concluded in *CAAS;* "but writing is a profession from which there is no retiring. The only way to kill off a writer is to shoot her; the very popular Agatha Christie finished her last book at eighty-six; Rex Stout, at eighty-nine. I fully intend to outlast all of them."

■ Works Cited

Arbur, Rosemarie, *Marion Zimmer Bradley,* Starmont House, 1985.

Arbur, Rosemarie, "Marion Zimmer Bradley," *Twentieth-Century Science Fiction Writers,* 2nd edition, St. James Press, 1986, pp. 75-77.

Bradley, Marion Zimmer, introduction to *The Best of Marion Zimmer Bradley,* edited by Martin H. Greenberg, DAW Books, 1988.

Bradley, Marion Zimmer, *Contemporary Authors Autobiography Series,* Volume 10, Gale, 1989, pp. 19-28.

Cushman, Carolyn, review of *The Forest House, Locus,* April, 1994, p. 29.

Deweese, Beverly, review of *The Mists of Avalon, Science Fiction Review,* summer, 1983, pp. 20-21.

Review of *The Firebrand, Publishers Weekly,* September 11, 1987, p. 79.

Review of *The Forest House, Kirkus Reviews,* February 1, 1994, pp. 81-82.

Herbert, Rosemary, "The Authors' Vision," *Publishers Weekly,* May 23, 1986, pp. 42-45.

Lamb, Sister Avila, review of *Thendara House, Kliatt Young Adult Paperback Book Guide,* November, 1983, p. 1.

Lane, Daryl, William Vernon, and David Carson, editors, *The Sound of Wonder: Interviews from "The Science Fiction Radio Show,"* Volume 2, Oryx, 1985, pp. 111-32.

Lefkowitz, Mary, review of *The Firebrand, New York Times Book Review,* November 29, 1987, p. 27.

McDaniel, Maude, review of *The Mists of Avalon, Washington Post,* January 28, 1983.

Miles, Margaret, review of *The Heirs of Hammerfell, Voice of Youth Advocates,* June, 1990, p. 113.

Murphy, Laura, "Marion Zimmer Bradley," *Dictionary of Literary Biography,* Volume 8: *Twentieth-Century American Science Fiction Writers,* Gale, 1981, pp. 77-80.

Quilligan, Maureen, "Arthur's Sister's Story," *New York Times Book Review,* January 30, 1983, pp. 11, 30.

See, Lisa, "PW Interviews: Marion Zimmer Bradley," *Publishers Weekly,* October 30, 1987, pp. 49-50.

Shwartz, Susan M., "Marion Zimmer Bradley's Ethic of Freedom," *The Feminine Eye: Science Fiction and the Women Who Write It,* edited by Tom Staicar, Ungar, 1982, pp. 73-88.

Spivack, Charlotte, *Merlin's Daughters: Contemporary Women Writers of Fantasy,* Greenwood Press, 1987.

■ For More Information See

BOOKS

Alpers, H. J., editor, *Marion Zimmer Bradley's Darkover,* Corian, 1983.

Arbur, Rosemarie, *Leigh Brackett, Marion Zimmer Bradley, Anne McCaffrey: A Primary and Secondary Bibliography,* G. K. Hall, 1982.

Breen, Walter, *The Gemini Problem: A Study of Darkover,* T-K Graphics, 1975.

Breen, Walter, *The Darkover Concordance: A Reader's Guide,* Pennyfarthing Press, 1979.

The Darkover Cookbook, Friends of Darkover, 1977, revised edition, 1979.

Paxson, Diana, *Costume and Clothing as a Cultural Index on Darkover,* Friends of Darkover, 1977, revised edition, 1981.

Roberson, Jennifer, *Return to Avalon,* DAW Books, 1996.

Wise, S., *The Darkover Dilemma: Problems of the Darkover Series,* T-K Graphics, 1976.

PERIODICALS

Algol, winter, 1977/1978.

Booklist, February 15, 1993, p. 1011; January 15, 1994, p. 875; March 15, 1995, p. 1313.

Entertainment Weekly, May 20, 1994, p. 57.

Fantasy Review of Fantasy and Science Fiction, April, 1984.

Journal of Popular Culture, summer, 1993, pp. 67-80.

Library Journal, December, 1990, p. 167; December 15, 1991, p. 117; March 15, 1992, p. 129; June 15, 1992, p. 106; March 15, 1993, p. 111; May 15, 1993, p. 100; June 15, 1993, p. 104; March 15, 1994, p. 104; June 15, 1994, p. 99; May 15, 1995, p. 99.

Los Angeles Times Book Review, February 3, 1983.

Mythlore, spring, 1984.

Publishers Weekly, March 15, 1993, p. 74; February 28, 1994, p. 72; February 27, 1995, p. 91.

San Francisco Examiner, February 27, 1983.

West Coast Review of Books, Number 5, 1986.

* * *

BRIDGERS, Sue Ellen 1942-

■ Personal

Born September 20, 1942, in Greenville, NC; daughter of Wayland Louis (a farmer) and Elizabeth (Abbott) Hunsucker; married Ben Oshel Bridgers (an attorney), March 17, 1963; children: Elizabeth Abbott, Jane Bennett, Sean McKenzie. *Education:* Attended East Carolina University, 1960-63; Western Carolina University, B.A. (summa cum laude), 1976.

■ Addresses

Home—628 Savannah Dr., Sylva, NC 28779. *Office*—P.O. Box 248, Sylva, NC 28779.

■ Career

Writer, 1970—. Member, board of directors, North Carolina Center for Public Television, Chapel Hill, NC, 1984—, Jackson County Library, Sylva, NC, 1985—, and North Carolina Humanities Council, 1990—.

■ Awards, Honors

Breadloaf Writer's Conference fellowship, 1976; *Boston Globe-Horn Book* Award for fiction, Christopher Award, named to American Library Association list of best books for young adults, all 1979, and American Book Award Nomination, 1981, all for *All Together Now;* American Book Award nomination, 1982, for *Notes for*

Another Life; ALAN Award, Assembly on Literature for Adolescents of the National Council of Teachers of English, 1985, for outstanding contributions to young adult literature; Parents' Choice Award, and North Carolina American Association of University Women (AAUW) Juvenile Fiction Award, both 1987, both for *Permanent Connections;* Western Carolina University Distinguished Service Award, 1991; Ragan-Rubin Award, 1992; North Carolina Arts Council fellowship, 1994-95.

■ Writings

YOUNG ADULT NOVELS

Home before Dark (originally appeared in *Redbook*), Knopf, 1976.
All Together Now, Knopf, 1979.
Notes for Another Life (originally appeared in *Redbook*), Knopf, 1981.
Permanent Connections, Harper, 1987.
Keeping Christina, HarperCollins, 1993.

ADULT NOVELS

Sara Will, Harper, 1985.
All We Know of Heaven, Banks Channel Books, 1996.

OTHER

Contributor of stories and articles to magazines including *ALAN Review, Carolina Quarterly, Ingenue, Mountain Living,* and *Redbook.* Also contributor to antholo-

gies, including *Visions: Short Stories by Outstanding Writers for Young Adults,* Delacorte, 1987; *Connections: Short Stories by Outstanding Writers for Young Adults,* Delacorte, 1989; and *Our Words, Our Ways: Reading and Writing in North Carolina.*

■ Sidelights

Sue Ellen Bridgers writes about a world she knows intimately—the rural South. A native of North Carolina, Bridgers has provided a geographical and emotional atlas of that territory in a series of critically acclaimed novels for young adults. With such award-winning novels as *All Together Now, Notes for Another Life,* and *Permanent Connections,* Bridgers has not only painted the landscape of that region, but also the ebb and flow of everyday life. Her portraits of young people facing difficult decisions and situations on the way to maturity reveal her belief in the ability of family and place to bring self-awareness, comfort, and healing. Her novels deal with emotional and physical trials, including social rejection, the death of parents, and mental illness. Often compared to other southern writers such as Flannery O'Connor, Carson McCullers, and William Faulkner, Bridgers is unique in that she writes mainly for young adult readers. "They deserve their literary giants, too," Ted Hipple noted in *ALAN Review.* "In Sue Ellen Bridgers, they have one."

Bridgers was raised in a small Appalachian town where generations of family on both sides had lived. She describes this upbringing in detail in her biographical essay for the *Something about the Author Autobiographical Series (SAAS).* "We lived between two houses," she wrote, meaning that her life was demarcated by the grandmothers' houses on two ends of the town of Winterville, North Carolina. Her paternal grandmother represented the strict, no-nonsense Germanic approach to life; when the family gathered at her home for Sunday dinners children "were relegated to the parlor." Her mother's family home, however, was "a house for the imagination," as Bridgers described it in *SAAS.* "In the window seat in the living room I was Jo reading and scribbling as in *Little Women.* On a chaise lounge in the front bedroom I died many deaths." And it was here she heard the old family stories: the tall tales and tragedies that make up family history. It was here, too, that she dealt with the life of emotion and drama. "Here family life was exposed," Bridgers recalled in *SAAS.* "Here I was afraid and yet loved. Here I was valued and accepted, but I felt responsibilities, too.... We were surrounded by kin. The lessons of such an upbringing are both difficult and joyful. There were perhaps too many eyes focused on us and yet there was an abundance of concern and well-intentioned affection." In short, Bridgers was educated about both the demands and the curative powers of family life. It was a lesson she would never forget.

Beyond the family and the tight community life of a small town, there were books in Bridgers's youth. "I have always wanted to be writer," she noted in *SAAS.* "The first sign was, I suppose, that I loved to be read

SUE ELLEN BRIDGERS

to." Her mother would read her Bible stories, especially those from the Old Testament, and then there were the adventures of Winnie the Pooh, the poetry from *A Child's Garden of Verses,* the Uncle Remus stories, and "a host of children's books, from *Poky Little Puppy* to *The Little Engine That Could,* and many more which I learned by heart." She learned to use the alphabet at an early age, not only for reading, but for writing. "I wanted to write as much as I wanted to read, maybe more so. There was a thrill about it that I still can't describe, a sort of letting go that is, at the same time, extremely focused so that in the process actual words appear on the page. I still revel in it." Bridgers began with poems suitable for every holiday occasion, several of which she published in local newspapers by the age of thirteen. Then she went on to writing short stories, searching for her own voice and themes. "During this time I frequently felt as if I were living two lives," Bridgers recalled in *SAAS.* "At school I was involved in

After moving from the suburbs of New Jersey to a small North Carolina town, seventeen-year-old Rob Dickson becomes depressed and withdrawn until a near tragic event almost kills his grandfather. (Cover illustration by Eric Velasquez.)

all the typical activities—band, chorus, clubs, cheerleading, piano practice, enjoying a social life; but in my private life, in my room, I was a writer." It was an early choice that was supported by her mother.

The one major disruption of her adolescent years came about when Bridgers's father suffered his first bout of mental depression. Hospitalized and treated with shock therapy and medications, he recovered for a time and returned to his family and farm, only to spiral back into depression. It was a cycle that lasted for fifteen years. "The effects of his illness on each of us children were individual and private," Bridgers wrote in *SAAS.* She later dealt with such effects in one of her own novels, *Notes for Another Life.*

Bridgers went to college in 1960, working on a literary magazine where her talents were discovered only after she had been utilized for a time as a volunteer typist. She met her husband, a young English instructor, at college; they were married before Bridgers finished her degree. There followed several years of roller-coaster change, including the birth of three children and a career move for her husband, who had gone from teaching to the Air Force, and from there to study law. It was not until the family was settled in a small town in the mountains of western North Carolina that Bridgers finally returned to her writing. Initial success with the publication of short stories encouraged her to try something longer. She did not have far to look for inspiration.

"I have always believed in visions," Bridgers wrote in *SAAS.* "Each of my books was begun because of a visionary moment, a scene that came to me spontaneously with images so potent I couldn't shake free of them." Her first novel, *Home before Dark,* began with a family she visualized. Slowly this germ of an idea grew to become the story of James Earl Willis, who returns with his family to his native North Carolina after years as a migrant worker in Florida. The family is given a small cottage on the tobacco farm now owned by James's brother, and everyone settles into the new life. Everyone but the wife, Mae, that is, who liked the itinerant life better. However, when she dies in a lightning storm, the mantle of family responsibility passes to young Stella, the daughter. When her father marries another woman, Stella at first refuses to leave the cottage that she has helped to transform into a new home. Eventually she joins the new family unit, achieving a heightened level of maturity in the process. Reviewing *Home before Dark* in *Horn Book,* Sally Holmes Holtz noted that it was "an outstanding first novel," and also commented on how well Bridgers details the emotions not only of young Stella, but also of her father. Barbara Helfgott also pointed out in the *New York Times Book Review* that Bridgers's portrayal of the adults in the story was "almost painfully real," and that "the author speaks with a voice that is intensely lyrical yet wholly un-selfconscious."

"My writing seems to find its expression in nostalgia," Bridgers once remarked in *Something about the Author.*

"My personal childhood experiences and the setting of a small southern town combine with a sense of the inevitable loss of that way of life. I feel very close to my roots when I'm working, as if the writing itself, although not autobiographical, is taking me back in time and is revealing some of the complexities of what seems to be a simple agrarian way of life." *Home before Dark* was a novel that explored the agrarian reality—a story about the land. Yet Bridgers is equally interested in connections between people, and it is the realm of emotions that she explored in her second novel, *All Together Now.* On one level, this is a deceptively simple story of a twelve-year-old girl's summertime friendship with an adult whose mind is forever locked in youth. A temporary "orphan" whose mother is working and whose father is fighting in Korea, young Casey comes to stay with her grandparents during a summer that changes her life. Dwayne Perkins, a man her father's age who suffered a childhood accident, befriends her, thinking she is a boy because she is dressed in jeans. Casey does nothing to disabuse him as Dwayne does not like girls, and slowly the two form a bond. But the simple story is widened with the cast of characters surrounding the grandparents, from a sports-car-loving uncle and his sweetheart, Gwen, to a dancing waiter named Hazard and his marriage to the aging daughter of the local doctor. Told from the point of view of eight characters, *All Together Now* ultimately focuses on Casey and Dwayne: When he is threatened with being institutionalized, the town rallies to save him. And though Dwayne discovers in the end that Casey is a girl, he still likes her and looks forward to her visit the next year.

The winner of the *Boston Globe-Horn Book* Award for fiction, *All Together Now* was lauded by critics for its story and technique. Katherine M. Flanagan commented in *Horn Book* that "the book is exceptional not only for its superb writing and skillful portrayal of human relationships, but also for its depiction of a small southern town." Katherine Paterson noted in a *Washington Post* review the technical risks Bridgers took with the multiple viewpoint and concluded that "she has certainly written a lovely book—a book for all of us who crave a good story about people we will come to care about deeply."

Bridgers's third novel tackled the difficult memories she had of her own father's mental depression. *Notes for Another Life* chronicles the experiences of thirteen-year-old Wren and her brother Kevin, who are staying with their grandparents. Their father is mentally ill and their mother, after years of suffering the ups and downs of her husband's illness, has chosen career over family. Kevin, feeling the rejection of his mother and of a girlfriend, attempts suicide, and the family bands together to save the troubled youth. "The author has succeeded in painting a portrait of mental illness that, for once, is not overburdened with melodrama and journalistic self-examination," noted Diane C. Donovan in a *Best Sellers* review of the book. Dick Abrahamson, writing in *English Journal*, commented on Bridgers's "fine sense of characterization," while Joan L. Atkinson noted in *Voice of Youth Advocates* that the story "is superbly

written" and portrays "incredibly strong women." Doris Betts, in a *Washington Post Book World* review of *Notes for Another Life*, also commented on the strong women in the novel: "Slowly and steadily the women teach the rest what has come naturally to them," Betts pointed out.

In a discussion of narrative technique in *ALAN Review*, Bridgers once wrote about the importance of characters, both male and female, in her fiction. "My subject matter is only clear to me in the context of the characters themselves, not as a theme to actively advance.... My decision to write about people struggling to find meaning in life is a moral choice. It is the same choice millions of women make in their daily lives—a choice to nurture, to heal, to make decisions that reflect care rather than justice.... My characters then are more crucial than any other element in my approach to writing fiction."

Further young adult titles include 1987's *Permanent Connections* and 1993's *Keeping Christina,* both of which continue Bridgers's exploration of the themes of family and friendship. The award-winning *Permanent Connections* was something of an experiment for Bridgers in that she employs a male character as the dominant protagonist, though there are ample strong women around to guide him through treacherous waters. Seventeen-year-old Rob Dickson unwillingly accompanies his father to North Carolina from the New Jersey suburbs to help take care of an ailing uncle. Left with his grandparents for a time, Rob is troubled and depressed. He meets another urban drop-out in this small town, Ellery, and the two become lovers, though the love does not grow, and ultimately Ellery breaks off the relationship. On the periphery and moving to center stage are Ellery's mother Ginny, who is finding herself after divorce, and Coralee, Rob's agoraphobic aunt. An incident that almost causes his grandfather's death finally brings Rob out of his shell, and he is able to acknowledge his place in the extended family. Writing in the *New York Times Book Review,* Hazel Rochman found that Bridgers's novel "affirms the bonds of extended family and community." A *Publishers Weekly* critic called it a "marvelous book" that "movingly evokes the tortured feelings of young people, and the viewpoints of their elders"; and a *Kliatt* reviewer concluded that "fine characterization, realistic situations, and wonderful descriptions throughout make this one of Bridgers' best works."

Keeping Christina explores the boundaries of friendship and is "an unsettling morality tale," according to one *Publishers Weekly* contributor. The novel finds ever-popular Annie befriending the new girl at school, with unwanted and totally unexpected consequences. When Christina begins to charm Annie's friends and family to manipulate them and turn them against Annie, there seems little that can be done. A near tragedy, however, finally exposes Christina's false nature, but she is unrepentant. "The smooth writing and authentic school dynamics ... will capture readers," noted Betsy Hearne in *Bulletin of the Center for Children's Books.*

In her novels for young adults, as well her adult novels, *Sara Will* and *All We Know of Heaven,* Bridgers has emphasized the central role of family and friendship in our lives. She also has brought spirituality and the power of prayer into play, though in a subtle and undidactic way. Her strong female characters anchor her stories and many times act as a compass to the action. But ultimately it is the interplay of Bridgers's teenage characters and the adults involved that sets her novels apart. Writing in *Dictionary of Literary Biography,* Hipple noted that, "Unlike their peers in many other novels, Bridgers's teenagers like, love, and respect those adults who deserve their affection. Similarly Bridgers's adults are well drawn and not merely pawns of fictional devices." Hipple went on to comment that Bridgers "possesses in abundance qualities much needed in young-adult fiction and seldom found there: the ability to tell a good story, to place it in a believable setting, to people it with real teenagers and adults, and to do it all with truly special linguistic talent."

For Bridgers, every book is an invitation to a journey of exploration and discovery. "Come and share a life," she wrote in *SAAS,* "accept its special reality, be one with it for a while. After all, we are fellow travelers; and our finest journeys, our most challenging explorations, are those of the spirit."

■ Works Cited

Abrahamson, Dick, "Old Friends with New Titles," *English Journal,* September, 1981, pp. 75-77.

Atkinson, Joan L., review of *Notes for Another Life, Voice of Youth Advocates,* October, 1981, p. 20.

Betts, Doris, "Themes and Variations on Family Life," *Washington Post Book World,* November 8, 1981, p. 17.

Bridgers, Sue Ellen, essay in *Something about the Author Autobiography Series,* Volume 1, Gale, 1986, pp. 39-52.

Bridgers, Sue Ellen, "Writing for My Life," *ALAN Review,* fall, 1995, pp. 2-7.

Donovan, Diane C., review of *Notes for Another Life, Best Sellers,* November, 1981, pp. 317-18.

Flanagan, Katherine M., review of *All Together Now, Horn Book,* April, 1979, pp. 197-98.

Hearne, Betsy, review of *Keeping Christina, Bulletin of the Center for Children's Books,* June, 1993, p. 309.

Helfgott, Barbara, review of *Home before Dark, New York Times Book Review,* November 14, 1976, p. 40.

Hipple, Ted, "Sue Ellen Bridgers: An Appreciation," *ALAN Review,* fall, 1990, pp. 8-9.

Hipple, Theodore W., "Sue Ellen Bridgers," *Dictionary of Literary Biography,* Volume 52: *American Writers for Children since 1960,* Gale, 1986, pp. 38-41.

Holtz, Sally Holmes, review of *Home before Dark, Horn Book,* April, 1977, pp. 165-66.

Review of *Keeping Christina, Publishers Weekly,* June 7, 1993, p. 71.

Paterson, Katherine, review of *All Together Now, Washington Post,* May 13, 1979, pp. K1, K4.

Review of *Permanent Connections, Publishers Weekly,* January 16, 1987, p. 75.

Review of *Permanent Connections, Kliatt,* May, 1988, p. 2.

Rochman, Hazel, review of *Permanent Connections, New York Times Book Review,* July 26, 1987, p. 21.

■ For More Information See

BOOKS

Children's Literature Review, Volume 18, Gale, 1989, pp. 20-28.

Contemporary Literary Criticism, Volume 26, Gale, 1983.

Hipple, Ted, *Presenting Sue Ellen Bridgers,* Twayne, 1990.

Salvner, Gary, and Virginia Monseau, editors, *Reading Their World: The Young Adult Novel in the Classroom,* Boynton/Cook Publishers, 1992.

PERIODICALS

ALAN Review, fall, 1985, pp. 44-47; winter, 1986, pp. 53-55, 61; fall, 1990, pp. 8-13; spring, 1994, pp. 53-55; fall, 1995.

Booklist, March 15, 1979, p. 1152; January 1, 1985, p. 602; March 1, 1990, p. 1355; July, 1993, p. 1957; October 15, 1994, p. 413.

New York Times Book Review, April 29, 1979, p. 38; November 25, 1979, p. 18; November 2, 1980, p. 43; November 15, 1981, p. 56.

School Library Journal, January, 1977, p. 99; May, 1979, p. 70; May, 1980, p. 48; September, 1983, p. 54; March, 1987, p. 168; November, 1989, p. 43; July, 1993, p. 98.*

—*Sketch by J. Sydney Jones*

*   *   *

BROWNE, Vee F(rances) 1956-

■ Personal

Born September 4, 1956, in Ganado, AZ; daughter of William Tully Brown, Sr. (a farmer) and Sarah F. Gorman (a weaver); foster daughter of Kenneth and Beth Ball and Stephen and Caroline Butler; children: Tye O'Harris, Delilah Violet, Coty Whitedove Lepkojus, WindSong LoVee Conrad. *Education:* Cochise Community College, A.A., 1977; Northern Arizona University, B.S., 1985; Western University of New Mexico, M.A., 1990; also attended writing courses at the University of Arizona, Tucson. *Politics:* Democrat. *Religion:* Native American—Navajo Beauty Way.

■ Addresses

Home and office—P.O. Box 1085, Chinle, AZ 86503.

■ Career

Author, journalist, storyteller, counselor, and educator. Chinle Pinon, Cottonwood, AZ, teacher, 1985-89; Many

Farms High School, grant writer/education specialist, 1990; Chinle High School, counselor, 1995—. Has done presentations at schools, libraries, and conferences, as well as poetry readings at universities. *Member:* Native American Wordcraft Circle, Native Writers and Storytellers (member of National Caucus board, 1994-96), Society of Children's Book Writers and Illustrators, Society of Southwest Authors, Arizona Reading Association, Arizona Press Association, Beta Phi Gamma, Delta Epsilon.

■ Awards, Honors

Western Heritage Award for best juvenile book, National Cowboy Hall of Fame, 1992, for *Monster Slayer;* Buddy Bo Jack National Award for Humanitarian for Children's Books, 1992; Works Award for books published in 1993, Society of Southwestern Authors, for *Monster Birds.*

■ Writings

(Reteller) *Monster Slayer: A Navajo Folktale,* illustrated by Baje Whitethorne, Northland, 1991.
(Reteller) *Monster Birds: A Navajo Folktale,* illustrated by Baje Whitethorne, Northland, 1993.
Maria Tallchief: Prima Ballerina, illustrated by Mary O'Keefe Young, Modern Curriculum, 1995.
(Reteller) *Owl: American Indian Legends,* additional text and book design by Vic Warren, illustrated by Diane Magnuson, Scholastic, 1995.

Work also represented in the anthologies *Neon Pow-Wow: New Native American Voices of the Southwest,* edited by Anna Lee Walters, Northland, 1993, and *Blue Dawn, Red Dawn,* Anchor, 1996, as well as in the literary quarterly *ELF: Eclectic Literary Forum.* Browne has also been a contributing reporter for the *Navajo-*

VEE F. BROWNE

Hopi Observer, a writer of sports articles for newspapers, and a consultant for *Highlights Magazine.*

■ Work in Progress

Cinnibah's First Valentine; My Dog Bunny.

■ Sidelights

Described by D. L. Birchfield in *News from Indian Country* as a "writer who is not afraid to find out where her many talents might lead," Vee Browne is the creator of works that draw on Native American lore for their subjects; she is also well known for writing a biography of Osage ballerina Maria Tallchief for young people. A member of the Bitter Water and Water Flows Together clans of the Navajo Nation, she vowed as a young girl to write a children's book based on Navajo stories and legends. Her first two books, *Monster Slayer* and *Monster Birds,* depict the adventures of the twins Child-Born-for-the-Water and Monster Slayer, heroes who save their people from cannibalistic giants called Yeis. In addition, she has recently retold a collection of Native American legends about the owl.

Browne told *SATA:* "I had concern for Navajo children who didn't have cultural books of their own. I especially wrote the Navajo folktales for them; as a classroom primary teacher, I missed these books in the library. I hope to share my Navajo-Dine culture with the world and help many children see that reading is fun. I believe fully that Native Americans should write their own children's books/novels. It upsets me and other Native Americans when non-natives treat our folktales as open-market. We should have first right to write/sell our own stories for cultural authenticity." The author concluded, "I write alone in a rural area of Cottonwood-Tselani. I like to write at night because there is a certain energy that goes with stars and full-moon. As a writer, I like Maurice Sendak—he likes to write Monster books and so do I—although I enjoy being in the same room as Eve Bunting. The two are my mentors."

■ Works Cited

Birchfield, D. L., review of *Neon Pow-Wow: New Native American Voices of the Southwest, News from Indian Country,* April, 1994, p. 32.*

*   *   *

BUCKLEY, Helen E(lizabeth) 1918-

■ Personal

Born June 6, 1918, in Syracuse, NY; daughter of James F. (an office manager) and Bridget (Horan) Buckley; married Francis E. Simkewicz (in newspapers), January, 1971; children: (stepdaughter) Niesha. *Education:* Syracuse University, B.S., 1945, M.S., 1949; Columbia University, Ed.D., 1962. *Religion:* Roman Catholic. *Hobbies and other interests:* Bowling, golf, swimming, reading, traveling.

HELEN E. BUCKLEY

■ Addresses

Home—Bradenton, FL.

■ Career

Public school elementary teacher, Syracuse, NY, 1942-49; State University College at Oswego, Oswego, NY, education department and campus school teacher, 1949-61, professor of English, 1961-76; Syracuse University Continuing Education Department, Syracuse, adjunct professor of teaching, 1978-88. *Member:* Authors Guild, Authors League of America, Society of Children's Book Writers and Illustrators.

■ Writings

Grandfather and I, illustrated by Paul Galdone, Lothrop, 1959, reprinted with illustrations by Jan Ormerod, 1994.
Grandmother and I, illustrated by Paul Galdone, Lothrop, 1960, reprinted with illustrations by Jan Ormerod, 1994.
Where Did Jose Go?, illustrated by Evaline Ness, Lothrop, 1962.
Some Cheese for Charles, illustrated by Evaline Ness, Lothrop, 1963.
My Sister and I, illustrated by Paul Galdone, Lothrop, 1963.
Josie and the Snow, illustrated by Evaline Ness, Lothrop, 1964.
The Little Boy and the Birthdays, illustrated by Paul Galdone, Lothrop, 1965.
Too Many Crackers, illustrated by Tony Chen, Lothrop, 1966.
Josie's Buttercup, illustrated by Evaline Ness, Lothrop, 1967.
The Little Pig in the Cupboard, illustrated by Ron Howard, Lothrop, 1968.

The Wonderful Little Boy, illustrated by Ron Howard, Lothrop, 1970.
Michael Is Brave, illustrated by E. McCully, Lothrop, 1971.
Someday with My Father, illustrated by Ellen Eagle, Harper & Row, 1985.
"Take Care of Things," Edward Said, illustrated by Katherine Coville, Lothrop, 1994.
Moonlight Kite, illustrated by Elise Primavera, Lothrop, 1997.

Contributor of several children's poems to books and journals, including "The Little Boy," which appeared in *Chicken Soup for the Soul,* and several other publications.

■ Work in Progress

The Leftover Bridge, illustrated by Oki S. Han, for Lothrop, expected in 1999.

■ Sidelights

After a fifteen-year layoff from children's books, Helen E. Buckley resumed her writing career in 1985 with the publication of *Someday with My Father.* Buckley, inspired by her husband to create a book about sports, decided to write a story that features a young girl daydreaming about all the fun activities she will do with her father one day. The young girl imagines she and her father will go hiking, skiing, and fishing, and after successfully completing each sport, he will praise her athletic talent. Just when the reader begins to wonder why the father isn't doing all of these things with his daughter, Buckley reveals that the young girl's leg is in a cast. Calling the ending "a complete surprise and delight," Marge Loch-Wouters wrote in *School Library Journal* that *Someday with My Father* shows a strong father-daughter relationship which is "homey and pleasing."

In 1994, Lothrop republished two re-illustrated classic picture books by Buckley, *Grandfather and I* and *Grandmother and I.* Originally published in 1959 and 1961, respectively, *Grandfather and I* and *Grandmother and I* feature a young boy and girl doing a wide range of activities with their grandparents, including walking around the neighborhood with grandfather and sitting on grandmother's lap. While the text remains basically the same, new pencil-and-watercolor illustrations of African American families by Jan Ormerod replace Paul Galdone's original pictures of white grandchildren and grandparents. Writing in *School Library Journal,* Jeanne Marie Clancy said she enjoyed the updated art and marveled at how Buckley's original text has passed "the test of time beautifully." Calling the book "warm without being mushy," *Booklist* contributor Ilene Cooper described Buckley's stories as "realistically portray[ing]" the therapeutic value that children receive while spending quiet time alone with their grandparents.

Buckley told *SATA:* "I have been publishing children's books for many years and have seen great changes in the

Republished with new illustrations by Jan Ormerod, Buckley delights another generation of children with *Grandfather and I,* her picture book about the special place grandfathers have in the lives of young children.

business. In the old days one had to wait only a month or two before hearing from an editor, and once the contract was signed, one was assured of publication in a year. Books also stayed in print much longer—*Grandfather and I* could be found on the bookstore shelves for twenty-seven years!

"Children do not seem to change, however—at least pre-schoolers. They give the same attention to thirty-year-old books as they do to the brand new ones, and perhaps this is the reason why many older but successful books of the past are being reissued. The above mentioned *Grandfather and I* and *Grandmother and I* have just been reissued with new illustrations by Jan Ormerod. The characters are now African American.

"I began my career by teaching preschool and elementary school children, which gave me an ear not only for what children like and think about, but how they sound. A late marriage to a man with a ten-year-old child brought the gift of motherhood and a fifteen-year-gap in my publishing any new books. *Someday with My Father* put me back on track after my husband said, 'Why don't you write a *good* book about fishing and hunting?' The resulting book was dedicated to him and our daughter. Now there are new books and, these many years later, a grandson, Tyler Sheffield."

■ Works Cited

Clancy, Jeanne Marie, review of *Grandfather and I* and *Grandmother and I, School Library Journal,* April, 1994, p. 96.

Cooper, Ilene, review of *Grandfather and I* and *Grandmother and I, Booklist,* February 15, 1994, p. 1092.

Loch-Wouters, Marge, review of *Someday with My Father, School Library Journal,* January, 1986, p. 54.

■ For More Information See

PERIODICALS

Booklist, December 15, 1985, p. 623.
Bulletin for the Center of Children's Books, September, 1991, p. 3.
Children's Book Review Service, January, 1986, p. 47.
Horn Book, July, 1994, p. 477.
Horn Book Guide, spring, 1992, p. 27; fall, 1994, p. 266.
Kirkus Reviews, July 15, 1991, p. 937.
New Advocate, winter, 1995, p. 50.
School Library Journal, October, 1991, p. 84.

*   *   *

BUTENKO, Bohdan 1931-

■ Personal

Born February 8, 1931, in Bydgoszcz, Poland; son of Jan (an engineer) and Anna (an artistic weaver) Butenko. *Education:* Academy of Fine Arts (Warsaw), M.A., 1955. *Hobbies and other interests:* Canoeing, biking, skiing, and playing volleyball.

■ Addresses

Home—Skrytka 715, 00-950 Warszawa 1, Poland.

■ Career

Illustrator, cartoonist, and painter. Nasza Ksiegarnia (publishing house), art editor, 1955-63; KAW (publishing house), art director, 1977-79. President of the Swiat Dziecka (Children's World) Foundation, 1990—; secretary general of the International Board on Books for Young People, Polish section, 1995—. Has made approximately thirty animated films (cartoons) and more than three hundred television programs (including trick programs, stage design, costumes, puppet theater); has done stage design and costumes with Compagne Rody in Paris and puppets and stage design with Marionetteatern in Stockholm. *Exhibitions:* Has held one-man shows, participated in numerous collective exhibitions, and has works held in private collections throughout the world. *Member:* International Theater Institute, Cartoonists and Writers Syndicate, Society of Authors—Poland (ZAIKS).

BOHDAN BUTENKO

■ Awards, Honors

Prizes of the Polish Publishers' Association, 1963, 1967, 1970, 1988, 1989, and 1996, all for the "Most Beautiful Books"; Silver Medal, 1967, for the Olympic poster "Verso Mexico"; Special TV Prize, 1967, for "Golden Lion"; Second Prize, International Book Exhibition, Best Artistic and Printing Setting, 1970, for *Ziemia;* Prize of the Polish Prime Minister, 1974; Premio Europeo di Letteratura Giovanile, 1976, for *The Whole Life of Marianne; or, the History of France;* Silver Medal on the Biennial of Art for Children, 1979, for *History of One Film* and *Good Morning!;* Prize of the International Board on Books for Young People (IBBY), 1990, for *About Felix, Wildcat, and the Little Mammoth;* Book of the Year, 1995, for *Encyklopedia Warszawy.*

■ Illustrator

IN ENGLISH

Franz Rottensteiner, *The Fantasy Book,* Thames & Hudson, 1972.

Edward Lear, *How Pleasant to Know Mr. Lear: Nonsense Poems,* Stemmer House (Owings Mills, MD), 1994.

IN POLISH

Jerzy Wittlin, *Vademecum dla tych, ktorzy pierwszy raz,* Iskry, 1972.

Jan Brzechwa, *Pali sie* (children's poetry), Krajowa Agencja Wydawnicza, 1977.

Wesola gromadka: wybor poemacikow i fotografii oraz reczne zdobienie (black humor), Mlodziezowa Agencja Wydawnicza, 1987.

Encyklopedia Warszawy (title means "The Dictionary of Warsaw"), Wydawnictwo Naukowe PWN, 1994.

Also illustrator of numerous other works, including *Ziemia, The Whole Life of Marianne or the History of France, History of One Film, Good Morning!,* and *About Felix, Wildcat, and the Little Mammoth.* Many of Butenko's works appear as posters for film, theater, and publicity, and as greeting cards. His comic strips and cartoons, especially the character Scatterbrain, are published in newspapers and periodicals in Poland and throughout Europe. Scatterbrain has also been developed for books and television.

■ Sidelights

Bohdan Butenko told *SATA:* "I was born in a very famous old town in the northern part of Poland and I spent my childhood in an old house near a big forest full of squirrels, deer, rabbits, wild boars, and wolves. When I was four or five years old I started to explore the forest with a big Irish setter, my favorite dog, to look after me. At home, I began to draw my first illustrations and comic strips, inventing different stories with the animals I had seen in the forest. Even today I enjoy drawing trees and animals! In primary school I often had problems with my teachers because I had drawn most of the sketches in my textbooks and—I must say—sometimes during the classes.

"Now I live in Warsaw illustrating books, teaching, and painting (mostly watercolors). I have illustrated over two hundred books published in Poland and abroad. One of my favorite characters—a boy named 'Scatterbrain' in England, 'Nigaudin' in France, 'Zipfelzapfel' in Germany, and 'Gapiszon' in Poland—has been the most popular and the most beloved character in comic strips in Poland for thirty years. I have done twelve books with the Scatterbrain's adventures (in Poland and in Germany), fifteen TV films (some of them were shown in the United States) and about one hundred TV programs. Since 1965, Scatterbrain's adventures appear constantly in the children's magazine *MIS* in Poland. My works are in collections of art all over the world and have received many awards. I also head the Children's World Foundation devoted to encouraging art by and for children.

"I have only one dog (a sheepdog named 'Jaga'). I like to canoe, bike, ski and play volleyball. I have travelled throughout Europe, Japan, the Sahara Desert (which has given me many ideas for future work!), and the East Coast of the United States, from New York City to Key West. In the United States I had a one-man exhibition of my works in the Milton S. Eisenhower Library in Baltimore (1993), and in 1994 I illustrated the book *How Pleasant to Know Mr. Lear,* by Edward Lear. Illustrating this book has given me a lot of pleasure because I adore those types of poems, and Edward Lear is one of my favorite poets!

"My latest big work was *Encyklopedia Warszawy* (The Dictionary of Warsaw), published in 1994, which has won nine prizes, including the very important prize 'The Book of the Year' in Poland in 1995!"

C

CABRERA, Marcela 1966-

■ Personal

Born November 22, 1966, in Bogota, Colombia; daughter of Rafael Cabrera Moreno (a civil engineer) and Mercedes Vanegas de Cabrera; married Victor Jay Rachootin (a computer artist), July 9, 1994. *Education:* Neumann Institute of Design, Venezuela, B.A., 1987; studied airbrush illustration and techniques, computer graphics, and printing processes at schools in Venezuela and the U.S. *Religion:* Catholic. *Hobbies and other interests:* "Sports, art, and travel, the latter being my favorite."

MARCELA CABRERA

■ Addresses

Home—1226 Smithwood Dr., #4, Los Angeles, CA 90035. *Agent*—Maggi Byer-Sprinzeles, 418 West 47th Street #5FW, New York, NY 10036, and/or Jane Feder, 305 East 24th Street, New York, NY 10010.

■ Career

Graphic designer and illustrator. Freelance artist, 1985—. Lagoven (an oil company), Venezuela, assistant art director, 1985; Montana Grafica, Venezuela, graphic designer and illustrator, 1987-88; Sound Source Interactive, illustrator and animator for interactive media and CD-ROM, 1995-96. Freelance graphic designer for publishing, packaging, and oil companies, advertising agencies, art galleries, the entertainment industry, foundations, and other institutions in both the United States and Venezuela; has conducted illustration seminars for children and adults. *Exhibitions:* Exhibitor at children's book and illustration exhibitions and competitions in Venezuela, Japan, Italy, and the United States. *Member:* Society of Children's Books Writers and Illustrators.

■ Awards, Honors

Named one of the "100 Best Children's Book Illustrators of the World," International Board on Books for Young People, 1994, for *El Libro de los Animales* ("The Book of the Animals"); several of Cabrera's books have been designated as Best Children's Books of the Year by the Venezuelan National Library.

■ Illustrator

Javier Rondon, *El Sapo Distraido,* Ediciones Ekare (Venezuela), 1988.
Clara Inez Olaya, *Fruitas Tropicales,* Ediciones Ekare, 1991.
Aquiles Nazoa, *El Libro de los Animales,* Monte Avila Editores (Venezuela), 1991.
Yolanda Pantin, *Raton y Vampiro se conocen,* Monte Avila Editores, 1993.
Barbara Brenner, *The Mystery of the Plumed Serpent,* Houghton, 1993.
Salvador Garmendia, *El dia que el armadillo vio su sombra,* Houghton, 1993.
Salvador Garmendia, *Galileo en su Reino,* Monte Avila Editores, 1993.
Javier Rondon, *The Absent-Minded Toad,* translated by Kathryn Miller, Kane-Miller, 1994.
Women (pop-up mini book), Intervisual Books, 1994.
Peter Gould (adapter), *Exosquad* (interactive book), Sound Source Interactive, 1995.
Mark Bankins (adapter), *The Adventures of Batman and Robin* (interactive book), Sound Source Interactive, 1995.
Mark Bankins (adapter), *Dragonheart* (interactive activity center), Sound Source Interactive, 1996.
Peter Gould (adapter), *The Land Before Time* (interactive book), Sound Source Interactive, 1996.
Yanitzia Canetti, *Sal de la Cama!,* Houghton Mifflin, 1996.

■ Work in Progress

A new interactive book and other freelance illustration jobs.

■ Sidelights

Marcela Cabrera told *SATA:* "I have a degree in graphic design, however I've always done a lot of work as an illustrator. Aside from doing traditional illustration, I'm also currently working in computer graphics producing both 2D and 3D illustration and animation. The technology is fascinating and I love my work."

*   *   *

CAMPBELL, Hugh 1930-

■ Personal

Born February 20, 1930, in Providence, RI; son of Wallace (a businessman) and Mary H. (a homemaker) Campbell; married Eleonore T. Campbell (a homemaker), June 13, 1954; children: Elizabeth Peters, Peggy Freeman, Jeanie Lero, Polly Moore, Erika Jezo, Hope McAndrew, Martina Price. *Education:* Yale University, B.A., 1951; Middlebury College, M.A., 1957. *Politics:* Republican. *Religion:* "Bible-believing Christian." *Hobbies and other interests:* Fly-fishing, watercolor painting.

■ Addresses

Home and office—RR 1, Box 328, Palmer Hill Rd., Waitsfield, VT 05673.

■ Career

Canterbury School, New Milford, CT, French teacher, 1953-57; Roxbury Latin School, West Roxbury, MA, French teacher and athletic coach, 1957-67; Rocky Hill School, East Greenwich, RI, headmaster, 1967-75; American Express Financial Advisor, financial advisor, 1977—. Selectman, Waitsfield, VT. *Military service:* U.S. Air Force National Guard, 1951-53. *Member:* Outdoor Writers Association of America.

■ Writings

(Self-illustrated) *Lightning's Tale: The Story of a Wild Trout,* Frank Amato Publications, 1994.

Also author of French readers (with Camille Bauer) published by Houghton in the 1960s, including *Contes pour Debutante, Arsene Lupin, La Robe et le Couteau,* and *La Dynamite.*

■ Sidelights

Hugh Campbell told *SATA,* "I started working on books when teaching French at the high school level in the late 50s. It was just when the emphasis was shifting from conjugating to speaking the language. We taught French in French from day one on. There were very few readers

HUGH CAMPBELL

with French to French vocabulary and audio-lingual exercises to help students learn to speak and use correctly the expressions that they had just read. So Camille Bauer and I put together a series of four readers that were published by Houghton Mifflin and carried for more than thirty years. That initial success was a great encouragement to me when I later wanted to do a book on the life of a trout.

"There really weren't any books that kids could read about how a trout lives; the dangers he faces, not only from man but animals; the winter cold and spring ice-out, etc. I wanted to write a story that would give kids some appreciation of how well designed and adapted a trout is to live surrounded by so many dangers. This appreciation will, hopefully, lead to releasing, rather than frying, what you catch. In that way the quality of fishing will improve, more people will enjoy it (and so will the trout!). It is my hope that *Lightning's Tale* will make a difference as this generation of young fisherfolk catch bigger trout that they in turn put back for their kids to enjoy.

"So I had a goal. The plot came together by combining experiences learned on the rivers and ponds I had fished. But where to find the illustrator? As I knew none and had no idea where to turn, I wondered about painting the illustrations myself. The only problem was that I hadn't used watercolors since grade school. I found a wonderful teacher, Lisa Beach, whose husband was a client of mine. With her skill developing what the good Lord had given me, I had the necessary watercolors and black and white sketches in five years.

"I am planning to retire in a few months, so I will have time for more writing and illustrating. Ideas abound."*

* * *

CARLSON, Nancy L(ee) 1953-

■ Personal

Born October 10, 1953, in Minneapolis, MN; daughter of Walter J. (a contractor) and Louise (a homemaker; maiden name, Carlson) Carlson; married John Barry McCool (a graphic designer), June 30, 1979; children: Kelly Louise, John Patrick, Michael Barry. *Education:* Attended University of Minnesota, Duluth, 1972-73, and Santa Fe Workshop of Contemporary Art, 1975; Minneapolis College of Art and Design, B.F.A., 1976. *Hobbies and other interests:* "Physical fitness, running, biking, watching my children do sports."

■ Addresses

Home—5900 Mount Normandale Dr., Bloomington, MN 55438.

■ Career

Artist and illustrator, 1975—. Visiting artist at schools, including Bemidji State University, 1983, Minnetonka Schools, MN, 1985, and Minneapolis School of Art and Design, 1986. Lecturer and public speaker. Card Buyer for Center Book Shop, Walter Art Center, 1977-80; arts and craft specialist for city of South St. Paul, MN, 1978; illustrator of greeting cards for Recycled Paper Prod-

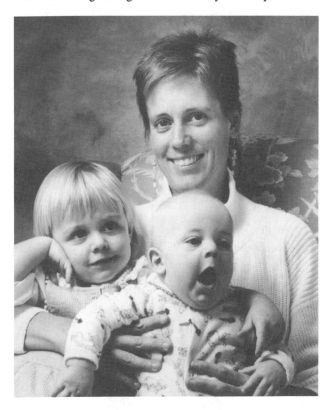

NANCY L. CARLSON

ucts, 1982. Creator of CD-ROM products. Illustrator of calendars, mugs, T-shirts, posters, hats, and gift wrap. *Exhibitions:* "Commencement Exhibition," Minneapolis College of Art and Design, 1976; "New Works by Three Artists," Honeywell Plaza, Minneapolis, MN, 1980; "Drawings: Scandinavian Reflections," Dolly Fiterman Gallery, 1980; "Minnesota Women," WARM Gallery, Minneapolis, 1981, 1982; Minnesota State Fair Art Exhibition, 1981; "American Art: The Challenge of the Land," Pillsbury World Headquarters, 1981; "Illustrator's Art," Inland Gallery, Minneapolis, 1982; "Young Minnesota Artists," University Gallery, University of Minnesota, 1982; "Hausman Years: 1975-1982," Minneapolis College of Art and Design, 1982; "Original Art," Master Eagle Gallery, New York City, 1983, 1985; "Alumni Show," Minneapolis College of Art and Design, 1986; "The Art of Author Illustrator Nancy Carlson," American Swedish Institute, Minneapolis, 1989; "Metaphorical Fish," University Art Museum, 1990; "Children's Book Illustration," Minneapolis College of Art and Design, 1993; "Children's Book Illustration," Plymouth Church, Minneapolis, 1994; "Whimsical World of Josie Winship and Nancy Carlson," Bloomington Art Center, Bloomington, MN, 1996.

■ Awards, Honors

Drawing awards from Northshore Arts Festival, 1975, Minnesota State Fair Art Exhibition, 1981, Young Minnesota Artists, University of Minnesota, 1982, Women in International Design, 1983, and Minneapolis Graphic Design Association, 1985; Parents' Choice Award, Parents' Choice Foundation, 1985, for *Louanne the Pig in the Talent Show;* Children's Choice Award, 1996, for *Sit Still.*

■ Writings

SELF-ILLUSTRATED

Harriet's Recital, Carolrhoda, 1982.
Harriet and Walt, Carolrhoda, 1982.
Harriet and the Roller Coaster, Carolrhoda, 1982.
Harriet and the Garden, Carolrhoda, 1982.
Harriet's Halloween Candy, Carolrhoda, 1982.
Loudmouth George and the Cornet, Carolrhoda, 1983.
Loudmouth George and the New Neighbors, Carolrhoda, 1983.
Loudmouth George and the Fishing Trip, Carolrhoda, 1983.
Loudmouth George and the Sixth-Grade Bully, Carolrhoda, 1983.
Loudmouth George and the Big Race, Carolrhoda, 1983.
Bunnies and Their Hobbies, Carolrhoda, 1984.
Louanne Pig in Making the Team, Carolrhoda, 1985.
Louanne Pig in the Mysterious Valentine, Carolrhoda, 1985.
Louanne Pig in the Perfect Family, Carolrhoda, 1985.
Louanne Pig in the Talent Show, Carolrhoda, 1985.
Louanne Pig in Witch Lady, Carolrhoda, 1985.
Bunnies and Their Sports, Viking, 1987.
Arnie and the Stolen Markers, Viking, 1987.
Arnie Goes to Camp, Viking, 1988.

I Like Me, Viking, 1988.
Poor Carl, Viking, 1988.
Arnie and the New Kid, Viking, 1990.
Take Time to Relax, Viking, 1991.
What If It Never Stops Raining?, Viking, 1992.
A Visit to Grandma's, Viking, 1993.
Life is Fun!, Viking, 1993.
How to Lose All Your Friends, Viking, 1994.
Arnie and the Skateboard Gang, Viking, 1995.
Sit Still, Viking, 1996.

ILLUSTRATOR

Joyce Kessel, *Halloween,* Carolrhoda, 1980.
Geoffrey Scott, *Egyptian Boats,* Carolrhoda, 1981.
(With Trina Schart Hyman, Hilary Knight, and Peter E. Hanson) Pamela Espeland and Marilyn Waniek, *The Cat Walked through the Casserole and Other Poems for Children,* Carolrhoda, 1984.
Susan Pearson, *The Baby and the Bear,* Viking, 1987.
Susan Pearson, *When the Baby Went to Bed,* Viking, 1987.
Rufus Klein, *Watch Out for These Weirdos,* Viking, 1990.
Susan Pearson, *Lenore's Big Break,* Viking, 1992.
Jacqueline K. Ogburg, *The Masked Maverick,* Lothrop, 1994.
Rick Walton, *What to Do When a Bug Climbs in Your Mouth and Other Poems to Drive You Buggy,* Lothrop, 1995.

OTHER

Carlson also wrote stage adaptations of *Louanne Pig in the Talent Show* and *Loudmouth George and the 6th Grade Bully,* both produced in Hopkins, MN.

■ Adaptations

CASSETTES

Harriet and Walt, Live Oak Media, 1984.
Harriet's Recital (with filmstrip), Random House, 1984, Live Oak Media, 1985.
Harriet and the Roller Coaster, Live Oak Media, 1985.
Harriet and the Garden, Live Oak Media, 1985.
Harriet's Halloween Candy, Live Oak Media, 1985.
Loudmouth George and the Cornet, Live Oak Media, 1986.
Loudmouth George and the Fishing Trip, Live Oak Media, 1986.
Loudmouth George and the Sixth-Grade Bully, Live Oak Media, 1986.
Loudmouth George and the Big Race, Live Oak Media, 1986.
Loudmouth George and the New Neighbors, Live Oak Media, 1987.
Louanne Pig in the Talent Show, Live Oak Media, 1987.
Louanne Pig in Witch Lady, Live Oak Media, 1987.
Louanne Pig in the Perfect Family, Live Oak Media, 1987.
Louanne Pig in Making the Team, Live Oak Media, 1987.
I Like Me ("Read Along" cassette series), Weston Woods, 1988, (with filmstrip), Weston Woods, 1988.

When a boy in a wheelchair enters a new school, Arnie joins the other students in teasing him until Arnie breaks his leg and discovers for himself what being disabled is like. (From *Arnie and the New Kid*, written and illustrated by Carlson.)

■ Work in Progress

A CD-ROM; *ABC, I Like Me Book.*

■ Sidelights

From the age of five, author and illustrator Nancy Carlson knew that she wanted to be an artist when she grew up; she began illustrating children's books soon after graduating from college. Quickly realizing she would rather illustrate books that she had written herself, Carlson began combining her own pictures with stories and produced her first book, *Harriet's Recital*, in 1982. She wrote four more books about Harriet before creating a series of books about Loudmouth George and another about Louanne Pig.

Another series by Carlson features the antics of Louanne and George's friend, Arnie the Cat. A cat who loves mice, Arnie first appeared in Carlson's books about Harriet before he received a book of his own, *Arnie and the Stolen Markers*, in 1987. One day Arnie sees a set of markers for sale at Harvey's Candy and Toy Shop and decides that he must have them. However, since he has wasted all his allowance on candy and his spendthrift friend Louanne refuses to lend him any money, Arnie slips the markers under his shirt and out of the store. Once he returns home, Arnie's mother discovers his thievery and returns him to the store, where the owner makes Arnie work for the stolen marker set. "Brightly spirited characters" help Carlson convey the message to children that stealing is wrong without the author "didactically haranguing the impropriety of stealing" according to Cathy Woodward in *School Library Journal*.

In *Arnie and the New Kid*, Carlson's 1990 picture book, a boy named Philip, who is in a wheelchair, enters Arnie's school. Arnie leads the other children in teasing Philip about his physical disability, but when Arnie injures his leg and finds out how difficult maneuvering on crutches is, he begins to sympathize with Philip. Philip and Arnie begin a friendship that continues long after Arnie's cast is removed. Writing in *School Library Journal*, Ellen Fader praised the happy ending, as well as Carlson's "lighthearted treatment of a common situation." *Bulletin of the Center for Children's Books* critic Deborah Stevenson applauded Carlson's illustrations, saying the characters complimented the text by "convey[ing] emotions that the text left unspoken."

While producing the *Arnie* series, Carlson also worked on other books to help youngsters calm their childhood fears and develop a healthy outlook on life. *Take Time to Relax*, the author's 1991 book, features a family of busy beavers who fill their every waking hour with activities from ballet classes and soccer games to tennis lessons and volleyball matches. When a terrible snowstorm prevents the beaver family from leaving their home, the ambitious family discovers that spending time alone with each other is more important than any other activity. A critic in *Publishers Weekly* liked the "hyperbole and humor" Carlson included in her text

Carlson tries to soothe the worries many children have over unfamiliar situations and other events out of their control in her self-illustrated picture book *What If It Never Stops Raining?*

and noted that *Take Time to Relax* reinforces "an important message to today's over-programmed families."

Carlson followed *Take Time to Relax* with *What If It Never Stops Raining?*, another book that concentrates on children coping with their anxieties. Young Tim constantly worries about everything, even about a never-ending rain flooding his house. However, with his mother's support, Tim learns how to distinguish between worrying about real dangers, like falling off of the playground equipment, and needless anxiety about unfamiliar situations, like his new school bus driver getting lost. While admitting the ending is "a bit too tidy," a reviewer in *Publishers Weekly* said Carlson "proficiently handled" the delicate subject of how to quiet a child's irrational fears.

Carlson once told *SATA:* "I'm an artist who enjoys making up stories for children. When I'm not writing for kids, I'm drawing pictures for shows and galleries."

■ Works Cited

Fader, Ellen, review of *Arnie and the New Kid, School Library Journal,* June, 1990, p. 97.

Stevenson, Deborah, review of *Arnie and the New Kid, Bulletin of the Center for Children's Books,* May, 1990, p. 209-10.

Review of *Take Time to Relax, Publishers Weekly,* December, 7, 1990, p. 81.

Review of *What If It Never Stops Raining?, Publishers Weekly,* November 9, 1992, p. 82.

Woodward, Cathy, review of *Arnie and the Stolen Markers, School Library Journal,* February, 1988, p. 58.

■ For More Information See

PERIODICALS

Booklist, May 15, 1990, p. 1797; October 15, 1992, p. 438; January 1, 1993, p. 810; February 1, 1994, p. 1010; September, 1, 1994, p. 49; June 1, 1995, p. 1782.

Bulletin of the Center for Children's Books, February, 1989, p. 143.

Five Owls, September, 1988, p. 8; May, 1990, p. 93; May, 1993, pp. 104, 122. *Junior Bookshelf,* April, 1993, p. 57.

Horn Book Guide, spring, 1993, p. 23; spring, 1994, p. 28; spring, 1995, p. 28.

Kirkus Reviews, March 15, 1989, p. 460; May 15, 1990, p. 726; August 15, 1991, p. 1086; August 15, 1994, p. 1122.

Magpies, March, 1992, p. 27.

Publishers Weekly, October 9, 1987, p. 84; April 29, 1988, p. 74; September 9, 1988, p. 130; December 9, 1988, p. 61; August 30, 1991, p. 81; March 1, 1993, p. 58; July 26, 1993, p. 70.

School Library Journal, September, 1988, p. 154; August, 1991, p. 143; November, 1991, p. 90; February, 1993, p. 70; November, 1993, p. 76; August, 1995, p. 121.

Times Educational Supplement, February 19, 1993, p. R2.

*　　*　　*

CARREL, Annette Felder 1929-

■ Personal

Born December 11, 1929, in San Francisco, CA; married Robert E. Carrel (a pediatric neurologist; died, 1989); children: three. *Education:* Notre Dame College, A.A.; Lone Mountain College, B.A.; University of California at San Francisco, M.A. (special education).

■ Addresses

Home—2010 Garden St., Santa Barbara, CA 93105-3615.

■ Career

Taught kindergarten and first grade in Marin County, CA, for ten years; former director of education at Sunny Hills, a residential treatment center for children with emotional problems. Docent for the Santa Barbara Historical Society, Trust for Historic Preservation, Symphony League, local court house, and the Santa Barbara Mission and Archive Library; public speaker;

ANNETTE FELDER CARREL

commissioner of the Juvenile Justice/Delinquency Prevention Commission. Board member of Saint Vincent's facility for female juvenile offenders, Catholic Charities, and Woman's Board of the Museum of Art.

■ Writings

It's the Law: A Young Person's Guide to Our Legal System, Volcano Press (Volcano, CA), 1994.

■ Sidelights

Annette Felder Carrel is a former kindergarten and first grade teacher who has become heavily involved in her home community of Santa Barbara as a docent—a teacher and tour guide—for libraries, museums, schools, and political organizations. The background for her book for young readers, *It's the Law: A Young Person's Guide to Our Legal System,* came from her experience at her local court house. As she explained to *SATA:* "I have taught the 'Law Experience' at the Santa Barbara Superior Courthouse for over fifteen years. I teach approximately twelve to fifteen hundred youths a year. This work is part of the large docent program at the courthouse. I teach in a courtroom and cover the material in my book including arrest (with handcuffs and jail clothing), arraignment, and a mock trial. This means I am current in thought about youth, education, juvenile justice, and law.

"I also present the 'Law Experience' to adults in 'English as a Second Language' classes and 'Citizenship Classes' conducted by our adult education program," Carrel continued. "I am asked to present the law program for special groups such as the Braille Institute, which translated my mock trial into braille. I have taken Russian, Chinese, and other foreign groups through the courthouse, giving me the delicious challenge of explaining our system of justice to many who have never lived in a democracy.

"I am asked often if I am an attorney, and when I reply that I am not, I am challenged whether I could or should be able to write about the law. I explain that my field and interest is political science, which is the development of society and how that society governs itself. We citizens are the law; we make laws, we break laws, we enforce laws and we adjudicate laws, we change and often ignore laws. Attorneys practice the law in that they apply our laws to the roles and actions of our citizens.... But this is done at our command. All citizens should know as much as I."

■ For More Information See

PERIODICALS

Booklist, February 15, 1995, p. 1068.
Los Angeles Times Book Review, October 9, 1994, p. 13.

CHANG, Cindy 1968-

■ Personal

Born April 21, 1968, in Taipei, Taiwan, Republic of China; daughter of Edward Chang and Irene Kao.

■ Addresses

Home—Sherman Oaks, CA. *Office*—MCA Publishing Rights, 100 Universal City Plaza, Universal City, CA 91608.

■ Career

Author, reteller, and editor. Random House, Inc., New York City, intern, 1990; Price, Stern, Sloan, Inc., Los Angeles, CA, editor, 1990-94; Intervisual Books, Santa Monica, CA, editor, 1994-96; MCA Publishing Rights, Universal City, CA, director, 1996—. *Member:* PEN USA West (member of editorial board), Society of Children's Book Writers and Illustrators.

■ Writings

Good Night, Kitty!, illustrated by Deborah Borgo, Price, Stern, 1994.
Good Morning, Puppy!, illustrated by Deborah Borgo, Price, Stern, 1994.
(Reteller) *The Seventh Sister: A Chinese Legend* (part of "Legends of the World" series), illustrated by Charles Reasoner, Troll, 1994.
(Adaptor) *Balto: The Junior Novelization,* Grosset & Dunlap, 1995.
(Compiler) *Food* (quote book), Andrews & McMeel, 1995.
(Compiler) *Gardens* (quote book), Andrews & McMeel, 1995.
(Compiler) *Golf* (quote book), Andrews & McMeel, 1995.
What's for Lunch?, Random House, 1996.
Where's the Mouse?, Random House, 1996.
Jump! Jump! All the Games, Rhymes, and Helpful Hints You'll Ever Need to Know about Jumping Rope!, Price, Stern, 1996.
Trucks All Around, Dutton, 1996.
(Compiler) *Reading* (quote book), Andrews & McMeel, 1996.
(Compiler) *Nature* (quote book), Andrews & McMeel, 1996.
(Compiler) *Thank You* (quote book), Andrews & McMeel, 1996.
(Compiler) *Family* (quote book), Andrews & McMeel, 1996.

Also co-editor of regional newsletter *Kitetales.*

■ Work in Progress

Train (tentative title), for Dutton.

CHAPMAN, Lee
See BRADLEY, Marion Zimmer

* * *

CHEKHONTE, Antosha
See CHEKHOV, Anton (Pavlovich)

* * *

CHEKHOV, Anton (Pavlovich) 1860-1904
(A Man without a Spleen, Antosha Chekhonte, My Brother's Brother, v)

■ Personal

Middle name (patronymic) also transliterated as Pavlo-vitch; surname also transliterated as Cechov, Cekov, Cexov, Chehov, Chekhoff, Chekov, Tchekhov, Tchek-hof, Tchekhoff, Tcheckhov, Tchekkof, and Tchekoff; born January 16, 1860, in Taganrog, Russia; died of tuberculosis, July 2, 1904, in Badenweiler, Germany; buried in Moscow, Russia; son of Pavell Yegorovitch (a grocer) and Yevgeniya Yakovlevna (Morozov) Chek-hov; married Olga Leonardovna Knipper (an actress), May 25, 1901. *Education:* University of Moscow, M.D., 1884.

■ Career

Physician and author. Editor of the literary section of *Russkaya mysl,* 1903; founder of two rural schools. *Member:* Society of Russian Dramatic Writers and Opera Composers, Society for Lovers of Russian Litera-ture (provisional president, 1903), Literary Fund.

■ Awards, Honors

Pushkin Prize, Division of Russian Language and Letters of the Academy of Sciences, 1888, for *In the Twilight;* elected Honorary Academician of Pushkin Section of Belle Lettres, Academy of Sciences, 1899; Order of St. Stanislav, 1899, for work in the cause of national education; Griboedov Prize, Society of Dra-matic Writers and Opera Composers, for *The Three Sisters.*

■ Writings

FOR CHILDREN

Kashtanka, translated by Charles Dowsett, illustrated by William Stobbs, Oxford University Press, 1959, H. A. Walck, 1961; translated by Richard Pevear, illustrated by Barry Moser, Putnam, 1991; illus-trated by Gennady Spirin, Harcourt, 1995.
Shadows and Light: Nine Stories, translated by Miriam Morton, Doubleday, 1968.
White Star, translated by Michelle MacGrath, illus-trated by N. Charushin, Malysh, 1980.

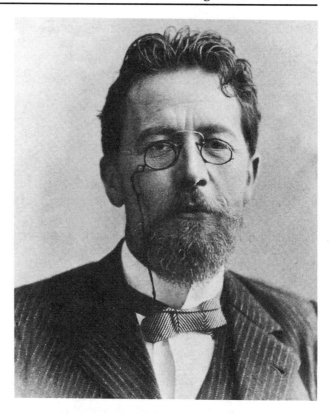

ANTON CHEKHOV

Also author of *Sbornik dlya detey* (title means "A Collection of Children's Stories," 1883) and *A Day in the Country,* 1985.

PLAYS

That Worthless Fellow Platonov (one-act), translated by John Cournos, Dutton, 1930; translated by Basil Ashmore as *A Play without a Title (Platonov),* P. Nevill, 1952; translated as *Don Juan (in the Russian Manner)* (produced in New York City at the Minor Latham Drama Workshop, April 23, 1954), preface by Sir Desmond MacCarthy, P. Nevill, 1952; trans-lated and adapted by Alex Szogyj as *A Country Scandal (Platonov)* (first produced in New York City at the Greenwich Mews Theater, May 5, 1960), Coward-McCann, 1960, published as *A Country Scandal: A Drama in Four Acts,* Samuel French, 1961; translated by Dimitri Makaroff as *Platonov: An Abridged Version of an Untitled Play,* introduc-tion by George Devine, Methuen (London), 1961; translated by David Magarshack as *Platonov: A Play in Four Acts and Five Scenes,* Hill & Wang, 1964; translated by Michael Frayn as *Wild Honey: The Untitled Play* (first produced in London at the National Theater, 1984, produced on Broadway at the Virginia Theater, December 18, 1986), Me-thuen, 1984 (originally written as *P'yessa bez nazva-niya (Platonov),* c. 1881).
On the Harmful Effects of Tobacco, translated by Milka Petrovich, adapted by Boris Zupetz, pictures by Patrick Couratin, Quist, 1977 (originally written as *O vrede tabaka: Stsens monolog,* c. 1886-1902).

Ivanoff: A Play in Four Acts, translated by Marian Fell, Brentano's (New York City), 1923; translated by Ariadne Nicolaeff as *Ivanov: A Drama in Four Acts* (first produced on Broadway at the Shubert Theater, May 3, 1966), adapted by John Gielgud, Theater Arts (New York City), 1966 (originally appeared as *Ivanov: Drama v chetryokh deystiviyakh;* produced in Moscow at the Korsh Theater, November 19, 1887).

A Bear, translated by Roy Temple House, Moods, 1909; translated by Hilmar Baukhage as *The Boor: A Comedy in One Act,* Samuel French, 1915; translated by Eric Bentley as *The Brute: A Joke in One Act,* Samuel French, 1956; translated as *The Bear,* adapted by Joellen Bland, Denver Pioneer Drama Service (Denver, CO), 1984 (originally produced as *Medved: Shutka v odnom deystvii,* in Moscow at the Korsh Theater, October, 1888).

A Marriage Proposal (one-act), translated by Hilmar Baukahage and Barett H. Clark, Samuel French, 1914; new edition edited by William-Alan Landes, Players Press, 1990 (originally written as *Predlozheniye: Shutka v odnom deystvii,* c. 1888-89).

The Wood Demon: A Comedy in Four Acts, translated by S. S. Koteliansky, Macmillan, 1926 (originally produced as *Leshy: Komedya v chetyryokh deystviyakh,* in Moscow at the Abramov Theatre, November, 1889).

The Sea-gull (four-act), translated by Fred Eisemann, R. G. Badger, 1913; translated by Julius West as *The Sea-gull: A Play in Four Acts,* Hendersons, 1915; translated by Stark Young as *The Sea Gull* (first produced on Broadway at the Shubert Theater, March 28, 1938), Scribner, 1939, reprinted as *The Sea Gull: A Drama in Four Acts,* Samuel French, 1950; translated by David Magarshack as *The Seagull: Produced by Stanislavsky,* edited and introduction by S. D. Balukhaty, Dobson, 1952; translated by David Iliffe as *The Seagull: A Play,* Samuel French (London), 1953; translated by Bernard W. Sznycer as *The Gull: A Comedy in Four Acts,* [New York], 1967, published in England as *The Gull,* Poets' and Painters' Press, 1974; translated by Jean-Claude Van Itallie as *Anton Chekhov's The Sea Gull: A New Version,* Dramatists Play Service (New York City), 1974, published as *The Sea Gull: A Comedy in Four Acts,* commentaries by William M. Hoffman and Daniel Seltzer, textual notes by Paul Schmidt, Harper & Row, 1977; translated by Ann Jellicoe as *The Sea Gull,* edited by Henry Popkin, Avon, 1975; translated by David French as *The Seagull,* Playwright's Co-op (Toronto), 1977, published as *The Seagull: A Play,* notes by Donna Orwin, General Paperbacks, 1978; translated by Thomas Kilroy as *The Seagull,* Methuen, 1981; translated and introduction Tania Alexander and Charles Sturridge as *The Seagull: A Comedy in Four Acts,* Amber Lane Press (Oxford), 1985; translated and introduction by Michael Frayn as *The Seagull: A Comedy in Four Acts,* Methuen, 1986 (originally produced as *Chayka: Komediya v chetyryokh deystviyakh,* in St. Petersburg at the Alexandrine Theater, October 17, 1896).

Uncle Vanya: A Comedy in Four Acts, translated by Jenny Covan, Brentano's, 1922; adapted and translated by Rose Caylor as *Uncle Vanya,* Covici, Friede, 1930; translated by Stark Young as *Uncle Vanya: Scenes from Village Life in Four Acts,* Samuel French, 1956; translated by Tyrone Guthrie and Leonid Kipnis as *Uncle Vanya: Scenes from Country Life in Four Acts,* University of Minnesota Press (Minneapolis), 1969; translated by Robert W. Corrigan as *Uncle Vanya: An Authoritative Text Edition of a Great Play,* Avon, 1974; translated by John Murrell as *Uncle Vanya: Scenes from Rural Life,* Theatrebooks (Toronto), 1978, translated by Pam Gems as *Uncle Vanya,* introduction by Edward Braun, Methuen, 1979; translated by Jean-Claude Van Itallie as *Uncle Vanya: Scenes from Country Life in Four Acts,* Dramatists Play Service, 1980; translated and introduced by Michael Frayn as *Uncle Vanya: Scenes from Country Life in Four Acts,* Methuen, 1987 (originally produced as *Dyadya Vanya: Stseny iz derevenskoy zhizni v chetyroykh deystviyakh,* in Moscow at the Moscow Art Theater, October 26, 1899).

The Three Sisters: A Drama in Four Acts, translated by Jenny Covan, Brentano's, 1922; translated by Stark Young as *The Three Sisters: A Drama in Four Acts,* Samuel French, 1941; translated by Tyrone Guthrie and Leonid Kipnis as *The Three Sisters: An Authoritative Text Edition,* critical material selected and introduction by Henry Popkin, Avon, 1965; translated and with notes by Randall Jarrell as *The Three Sisters,* Macmillan, 1969; translated by Moura Budberg as *Three Sisters,* Davis-Poynter, 1971; translated by Jean-Claude Van Itallie as *Anton Chekhov's Three Sisters: A New English Version,* Dramatists Play Service, 1979; translated by Brian Friel as *Anton Chekhov's Three Sisters: A Translation,* Gallery Books (Dublin), 1981; translated by Michael Frayn as *Three Sisters: A Drama in Four Acts,* Methuen, 1983; translated by Lanford Wilson as *Three Sisters: A Play* (first produced in Hartford, CT, at the Hartford Stage, 1984), Dramatists Play Service, 1984 (originally produced as *Tri syostry: Drama v chetyryokh deystviyakh,* in Moscow at the Moscow Art Theater, January 21, 1901).

The Cherry Garden: A Comedy in Four Acts, translated and with introduction by Max S. Mandell, C. G. Whaples, 1908; translated by Jenny Covan as *The Cherry Orchard: A Comedy in Four Acts,* Brentano's, 1922; translated by Hubert Butler as *The Cherry Orchard: A Play in Four Acts,* introduction by Tyrone Guthrie, Baker International Play Bureau, 1934; translated by Irina Skariatina and produced as *The Cherry Orchard* on Broadway at the National Theater, January 25, 1944; translated by Stark Young as *The Cherry Orchard: A Drama in Four Acts,* [New York], 1947; adapted by Joshua Logan as *The Wistoria Trees* (first produced on Broadway, 1950), Random House, 1950; published as *The Cherry Orchard,* Foreign Languages Publishing House (Moscow), 1956; translated by John Gielgud as *The Cherry Orchard: A Comedy in Four Acts,* introduction by Michel Saint-Denis, Theater

Arts, 1963; translated by W. L. Goodman as *The Cherry Orchard*, dialogue and adaptation by Henry S. Taylor, Ginn, 1964; published as *Chekhov's The Cherry Orchard*, edited by Herbert Goldstone, Allyn & Bacon (Englewood Cliffs, NJ), 1965; translated by Avrahm Yarmolinsky as *The Cherry Orchard*, critical material selected and introduced by Henry Popkin, Avon, 1965; translated by Tyrone Guthrie and Leonid Kipnis as *The Cherry Orchard: A Play in Four Acts*, University of Minnesota Press, 1965; translated by Jean-Claude Van Itallie as *The Cherry Orchard*, Dramatists Play Service, 1977, published as *The Cherry Orchard: A Comedy in Four Acts*, Grove Press, 1977, revised edition, Dramatists Play Service, 1979; translated by Helen Rappaport as *The Cherry Orchard*, new version by Trevor Griffiths, Pluto Press (London), 1978; translated by Michael Frayn as *The Cherry Orchard: A Comedy in Four Acts*, Methuen, 1978 (originally produced as *Vishnyovy Sad: Komediya v chetyryokh deystriyakh*, in Moscow at the Moscow Art Theater, January 17, 1904).

Chekhov also published a collection of plays in 1897.

COLLECTED PLAYS; IN ENGLISH TRANSLATION

Plays, translated by Marian Fell, first series, Scribner, 1912.

Two Plays by Tchekhof: The Seagull and The Cherry Orchard, translated by George Calderon, G. Richards, 1912.

Plays by Anton Tchekoff, translated by Julius West, second series, Scribner, 1916.

Plays from the Russian, two volumes, translated by Constance Garnett, Chatto & Windus, 1923.

The Plays of Anton Tchekov, translated by Constance Garnett, Modern Library, 1930.

Plays: The Seagull, The Cherry Orchard, On the High Road, The Wedding, The Proposal, The Anniversary, The Bear, The Three Sisters, woodcuts by Howard Simon, Three Sirens Press, 1935, published as *Plays*, Perma Giants, 1950.

The Cherry Orchard and Other Plays, woodcuts by Howard Simon, Grossett & Dunlap, 1936.

Five Famous Plays, translated by Julius West and Marian Fell, Scribner, 1939.

Three Plays, translated by S. S. Koteliansky, Penguin, 1940.

The Plays of Anton Chekhov: Nine Plays, translated by Constance Garnett, Caxton House, 1945.

Six Famous Plays, translated by Julius West and Marian Fell, Scribner, 1949.

Four Short Plays, translated by Julius West, Duckworth, 1950.

Plays, Doric Books, 1950.

Chekhov Plays, translated by Elisaveta Fen, Penguin, 1951.

The Seagull, Uncle Vanya, The Bear, The Proposal, A Jubilee, translated by Elisaveta Fen, Penguin, 1953, published as *The Seagull and Other Plays*, 1954.

Best Plays, translated by Stark Young, Modern Library, 1956.

Three Plays: The Cherry Orchard, Three Sisters, Ivanov, translated by Elisaveta Fen, Penguin, 1956.

The Brute and Other Farces, edited by Eric Bently, translated by Bently and Theodore Hoffman, Samuel French, 1958.

Plays, translated by Elisaveta Fen, Penguin, 1959.

Six Plays of Chekhov, translated by Robert W. Corrigan, foreword by Harold Clurman, Holt, 1962.

Chekhov: The Major Plays, translated by Ann Dunnigan, New American Library, 1964.

Uncle Vanya; The Cherry Orchard; and The Wood Demon, translated by Ronald Hingley, Oxford University Press (Oxford), 1964.

The Sea Gull [and] *The Tragedian in Spite of Himself*, translated by Fred Eisemann and Olive Frances Murphy, International Pocket Library, 1965.

Uncle Vanya, and The Cherry Orchard, translated by Ronald Hingley, Oxford University Press, 1965.

Ten Early Plays, translated by Alex Szogyi, Bantam, 1965.

Two Plays: The Cherry Orchard and Three Sisters, translated by Constance Garnett, introduction by John Gielgud, Heritage Press, 1966.

Four Plays, translation by Alex Szogyi, Washington Square Press, 1968.

Ivanov, The Seagull, and Three Sisters, translated by Ronald Hingley, Oxford University Press, 1968.

Four Plays, translated by David Magarshack, Hill & Wang, 1969.

Chekhov Plays, Heron Books (Portland, OR), 1969.

Eight Plays, translated by Elisaveta Fen, Franklin Library, 1976.

Anton Chekhov's Plays, translated and edited by Eugene Kerr Bristow, Norton, 1977.

Chekhov: Five Major Plays, translated by Ronald Hingley, Oxford University Press, 1977.

The Cherry Orchard and The Seagull, translated by Laurence Senelick, AHM Publishing, 1977.

Five Plays, translated by Ronald Hingley, Oxford University Press, 1977.

Two Plays: The Three Sisters; The Cherry Orchard, translated by Elisaveta Fen, Franklin Library, 1980.

Chekhov's Great Plays: A Critical Anthology, edited by Jean-Pierre Barricelli, New York University Press, 1981.

SHORT FICTION

Contributor, sometimes under the pseudonyms A Man without a Spleen, Antosha Chekhonte, My Brother's Brother, or "v," of more than four hundred short stories, including "An Anonymous Story," "Anyuta," "Ariadne," "At Christmas," "At Home," "An Awkward Business," "The Beauties," "The Beggar," "The Butterfly," "Concerning Love," "The Daughter of Albion," "The Death of a Government Official," "A Dreadful Night," "A Dreary Story," "Easter Night," "The Encounter," "Enemies," "Excellent People," "Fat and Thin," "Gooseberries," "Grisha," "Gusev," "A Hard Case," "Heartache," "The Huntsman," "In Exile," "In the Cart," "In the Ravine," "In Trouble," "The Malefactor," "A Marriageable Girl," "Mire," "The Misfortune," "Murder," "My Life," "My Wife," "The Name-Day Party," "New Villa," "On Official Business,"

"Oysters," "Peasant Women," "Peasants," "Revenge," "Romance with Double Bass," "Sergeant Prishibeyev," "Sleepy," "A Trifle from Life," "The Two Volodyas," "Typhus," "Vanka," "Verochka," "A Woman's Kingdom," "The Witch," and "The Work of Art." Contributor to numerous periodicals, including *budil'nik, Novoye vremya, Oskolki, Peterburgkaya gazeta, Russkaya mysl, Russkiye vedemosti, Severny vestnik, Strekoza,* and *Zhrnal dlya vsekh.*

Chekhov published a number of collections of his works during his lifetime, including *Pestrye rasskazy* (title means "Motley Tales"; 1886), *V sumerkakh* (title means "In the Twilight"; 1887), *Nevinnye rechi* (title means "Innocent Speeches"; 1887), *Rasskazy* (title means "Tales"; 1888), and *Detvora* (title means "Children"; 1889).

COLLECTED SHORT FICTION; IN ENGLISH TRANSLATION

The Black Monk and Other Stories, translated by R. E. C. Long, Duckworth, 1903, F. A. Stokes, 1915.

The Kiss and Other Stories, translated by Long, Duckworth, 1908, F. A. Stokes, 1916.

Stories of Russian Life, translation by Marion Fell, Scribner, 1914.

The Bet and Other Stories, translated by S. S. Koteliansky and J. M. Murry, J. W. Luce, 1915.

Russian Silhouettes: More Stories of Russian Life, translated by Marion Fell, Scribner, 1915.

The Steppe and Other Stories, translated by Adeline Lister Kaye, F. A. Stokes, 1915.

The House with the Mezzanine and Other Stories, translated by S. S. Koteliansky and Gilbert Cannan, Scribner, 1917.

Rothschild's Fiddle and Other Stories, Boni & Liveright (New York City), 1917.

The Tales of Chekhov, two volumes, translated by Constance Garnett, Macmillan, 1917.

Nine Humorous Tales, translated by Isaac Goldbert and Henry T. Shnittkind, Stratford, 1918, 2nd revised edition, Books for Libraries Press, 1970.

My Life and Other Stories, translated by S. S. Koteliansky and Gilbert Cannan, C. W. Daniel, 1920.

The Grasshopper and Other Stories, translated by A. E. Chamot, McKay, 1926.

The Shooting Party, translated by A. E. Chamot, Stanley Paul, 1926, McKay, 1927, revised by Julian Symons, Deutsch, 1986.

Select Tales of Tchehov, two volumes, translated by Constance Garnett, Chatto & Windus, 1927.

Short Stories, translated by Constance Garnett, Macmillan, 1928.

The Stories of Anton Tchekov, edited and introduced by Robert N. Linscott, Modern Library, 1932, published as *The Stories of Anton Chekhov,* 1959.

Tales from Tchekhov, translated by Constance Garnett, Penguin, 1938.

My Life, translated by E. R. Schimanskaya, Staples, 1943.

Short Stories, translated by A. E. Chamot, Commodore Press, 1946.

The Beggar, and Other Stories, illustrated by George W. Rickey, Story Classics, 1949.

Selected Stories, translated by Constance Garnett, Chatto & Windus, 1953.

The Woman in the Case and Other Stories, translated by April FitzLyon and Kyril Zinovieff, Spearman & Calder (London), 1953, British Book Centre (New York City), 1954.

Short Novels and Stories, translated by Ivy Litviov, Foreign Languages Publishing (Moscow), 1954.

Peasants and Other Stories, Doubleday, 1956.

Tales, State Press of Artistic Literature (Moscow), 1956.

Three Years, translated by Rose Prokofieva, Foreign Languages Publishing, 1958.

Great Stories, translated by Constance Garnett, Dell, 1959.

St. Peter's Day and Other Tales, translated by Frances H. Jones, Capricorn Books, 1959.

Wife for Sale, translated by David Tutsev, J. Calder, 1959.

Early Stories, translated by Nora Gottlieb, Bodley Head, 1960, Doubleday, 1961.

Selected Stories, translated by Ann Dunnigan, New American Library, 1960.

The Image of Chekhov: Forty Stories in the Order in Which They Were Written, translated by Robert Payne, Knopf, 1963.

Selected Stories, translated by Jessie Coulson, Oxford University Press, 1963.

Lady with Lapdog and Other Stories, translated by David Magarshack, Penguin, 1964.

Late-blooming Flowers and Other Stories, translated by I. C. Chertok and Jean Gardner, McGraw, 1964.

The Thief and Other Tales, translated by Ursula Smith, Vantage, 1964.

Ward Six and Other Stories, translated by Ann Dunnigan, New American Library, 1965.

The Wolf and the Mutt, translated by Guy Daniels, McGraw, 1971.

The Sinner from Toledo and Other Stories, translated by Arnold Hinchliffe, Farleigh Dickinson University Press, 1972.

The Short Stories of Anton Chekhov, Cardavon Press, 1973.

Seven Stories, translated by Ronald Hingley, Oxford University Press, 1974.

Short Stories, translated by Elisaveta Fen, Folio Society (London), 1974.

Eleven Stories, translated by Ronald Hingley, Oxford University Press, 1975.

Chuckle with Chekhov: A Selection of Comic Stories, translated by Harvey Pitcher and James Forsyth, Swallow House Books, 1975.

Boys, translated by James Riordan, Progress, 1979.

The Kiss and Other Stories, translated by Ronald Wilks, Penguin, 1982.

Chekhov: The Early Stories, 1883-1888, selected and translated by Patrick Miles and J. Murray Pitcher, Macmillan, 1983.

The Duel and Other Stories, translated by Ronald Wilks, Penguin, 1984.

The Russian Master and Other Stories, translated by Ronald Hingley, Oxford University Press, 1984.

The Black Monk and Other Stories, Alan Sutton, 1985.

The Party and Other Stories, translated and introduction by Ronald Wilks, Penguin, 1985.

The Fiancee and Other Stories, translated and introduction by Wilks, Penguin (Harmonsdworth), 1986.

The Shooting Party, University of Chicago Press, 1987.

Ward Number Six and Other Stories, translated by Ronald Hingley, Oxford University Press, 1988.

The Crooked Mirror and Other Stories, Kensington Publishing, 1992.

LETTERS

Letters of Anton Chekhov to His Family and Friends, translated by Constance Garnett, Macmillan, 1920.

Letters on the Short Story, the Drama, and Other Literary Topics, edited by Louis S. Friedland, Milton, Balch, 1924.

The Life and Letters of Anton Tchekhov, edited by S. S. Koteliansky and Philip Tomlinson, G. H. Doran (London), 1925, B. Blom (New York City), 1965.

The Letters of Anton Pavlovitch Tchehov to Olga Leonardovna Knipper, edited and translated by Constance Garnett, G. H. Doran, 1925, B. Blom, 1966.

Selected Letters, edited by Lillian Hellman, translated by Sidonie K. Lederer, Farrar, Straus, 1955.

Letters of Anton Chekhov, translated by Michael Henry Heim and Simon Karlinsky, Harper & Row, 1973, published as *Anton Chekhov's Life and Thought: Selected Letters and Commentary,* University of California Press (Berkeley), 1975.

Letters of Anton Chekhov, translated by Bernard Guilbert Guerney and Lynn Solotaroff, Viking, 1973.

OTHER

The Diary of Anton Tchehov, translated by S. S. Koteliansky and Katherine Mansfield, Atheneum, 1920.

Note-book of Anton Chekhov, translated by S. S. Koteliansky and Leonard Woolf, B. W. Heubsch, 1921, published with *Reminiscences of Tchekhov by Maksim Gorky,* translated by S. S. Koteliansky and Leonard Woolf, Hogarth Press, 1921.

Anton Tchekhov: Literary and Theatrical Reminiscences, translated by S. S. Koteliansky, G. H. Doran, 1927.

The Personal Papers of Anton Chekhov, translated by Constance Garnett, Lear, 1948.

The Unknown Chekhov: Stories and Other Writings Hitherto Untranslated, translated by Avrahm Yarmolinsky, Noonday Press, 1954.

The Island: A Journey to Sakhalin (nonfiction), translated by Luba and Michael Terpak, Washington Square Press, 1967.

SELECTED COLLECTIONS

The Tales of Tchehov, thirteen volumes, translated by Constance Garnett, Macmillan, 1916-22.

The Plays of Tchehov, two volumes, translated by Constance Garnett, Chatto & Windus, 1922-23.

The Works of Anton Chekhov, W. J. Black, 1929, published as *The Best Known Works of Anton Chekhov,* Blue Ribbon Books, 1936.

Plays and Stories, translated by S. S. Koteliansky, Dent, 1937, Dutton, 1938.

The Portable Chekhov, Viking, 1947.

Izbrannie proizvdeniya v trekh tomakh, three volumes, [Moscow], 1964.

Anton Chekhov—Plays and Stories, translated by Ann Dunnigan, International Collectors Library, 1965.

Selected Works in Two Volumes, translated by Ivy Litviov, Progress, 1973.

Chekhov, translated by Patrick Miles and Harvey Pitcher, Abacus, 1984.

COMPLETE WORKS

Polnoe sobranie sochinenii i pisem A. P. Chekhova, twenty volumes, edited by S. D. Balukhatyi and others, [Moscow], 1944-51.

The Oxford Chekhov, nine volumes, translated and edited by Ronald Hingley, Oxford University Press, 1964-75.

Polnoe sobranie sochinenii i pisem A. P. Chekhova, thirty volumes, edited by N. F. Bel'chikov and others, Gorky Institute of World Literature of the U.S.S.R. Academy of Sciences, 1974-83.

■ Adaptations

Many of Chekhov's writings have been adapted for the stage and screen by other authors, including Joseph Buloff, Michael Chekhov, Maria Irene Fornes, Spalding Gray, John Guare, David Mamet, Nicholasa Mohr, Michael O'Hara, Luba Kadison, Evrom Allen Mintz, Thomas Pasatierei, Harold Poppe, Mark Schweid, Wendy Wasserstein, Michael Weller, Robert Whittier, Samm-Art Williams, Avrahm Yarmolinsky, and Alek Zolin.

■ Sidelights

As well as being hailed as one of the most famous Russian writers of the last century, Anton Pavlovich Chekhov is considered by many scholars to be the father of the modern short story. Because of his experiments with style in both short fiction and drama, Chekhov helped to mold the well-defined focus and stylistic artistry of the twentieth-century fictional story; his works are read world-wide for their literary quality as well as for their sensitive insights into the lives of working-class people.

Chekhov—whose name has been transliterated from the Russian Cyrillic alphabet to our Roman alphabet in a variety of spellings—was born in Taganrog, Russia, a seaside town on the Black Sea, in 1860. The third of six children, he was the son of a fanatically religious grocer and the grandson of a serf, or peasant, who had bought his family's freedom in the days before Russia eliminated the ability of wealthy people to "own" the less fortunate. Raised in a lower-middle-class home and aware of the hardships of peasant life, Chekhov would find in his family history and circumstances much of the subject-matter for his later writing. While Chekhov's father, Pavell, was religious to the point of inspiring fear in his offspring, his mother, Yevgeniya, was a wonderful storyteller. She is most likely the source of much of her son's gift in that area; she is also the one who inspired in him an interest in reading and writing, schooling

Chekhov at home until he was sent to the grammar school at the age of eight.

While not a particularly outstanding student, young Chekhov quickly gained a reputation as a wiseacre, making satirical comments, playing pranks, and dubbing each of his teachers with a laughable nickname. He also began to develop an interest in the theater, both as an actor in school productions and as an observer. As a teenager, he began to try his hand at short story writing, oftentimes employing a now-customary satirical approach. He also wrote a play, "Fatherless," which he would later destroy. The fifteen-year-old Chekhov's relatively peaceful childhood would be turned upside down in 1875, when his father's grocery business failed. Facing a jail sentence because of his large debts, Pavell left his family and went to the city of Moscow to seek work; Yevgeniya soon lost the family home to a dishonest local official and was forced to follow her husband to Moscow. She took her three youngest children with her, leaving Chekhov behind to finish his studies. Tutoring young students and selling some of the family's possessions to keep a roof over his head, the teenager managed to pass his exams in 1879 and join his family in Moscow, where his father had found a new position in a warehouse. Chekhov entered that city's university the following year on a scholarship, intending to study medicine.

University study did not bring much-needed income into his family's coffers, so Chekhov decided to use his talents for writing to help cover their living expenses. His first works were directed at the unsophisticated humor magazines that were so popular in the politically repressive Russia of the late 1800s. Disinterested in politics, Chekhov's humor was not directed at the autocratic Russian Tsar, and he had no fear of being sent to a work farm in the cold outreaches of Siberia, as were many Russian writers who attempted to criticize the government through humor. Chekhov wrote to earn money, and the fact that hundreds of his stories were published in the next few years—often under pseudonyms like "Antosha Chekhonte"—shows that his efforts yielded some success on that score. However, most of them were so trivial that few of his stories from this period are still read as "literature."

In fact, Chekhov's work for comic weeklies such as *Strekoza* ("Dragonfly") and the well-respected *Oskolki* ("Fragments") would greatly impact his later style. *Oskolki*'s editor, Nicolas Leykin, insisted that contributors keep to a two-and-a-half-page maximum in each of their story submissions. Such length restrictions would force the young writer to eliminate many of the long, descriptive passages common to nineteenth-century literature, and he began to develop a spare and economical prose style in his fiction. In addition, themes that included dishonest government officials, the sufferings of the poor, the misunderstandings that lie at the heart of most human conflict, as well as Chekhov's interest in focussing on a particular character's point of view, began to emerge in his writing. While in Moscow the young Chekhov also completed his first surviving play,

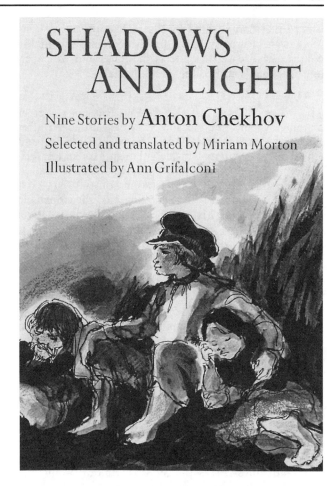

A collection of nine short stories, *Shadows and Light* features Chekhov's warmest tales about people from all walks of life. (Cover illustration by Ann Grifalconi.)

P'yessa bez nazvaniya—often translated as *That Worthless Fellow, Platonov,* although a more literal translation would be "Play without a Title." A fairly conventional work, the play was written in 1881.

Chekhov's medical training, which he completed three years later, would provide the young writer with a great deal of practical insight, not only into medical science, but into human character as well. Gradually, inevitably, Chekhov's satiric edge began to soften and his stories became imbued with a more serious tone. No longer as popular with comic magazines, in 1885 Chekhov began to submit his short stories to periodicals in St. Petersburg, where he was introduced to A. S. Suvorin, the editor of *Novoe vremja,* a literary journal. Impressed with the young man's work, Suvorin encouraged Chekhov to develop his talent as a serious writer.

Meanwhile, despite Chekhov's continuous and prodigious output of saleable writing, the family's financial needs had not abated; the wild spending of his older brothers kept the Chekhovs in constant debt. While by 1892 he and his family would experience a rise in fortunes that would enable them to move to a country estate at Melikhovo, Chekhov continued to work at a furious pace, attempting to balance his need for income with his potential as a creative talent. His stressful life was further complicated by the realization, as early as 1884, that he was suffering from tuberculosis, a highly contagious disease that affects the lungs and which, in one Chekhov's age, often proved fatal.

The works of Leo Tolstoy, a famous Russian writer of an older generation, became a strong influence after they were introduced to the then-twenty-five-year-old Chekhov, particularly Tolstoy's thoughts on antimaterialism, moral education, and the belief that man should ultimately accept the manifestations of evil that exist naturally in the world. Believing, as the idealistic Tolstoy had, that his writing should be instructive, Chekhov penned stories that concealed a clear but subtle message within their plots. "A Boring Story," considered one of the masterpieces of this period of his writing, paints a picture of an unmotivated, ineffective person who goes through life without purpose or effort.

Tolstoy's ideas would remain the prime influence on Chekhov's own work until 1890, when the young Russian visited a penal colony on the Eastern Siberian island of Sakhalin. Motivated by his desire to "pay off my debt to medicine," as he would write to a friend, Chekhov intended to take a census of the people living under the island's harsh conditions, interview resident government officials, and write a report on the overall situation within the colony of political prisoners. The experience, which took the already weak Chekhov five thousand miles across the Siberian tundra, would become the subject of the humanitarian study *Ostrov Sakhalin,* translated as *Sakhalin Island.* He carefully recorded the misery of the inhabitants of the five-hundred-mile-long island by speaking to up to 160 people each day. The experience at Sakhalin profoundly influenced the writer, and he began to seriously question a moral code such as Tolstoy's that would passively accept such human suffering. In the short story "Ward Number 6," Chekhov directly attacks Tolstoy's advocacy of non-resistance to evil by portraying the downfall of a Tolstoy-esque hero into madness and misery.

Abandoning the idealism of his literary elder, Chekhov began to exhibit an even greater realism within his writing, focussing on situations of hardship, boredom, futility, and the suffering common to many people of the middle and lower classes. Although labeled somewhat pessimistic by several European and American critics due to their more somber tone and repeated exploration of the darker side of life, the stories and plays that Chekhov created in his "third" period would, surprisingly, also be hailed for their optimism. After the Russian Revolution and the overthrow of Tsar Nicholas II in November, 1917, Chekhov was lauded as a hero in the newly formed U.S.S.R., a writer whose works prefigured the onset of a Russian revolution born of the discontent of the ill-used working classes. Interestingly, in many of his journals and letters Chekhov expressed a great deal of personal optimism for the social progress he saw emanating from the scientific advances of his day.

During the third period of Chekhov's literary career, such plays as *Uncle Vanya, The Sea-gull,* and *The Cherry Orchard* seemed almost radical. They broke with tradition in their depiction of the pivotal, sometimes violent, and often intensely dramatic moments of their characters' lives confined offstage. *The Sea-gull,* the first drama to utilize such "indirect action," ignores the conventions of nineteenth-century theater by containing no starring role, no sense of heightening dramatic tension, and no perceptible conclusion. While debuting disastrously at Moscow's Art Theater—in fact, the lack of a role for a favorite local actress actually sparked a riot outside the theater building—*The Sea-gull* would be performed to acclaim two years later. The prestigious Moscow Art Theater, which would debut most of Chekhov's dramatic works, was also where the playwright met his wife-to-be, actress Olga Knipper. Married in 1901, the couple was forced to spend a great deal of time apart: Chekhov because his ongoing battle with tuberculosis kept him confined to European health resorts for much of the year, and Olga because of the demands of her successful acting career.

By the late 1890s, Chekhov had reached what many critics consider his mature style. While the quantity of his writing had declined, the quality had increased, and he began to indulge in longer stories, such as "The

In Chekhov's *Kashtanka,* a small lost dachshund is befriended by a clown who teaches him new tricks for the travelling circus. (Illustration by Ruben Vardzigulyants.)

Beauties," "The Name-Day Party," and the brilliant "A Dreary Story," without sacrificing his concise style. In the latter work, a dying professor of medicine recalls the last months of his life: his fear of death; his battle with academic colleagues; and his growing apathy regarding family concerns, including his daughter's elopement with a local scoundrel. Realizing that life is indeed meaningless, he, in turn, becomes incapable of discovering meaning, and cannot help his beloved ward, Katya, when she pleads for his advice. Many scholars have perceived in "A Dreary Story" in particular the inner cynicism of its author, an attitude that, in fact, shadows many of his written works.

Even today, Chekhov's works are reread in many translations. *Kashtanka,* the story of a small dachshund who strays from home and is adopted by a travelling circus, has been illustrated and provides an excellent introduction for younger readers to his short fiction. Characteristic of Chekhov's interest in point-of-view, the story is told from the dog's perspective. Her master loses her one day when he is too drunk to retrieve his dog. The story then focuses on Kashtanka's new life with a circus clown who treats her with great kindness, feeding her better and being much less harsh than the dog's former owner. However, when Kashtanka is performing her first tricks at the circus, she hears the voice of her former master's son and immediately runs to him. As Patricia Dooley pointed out in a *School Library Journal* review of the picture book, the fact that Kashtanka returns to her former, less kind owners might not make sense to some young readers at first, but taken from a "dog's-eye view ... her dogged, illogical loyalty makes perfect sense." Chekhov also wrote other stories suitable for young people, some of which are collected in the 1968 anthology *Shadows and Light: Nine Stories.* The tales in this volume are again told from points-of-view that children will find sympathetic, including those of animals and children. These short stories will also serve as fine introductions to younger readers of Chekhov.

Noted literary critic John Middleton Murry wrote that Chekhov's works provide "a standard by which modern literary effort must be measured, and the writer of prose or poetry who is not sufficiently single-minded to apply the standard to himself is of no particular account." Succumbing to the tuberculosis which he had battled since 1884, Chekhov, an undisputed literary talent of international stature, died in 1904, at the age of forty-four.

■ Works Cited

Dooley, Patricia, review of *Kashtanka, School Library Journal,* November, 1991, p. 116.
Murry, John Middleton, "Thoughts on Tchehov," *Aspects of Literature,* Collins, 1920, p. 78.

■ For More Information See

BOOKS

Aiken, Conrad, *Collected Criticism,* Oxford University Press, 1968.
Bruford, W. H., *Chekhov's Art: A Stylistic Analysis,* Ardis Press, 1983.
Clyman, Toby W., editor, *A Chekhov Companion,* Greenwood Press, 1985.
Davies, Ruth, *The Great Books of Russia,* University of Oklahoma Press, 1968.
Gilman, Richard, *The Making of Modern Drama,* Farrar, Straus, 1974.
Hahn, Beverly, *Chekhov, A Study of the Major Stories and Plays,* Cambridge University Press, 1977.
Hingley, Ronald, *A New Life of Anton Chekhov,* Knopf, 1976.
Magarshack, David, *Chekhov the Dramatist,* Hill & Wang, 1960.
Short Story Criticism, Volume 2, Gale, 1989, pp. 124-60.
Simmons, Ernest J., *Chekhov: A Biography,* University of Chicago Press, 1962.
Stowall, Peter, *Literary Impressionism: James and Chekhov,* University of Georgia Press, 1980.
Twentieth-Century Literary Criticism, Gale, Volume 3, 1980, Volume 10, 1983.

PERIODICALS

Bulletin of the Center for Children's Books, December, 1991, p. 85.
Horn Book, February, 1962, p. 46; October, 1968, pp. 562-63.
Kirkus Reviews, November 15, 1991, p. 1468.
Quill & Quire, November, 1991, p. 25.
School Library Journal, December, 1995, p. 73.*

* * *

CHRISTELOW, Eileen 1943-

■ Personal

Born April 22, 1943, in Washington, DC; daughter of Allan (an historian and business executive) and Dorothy (an economist; maiden name, Beal) Christelow; married Albert B. Ahrenholz (a potter), December, 1965; children: Heather. *Education:* University of Pennsylvania, B.A. (architecture), 1965; graduate study, University of California, Berkeley.

■ Addresses

Agent—Dilys Evans, 40 Park Ave., New York, NY 10016.

■ Career

Freelance photographer in Philadelphia, PA, 1965-71, and graphic designer and illustrator in Berkeley, CA, 1973-81; author and illustrator of books for children, 1982—. *Member:* Society of Children's Book Writers and Illustrators.

■ Awards, Honors

Little Archer Award (Wisconsin), 1982, for *Henry and the Red Stripes;* Junior Literary Guild selections for *Henry and the Red Stripes, Mr. Murphy's Marvelous Invention,* and *Henry and the Dragon;* Washington Irving fiction award, 1984, Land of Enchantment award, 1986, and Maud Hart Lovelace award, 1986, all for *Zucchini; School Library Journal* Best Books list, 1995, for *What Do Authors Do?*

■ Writings

SELF-ILLUSTRATED BOOKS FOR CHILDREN

Henry and the Red Stripes, Clarion, 1982.
Mr. Murphy's Marvelous Invention, Clarion, 1983.
Henry and the Dragon, Clarion, 1984.
Jerome the Babysitter, Houghton Mifflin, 1987.
Olive and the Magic Hat, Houghton Mifflin, 1987.
Jerome and the Witchcraft Kids, Clarion, 1988.
The Robbery at the Diamond Dog Diner, Houghton Mifflin, 1988.
(Reteller) *Five Little Monkeys Jumping on the Bed,* Clarion, 1989.
Glenda Feathers Casts a Spell, Clarion, 1990.
Five Little Monkeys Sitting in a Tree, Clarion, 1991.
Don't Wake Up Mama: Another Five Little Monkey's Story, Clarion, 1992.
Gertrude, the Bulldog Detective, Clarion, 1992.
The Five-Dog Night, Clarion, 1993.
The Great Pig Escape, Clarion, 1994.
What Do Authors Do?, Clarion, 1995.
Five Little Monkeys with Nothing to Do, Houghton Mifflin, 1996.

ILLUSTRATOR

(With others) Diane Downie, *Math for Girls and Other Problem Solvers,* University of California Press, 1981.
Barbara Dana, *Zucchini,* Harper, 1982.
Thomas Rockwell, *Oatmeal Is Not for Mustaches,* Holt, 1984.
Sue Alexander, *Dear Phoebe,* Little, Brown, 1984.
Barbara Steiner, *Oliver Dibbs and the Dinosaur Cause,* Simon & Schuster, 1986.
Jim Aylesworth, *Two Terrible Frights,* Simon & Schuster, 1987.
Joy Elizabeth Handcock, *The Loudest Little Lion,* A. Whitman, 1988.
Barbara Steiner, *Oliver Dibbs to the Rescue!* Avon Books, 1988.
Myra Cohn Livingston, selector, *Dilly Dilly Piccalilli: Poems for the Very Young,* McElderry Books, 1989.
Mary Elise Monsell, *The Mysterious Cases of Mr. Pin,* Atheneum, 1989.
Jim Aylesworth, *The Completed Hickory Dickory Dock,* Atheneum, 1990.
Mary Elise Monsell, *Mr. Pin: The Chocolate Files,* Atheneum, 1990.
Peggy Christian, *The Old Coot,* Atheneum, 1991.
Barbara Steiner, *Dolby and the Woof-Off,* Morrow, 1991.
Jan Wahl, *Mrs. Owl and Mr. Pig,* Lodestar, 1991.

Mary Elise Monsell, *Mr. Pin: The Spy Who Came North from the Pole,* Atheneum, 1993.
Jennifer Brutschy, *Celeste and Crabapple Sam,* Lodestar, 1994.
Maryann Macdonald, *Secondhand Star,* Hyperion, 1994.
Mary Elise Monsell, *Mr. Pin: A Fish Named Yum,* Atheneum, 1994.
Maryann Macdonald, *No Room for Francie,* Hyperion, 1995.

Christelow's photographs have appeared in *Progressive Architecture, Colloquy, Ford Foundation, Home, Media and Method, New York Times Book Review, Pennsylvania Gazette, Youth, Teacher,* and in various textbooks. Creator of posters for the Children's Book Council.

■ Sidelights

Eileen Christelow is an award-winning author/illustrator who produces humorous, bright, and energetic picture books. Whether she is illustrating her own stories or those of other authors, her animal characters—from cats and dogs to alligators and penguins—are charming and expressive. Christelow once explained to *SATA* that her career as a picture-book creator developed from her interests in architecture and photography.

"I majored in architecture at the University of Pennsylvania in Philadelphia," she explained. "While I was there, I discovered the darkroom in the graphics department. I spent more time there than I should have, taking photographs. After graduation, I earned my living as a freelance photographer, photographing buildings rather than designing them. I also photographed in the Philadelphia public school classrooms, skid row, and Chinatown. I took several trips with my cameras across the United States and one trip to Mexico. My photos appeared in various magazines and textbooks."

After a visit to Cornwall, England, and the birth of a daughter, Christelow and her family moved to Berkeley, California. There, she "found that I was tired of constantly looking at the world through a camera lens, so I began to learn about type, graphic design, and illustration. I eventually started freelancing as a designer producing ads, brochures, catalogues, and books.

"When my daughter was fourteen months old, I decided that I wanted to write and illustrate picture books for young children. For several years my daughter and I researched the problem together, taking weekly trips to the library and reading at naptime and bedtime. I found the picture book format a fascinating and frustrating challenge. I learned about pacing and I learned to keep my text spare. I also found that the years I'd spent as a photographer, trying to capture one photo that would tell an entire story, were invaluable to the process of creating stories with pens and pencils." One of the results of her efforts was a large collection of children's books, which helped her daughter to read and write. "And I wrote and illustrated several books—one of which is *Henry and the Red Stripes.*

Farmer Bert's efforts to sell his pigs at the market meet with comical resistance in Eileen Christelow's self-illustrated picture book *The Great Pig Escape*, which is based in part on a true story.

"The idea for *Henry and the Red Stripes* first came to me when I was half asleep in a hot, steamy bath. It had been percolating in the back of my mind for months as I researched and illustrated a poster picturing twenty-six insects, reptiles, birds, and mammals camouflaged in a forest setting. That poster, combined with observing my daughter and her friends decorating themselves with paints and magic markers, led to the creation of Henry Rabbit."

Henry and the Dragon, the second "Henry" book, portrays the rabbit after a bedtime story. He thinks there must be a dragon about, and builds a trap to catch

it. As Christelow said in a *Junior Literary Guild* article, *Henry and the Dragon* "was inspired by memories" of her young daughter asking if any bears walked around the family house at night.

Jerome the Babysitter introduces a young alligator boy just as he begins his first job babysitting. His twelve charges trick and mistreat him, and even trap him on the roof, but in the end Jerome proves he is a clever as well as competent caretaker. According to Lisa Redd in *School Library Journal,* the alligator characters are "delightful," and rendered with "expressive faces." In the words of a *Publishers Weekly* critic, the book

In *What Do Authors Do?*, Christelow explains to young readers how authors and illustrators turn a simple idea into a colorful picture book.

presents a "side-splitting story" and "luridly colored cartoons."

The Robbery at the Diamond Dog Diner features a little hen who can't keep her mouth shut. When she hides her dog friend's diamonds in her hollowed-out eggs, diamond thieves think she's a diamond-egg-laying hen, and kidnap her. *The Five-Dog Night,* which a *Kirkus Reviews* critic calls a "good-natured, entertaining yarn," surprises readers by demonstrating that a five-dog night is one so cold that five dogs in the bed make the best blanket. A young dog, intent on becoming a detective, spies on her neighbors in *Gertrude, the Bulldog Detective;* although the neighbors provide her with some fake clues in an effort to discourage her, Gertrude manages to catch some real thieves.

In *The Great Pig Escape* a pair of vegetable farmers decide to raise pigs. When it is time for the farmers to sell the pigs at the market, the pigs escape both the market and certain death by stealing clothes, disguising

themselves as people, and blending in with the crowd. After safely reaching Florida, the pigs return the clothes, along with a postcard for their owners with the comment, "Oink!" *School Library Journal* contributor Cynthia K. Richey described the text as "lively" and "funny," and notes that the book's pen and ink and watercolor illustrations are "filled with humor." And a *Publishers Weekly* critic describes the book as a "strategic endorsement of vegetarianism."

Fans of Christelow's, as well as aspiring authors, may appreciate her book *What Do Author's Do?* By following the efforts of two writers who have witnessed the same event, Christelow demonstrates how writers begin their books and prepare them for publication. According to *Horn Book* contributor Elizabeth S. Watson, "If ever there was a book to encourage youngsters to try their hand at writing, this is one."

■ Works Cited

Review of *The Five-Dog Night, Kirkus Reviews,* July 1, 1993, p. 857.

Review of *The Great Pig Escape, Publishers Weekly,* June 27, 1994, p. 78.

Review of *Henry and the Dragon, Junior Literary Guild,* March, 1984.

Review of *Jerome the Babysitter, Publishers Weekly,* February 22, 1985, p. 158.

Redd, Lisa, review of *Jerome the Babysitter, School Library Journal,* March, 1986, p. 145.

Richey, Cynthia K., review of *The Great Pig Escape, School Library Journal,* November, 1994, p. 73.

Watson, Elizabeth S., review of *What Do Authors Do? Horn Book,* November/December, 1995, p. 754.

■ For More Information See

PERIODICALS

Booklist, March 15, 1992, p. 1397.

Bulletin of the Center for Children's Books, July-August, 1985.

Horn Book, September-October, 1989, pp. 633-34.

Publishers Weekly, June 28, 1993, p. 77.

School Library Journal, February, 1987, p. 66; June, 1992, p. 90.

*   *   *

CLEM, Margaret H(ollingsworth) 1923-

■ Personal

Born February 25, 1923, in Terre Haute, IN; married James Harry Clem, February 18, 1984; children: Dr. R. Michael Myers, Susan Myers Beeson, Dr. Brent Myers. *Education:* Attended Indiana State University. *Politics:* Independent. *Religion:* Protestant. *Hobbies and other interests:* Decorating, gardening, reading, grandchildren.

■ Addresses

Home—140 South 26th St. Dr., Terre Haute, IN 47803.

■ Career

MEIS Department Store, Terre Haute, IN, assistant to the buyer/manager of the Boulevard Room (customer relations, community relations, ad-writing, displays), weekly column writer for the Women's Department, 1962-86. *Member:* Society of Children's Book Writers and Illustrators, Vigo County Library, Vigo County Historical Society, Central Presbyterian Church.

■ Writings

(And illustrator) *Elbert Ein Swine, Genius Pig,* Mayhaven, 1994.

(And illustrator) *Elbert Ein Swine Learns Line Dancing,* Mayhaven, 1995.

Little Candles: A Collection of Poems and Stories, Mayhaven, 1995.

MARGARET H. CLEM

Also author of several unpublished books for children, including *My Dad Doodles, Me and the Car Chase, Mud Kids, Thinking Kaps, Earth Bank, Insect Fashion Parade, Spaghetti-Whos?, One Little Light, Little Buffalo, Give Me an "S,"* and *Polly, Our Poodle.*

■ Work in Progress

Plant Zoo, Elbert Ein Swine Teaches Pig Latin, Elbert Ein Swine Saves Pigdom Park, all for Mayhaven Publishing; *Little Buffalo,* the story of a Native American boy, and *Children's Choices: What Children Like to Read,* a "nonfiction handbook for teachers, parents, authors, publishers, and childcare providers," also for Mayhaven; a three-hundred-page novel, tentatively titled *Champagne Velvet* or *Bottles;* research on Eugene V. Debs, the brewing industry, forensic medicine, folk stories of the Wabash Valley.

■ Sidelights

When Margaret H. Clem learned that her first children's book, *Elbert Ein Swine, Genius Pig,* was to be published, she "had a lifetime dream come true!" That dream is to encourage children "in the love of reading and writing and to love and respect their own voices." *Elbert Ein Swine, Genius Pig,* "addresses mental exercise and motivates children to 'problem-solve.'" Its sequel, *Elbert Ein Swine Learns Line Dancing,* "addresses physical exercise and shows children the joys of learning something new."

Clem is also the illustrator of her Elbert Ein Swine books. She told *SATA* that "simple, action-filled drawings are what I do . . . . Children love action, familiar scenes, maps, identifiable characters involved in identifiable or novel activities . . . . As I write I envision which pictures will go where in the book. Variety of placement, size, focus, and gradation of colors or intensity gives texture to the book."

"Determining the physical characteristics of the characters—how they look, their apparel, unique features which identify them—is the most critical illustrative challenge. Once you know your character has white hair, wears glasses, has a sweet smile, wears a sweater and jeans, and is pink ... well, see, the hard part is done! Then you just draw him! And that is Elbert Ein Swine, Genius Pig!"

* * *

CONRAD, Pam 1947-1996

OBITUARY NOTICE—See index for *SATA* sketch: Born June 18, 1947; died of breast cancer, January 22, 1996, in Rockville Center, NY. Writer. Educated at Hofstra University and the New School for Social Research, Conrad began writing for children and young adult readers in 1979. She was well-known for exploring such contemporary themes as divorce, alcoholism, mental illness, and youthful feelings of rejection and alienation in her works. One of her most popular books, *Prairie Songs,* published in 1985, is set in Nebraska, where a young family struggles with the strain of austere pioneer life. Conrad won several awards for the book, including the International Reading Association Children's Book Award, and the American Library Association/*Booklist* "Best of the '80s" books for children citation. Conrad also produced picture books and novels for younger and reluctant readers. Among Conrad's most recent works are *Prairie Vision: The Life and Times of Solomon Butcher,* 1991, *Pedro's Journal: A Voyage with Christopher Columbus,* 1991, *Molly and the Strawberry Day,* 1994, *Doll Face Has a Party,* 1994, *The Rooster's Gift,* 1995, *Call Me Ahnighito,* 1995, and *Animal Lingo,* 1995.

OBITUARIES AND OTHER SOURCES:

BOOKS

Children's Literature Review, Vol. 18, Gale Research, 1989.
Something about the Author Autobiography Series, Vol. 19, Gale Research, 1995.
Twentieth-Century Young Adult Writers, St. James Press, 1994.

PERIODICALS

New York Times, January 26, 1996, p. B9.

* * *

COUSINS, Linda 1946-
(Amasewa Okomfo)

■ Personal

Born January 19, 1946, in Knoxville, TN; daughter of Raymond Hall (in the military) and Bertha Cousins-Reynolds (a housekeeper); children: Nadage. *Education:* University of Tennessee, B.S. *Politics:* Independent. *Religion:* "New Thought." *Hobbies and other interests:* Historical research.

■ Addresses

Home—P.O. Box 5, Radio City Station, New York, NY 10101-0005.

■ Career

Children's book writer. New York City Board of Education, Brooklyn, social studies teacher, 1987—. Conducts workshops on publishing and distribution, poetry writing, travel writing, starting and operating a home-based business, motivation and self-esteem, and spiritual woman awareness. Has also taught in an alternative high school as a lead teacher; has taught adult education, written high school curricula on African, African-American, and Caribbean history; has worked as a continuing education instructor for Medgar Evers College, Brooklyn, NY, and Malcolm-King College, Harlem, NY. Has produced and hosted a travel talk show for WNYE radio station, Medgar Evers College, Brooklyn. *Member:* International Association of Independent Publishers, Poets and Writers, United Federation of Teachers, Black Women in Publishing.

■ Awards, Honors

Proclamation and key to the city, Mayor's Office, Knoxville, TN; Fannie Lou Hamer Award, Women's Center, Medgar Evers College; Women of Influence Award, Brooklyn YWCA; Excellence in Teaching Award, Vocational Education Department, Brooklyn YWCA; African Youth Diaspora Foundation, U.S. Virgin Islands, for promotion of tourism to the U.S. Virgin Islands; Bahamas Loving Care Association Award, Nassau, for promotion of Bahamian business and tourism to the Bahamas; Black Playwrights Award, WWRL radio station, Queens, NY. Has also received awards from the Central Brooklyn Coordinating Council, Inc., and *The West Indian Tribune* newspaper.

■ Writings

(Editor) *Ancient Black Youth and Elders Reborn: Anthology of the Poetry, Short Stories, Oral Histories, and Deeper Thoughts of African-American Youth and Elders,* Universal Black Writer Press, 1985.
Huggy Bean and the Origin of the Magic Kente Cloth (juvenile), Gumbs & Thomas Publishers, 1991.
Huggy Bean: A Desert Adventure (juvenile), Gumbs & Thomas Publishers, 1992.
Huggy Bean: We Happened upon a Beautiful Place (juvenile), Gumbs & Thomas Publishers, 1992.
Caribbean Bound! Culture Roots, Places, and People, Universal Black Writer Press, 1994.
Monica Made Me Promise (young adult), illustrated by Jim Webb, DARE Books, 1994.

Also author of *Proverbs of a Contemporary AfrICAN* and *This Ancestral Poetsong* (audiotape).

Work in Progress

Cultural Travel Rootswoman-Style and *A Silent Woman Now Sings,* a novel; researching Caribbean Healing Spots.

For More Information See

PERIODICALS

Library Journal, March 1, 1995, p. 42.*

* * *

COWLEY, (Cassia) Joy 1936-

Personal

Born August 7, 1936; daughter of Peter (a builder) and Cassia (Gedge) Summers; married Malcolm Mason (an accountant and writer), 1970 (died 1985); married Terry Coles, 1989; children: (from a previous marriage) Sharon, Edward, Judith, James. *Education:* Attended Girls' High School, Palmerston North, Wellington, New Zealand. *Politics:* None. *Religion:* Catholic. *Hobbies and other interests:* Spinning, fishing, and "other soothing pastimes."

Addresses

Home—Te Mangawa, Fish Bay, Kenepuru, R.D.2, Picton, New Zealand.

Career

Writer, 1967—. Pharmacists' apprentice in New Zealand, 1953-56.

Awards, Honors

New Zealand Buckland Literary Award, 1970, for *Man of Straw;* New Zealand Literary Achievement Award, 1980; New Zealand AIM Children's Book Awards, 1982, for *The Silent One,* 1992, for *Bow Down Shadrach,* and 1996, for *The Cheese Trap;* Children's Book of the Year awards, 1983, for *The Silent One,* and 1993, for *Bow down Shadrach;* Russell Clark Award, 1985, for *The Duck in the Gun;* New Zealand Commemoration Medal, 1990; Order of the British Empire, 1992, for services to children's literature; Margaret Mahy Lecture Award, 1993; Women's Suffrage Centennial Medal, 1993; Honorary Doctorate of Literature, Massey University, 1994.

Writings

FOR CHILDREN

The Duck in the Gun, illustrated by Edward Sorel, Doubleday, 1969, illustrated by Robyn Belton, Shortland (Auckland), 1984.
The Silent One, illustrated by Hermann Greissle, Knopf, 1981, illustrated by Sherryl Jordan, Whitcoulls, 1981.

JOY COWLEY

The Terrible Taniwha of Timberditch, Oxford University Press (Auckland), 1982.
Old Tuatara, illustrated by Clare Bowes, Department of Education School Publications Branch (Wellington), 1983, published as *Old Lizard,* Nelson (London), 1985.
(With Mona Williams) *Two of a Kind* (stories), illustrated by Jane Amos, Blackberry Press (Upper Hutt, New Zealand), 1984.
The Fierce Little Woman and the Wicked Pirate, illustrated by Jo Davies, Shortland, 1984.
Salmagundi, illustrated by Philip Webb, Oxford University Press, 1985.
Brith the Terrible, Shortland, 1986.
Captain Felonius, illustrated by Elizabeth Fuller, Shortland, 1986.
The Lucky Feather, illustrated by Philip Webb, Shortland, 1986.
My Tiger (stories), illustrated by Jan van der Voo, Shortland, 1986.
The King's Pudding, illustrated by Martin Bailey, Shortland, 1986.

Mrs. Grindy's Shoes, illustrated by Val Biro, Shortland, 1986.

The Train Ride Story, illustrated by Val Biro, Shortland, 1987.

Giant on the Bus, illustrated by Ian McNee, Shortland, 1987.

Seventy Kilometers from Ice Cream, photographs by Winto Cleal, Department of Education School Publications Branch, 1987.

Turnips for Dinner, illustrated by Jan van der Voo, Shortland, 1986.

Pawprints in the Butter, Mallinson Rendel (Wellington, New Zealand), 1991.

Bow down Shadrach, illustrated by Robyn Belton, Hodder & Stoughton (Auckland), 1991, Wright Group (Seattle, WA), 1996.

Happy Birthday Mrs. Felonius, Omnibus (Australia), 1992.

The Day of the Rain, Mallinson Rendel, 1993.

The Screaming Mean Machine, Scholastic, 1993.

Gladly Here I Come, Penguin (Harmondsworth), 1994, Wright Group, 1996.

Beyond the Rivers, Scholastic New Zealand, 1994.

Song of the River, Wright Group, 1994.

Write On, Scholastic New Zealand, 1994.

Guide for Young Authors, Wright Group, 1994.

The Day of the Snow, illustrated by Bob Kerr, Mallinson Rendel, 1994.

Papa buys Miguel a turkey to fatten for Thanksgiving, not realizing the turkey will become Miguel's special pet. (Cover illustration by Joe Cepeda.)

Tulevai, Scholastic New Zealand, 1995.

The Happy Hens Series, Scholastic New Zealand, 1995.

The Day of the Wind, Mallinson Rendel, 1995.

Sea Daughter, Scholastic New Zealand, 1995.

The Mouse Bride, paintings by David Christiana, Scholastic, 1995.

The Cheese Trap, Scholastic New Zealand, 1995.

Nicketty-Nacketty-Noo-Noo-Noo, Scholastic New Zealand, 1995.

Joy Cowley Answers Kids' Questions, Scholastic New Zealand, 1995.

Brave Mama Puss ("Puss Quartet"), Reed (Auckland), 1995.

Papa Puss to the Rescue ("Puss Quartet") Reed, 1995.

Mabel and the Marvelous Meow ("Puss Quartet"), Reed, 1995.

Oscar in Danger ("Puss Quartet"), Reed, 1995.

Gracias the Thanksgiving Turkey, illustrated by Joe Cepeda, Scholastic, 1996.

Snake and Lizard, Wright Group, 1996.

JUVENILE READERS

Author of readers *Fish in the Trough, A New Friend, Johnny's Guitar, The Fire-Fighters, The Meeting House,* and *Wendy Makes a Poi,* all illustrated by Nancy Parker, Kea Press (Wellington), 1968, published as *The Tui and Sis Books,* Price Milburn (Wellington), 1977.

Author, with June Melser, of "Story Chest Read-To-gether" series: *Mrs. Wishy-Washy, Smarty Pants, The Big Toe, Boo-Hoo, Grandpa Grandpa, Hairy Bear, The Hungry Giant, In a Dark Dark Wood, Lazy Mary, Obadiah!, One Cold Wet Night, Poor Old Polly, Sing a Song, Three Little Ducks, Woosh!, Yes Ma'am, The Red Rose, To Town, Dan the Flying Man, The Farm Concert, The Jigaree, Meanies, The Monster's Party,* and *Who Will Be My Mother?,* Shortland, 1980-83.

Author, with June Melser, of "Story Chest Books" series: *The Birthday Cake, The Dragon, A Terrible Fright, A Barrel of Gold, Clever Mr. Brown, Hungry Monster, Jack-in-the-Box, The Kick-a-Lot Shoes, The Pirates, Wet Grass, Where Is My Spider?, Yum and Yuk, Captain Bumble, Countdown, A Day in Town, The Big Tease, Cat on the Roof, The Ghost and the Sausage, Grandma's Stick, Hatupatu and the Birdwoman, Little Brother's Haircut, The Sunflower That Went FLOP, Tell-Tale,* and *Sun Smile,* Shortland, 1981-82.

Author, with June Melser, of "Story Chest Ready-Set-Go" series: *The Bee, The Chocolate Cake, Come with Me, Copy-Cat, Flying, I Want an Ice Cream, Little Pig, Lost, My Home, Plop!, Round and Round, Splosh, To New York, Who Lives Here?, Where Are They Going?, Who's Going to Lick the Bowl?, Horace, The Night Train, The Pumpkin, Rum-Tum Tumm, Sleeping Out, Too Big for Me, What a Mess!,* and *Look for Me,* Shortland, 1981-82.

Author, with June Melser and Margaret Mahy, of *Cooking Pot, Fast and Funny, Roly Poly, Sing to the Moon,* and *Tiddalik,* Shortland, 1982.

while I had to stay down on the ground and watch them all.

A young girl is finally big enough to ride on the scariest roller coaster, but is she brave enough to climb aboard? (From *The Screaming Mean Machine*, written by Cowley and illustrated by David Cox.)

Author of "Story Box Books" series: *The Pie Thief, The Tale of the Cook, The Trader from Currumbin, The War of the Winds,* and *Poor Old Robot,* Shortland, 1982-85.

Author of "Story Chest Ready-to-Read" series: *Number One, The Biggest Cake in the World, Fasi Sings, Fasi's Fish, Greedy Cat, Our Teacher Miss Pool, Rain Rain, Words, I'm the King of the Mountain, Rosie at the Zoo, The Wild Wet Wellington Wind, Did You Say Five?, The Smile,* and *Where Is Miss Pool?,* Department of Education School Publications Branch, 1982-87.

Author, with June Melser, of "Story Chest Get Ready Books": *The Bicycle, The Big Hill, Feet, The Ghost, Go Go Go, Houses, If You Meet a Dragon, In the Mirror, A Monster Sandwich, Mouse, Night-Time, On a Chair, Painting, The Party, The Storm,* and *The Tree-House,* Arnold Wheaton (Leeds, England), 1983.

Author of "Sunshine Books" series: *Yuk Soup, Baby Gets Dressed, Big and Little, Buzzing Flies, Dinner!, Down to Town, A Hug Is Warm, Huggles' Breakfast, Huggles Can Juggle, Huggles Goes Away, I Am a Bookworm, I Can Fly, I Can Jump, I Love My Family, Ice Cream, Little Brother, The Long Long Tail, Major Jump, My Home, My Puppy, Our Granny, Our Street,* *The Race, Scat! Said the Cat, Shark in a Sack, Shoo! Snap!, Uncle Buncle's House, Up in a Tree, What Is a Huggles?, When Itchy Witchy Sneezes, Along Comes Jake, Bread, Come for a Swim, The Cooking Pot, Dad's Headache, Don't You Laugh at Me!, The Giant's Boy, Good for You, Goodbye Lucy, I'm Bigger Than You!, Let's Have a Swim!, Little Car, The Monkey Bridge, Mr. Grump, Mr. Whisper, My Boat, My Sloppy Tiger, Noise, Nowhere and Nothing, Old Grizzly, One Thousand Currant Buns, The Poor Sore Paw, Ratty-Tatty, Red Socks and Yellow Socks, The Seed, Spider Spider, The Terrible Tiger, The Tiny Woman's Coat, Wake Up, Mum!, What Would You Like?, Where Are You Going Aja Rose?,* and *The Wind Blows Strong,* Heinemann (London), 1986-87.

Author of "Windmill" series: *Growing, The Little Red Hen, My Little Brother, Splish Splash!, Where Can We Put an Elephant?, Where's the Egg Cup, Lucy's Sore Knee,* and *My Wonderful Chair,* Heinemann, 1986-88.

Author of "Jellybeans" series: *Don't Wake the Baby, The Kangaroo from Wooloomooloo, Lavender the Library Cat, Let's Get a Pet, The Little Brown House, The Magician's Lunch, Morning Dance, The Most Scary Ghost, Mouse Monster, The Plants of My Aunt, Ten*

"Oh, house, handsome house!" she cried.
"Please, will you marry me?"

The house did not answer her.

Illustrated from a mouse's perspective, Cowley's whimsical adaptation of a multi-cultural folktale follows the little creature on her journey to find the strongest mate in the world. (From *The Mouse Bride*, illustrated by David Christiana.)

Loopy Caterpillars, The Terrible Armadillo, The Train That Ran Away, The Yukadoos, Monster, The Amazing Popple Seed, The Bull and the Matador, Cow Up a Tree, The Difficult Day, The Gumby Shop, A Handy Dragon, The Horrible Thing with Hairy Feet, Mr. Beep, Boggity-Bog, Do-Whacky-Do, The Shoe Grabber, A Silly Old Story, A Walk with Grandpa, The Wonder-Whizz, and *The Wild Woolly Child,* Allan, 1988-89.

ADULT FICTION

Nest in a Falling Tree, Doubleday, 1967.
Man of Straw, Doubleday, 1970.
Of Men and Angels, Doubleday, 1973.
The Mandrake Root, Doubleday, 1976.
The Growing Season, Doubleday, 1979.
Heart Attack and Other Stories, Hodder & Stoughton, 1985.

OTHER

Whole Learning: Whole Child, Wright Group, 1994.

Contributor, *New Zealand Short Stories,* Volume 3, Oxford University Press, 1975. Stories have appeared in New Zealand literary periodicals and school readers; writer of radio scripts for New Zealand Broadcasting Corporation. Several of Cowley's books have been translated into Spanish.

■ **Adaptations**

Carry Me Back, a film produced by Kiwi Film Production/New Zealand Film Commission, and shown at the 1982 Cannes film festival, was based on a story by Cowley. *Nest in a Falling Tree* was adapted by Roald Dahl as the film *The Night Digger,* starring Patricia Neal. *The Silent One* has been adapted for film and aired on The Disney Channel.

■ **Work in Progress**

Starbright and the Dream Eater, a children's book.

■ **Sidelights**

Joy Cowley, a prolific, award-winning writer of children's picture books and readers, first earned her reputation as a writer with adult novels. *Nest in a Falling Tree,* about a love affair between a woman over forty and a man under twenty, won praise from Seymour Epstein, a critic for the *New York Times Book Review.* According to Epstein, Cowley's first novel is "hauntingly beautiful" and eminently well-formed.

The Silent One first brought Cowley attention for her work for children. This story, set in the South Pacific, tells how a deaf, mute boy named Jonasi is dreaded and ostracized by superstitious islanders because of his silence and because of his friendship with a rare albino turtle. Jonasi and the turtle are perceived as demons, and blamed for both a hurricane and a fatal shark attack. When Jonasi gets his chance to leave the island for a new life and an education at a school for the deaf, the life of his turtle is threatened. Jonasi jumps into the ocean to save it, and disappears forever.

The Silent One was favorably received by many critics, and it earned Cowley her first AIM Children's Book Award. Virginia Haviland, writing in *Horn Book,* found the prose in *The Silent One* to be "brilliantly evocative of the physical background as well as of the emotional atmosphere." The book "has a haunting quality," asserted a critic for *Bulletin of the Center for Children's Books.* And *Times Educational Supplement* critic Fred Urquhart declared that *The Silent One* "will not be forgotten easily."

More recently, Cowley has gained critical recognition for her picture book *The Mouse Bride,* illustrated by David Christiana. In this work, based on a traditional folktale spanning many cultures, a small mouse laments her weakness and desires to marry the strongest husband in the world, thereby seemingly ensuring strong children. Her search takes her to the sun, the cloud, the wind, and finally back again to a house before her quest is resolved.

Cowley, who has also penned books on the education of children and on children's writing, once told *SATA* how she approaches her work for children. "Writing for young people requires a memory; more than that—before starting a book it's necessary to peel away years of adult experience like the layers of an onion, and expose a self that's of an age corresponding with character and reader. Only by being once more ten or fourteen or whatever age I'm writing for, can I evaluate the work. I can 'live' with my characters and understand them as equals."

■ Works Cited

Epstein, Seymour, review of *Nest in a Falling Tree, New York Times Book Review,* August 13, 1967, p. 5.
Haviland, Virginia, review of *The Silent One, Horn Book,* June 1981, pp. 301-302.
Review of *The Silent One, Bulletin of the Center for Children's Books,* June 1981, p. 189.
Urquhart, Fred, review of *The Silent One, Times Educational Supplement,* August 20, 1982.

■ For More Information See

PERIODICALS

Best Sellers, August 15, 1967.
Kirkus Reviews, March 15, 1978, p. 321.
Library Journal, February 1, 1975, p. 310.
Magpies, March, 1996.
New York Times Book Review, December 24, 1972, p. 14.
Observer Review, October 22, 1967.

Publishers Weekly, January 20, 1975, p. 65; April 3, 1978, p. 69; September 30, 1996, p. 86.
Reading Time, May, 1996, p. 23.

* * *

CRAIG, A. A.
See ANDERSON, Poul (William)

* * *

CURRY, Jane L(ouise) 1932-

■ Personal

Born September 24, 1932, in East Liverpool, OH; daughter of William Jack, Jr. (a ceramic engineer) and Helen Margaret (a teacher; maiden name, Willis) Curry. *Education:* Attended Pennsylvania State University, 1950-51; Indiana State Teachers College (now Indiana University of Pennsylvania), B.S., 1954; attended University of California, Los Angeles, 1957-59; University of London, graduate study, 1961-62, 1965-66; Stanford University, M.A., 1962, Ph.D., 1969. *Hobbies and other interests:* Cooking, gardening, painting, travel, theater.

■ Addresses

Home—Los Angeles, CA. *Office*—c/o McElderry Books, Simon & Schuster Children's Publishing Division, 1230 Avenue of the Americas, New York, NY 10020.

JANE L. CURRY

■ Career

Writer and artist. Art teacher in Los Angeles, CA, city schools, 1955-59; Stanford University, Stanford, CA, teaching assistant, 1959-61 and 1964-65, acting instructor in English literature, 1967-68 and 1983-84, lecturer, 1987. *Exhibitions:* Paintings shown in London at group exhibitions, including Royal Society of British Artists, 1962. *Member:* International Arthurian Society, Authors Guild, Authors League of America, Southern California Council on Literature for Children and Young People.

■ Awards, Honors

Spring Children's Book Festival honor book designation, *Book World,* 1970, and Notable Book by a California Author Award, Southern California Council on Literature for Children and Young People, 1971, both for *The Daybreakers;* German translation of *Over the Sea's Edge* was named Book of the Month by Deutsche Akademie fuer Kinder und Jungendliteratur (Volkach), 1971; *New York Times* Outstanding Book of the Year citation, 1975, for *The Watchers;* Ohioana Book Award, Martha Kinney Cooper Ohioana Library Association, 1978, for *Poor Tom's Ghost,* and 1987, for *The Lotus Cup;* Edgar Allan Poe Award runner-up, Mystery Writers of America, 1978, for *Poor Tom's Ghost,* and 1979, for *The Bassumtyte Treasure;* award for Distinguished Contribution to the Field of Children's Literature, Southern California Council of Literature for Children and Young People, 1979, for body of work.

■ Writings

FOR CHILDREN

(Reteller) *Down from the Lonely Mountain: California Indian Tales,* illustrated by Enrico Arno, Harcourt, 1965, self-illustrated edition, Dobson, 1967.
The Sleepers, illustrated by Gareth Floyd, Harcourt, 1968.
Mindy's Mysterious Miniature, illustrated by Charles Robinson, Harcourt, 1970, published in England as *The Housenapper,* Longman, 1971.
The Ice Ghosts Mystery, Atheneum, 1972.
The Lost Farm, illustrated by Charles Robinson, Atheneum, 1974.
Parsley Sage, Rosemary, and Time, illustrated by Charles Robinson, Atheneum, 1975.
The Magical Cupboard, illustrated by Charles Robinson, Atheneum, 1976.
Poor Tom's Ghost, illustrated by Janet Archer, Atheneum, 1977.
The Bassumtyte Treasure, Atheneum, 1978.
Ghost Lane, Atheneum, 1979.
The Great Flood Mystery, Atheneum, 1985.
The Lotus Cup, Macmillan, 1986.
(Reteller) *Back in the Beforetime: Tales of the California Indians,* illustrated by James Watts, Macmillan, 1987.
Me, Myself, and I, Macmillan, 1987.
The Big Smith Snatch, Macmillan, 1989.

Little, Little Sister, illustrated by Erik Blegvad, Macmillan, 1989.
What the Dickens!, Macmillan, 1991.
The Christmas Knight, illustrated by DyAnne DiSalvo-Ryan, Macmillan, 1993.
The Great Smith House Hustle, Macmillan, 1993.
(Reteller) *Robin Hood and His Merry Men,* illustrated by John Lytle, Macmillan, 1994.
(Reteller) *Robin Hood in the Greenwood,* illustrated by Julie Downing, Macmillan, 1995.
Moon Window, Margaret K. McElderry, 1996.

"ABALOC" SERIES

Beneath the Hill, illustrated by Imero Gobbato, Harcourt, 1967.
The Change-Child, illustrated by Gareth Floyd, Harcourt, 1969.
The Daybreakers, illustrated by Charles Robinson, Harcourt, 1970.
Over the Sea's Edge, illustrated by Charles Robinson, Harcourt, 1971.
The Watchers, illustrated by Trina Schart Hyman, Atheneum, 1975.
The Birdstones, Atheneum, 1977.
The Wolves of Aam, Atheneum, 1981.
Shadow Dancers, Atheneum, 1983.

OTHER

Contributor to anthologies, including *King Arthur through the Ages,* Volume 2, edited by Valerie M. Lagorio and Mildred Leake Day, Garland Publishing, 1990, and *Sitting at the Feet of the Past,* edited by Gary B. Schmidt and Donald R. Hettinga, Greenwood Press, 1992. Also contributor of notes on Middle English poetry to journals. Book reviewer for *Times Educational Supplement* (London), 1969-70.

Curry's works are included in the Kerlan Collection at the University of Minnesota. Some of her works have been translated into German.

■ Sidelights

Since the 1960s Jane L. Curry has written some of the most acclaimed works of historical fantasy in children's literature. Many of her novels for upper elementary and middle school readers feature modern-day children who mysteriously become involved with people and places of the past. Her work also includes a number of retellings, from the legends of California Native Americans to the classic medieval stories of Robin Hood and King Arthur. "I am always aware of and fascinated by the power which past—even long-past—actions and choices have over the present," Curry admitted in an essay for the *Something about the Author Autobiography Series* (*SAAS*). In addition, the author revealed, "I am drawn again and again to the theme of a young person's search for a truer self, in which that search involves a fresh look not only at his or her past self, but the wider, deeper past of family and culture." Critics especially praise Curry for making history interesting and meaningful to children.

Growing up in the small industrial town of East Liverpool, Ohio, Curry always loved to read, "as many books as I could comfortably carry home from school and public libraries," she remarked. "I had no favorite kind of book—I simply went along the library shelves like a two-legged vacuum cleaner, sweeping up anything that had an interesting-sounding title." In the fifth grade, Curry came across a book that ultimately directed the course of her life—*The Enchanted Castle* by E. Nesbit. "Looking back, I cannot recall whether I read *The Enchanted Castle* in an hour or a day, for the experience was utterly unlike those I had with other books. It seems to me as if I must have not simply devoured, but inhaled it. I lived it. And when I finished, I dreamed it," she recalled in her autobiographical essay.

When her family moved to Johnstown, Pennsylvania, the following year, Curry was dismayed to find that her new school did not have a copy of the book in its library. The thrill of reading *The Enchanted Castle* gradually faded from her memory over the years until, while she was in England as a graduate student at the University of London, she happened to see the book on a shelf in a bookstore. "I stood rooted amidst the bustle of the world's largest bookshop, twenty-nine years old, my heart hammering, clutching to my chest a book I hadn't read since fifth grade. I felt a horrible inclination to burst into tears. I was amazed and amused at the depth of my delight, but that glimmer of detachment hadn't a chance against the vividness of childhood memory," Curry noted in *SAAS*. She reread the book and rediscovered the pleasure she had once taken in it; "a few months afterward I was to begin my own first book for children."

During this same stay in London, Curry had discovered the pleasure of storytelling. As a troop leader for the British equivalent of the Girl Scouts, Curry captivated her young audience by relating the legends of California Native American tribes. The girls' persistent requests for new stories led Curry to conduct extensive research on the subject. Her troop finally suggested that she collect the tales into a book, and *Down from the Lonely Mountain: California Indian Tales* was accepted for publication in 1965—much to Curry's astonishment. She had begun to translate her own passion for children's literature into a career as a writer.

Curry is perhaps best known for her "Abaloc" books, a series of eight related fantasy novels featuring a mythological world she invented by combining elements of Welsh mythology and American history. "A great part of the pleasure as I wrote was in planting a slip of the fairy tradition in an American landscape, where it had not in the past taken root," she commented in *SAAS*. In *Beneath the Hill,* the first book in the series, a group of young people spending the summer on a Pennsylvania farm find a mysterious people living under a mountain in caverns that date back to the Ice Age. As the children soon discover, the area was once part of a great mythical kingdom populated by fairies and other magical creatures. When strip-mining threatens the farm, the chil-

dren find that present-day events are intimately connected with ancient Abaloc. A reviewer for *Times Literary Supplement* called *Beneath the Hill* "a blissfully enjoyable book" that "carries the reader along in unquestioning suspension of disbelief."

Subsequent volumes in the series have similarly explored the relationship between past and present. In *The Daybreakers,* for instance, a multiracial group of friends in Apple Lock, West Virginia, led by black twins Callie and Harry, find a path to Abaloc through an underground chamber in an ancient mound and are caught up in a struggle against the inimical forces of Cibotlan. "The gift for fantasy and the superb craftsmanship that marked Jane Louise Curry's earlier books are richly manifest in this engrossing, intricately wrought story," Polly Goodwin asserted in *Children's Book World. The Watchers* similarly involves Ray—an outsider who comes to live in West Virginia with his late mother's relatives—with a threat from the past that is somehow tied to his extended family's history. *Junior Bookshelf* contributor J. Russell found the book so involving that "[I] rushed off to the library and ordered the author's other books, so constrained was I at having missed so outstanding a writer before." A visitor from ancient Abaloc appears in modern-day Apple Lock in *The Birdstones,* and six friends must help her escape her enemies and return to her own time. According to *Junior Bookshelf*'s Marcus Crouch, the book "confirms the impression that here is one of the most promising new voices from America. [Curry] blends the most convincing naturalistic presentation of modern society with the supernatural in masterly fashion."

Curry has also created several variations of the time-travel story outside of the Abaloc series. In *The Sleepers,* four children are among an archaeological party that discovers the cave where King Arthur slumbers, waiting for the time when Britain needs him again. An ancient prophecy and thirteen Treasures all come into play as the children try to save the king from his old nemesis, the evil enchantress Morgana. The result is "an exciting, varied, fast-moving fantasy with its heart in the right place," a *Times Literary Supplement* critic noted, which "shows some skill in the full use of a big bunch of characters, young and older, second-sighted and down-to earth, all delineated with zest and some conviction." *Poor Tom's Ghost* involves a haunted Elizabethan manor whose former occupant, a Shakespearean actor, comes to possess young Roger's father; Roger then must travel back to the 1600s to set things aright. Calling the novel "a *tour de force*," Patrick Verriour added in *The World of Children's Books* that "each tiny piece of this complex mosaic is exactly right.... *Poor Tom's Ghost* is a triumph for Jane Louise Curry." Another mystery with a hint of time fantasy is *The Bassumtyte Treasure,* in which ten-year-old Tommy returns to his family's ancestral home in England with an heirloom which could help him find a lost treasure. The book is a "adroitly conceived mystery," as Barbara Elleman stated in *Booklist,* which has "a strong, readable line, with time for the characters and a clever integration of historical incident."

More recently, Curry has produced two "oddball mysteries" featuring the five Smith children, *The Big Smith Snatch* (1989) and *The Great Smith House Hustle* (1993). She explained to *SATA* that the ideas for these books "came from that very ordinary source, the morning newspaper. I clip out any story with a promising quirk to it, and quirkiest of all were the accounts of a crooked couple who organized a pint-sized burglary ring." In *The Big Smith Snatch,* the children are separated from their parents when their father takes a job across the country and their mother is hospitalized just before they begin their move. A suspicious couple, J. D. and Peachie, immediately steps in to become their foster parents. At first the Smiths' new life is wonderful, as J. D. and Peachie pamper them and teach them exciting new games. Before long, however, the children find themselves "playing games" in other people's houses in the middle of the night as part of the couple's burglary operation. "Highly entertaining, this also carries an underlying message about how easy it is to become homeless," Denise Wilms observed in *Booklist.*

In the sequel, *The Great Smith House Hustle,* the Smith children go to Pennsylvania to live with their elderly grandmother. Granny Smith soon finds herself at the center of a mystery, as her house is sold without her knowledge and she is about to be evicted. After learning that the same thing has happened to several other elderly people in the neighborhood, the Smith children are able to expose the scam after some research in their local library. "Watch out," *School Library Journal* reviewer Susan Hepler proclaimed. "This book might jump-start some young historians and/or detectives." A writer for *Kirkus Reviews* added that "the zippy plot, general good humor, and nail-biting suspense make this a real page-turner."

"I enjoy the Smiths because, in the words of the old commercial, they 'take a licking and keep on ticking,'" Curry told *SATA.* "In the nineteenth century and in the early years of our own, family stories quite often involved families who had to struggle to 'make do,' but for a long while now, the fictional families have been predominantly middle-class, in more-or-less comfortable circumstances. I don't pretend to know why that shift in fashion has come about, but I do rather enjoy echoing the older tradition. The Smiths may return one day not too distant, but I do not yet know what disaster is to befall them or what mystery the children will have to unravel."

The Christmas Knight, published in 1993, was created out of Curry's love of "the Middle Ages and its romances and ballads," as she explained to *SATA.* "Years before I ever thought to make a picture-book story of it, I came upon a version of the old romance of *Sir Cleges* in a used-book shop in Brighton, on the south coast of England. Then, one day long afterward, when I was looking for a story that would make a lively picture book, I reached my hand up to one of my bookshelves, and that old volume almost jumped into it. Sir Cleges, that good-hearted, open-handed—and sharp-witted—Christmas hero, turns the tables on the king's greedy

servants and is rewarded by being ordered to do what he loves best: to feed and care for the homeless and hapless." Curry's retelling of the fifteenth-century tale describes how Sir Cleges gives an annual Christmas feast for the poor until he finally goes broke. Before long, however, God recognizes his goodness and sends him a gift of a branch from a cherry tree, laden with fruit in the middle of the winter. Cleges takes the branch to the king for Christmas, and the king shows his appreciation by naming Cleges the Christmas Knight. From then on, Cleges is in charge of taking care of the poor and the hungry on behalf of the king. Curry continued in this vein by publishing two retellings of the adventures of Robin Hood in 1994 and 1995. "I like to think that for young readers that concern for folk who need help might linger in the wake of adventure," she explained to *SATA.*

■ Works Cited

Review of *Beneath the Hill,* "Kingdoms of the Mind," *Times Literary Supplement,* October 3, 1968, p. 1113.

Crouch, Marcus, review of *The Birdstones, Junior Bookshelf,* February, 1979, p. 48.

Curry, Jane L., essay in *Something about the Author Autobiography Series,* Vol. 6, Gale, 1988, pp. 87-102.

Elleman, Barbara, review of *The Bassumtyte Treasure, Booklist,* April 15, 1978, p. 1347.

Goodwin, Polly, review of *The Daybreakers, Children's Book World,* May 17, 1970, p. 5.

Review of *The Great Smith House Hustle, Kirkus Reviews,* May 1, 1993, p. 595.

Hepler, Susan, review of *The Great Smith House Hustle, School Library Journal,* August, 1993, p. 163.

Russell, J., review of *The Watchers, Junior Bookshelf,* August, 1976, pp. 223-24.

Review of *The Sleepers,* "Crusaders, Monks, and Britons," *Times Literary Supplement,* April 3, 1969, p. 351.

Verriour, Patrick, review of *Poor Tom's Ghost, The World of Children's Books,* Volume 2, number 2, 1977, pp. 22-23.

Wilms, Denise, review of *The Big Smith Snatch, Booklist,* September 1, 1989, p. 68.

■ For More Information See

BOOKS

Cameron, Eleanor, *The Green and Burning Tree: On the Writing Enjoyment of Children's Books,* Atlantic/Little, Brown, 1969.

Children's Literature Review, Vol. 31, Gale, 1994.

Twentieth-Century Children's Writers, 4th edition, St. James Press, 1995.

PERIODICALS

Booklist, May 1, 1993, p. 1588; September 15, 1993, p. 153.

Bulletin of the Center for Children's Books, September, 1977, p. 12; May, 1987, p. 165.

Growing Point, May, 1979, p. 3516.

Horn Book, August, 1965, p. 390; August, 1967, p. 461;
    April, 1981, pp. 196-97; October, 1983, p. 580.
Kirkus Reviews, March 1, 1986, p. 390; September 15,
    1987, p. 1391; November 1, 1993, p. 1388.
Publishers Weekly, September 20, 1993, p. 40.
School Library Journal, May, 1986, pp. 100-101; Octo-
    ber, 1993, p. 42.
Times Literary Supplement, December 11, 1970, p.
    1449; July 15, 1977, p. 864.
The World of Children's Books, Volume 6, 1981, p. 53.

* * *

CURTISS, A(rlene) B. 1934-

■ Personal

Born March 29, 1934, in New York; married Raymond
G. Curtiss (a stockbroker), September 8, 1956; children:
Deane, Ford, Demming Forsythe, Sunday, Wolf. *Educa-
tion:* University of Maryland, B.A.; San Diego State
University, M.A. *Politics:* Conservative.

■ Addresses

Home—3415 Laredo Ln., Escondido, CA 92025.

■ Career

Author. Has worked as a psychotherapist, a hypnothera-
pist, and a family therapist.

■ Awards, Honors

Benjamin Franklin Award, 1995, for *In the Company of
Bears.*

■ Writings

In the Company of Bears (picture book), illustrated by
    Barbara Stone, Oldcastle, 1994.
Children of the Gods, Oldcastle, 1995.
Hallelujah, a Cat Comes Back, Oldcastle, 1995.

Curtiss has also published essays in several newspapers
and has had her poetic fiction quoted in greeting cards.

■ Sidelights

A. B. Curtiss told *SATA:* "By the time I was four I
wanted to write, though half my life was over before I
figured out what I was supposed to say. Then, with
incredible beginner's luck, the first essay I ever wrote,
about my son going off to college, was published on the
op-ed page of both the *New York Times* and the *Boston
Globe.*"

Curtiss began creating books in order to buy and
conserve wilderness land in Hidden Meadows, California, where she does much of her writing. Her first work,
the picture book *In the Company of Bears,* was a critical
and popular success, while her second book, *Children of
the Gods,* has achieved similar acclaim. This book takes

place in 1929 and is written as the journal of a man who
has a vision about the creation of Earth. In this vision,
he learns that the earth has been created as an experiment in altered consciousness by children of higher
beings who eventually forget their original awareness.
Curtiss told the *Golden Thread,* "I had in mind a new
translation of the *Tibetan Book of the Dead.* I had
become a hypnotist and I was dong some light trances,
just to limber up and let the juices flow.... And then
something quite different started to come along." Curtiss says that she wrote a lot of *Children of the Gods* "in
what some people might call a channeling.... This was
when I first started the work—this was about ten years
ago—but I don't do that anymore. I feel like in my work
I need to be aware. I concentrate full energy on trying to
understand where I am in the moment." Curtiss said
that *Children of the Gods* "is not a book for everybody.
In fact the work in there is really on a different level
than what most people are used to dealing with—at the
level of the awareness of these things rather than fixing
them, you take a more cosmic view of things. And that's
what this book is. It shows you and takes you a little bit
farther away so that you can have a less attached way of
looking at things.

"I work hard," the author added. "I'll do something
over thirty times to get it as close to true as I can. Still,
most of my life consists of doing things other than
writing. I raised five children, then went to graduate
school and became a psychotherapist. It was good for

A. B. CURTISS

me, I think, to become a writer second and many other things first so that I became a person who sometimes writes instead of a writer who is sometimes a person.

"There's something magical and exciting and special about writing. As writers, whatever we have done, or failed at, or thought about, or suffered, or missed, takes on new meaning as it enriches the personal mythology from which we create our stories. The bitter disappointments that can break your heart and have you wondering about the worth of your soul are the writer's best raw materials.

"And when something really works, when you get something just right, you walk a little freer and taller under the sky of your understanding. The scales fall from your eyes and you begin to love the wonderful oddments of your world. And when you share where you have been and what you have seen, you learn, with humility, that only at the exact moment when you can give something away do you finally possess it for the first time."

■ Works Cited

"A. B. Curtiss," *The Golden Thread,* mid-May to mid-June, 1995, p. 1.

D

DAWSON, Imogen (Zoe) 1948-

■ Personal

Born April 18, 1948, in England; children: two sons. *Education:* University of Sussex, B.A. *Hobbies and other interests:* Travel, reading and historical research, writing books, taking photographs, cooking and eating a wide variety of food, running.

■ Career

Author and publisher of children's information books.

■ Writings

(Compiler) *Chata, Choctaw Hymn Book: Uba Isht Taloa Holissa,* Holitopa, 1990.
Indian Food for the Body, Food for the Soul: Truly, a Book of Art, illustrated by Doug Maytubbie, Holitopa, 1992.
American Indian Food: Sixty-one Indian Recipes, Holitopa, 1993.
Food and Feasts in the Middle Ages, Silver Burdett, 1994.
Food and Feasts in Ancient Greece, Silver Burdett, 1995.
Food and Feasts with the Aztecs, Silver Burdett, 1995.

■ Sidelights

Imogen Dawson's "Food and Feasts" books describe the way food is used in various cultures, as well as the differences within those cultures. For example, she explains the sort of food one could expect farmers in the Middle Ages to consume and then the sort of food someone living in the city would favor. In the same manner she tells of the meals reserved for special occasions in rural and urban areas. Her books also include history about the culture, color photographs, and recipes. Deborah Stevenson wrote in *Bulletin of the Center for Children's Books* that this series offers "an appealing social history with a tasty theme."

■ Works Cited

Stevenson, Deborah, review of *Food and Feasts in the Middle Ages, Bulletin for the Center for Children's Books,* October, 1994, p. 41.

■ For More Information See

Horn Book, spring, 1995, p. 157.
School Library Journal, December, 1994, p. 120.*

* * *

de GROAT, Diane 1947-

■ Personal

Born May 24, 1947, in Newton, NJ; married Daniel Markham, 1975; children: Amanda Lee. *Education:* Attended Phoenix School of Design, New York, NY, 1964; Pratt Institute, B.F.A., 1969.

■ Addresses

Agent—Crown Publishers, One Park Ave., New York, NY 10016.

■ Career

Illustrator and author of books for children, 1971—. Holt, Rinehart & Winston (book publishers), Basic Reading Program, New York City, 1969-72, began as book designer, became art director. *Exhibitions:* Work has appeared in shows, including Society of Illustrators Annual National Exhibition, New York, NY, 1973, 1975; Art Directors Club, New York, 1974; and American Institute of Graphic Arts Annual Book Show, New York, 1978.

■ Writings

SELF-ILLUSTRATED

Alligator's Toothache, Crown, 1977.
Annie Pitts, Artichoke, Simon & Schuster, 1992.

Once again Annie Pitts has gotten herself in trouble at school, but this time her teacher decides to punish her in an unusual way—assigning her the role of the artichoke in the school play. (From *Annie Pitts, Artichoke*, written and illustrated by Diane de Groat.)

Annie Pitts, Swamp Monster, Simon & Schuster, 1993.
Roses Are Pink, Your Feet Really Stink, Morrow, 1995.

ILLUSTRATOR

Eleanor L. Clymer, *Luke Was There*, Holt, 1973.
Elinor Parker, *Four Seasons, Five Senses*, Scribner, 1974.
Marcia Newfield, *A Book for Jodan*, Atheneum, 1975.
Lucy Bate, *Little Rabbit's Loose Tooth*, Crown, 1975.
Mamie Hegwood, *My Friend Fish*, Holt, 1975.
Anne Snyder, *Nobody's Family*, Holt, 1975.
Miriam B. Young, *Truth and Consequences*, Four Winds Press, 1975.
Sylvia Sunderlin, *Antrim's Orange*, Scribner, 1976.
Maria Polushkin, *Bubba and Babba: Based on a Russian Folktale*, Crown, 1976.
Harriett M. Luger, *Chasing Trouble*, Viking, 1976.
Kathryn F. Ernst, *Mr. Tamarin's Trees*, Crown, 1976.
Eve Bunting, *One More Flight*, Warne, 1976.
K. F. Ernst, *Owl's New Cards*, Crown, 1977.
Ann Tompert, *Badger on His Own*, Crown, 1978.
Tobi Tobias, *How Your Mother and Father Met, and What Happened After*, McGraw, 1978.

Lois Lowry, *Anastasia Krupnik*, Houghton, 1979.
Seymour Simon, *Animal Fact/Animal Fable*, Crown, 1979.
Elizabeth T. Billington, *Part-Time Boy*, Warne, 1980.
Valerie Flournoy, *The Twins Strike Back*, Dial, 1980.
Lois Lowry, *Anastasia Again!*, Houghton, 1981.
Christine McDonnell, *Don't Be Mad, Ivy*, Dial, 1981.
Barbara Dillon, *Who Needs a Bear?*, Morrow, 1981.
Lynn Luderer, *The Toad Intruder*, Houghton, 1982.
Christine McDonnell, *Toad Food and Measle Soup*, Dial, 1982.
Johanna Hurwitz, *Tough Luck Karen*, Morrow, 1982.
Susan Shreve, *Bad Dreams of a Good Girl*, Knopf, 1982.
Lois Lowry, *Anastasia at Your Service*, Houghton, 1982.
Johanna Hurwitz, *DeDe Takes Charge!*, Morrow, 1984.
Susan Shreve, *The Flunking of Joshua T. Bates*, Knopf, 1984.
Bonnie Pryor, *Amanda and April*, Morrow, 1986.
Johanna Hurwitz, *Hurricane Elaine*, Morrow, 1986.
Niki Yektai, *Bears in Pairs*, Simon and Schuster, 1987.
Barbara Cohen, *The Christmas Revolution*, Lothrop, 1987.
Robin A. Thrush, *The Gray Whales Are Missing*, Harcourt, 1987.
Christine McDonnell, *Just for the Summer*, Viking, 1987.
Barbara Isenberg, *Albert the Running Bear Gets the Jitters*, Houghton, 1988.
Lois Lowry, *All about Sam*, Houghton, 1988.
Barbara Cohen, *The Orphan Game*, Lothrop, 1988.
Kate McMullan, *Great Advice from Lila Fenwick*, Puffin, 1989.
Johanna Hurwitz, *Aldo Peanut Butter*, Morrow, 1990.
Joanne Rocklin, *Jace the Ace*, Simon and Schuster, 1990.
Bonnie Pryor, *Merry Christmas, Amanda and April*, Morrow, 1990.
Barbara Cohen, *The Long Way Home*, Lothrop, 1990.
Kate McMullan, *The Great Eggspectations of Lila Fenwick*, Farrar, Straus, 1991.
Jamie Gilson, *Itchy Richard*, Houghton, 1991.
Eve Bunting, *A Turkey for Thanksgiving*, Houghton, 1991.
Lois Lowry, *Attaboy, Sam!*, Houghton, 1992.
Lisa G. Evans, *An Elephant Never Forgets Its Snorkel: How Animals Survive without Tools and Gadgets*, Crown, 1992.
Jean Van Leeuwen, *The Great Summer Camp Catastrophe*, Dial, 1992.
Kevin Roth, *Lullabies for Little Dreamers*, Random House, 1992.
Carol P. Saul, *Peter's Song*, Simon & Schuster, 1992.
Eve Bunting, *Our Teacher's Having a Baby*, Clarion, 1992.
Susan Shreve, *Wait for Me*, Morrow, 1992.
Eve Merriam, *Where Is Everybody?: An Animal Alphabet*, Simon & Schuster, 1992.
Susan Shreve, *Amy Dunn Quits School*, Morrow, 1993.
Ruth Westheimer, *Dr. Ruth Talks to Kids: Where You Came From, How Your Body Changes, and What Sex Is All About*, Simon & Schuster, 1993.
Teddy Slater, *The Wrong-Way Rabbit*, Scholastic, 1993.

A. C. LeMieux, *Fruit Flies, Fish, and Fortune Cookies,* Morrow, 1994.

Jamie Gilson, *It Goes Eeeeeeeeeee,* Houghton, 1994.

Stephanie Calmenson, *Kinderkittens: Show and Tell,* Scholastic, 1994.

P. J. Petersen, *Some Days, Other Days,* Scribner, 1994.

Eve Bunting, *Sunshine Home,* Houghton, 1994.

Jamie Gilson, *You Don't Know Beans about Bats,* Houghton, 1994.

John Dennis Fitzgerald, *The Great Brain Is Back,* Dial, 1995.

■ Sidelights

Besides writing four picture books of her own, Diane de Groat has illustrated over sixty books by some of the most prominent authors in children's literature. De Groat's interest in art began during her childhood, growing up in the small town of Newton, New Jersey. She took her first painting lessons at the age of seven, and by the time she reached her junior year of high school she had won a scholarship to study at the Phoenix School of Design in New York City for a summer. She attended college at the highly regarded Pratt Institute, which "opened new doors and cast a new perspective on the dimensions of the field" of art, as de Groat explained in *Illustrators of Children's Books, 1967-76.*

Immediately following her graduation, however, de Groat had trouble finding work as an artist. "I was broke and staying with friends in a one-room apartment while trying to peddle my talent," she recalled in *Illustrators of Children's Books.* "This included selling all the drawings I had done in school for one dollar each." One of her paintings ended up hanging on a friend's wall, where it was spotted by a man who happened to be the head of a children's reading program at the publishing company Holt, Rinehart & Winston. On the strength of her portfolio, de Groat ended up getting a job as a book designer at the company and also did some illustrations for the reading program. Within two years, she was successful enough to be able to make a living as a freelance children's book illustrator.

De Groat was inspired to write her first book, *Alligator's Toothache,* by a dream she had about her editor, who was then undergoing extensive dental work. In this wordless story, Alligator gets a terrible toothache after eating too much cake at his birthday party. He tries to ease the pain by tying a giant bandage around his snout, but it does not work. His friends decide to call the dentist, Dr. Possum, but Alligator is afraid of him and hides when he arrives at the house. Finally, Alligator's friends trick him into getting his tooth pulled, and then he feels better and they go on with the party. A contributor in *Kirkus Reviews* remarked that "the animals' clearly communicative expressions and gestures tell the story without words," while a reviewer in *Publishers Weekly* called the book "an uncommon treat for older children as well as for beginners."

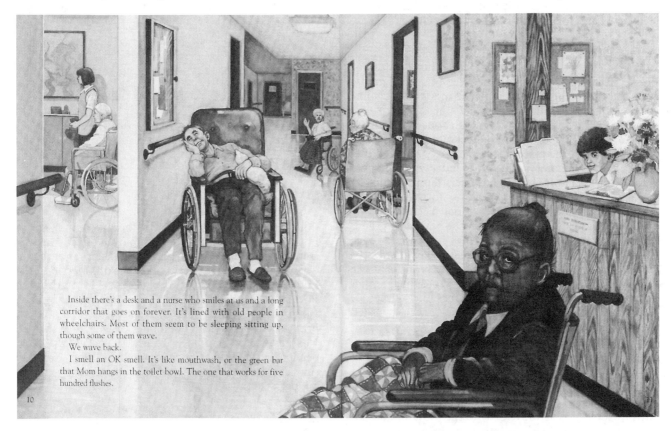

Inside there's a desk and a nurse who smiles at us and a long corridor that goes on forever. It's lined with old people in wheelchairs. Most of them seem to be sleeping sitting up, though some of them wave.

We wave back.

I smell an OK smell. It's like mouthwash, or the green bar that Mom hangs in the toilet bowl. The one that works for five hundred flushes.

10

In *Sunshine Home,* Young Timmie sees through his parents false cheerfulness and helps his grandmother express her true feelings about life in a nursing home. (Written by Eve Bunting and illustrated by Diane de Groat.)

In 1992, de Groat published the first of her amusing stories about third-grader Annie Pitts, who wants nothing in the world more than to be a famous actress. She thinks that her big break to stardom is waiting around every corner, which leads her into many funny situations. In *Annie Pitts, Artichoke,* Annie accompanies her class on a field trip to the supermarket. While there, she hopes that the store manager will notice her and ask her to appear in his next commercial. When Annie winds up hitting her classmate Matthew in the head with a dead fish, however, the class is asked to leave the store. As punishment, the teacher makes Annie play the undesirable role of an artichoke in the school play. In a *Booklist* review, Ellen Mandel called *Annie Pitts, Artichoke* "amusing and highly palatable reading fare, with sprightly, realistically drawn illustrations that enhance the book's energy and fun."

In 1993's *Annie Pitts, Swamp Monster,* Annie jumps at the chance to star in a low-budget horror movie being produced by a high-school student as a class project. She takes her role as the swamp monster very seriously, hoping it could be the opportunity she has been waiting for to get into show business. The filming turns into one hilarious disaster after another, however, and Annie is embarrassed when the video is shown to her grade-school class. Lucinda Snyder Whitehurst, writing in *School Library Journal,* called the book "breezy and lighthearted" and noted that "the slapstick humor will have young readers giggling." *Booklist* reviewer Chris Sherman added that "the black-and-white illustrations are delightful" and claimed that the book was "sure to win new fans for author-illustrator de Groat."

Among the many books that de Groat has illustrated for other authors is Eve Bunting's 1994 book *Sunshine Home.* The story centers around seven-year-old Timmy, whose grandmother has been placed in a nursing home after injuring herself in a fall. On his first visit to Sunshine Home, Timmy is nervous about what he will find there. Although he does not like the "barf green" walls or the way the place smells, Timmy is relieved that his grandmother seems the same and their visit goes well. After his family leaves, however, Timmy's mother begins to cry. Discovering that he has forgotten to give his grandmother a copy of his school picture, Timmy runs back into the nursing home and finds his grandmother crying too. When he brings his parents back inside to talk to his grandmother again, everyone in the family is able to confront their true feelings about the situation. In *Booklist,* Ellen Mandel wrote that "in her realistic watercolors, de Groat defines the images of Bunting's tender, true-to-life story." Jody McCoy added in *School Library Journal* that de Groat's illustrations "are appropriately heavy on institutional green and poignantly support the text."

De Groat has enjoyed the varied demands of her multifaceted career as an illustrator, author, and artist. "My picture books enable me to explore the world of fantasy, while the novels I've illustrated are very realistic in style," she explained in *Illustrators of Children's Books.* "My work in fine art is an infusion of these two styles."

■ Works Cited

Review of *Alligator's Toothache, Kirkus Reviews,* January 1, 1977, p. 1.
Review of *Alligator's Toothache, Publishers Weekly,* January 24, 1977, p. 333.
De Groat, Diane, comments in *Illustrators of Children's Books, 1967-1976,* Compiled by Lee Kingman and others, Horn Book, 1978.
Mandel, Ellen, review of *Annie Pitts, Artichoke, Booklist,* October 15, 1992, p. 428.
Mandel, Ellen, review of *Sunshine Home, Booklist,* March 15, 1994, p. 1371.
McCoy, Jody, review of *Sunshine Home, School Library Journal,* April, 1994, p. 100.
Sherman, Chris, review of *Annie Pitts, Swamp Monster, Booklist,* June 1, 1994, p. 1815.
Whitehurst, Lucinda Snyder, review of *Annie Pitts, Swamp Monster, School Library Journal,* July, 1994, p. 102.

■ For More Information See

PERIODICALS

Bulletin of the Center for Children's Books, May, 1977, p. 140.
Horn Book, July/August, 1989, p. 476.
Kirkus Reviews, September 15, 1992, p. 1185; June 15, 1994, p. 843.
Publishers Weekly, May 19, 1989, p. 81; February 5, 1996, p. 89.
School Library Journal, July, 1989, p. 73; September, 1992, p. 202.*

*   *   *

DEXTER, John
See BRADLEY, Marion Zimmer

*   *   *

DRISKILL, J. Lawrence 1920-

■ Personal

Born August 18, 1920, near Rustburg, Virginia; son of Elijah Hudson (a farmer and employee of the Highway Department) and Annie (a homemaker and factory worker; maiden name, Carwile) Driskill; married Ethel Lillian Cassel (a missionary), May 28, 1949; children: Edward L., Mary Driskill McCurry. *Education:* Pennsylvania State College (now University), B.A., 1946; San Francisco Theological Seminary, B.D., 1949, S.T.D., 1969; Princeton Seminary, Th.M., 1957. *Politics:* "Independent, usually vote Democratic." *Religion:* Presbyterian. *Hobbies and other interests:* Photography, tennis, hiking, swimming.

■ Addresses

Home and office—1420 Santo Domingo Avenue, Duarte, CA 91010.

J. Lawrence Driskill with his wife, Lillian.

■ Career

Presbyterian minister and author. Missionary to Japan
(Osaka area), 1949-72; Highland Presbyterian Church,
Maryville, TN, pastor, 1973-82; interim pastor at Madison Square Presbyterian Church, San Antonio, TX,
1973, Grace Presbyterian Church, Long Beach, CA,
1984-85, and Christ Presbyterian Church, Los Angeles,
CA, 1987-89; Nichigo (Japanese-speaking) pastor at
First Presbyterian Church, Altadena, CA, 1990—. Visiting professor, University of Dubuque seminary, 1961-
62, and Trinity University, San Antonio, TX, 1972-73;
part-time professor, Maryville College, 1974-75. Member of board of directors of Osaka Jo Gakuin and Seikyo
Gakuen Christian High School, Japan, and of the Synod
of Texas, UPC staff. Volunteer with Asian American
churches in the Los Angeles area and mission advocate
for the San Gabriel Presbytery. *Military service:* U.S.
Navy, 1942-45, aviation radio and V-12 officer training.
Member: American Academy of Religion, American
Association of Retired Persons, Bread for the World,
Common Cause, Sierra Club.

■ Writings

Mission Adventures in Many Lands, illustrated by Russ
Jackson, Hope, 1992.

(With Lillian Cassel Driskill) *Japan Diary of Cross-
Cultural Mission,* Hope, 1993.
Mission Stories from Around the World, illustrated by
Betty Harter, Hope, 1994.
*Cross-Cultural Marriages and the Church: Living the
Global Neighborhood,* Hope, 1995.
Worldwide Mission Stories for Young People, illustrated
by Betty Harter, Hope, 1996.
(Editor and contributor) *Christmas Stories from Around
the World,* Hope, 1996.

■ Sidelights

Appointed to the former Board of Foreign Missions of
the Presbyterian Church, U.S.A., and assigned to Japan
in 1949, the Reverend J. Lawrence Driskill has helped
to establish Christian groups and schools throughout the
Osaka area; he has also been a pastor to several Asian
American churches in the United States. He published
his first book, *Mission Adventures in Many Lands,* after
his retirement. Driskill told *SATA:* "Looking around at
my fellow retirees, I discovered that together we had
served in about thirty countries around the world. Some
served as teachers, some as doctors or nurses, and some
as new church developers. Then I heard that churches
were looking for good mission stories to use with their
members, especially young people. Realizing I was

sitting on top of a 'gold mine,' I decided to start digging. The result has been three mission story books with a total of about 140 mission stories. About 800 of these books were sold in Japan.

"My first fifty-three mission stories were published as 'take home stories' for young people in Presbyterian and Baptist churches across the U.S.A. In 1992 I brought them together in my first mission story book. Two others followed.

"Also, with my wife's assistance, I wrote a book, *Japan Diary.* It records our struggle to work effectively in Japan, meeting opportunities, accepting challenges, and overcoming problems serving in a different culture and using the Japanese language. It deals with the critical early years in Japan.

"As part of my retirement ministry I served interim pastorates in two Japanese American churches in the Los Angeles area and am now part-time pastor in a Japanese American church in Altadena, CA (First Presbyterian). In these churches I met many cross-cultural marriage couples. Knowing I had written other books, the drummer for the famous black singer Lou Rawls requested that I write a book about cross-cultural marriages. He said he needed help in meeting the challenges and overcoming the problems in his marriage to a Japanese music major. The resulting book, *Cross-Cultural Marriages and the Church,* is selling well, as are my other books. My goal in writing books is to try to help people, and I am grateful to hear many people say they have been helped by my books. I do not profit financially from most of them.

"I had always wanted to write books while working full time in Japan and the U.S.A. but could manage to write only a few magazine articles before retirement. My first book, *Mission Adventures in Many Lands,* was published in 1992 when I was age seventy-one. My suggestion to new writers is to look around you for promising topics to write about. Surprising opportunities may exist nearby. It is always best to write about topics or people that you know well. My favorites are stories about real people, many of whom can be helpful role models for us. If possible, join a writer's group where you can support each other, evaluate each other's writings, and profit from suggestions by others."

*   *   *

DUKE, Kate 1956-

■ Personal

Born August 1, 1956, in New York City; daughter of Robert (a lawyer) and Jeannette Duke; married Sidney Harris (a cartoonist), 1985. *Education:* Attended Duke University, 1975-76. *Hobbies and other interests:* Gardening, reading, cooking, visiting museums, mural-painting.

■ Addresses

Office—c/o Lisa Sandik, Dutton Children's Books, 375 Hudson St., New York, NY 10014.

■ Career

Children's book writer and illustrator, 1983—. Also lectures at schools and other educational institutions. *Member:* Society of Children's Book Writers and Illustrators, Writers Union, PEN, Authors Guild, Authors League of America.

■ Awards, Honors

Library of Congress Book of the Year, Parents Choice Award, Remarkable Books for Literature, IRA-CBC Children's Choice Award, International Reading Association/Children's Book Council, *Boston Globe-Horn Book* Illustration Honor Book, *Booklist* Children's Editors' Choice, *Horn Book* Honor List, Junior Library Guild Selection, all 1983, and Children's Picture Book of the Year award, *Redbook,* 1986, all for *The Guinea Pig ABC;* Junior Library Guild Selection, 1984, for *Guinea Pigs Far and Near;* IRA-CBC Children's Choice Award and Junior Library Guild Selection, both 1985, both for *Seven Froggies Went to School;* Year's Top Prizes Selection, *Publishers Weekly,* 1986, for *Bedtime; Clean-up Day; The Playground; What Bounces* (board books); ABA Pick of the Lists, American Booksellers Association, 1988, for *What Would a Guinea Pig Do?;* IRA-CBC Children's Choice Award, 1989, for *It's Too Noisy!;* IRA-CBC Children's Choice Award, Children's Book of the Year, Bank Street Child Study Children's Book Committee, and featured book on PBS television series "Storytime" and ABC radio series "Mrs. Bush's Story Hour," all 1992, all for *Aunt Isabel Tells a Good One;* Best Books, *School Library Journal,* Parents Choice Award, and Junior Library Guild Selection, all 1995, all for *One Saturday Morning.*

■ Writings

SELF-ILLUSTRATED

The Guinea Pig ABC, Dutton, 1983.
Guinea Pigs Far and Near, Dutton, 1984.
Seven Froggies Went to School, Dutton, 1985.
Guinea Pig Board Books (Bedtime, What Bounces?, The Playground, Clean-up Day,), Dutton, 1986.
What Would a Guinea Pig Do?, Dutton, 1988.
Roseberry's Great Escape, Dutton, 1990.
Aunt Isabel Tells a Good One, Dutton, 1992.
If You Walk Down This Road, Dutton, 1993.
Aunt Isabel Makes Trouble, Dutton, 1996.
Archaeologists Dig For Clues, HarperCollins, 1996.

ILLUSTRATOR

Raffi, *Tingalayo,* Crown, 1989.
Joanna Cole, *It's Too Noisy!,* HarperCollins, 1989.
Joanna Cole, *Don't Tell the Whole World!,* HarperCollins, 1990.
Barbara Brenner, *Good News!,* Bantam/Bank Street, 1991.

KATE DUKE

Miriam Schlein, *Let's Go Dinosaur Tracking!,* Harper-
Collins, 1991.
Joann Oppenheim, *Show-and-Tell Frog,* Bantam/Bank
Street, 1993.
Barbara Baker, *One Saturday Morning,* Dutton, 1995.
William Hooks, *Mr. Garbage,* Bantam/Bank Street,
1996.

■ Work in Progress

Soup of the Day at the Rundown Cafe, "starring a rude,
mean rabbit"; *Petunia Paints,* "starring an artistic
wallaby"; *Melrose & Elizabeth and the Bundle of Joy,*
"about two storks in the baby-delivery business."

■ Sidelights

Kate Duke is the award-winning author and illustrator
of picture books for children which introduce concepts
ranging from the alphabet to spatial relationships to the
how-to's of creative writing. The characters in Duke's
books are humorous and endearing animals of all sorts:
pigs, mice, squirrels, a mole or two, and her trademark
guinea pigs. "The heroes of Ms. Duke's stories are no
ordinary guinea pigs," Rebecca Lazear Okrent noted in
the *New York Times Book Review.* "They are whimsical
creatures with serious ideas who always seem to be

suppressing a giggle, especially in the face of disaster."
Duke has used her bemused and amusing guinea pigs in
four picture books that have garnered much critical
praise and have drawn many fans at reading hour. Her
audience includes both children and adults: "As in the
best toddler books ... there is humor here for both
child and parent," Linda Wicher pointed out in a *School
Library Journal* review of Duke's *Guinea Pig Board
Books,* and the same can be said for all of Duke's books
with their vibrant and action-packed illustrations and
frequently droll humor.

An early love of books spurred Duke's ambition to
become a writer. "I was born in New York City and
grew up there, the oldest of four children," Duke told
SATA. "Both my parents were and are great readers, and
we children were always amply supplied with books. My
experience of the world of literature was satisfying from
the start, for my parents seemed to enjoy reading to me
as much as I enjoyed being read to." An active child—
often roller skating and riding bikes in the park across
the street from her apartment building or in the country
where she spent summers with her grandmother—
Duke's favorite activity was reading. "I read in the
summer and in the winter, in the city and in the country,
in school and on vacation. I liked books that had

adventures in them, and books with talking animals, and books that made me laugh. I still do!"

One of her favorite fictional characters was Doctor Doolittle: "I yearned passionately to be able to talk to animals as he did," Duke told *SATA*. Another was Nancy Drew, and a third and most influential was Harriet the Spy, "whose exploits prompted me at age eleven to start following pedestrians around my neighborhood, taking notes on their every 'suspicious' move. I think I owe Harriet my first conscious awareness of the act of writing as important and meaningful work." Accompanying this realization about words was another, equally important discovery. "At about that same time ... sixth grade ... I also discovered that I could draw," Duke recalled for *SATA*. "In art class one day, the picture of a dog that I was copying from a how-to-draw book came out looking pretty much like a dog. Since my artistic abilities had not previously been particularly notable, I remember being quite surprised by this new development. Pleased, of course, but definitely surprised."

After finishing high school, Duke attended college for a couple of years; then she left school and "floundered around for a long while," as Duke described it, trying to figure out what she really wanted to do. Art classes in New York reminded her of how much she had enjoyed picture books as a child. "I got the idea that I could write stories to go with my pictures, and turn them into books for children. I hoped that the children who read

Duke's popular and highly regarded *Guinea Pig ABC* features colorfully drawn guinea pigs humorously acting out the meaning of adjectives chosen to represent each letter of the alphabet. (Illustration by Kate Duke.)

them would love them as much as I loved the books I had read as a child." Such aspirations eventually led to her first picture book, *The Guinea Pig ABC*. Different from other alphabet books, Duke's work is based on adjectives rather than nouns, and carefully places the animal character within the shape of each letter so as to focus the eye of the child on it. For example, with the letter "K" for "kind," a solicitous guinea pig is leaning against the downward sloping extension of the letter, while an obviously sick guinea pig lies in bed, propped for support against the perpendicular spine of the letter. A contributor in *Kirkus Reviews* felt that the book was "wholly pleasing—a homespun, direct alternative to lots of artifice," and Selma G. Lanes, writing in the *New York Times Book Review*, called Duke's first book a "refreshingly different alphabet with heady possibilities." Ann A. Flowers, in *Horn Book*, noted that Duke's idea was "cleverly carried out" with "bright-colored illustrations," and that the "overall feeling is one of gaiety and happiness.... Destined perhaps to become a classic." Margery Fisher in *Growing Point* commended Duke for "opening up an unusual aspect of vocabulary for young children," adding that "this alphabet from America is comic and interesting, not only for the choice of words but also for the light-hearted but still sufficiently natural view of bustling guinea pigs...." *The Guinea Pig ABC* won the *Boston Globe-Horn Book* Illustration Honor among many others awards, making it an auspicious debut for Duke.

Duke stuck with her guinea pigs, or "sprightly company of entertainers," as a *Publishers Weekly* reviewer described them, for her next picture book. *Guinea Pigs Far and Near* illustrates words of both physical and personal relationship, such as "apart," "far," "near," "beside," and "between." Each picture is a complete story that involves adventure, suspense, and humor. In the initial illustration, a female guinea pig gets on a railroad car with her brother in the car behind her. The two are separated when the coupling breaks, and their ensuing chase illustrates spatial relationships of far and near. Diane S. Rogoff, writing in *School Library Journal*, described *Guinea Pigs Far and Near* as "charming, entertaining and full of fun," but added that it could also be "very confusing to young people." Rogoff faulted the lack of a central character in the book, contending that children would have difficulty determining which character the featured word describes. Other commentators focused on Duke's humor and the quality of her illustrations; a critic in *Kirkus Reviews* called the book "sunny and good-humored, and quirky," while a reviewer in *Publishers Weekly* lauded Duke's "brightly colored, action-packed pictures."

Duke's third picture book took frogs as an inspiration, telling the rhyming story of school-bound amphibians in *Seven Froggies Went to School*. Duke adapted an old poem for her text, sending her frogs to a rush-filled pond where "Master Bullfrog, grave and stern / called the classes in their turn. / From his seat upon a log, / he taught the wisdom of the bog." Duke employed shades of green in her illustrations, and "zippy little amphibians in waistcoated dress," according to Denise M. Wilms in *Booklist*. "The sense of fun is strong," Wilms

Aunt Isabel and her niece develop a charming story by combining a heroine, plenty of action, and a touch of romance in this delicately illustrated picture book. (From *Aunt Isabel Tells a Good One*, written and illustrated by Kate Duke.)

concluded. A contributor in *Childhood Education* commented that "action abounds" in this text relating the "amusing antics" of the seven frogs who are learning about survival from Master Bullfrog. A critic in *Kirkus Reviews* found the illustrations "entertaining," but maintained that *Seven Froggies Went to School* "hasn't the conceptual eclat, or the masterly characterization, of [Duke's] previous entries."

Duke returned to her frisky and endearing guinea pigs with a set of four story board books, *Bedtime, Clean-up Day, The Playground,* and *What Bounces?* "The irrepressible family of guinea pigs ... star in the sunniest board books of the season," asserted a *Publishers Weekly* reviewer, who added: "This is the series for which Duke's pigs were born." The characters here represent a patient mother or a very active child with very simple, caption-like text. Daily activities are dealt with—cleaning up, going to bed, playing—as well as concepts, as in *What Bounces?* Here the young guinea pig climbs on a stool to explore the insides of the refrigerator, soon discovering that while balls bounce, eggs, milk, and butter most decidedly do not. They break, splash, and squish. A *Bulletin of the Center for Children's Books* contributor called the four-book set "funny" and "clever," and Ellen Mandel in *Booklist*

noted that the instructive nature of the books was "embellished by [Duke's] critters' perky personalities and by her own sense of humor," adding: "These four titles are especially engaging." Linda Wicher, in a *School Library Journal* review, concluded that the books were "very nicely done," while in *Publishers Weekly* Diane Roback picked Duke's board book set for the magazine's 1986 Top Prizes list, noting that "this sunny, delightfully childlike set ... stands out in a crowded field."

Duke stayed with her anthropomorphic rodents in *What Would a Guinea Pig Do?*, providing further adventures in domesticity. "What if a guinea pig wanted to clean up his house? ... What if some guinea pigs wanted to bake a cake? ... What if a guinea pig wanted to be like somebody else?" These three questions spawn interesting and often humorous results. "The irrepressible cast romps through each situation in merry mayhem," commented Starr LaTronica in a *School Library Journal* review of the book. "A delightful addition to the series," LaTronica concluded. "Duke's pigs make disasters look like terrific fun," noted a critic in *Publishers Weekly*. "The entire book is a joyful offering." And Rebecca Lazear Okrent, in the *New York Times Book Review*, pointed out the subtle lessons to be learned in each of the situations: Once the guinea pigs clean their house, for instance, they have a party and start all over again, a lesson in celebrating success. Okrent concluded: "The text is minimal and easy to read. The brightly colored illustrations ... are cheerful and captivating. As in all the best books, the rules for living are discreet. You have to be looking for them."

More recent books by Duke feature different animals: mice in *Aunt Isabel Tells a Good One,* an adventurous pig in *Roseberry's Great Escape,* and a menagerie of rabbits, lizards, mice, squirrels, and owls in *If You Walk Down This Road.* In the first title, a mouse child, Penelope, is staying overnight with her slightly bohemian Aunt Isabel. Duke's storytelling talents come to the fore in a story-within-a-story format in this work, in which the reader experiences not only the relationship between aunt and niece, but also the adventures of the tale Aunt Isabel creates with the child's assistance. Isabel's story involves a romance between Lady Penelope and Prince Augustus that is broken up by the mouse

king and queen, who believe the girl is too common for their royal son. However, Lady Penelope, in this interior tale, proves herself when she rescues Augustus from kidnappers, and a further feminist note is struck when any possible marriage is postponed until after careers are established. "The framing story has an appealing warmth and is deftly interwoven with Aunt Isabel's tale so that both narratives move briskly," noted a *Kirkus Reviews* contributor, who added that the book "should be invaluable to creative-writing programs for young children." Sheilamae O'Hara in *Booklist* concurred, noting that *Aunt Isabel Tells a Good One* is "a fine book to enjoy on its own merits, but it will also be useful for teachers instructing primary students in the elements of creative writing." O'Hara also commented on Duke's "droll, neatly executed water color illustrations," describing them as "an integral part of the story." A reviewer in *Publishers Weekly* called Duke a "gifted artist," and noted the "winsome borders, adorned with tiny, appropriate decorative touches" in the illustrations. Of this work, Duke told *SATA:* "I've been

The whole Bear family spends a busy day-off together eating breakfast, walking in the park, and reading books in Barbara Baker's *One Saturday Morning*, illustrated by Kate Duke.

The whole Lizard family lives in the log.

All of the animals in Shady Green love to have visitors and warmly welcome two travelers into their homes. (From *If You Walk Down This Road,* written and illustrated by Kate Duke.)

enormously pleased to find that teachers like to use *Aunt Isabel Tells a Good One* to help their students learn about writing. One reason the book works well in the classroom must be because the way Aunt Isabel and her niece make up the story is honestly the way *I* made up the story: by asking questions. I wrote the first draft of *Aunt Isabel* as if I were talking to another person. This other person kept asking (or sometimes telling) me what we should put in the story next, and I wrote down both the questions and the answers. Later I imagined the two 'voices' as mice, and named them Aunt Isabel and Penelope."

With *If You Walk Down This Road*, Duke created a picture book of the anthropomorphic forest folk in Shady Green who are curious about and welcome some newcomers. "Soft watercolor illustrations burst with humorous detail and activity totally appropriate to the homes and residents" of each creature featured, notes Virginia Opocensky in *School Library Journal*. Opocensky adds that Duke's illustrations will "demand multiple readings."

Duke has also illustrated several books by other authors, and her work on these has won praise similar to that for her own picture books. In *Booklist*, Denia Hester, reviewing *Let's Go Dinosaur Tracking!* by Miriam Schlein, concluded that "Duke's bright, playful pen-and-watercolor illustrations are perfect for this not-so-serious science book." *One Saturday Morning*, Barbara Baker's popular story of the busy Saturday activities of the Bear family, has also been illustrated by Duke. Chris Sherman, reviewing the work in *Booklist*, asserted that "Duke's bright colors, which grace every page, enhance the warmth and bustle of the story." Gale W. Sherman, writing in *School Library Journal*, described *One Saturday Morning* as "a winner," noting that "Duke's watercolor-and-pen illustrations are filled with humor and will delight children."

Duke, who lives in Connecticut, maintains a busy schedule to allow her to manage so many projects. "I work every day, from early morning to early afternoon," Duke told *SATA*. "My studio is in the upstairs of my house, and it's there that I spend most of my time. My typewriter is there, and all my paints and paper, and a comfortable chair for me to sit in while I try to think of new ideas for books." But when time permits, Duke is out in her garden or off lecturing at schools. "Since writing and drawing are both solitary pursuits, I try to make a point of getting out into the real world. A little human contact is important to keeping one's equilibrium. Indeed, one of the great pleasures I have these days is in going out to visit schools and talk to children about what I do. These occasions are a chance to get in touch with my books' intended audience and to recharge my memories of what it was like to be a child. I don't have children of my own, so it's a real treat to be able to interact with them once in a while. I'm always cheered and inspired by their energy and imagination. Plus, they laugh at my jokes!"

■ Works Cited

Review of *Aunt Isabel Tells a Good One*, *Kirkus Reviews*, December 15, 1991, p. 1589.

Review of *Aunt Isabel Tells a Good One*, *Publishers Weekly*, November 29, 1991, p. 591.

Duke, Kate, *Seven Froggies Went to School*, Dutton, 1985.

Duke, Kate, *What Would a Guinea Pig Do?*, Dutton, 1988.

Fisher, Margery, review of *The Guinea Pig ABC*, *Growing Point*, July, 1987, p. 4838.

Flowers, Ann A., review of *The Guinea Pig ABC*, *Horn Book*, February, 1984, pp. 42-3.

Review of *The Guinea Pig ABC*, *Kirkus Reviews*, November 1, 1983, p. 369.

Review of *Guinea Pigs Far and Near*, *Kirkus Reviews*, November 1, 1984, p. 88.

Review of *Guinea Pigs Far and Near*, *Publishers Weekly*, August 24, 1984, p. 80.

Review of *Guinea Pig Board Books*, *Publishers Weekly*, May 30, 1986, p. 60.

Review of *Guinea Pig Board Books*, *Bulletin of the Center for Children's Books*, July-August, 1986, p. 206.

Hester, Denia, review of *Let's Go Dinosaur Tracking!*, *Booklist*, January 1, 1992, p. 832.

Lanes, Selma G., review of *The Guinea Pig ABC*, *New York Times Book Review*, October 9, 1983, p. 38.

LaTronica, Starr, review of *What Would a Guinea Pig Do?*, *School Library Journal*, June-July, 1988, p. 90.

Mandel, Ellen, review of *Guinea Pig Board Books*, *Booklist*, June 1, 1986, p. 1459.

O'Hara, Sheilamae, review of *Aunt Isabel Tells a Good One*, *Booklist*, January 15, 1992, p. 950.

Okrent, Rebecca Lazear, review of *What Would a Guinea Pig Do?*, *New York Times Book Review*, June 5, 1988, p. 50.

Opocensky, Virginia, review of *If You Walk Down This Road*, *School Library Journal*, June, 1993, p. 72.

Roback, Diane, "The Year's Top Prizes—Children's Books," *Publishers Weekly*, January 9, 1987, p. 52.

Rogoff, Diane S., review of *Guinea Pigs Far and Near*, *School Library Journal*, December, 1984, pp. 69-70.

Review of *Seven Froggies Went to School*, *Childhood Education*, January-February, 1986, p. 216.

Review of *Seven Froggies Went to School*, *Kirkus Reviews*, March 1, 1985, p. J-4.

Sherman, Chris, review of *One Saturday Morning*, *Booklist*, January 1, 1995. p. 827.

Sherman, Gale W., review of *One Saturday Morning*, *School Library Journal*, November, 1994, p. 72.

Review of *What Would a Guinea Pig Do?*, *Publishers Weekly*, January 29, 1988, p. 429.

Wicher, Linda, review of *Guinea Pig Board Books*, *School Library Journal*, October, 1986, p. 159.

Wilms, Denise M., review of *Seven Froggies Went to School*, *Booklist*, March 15, 1985, p. 1058.

■ For More Information See

PERIODICALS

Childhood Education, May, 1984, p. 361; fall, 1992, p. 45.

Horn Book, September, 1986, p. 577; May, 1990, p. 322.
Los Angeles Times Book Review, October 30, 1983, p. 9.
Times Educational Supplement, August 8, 1986, p. 20.

—Sketch by J. Sydney Jones

*   *   *

DuQUETTE, Keith 1960-

■ Personal

Born May 2, 1960, in Freeport, NY; son of Steven (a
cartoonist and illustrator) and Suzanne (a library clerk;
maiden name Eppner) DuQuette; married Virgina
Hedges (a graphic designer), September 13, 1987. *Education:* Attended Art Students League, 1980, and Yale
University at Norfolk, VA, 1981; State University of
New York at Purchase, B.F.A., 1982.

■ Addresses

Home and office—333 Flatbush Ave., Brooklyn, NY
11217.

■ Career

Author and illustrator. Library preservationist at the
Brooklyn Museum Library.

■ Awards, Honors

Happy as a Tapir was named a Junior Library Guild
selection, 1992; *Hotel Animal* was placed on the International Reading Association's Children's Choice List,
1995, and was named a "Reading Rainbow" feature
book, 1996.

■ Writings

SELF-ILLUSTRATED

A Ripping Day for a Picnic, Viking, 1990.
Hotel Animal, Viking, 1994.

ILLUSTRATOR

Terry Carbone, *Happy as a Tapir,* Viking, 1992.

■ Sidelights

Keith DuQuette told *SATA:* "I was fortunate to grow up
in a home where drawing was seen as a way of life. My
father is a cartoonist and my mother, brother, and
sisters are all visually-oriented people with remarkable
and varied talents.

"It's hard to say exactly when I began working on
children's books because the desire to draw and tell
stories has been with me as long as I can remember. I do
know my first serious attempt was made in 1982 when
graduating from college. I attended an art school where I

**Feeling slightly overwhelmed by the enormousness of
the hotel at which they are staying, Mr. and Mrs.
Lizard find it difficult to adjust to their surroundings
until they come upon a tiny place just their size.** (From
Hotel Animal, written and illustrated by Keith
DuQuette.)

received an excellent foundation from a few marvelous
and challenging teachers. Since then I've tried my hand
at many forms of expression; abstract and landscape
painting, cartooning, sculpture, decorative arts, animation, and writing have all played a role in my artistic
development.

"I've been working in museums and libraries all of my
adult life. I can think of no better environment to
inspire a developing artist. They have been ideal places
to stimulate and influence the work in my studio. In
children's books, I've found an ideal form to use these
stimuli to find my voice as an artist and writer."

■ For More Information See

PERIODICALS

Booklist, May 15, 1994, p. 1371.
Publishers Weekly, March 14, 1994, p. 71.
School Library Journal, June, 1994, p. 98.

E–F

ELLER, Scott
See HOLINGER, William (Jacques) and SHEPARD, Jim

*   *   *

EL-MOSLIMANY, Ann P(axton) 1937-

■ Personal

Born August 2, 1937, in Fullerton, CA; daughter of Donald Dorn (a mechanical engineer) and Sarah Frances (a housewife; maiden name, Turman) Paxton; married Mohammad Ahmad El-Moslimany (an electrical engineering professor), May 31, 1962; children: Samia, Ahmad, Rasheed. *Education:* New Mexico State University, B.S., 1959; American University of Beirut, M.S., 1961; University of Washington, Ph.D., 1983. *Religion:* Muslim.

■ Addresses

Home—P.O. Box 367, Seahurst, WA 98062. *Office*—Islamic School of Seattle, P.O. Box 22956, Seattle, WA 98122.

■ Career

Various teaching positions, from elementary to university levels, 1959-83; Kuwait University, Kuwait, 1984-86; Seattle Central Community College, Seattle, WA, 1986-1990; Islamic School of Seattle, Seattle, principal and teacher, 1989—. Palynological Consultants, paleoecological research, 1987—. *Member:* Amnesty International, American Quaternary Association, National Council Teachers of Mathematics, Geographic Alliance of Washington, Seattle Islamic Sisterhood.

■ Writings

Zaki's Ramadan Fast, Amica, 1994.

ANN P. EL-MOSLIMANY

Also author of several scientific articles in journals such as *Vegetatio* and *Review of Paleobotany and Palynology.* Member of advisory Board for *Muslim Kaleidoscope* (magazine for Muslim children).

■ Work in Progress

A second book about Zaki; research on the lives of "notable twentieth-century Muslims" for young adults; scientific research on "climate change associated with [the] incense trade in Oman" and on "origins of agriculture in the Middle East."

■ Sidelights

"Apparently I am what they call a late-bloomer," Ann P. El-Moslimany explained to *SATA*. "I earned my Ph.D. at the age of forty-five and published my first children's book at fifty-seven. In college I had anguished over choosing among three career choices, biological science, writing, or elementary education. I am shocked to realize that as I approach sixty I am doing all three!

"I grew up in a typical American family and attended an all-white neighborhood school in a similarly homogeneous neighborhood. My identity was unquestioned. I was aware of 'others.' One night as we returned from shopping my mother explained why all of the colored women were running to catch their buses. 'It's against the law for them to be in Burbank after sunset,' she said. I was astounded.

"Later we moved to a rural community near Tucson. On clear, still summer nights I fell asleep listening to the music that drifted from a field half a mile away where the Mexican men had gathered under a tree to play their guitars, drink a little beer, and sing. My view of the world began to expand just a little.

"During my college days I was drawn to the foreign students. When I graduated and sailed off to Beirut to do graduate work my world view virtually exploded.

"Years later I was living in a neighborhood similar to the neighborhood where I had grown up and sending my children to a school similar to the one that I had attended. Except that my children were half-Egyptian, had strange names, and practiced Islam. They were 'others,' and it was tough. I too had become an 'other' but by my choice and according to my own time frame.

"Although too late for our children, it was a dream fulfilled when a group of Muslim women opened the Islamic School of Seattle. Children of many ethnic groups were linked to one another by their common religious background. My love for this school and the ideas it represented resulted in my recently retired husband and me jumping in with both feet when, after several years, the school was on the verge of failing. As we nursed it back to health, it became our lives.

"Although apparently more comfortable with their identities than my own children had been, there was little published material that reflected the unique culture of these American Muslim children and so *Zaki's Ramadan Fast* was born. Any Muslim child can relate to this story of a child who is fasting a whole day for the first time. Zaki's name is that of my grandson, but his family is patterned after the family of my closest friend who is an African American Muslim married to a Pakistani.

"Although the book was initially conceived as a book for Muslim children I am pleased to know that it is providing a glimpse of the Muslim way of life for many other children. May their worlds continue to grow."*

FORRESTER, Sandra 1949-

■ Personal

Born April 8, 1949, in Cullman, AL; daughter of Robert Martin (a transportation specialist) and Dorothy (a government employee; maiden name, Fine) Forrester. *Education:* Judson College, B.A., 1970; attended University of Virginia, 1972; University of North Carolina at Greensboro, M.L.I.S., 1996. *Hobbies and other interests:* Reading ("everything from mysteries to poetry to history"), restoring old doll houses, beachcombing, researching, collecting nineteenth- and early twentieth-century children's books, Majolica pottery, and Santa Clauses.

■ Addresses

Home—1001 Park Ridge Rd., Durham, NC 27713. *Office*—National Institute of Environmental Health Sciences, 101 Alexander Dr., Research Triangle Park, NC 27709. *Agent*—Barbara S. Kouts, P.O. Box 558, Bellport, NY 11713.

■ Career

Department of the Army, Alexandria, VA, occupational analyst, 1974-85, Falls Church, VA, management analyst, 1985-92; National Institute of Environmental Health Sciences, Research Triangle Park, NC, management analyst, 1992—. *Member:* American Library Association, Society of Children's Book Writers and Illustra-

SANDRA FORRESTER

tors, American Society for the Prevention of Cruelty to Animals.

■ Awards, Honors

Sound the Jubilee was selected as a notable children's trade book in the field of social studies, and as a Bank Street children's book of the year, both for 1996.

■ Writings

Sound the Jubilee (young adult novel), Dutton/Lodestar, 1995.

■ Work in Progress

A young adult novel, sequel to *Sound the Jubilee,* set in North Carolina during the Reconstruction.

■ Sidelights

Sandra Forrester told *SATA:* "*Sound the Jubilee* is based on actual events that occurred on the Outer Banks during the Civil War. After the Union Army captured Roanoke Island in February 1862, runaway slaves began to arrive almost immediately seeking sanctuary. Their numbers grew rapidly, until there were more than three thousand people living on the island in what was called the 'Contraband Camp.' The federal government gave each family an acre of land upon which to build a house and plant a garden—and the result was the largest, most prosperous community on the Outer Banks up to that time. *Sound the Jubilee* is the story of a young girl named Maddie who fled to Roanoke Island with her family in search of freedom. The reality of their lives on the island was often difficult and quite different from what they had envisioned." Laura J. Mikowski wrote in *Voice of Youth Advocates* that "the beauty of the book lies in two things: Maddie's growth and Forrester's balancing of the realities of the Civil War." Elizabeth M. Reardon stated in *School Library Journal* that "the author's use of a modified dialect adds substance to her characterization."

Forrester explained to *SATA* what inspired her to write *Sound the Jubilee:* "I learned about the Contraband Camp several years ago when I was vacationing on 'The Banks' and came across a brief reference to the camp's residents in a book on Outer Banks history. I searched for more information on these people but found that practically nothing had been written about them. Eventually I located letters that had been written by some of the camp's men when they were serving in the Union Army, as well as journals and privately-printed memoirs of Union soldiers who were stationed on Roanoke Island during the war. Many of the incidents experienced by Maddie and her friends and family are based on these first-hand accounts. Sadly, nothing remains on the island to remind us that a thriving business and residential community once stood there. The buildings were destroyed long ago, and the land has reverted to forest and undergrowth. I wrote *Sound the Jubilee*

because I was inspired by the courage of these self-freed slaves and moved by the poignancy of their experience."

"The many hours spent in libraries and archives researching Maddie's story rekindled a childhood aspiration," Forrester told *SATA.* "When I was growing up I loved libraries and always wanted to work in one. My recent collaborative efforts with librarians, who were as excited by my research as I was, convinced me to return to school for a degree in library studies.

"My passion for books is rivaled only by my love for animals. I have been active in animal rescue for years because I believe strongly that all animals, wild and domesticated, deserve our respect and protection. Unfortunately, a majority of cats and dogs born in this country are 'throwaways' who never know the comforts of a secure home and a loving family. I can only hope that we will someday learn to value the lives of these innocents, who require so little and give so much. I currently live with two cats, Oliver and Cayenne, who have taught me to worry less, to play more, and to never sit in the cats' chair wearing my good navy suit."

■ Works Cited

Mikowski, Laura J., review of *Sound the Jubilee, Voice of Youth Advocates,* August, 1995, p. 158.

Reardon, Elizabeth M., review of *Sound the Jubilee, School Library Journal,* May, 1995, p. 118.

*   *   *

FRADIN, Dennis Brindell 1945-

■ Personal

Born December 20, 1945, in Chicago, IL; son of Myron (an accountant) and Selma (a political activist; maiden name, Brindell) Fradin; married Judith Bloom (an author and college English teacher), March 19, 1967; children: Anthony, Diana, Michael. *Education:* Northwestern University, B.A. (creative writing), 1967; graduate study at University of Illinois, 1968. *Politics:* Independent. *Religion:* Jewish. *Hobbies and other interests:* Baseball, astronomy.

■ Addresses

Home and office—2121 Dobson, Evanston, IL 60202.

■ Career

Teacher (mostly second grade) in Chicago, IL, public schools, 1968-79; children's book author, 1976—. *Member:* Phi Delta Kappa.

■ Awards, Honors

Educator of the Year, National College of Education, 1989.

DENNIS BRINDELL FRADIN

■ Writings

NONFICTION FOR CHILDREN

Archaeology, Children's Press (Chicago), 1983.
Astronomy, Children's Press, 1983.
Blizzards and Winter Weather, Children's Press, 1983.
Droughts, Children's Press, 1983.
Olympics, Children's Press, 1983.
Farming, Children's Press, 1983.
Movies, Children's Press, 1983.
Comets, Asteroids, and Meteors, Children's Press, 1984.
Explorers, Children's Press, 1984.
Pioneers, Children's Press, 1984.
Skylab, Children's Press, 1984.
Space Colonies, Children's Press, 1985.
Halley's Comet, Children's Press, 1985.
Moon Flights, Children's Press, 1985.
The Voyager Space Probes, Children's Press, 1985.
Voting and Elections, Children's Press, 1985.
Continents, Children's Press, 1986.
Famines, Children's Press, 1986.
Space Telescope, Children's Press, 1987.
The Search for Extraterrestrial Intelligence, Children's Press, 1987.
Heredity, Children's Press, 1987.
Nuclear Energy, Children's Press, 1987.
Remarkable Children: Twenty Who Changed History, Little, Brown (Boston), 1987.
Cancer, Children's Press, 1988.

The Shoshoni, Children's Press, 1988, revised edition, 1993.
The Flag of the United States, Children's Press, 1988.
The Declaration of Independence, Children's Press, 1988.
The Thirteen Colonies, Children's Press, 1988.
Drug Abuse, Children's Press, 1988.
The Cheyenne, Children's Press, 1988, revised edition, 1992.
Ethiopia, Children's Press, 1988.
Earth, Children's Press, 1989, revised edition, 1993.
Mars, Children's Press, 1989, revised edition, 1992.
Venus, Children's Press, 1989, revised edition, 1993.
Medicine: Yesterday, Today, and Tomorrow, Children's Press, 1989.
Uranus, revised edition, Children's Press, 1990.
Amerigo Vespucci, F. Watts (New York City), 1991.
The Nina, the Pinta, and the Santa Maria, F. Watts, 1991.
Hiawatha: Messenger of Peace, McElderry Books (New York City), 1992.
The Pawnee, revised edition, Children's Press, 1992.
Jupiter, revised edition, Children's Press, 1992.
Mercury, revised edition, Children's Press, 1992.
Neptune, revised edition, Children's Press, 1992.
Pluto, revised edition, Children's Press, 1993.
Saturn, revised edition, Children's Press, 1993.
"We Have Conquered Pain": The Discovery of Anesthesia, McElderry Books, 1996.

"BEST HOLIDAY BOOK" SERIES; FOR CHILDREN; PUBLISHED BY ENSLOW PUBLISHERS

Christmas, 1990.
Columbus Day, 1990.
Halloween, 1990.
Hanukkah, 1990.
Lincoln's Birthday, 1990.
Thanksgiving Day, 1990.
Valentine's Day, 1990.
Washington's Birthday, 1990.

"COLONIAL PROFILES" SERIES; FOR CHILDREN; PUBLISHED BY ENSLOW PUBLISHERS

Abigail Adams: Adviser to a President, illustrated by Tom Dunnington, 1989.
John Hancock: First Signer of the Declaration of Independence, illustrated by Dunnington, 1989.
Anne Hutchinson: Fighter for Religious Freedom, illustrated by Dunnington, 1990.
King Philip: Indian Leader, 1990.

"YOUNG PEOPLE STORIES OF OUR STATES" SERIES; FOR CHILDREN; ILLUSTRATED BY RICHARD WAHL, EXCEPT AS NOTED; PUBLISHED BY CHILDREN'S PRESS

Illinois in Words and Pictures, 1976.
Virginia in Words and Pictures, 1976.
Alaska in Words and Pictures, illustrated by Robert Ulm, 1977.
California in Words and Pictures, illustrated by Ulm, 1977.
Ohio in Words and Pictures, illustrated by Ulm, 1977.
Wisconsin in Words and Pictures, 1977.

Alabama in Words and Pictures, 1980.
Arizona in Words and Pictures, 1980.
Arkansas in Words and Pictures, 1980.
Colorado in Words and Pictures, 1980.
Connecticut in Words and Pictures, illustrated by Wahl and Len Meents, 1980.
Delaware in Words and Pictures, 1980.
Florida in Words and Pictures, 1980.
Hawaii in Words and Pictures, 1980.
Idaho in Words and Pictures, 1980.
Indiana in Words and Pictures, 1980.
Iowa in Words and Pictures, 1980.
Kansas in Words and Pictures, 1980.
Maine in Words and Pictures, 1980.
Maryland in Words and Pictures, 1980.
Michigan in Words and Pictures, 1980.
Minnesota in Words and Pictures, 1980.
Mississippi in Words and Pictures, 1980.
Missouri in Words and Pictures, 1980.
Nebraska in Words and Pictures, 1980.
New Jersey in Words and Pictures, 1980.
North Carolina in Words and Pictures, 1980.
Oklahoma in Words and Pictures, 1980.
Oregon in Words and Pictures, 1980.
Pennsylvania in Words and Pictures, 1980.
South Carolina in Words and Pictures, 1980.
Tennessee in Words and Pictures, 1980.
Utah in Words and Pictures, 1980.
Vermont in Words and Pictures, 1980.
Washington in Words and Pictures, 1980.
West Virginia in Words and Pictures, 1980.
Wyoming in Words and Pictures, 1980.
Georgia in Words and Pictures, 1981.
Kentucky in Words and Pictures, 1981.
Louisiana in Words and Pictures, 1981.
Massachusetts in Words and Pictures, 1981.
Montana in Words and Pictures, 1981.
Nevada in Words and Pictures, 1981.
New Hampshire in Words and Pictures, 1981.
New Mexico in Words and Pictures, 1981.
New York in Words and Pictures, illustrated by Wahl, maps by Meents, 1981.
North Dakota in Words and Pictures, 1981.
Rhode Island in Words and Pictures, illustrated by Wahl, maps by Meents, 1981.
South Dakota in Words and Pictures, 1981.
Texas in Words and Pictures, 1981.

"DISASTER!" SERIES; PUBLISHED BY CHILDREN'S PRESS

Earthquakes, 1982.
Fires, 1982.
Floods, 1982.
Hurricanes, 1982.
Tornadoes, 1982.
Volcanoes, 1982.

"THIRTEEN COLONIES" SERIES; PUBLISHED BY CHILDREN'S PRESS

The Massachusetts Colony, 1986.
The Virginia Colony, 1986.
The New Hampshire Colony, 1987.
The New York Colony, 1988.

The Pennsylvania Colony, 1988.
The Georgia Colony, 1989.
The Rhode Island Colony, 1989.
The Connecticut Colony, 1990.
The Maryland Colony, 1990.
The New Jersey Colony, 1991.
The North Carolina Colony, 1991.
The Delaware Colony, 1992.
The South Carolina Colony, 1992.

"FROM SEA TO SHINING SEA" SERIES; PUBLISHED BY CHILDREN'S PRESS

Georgia, 1991.
Illinois, 1991.
Massachusetts, 1991.
California, 1992.
Florida, 1992.
Michigan, 1992.
New Hampshire, 1992.
North Carolina, 1992.
South Carolina, 1992.
Tennessee, 1992.
Texas, 1992.
Virginia, 1992.
Washington, D.C., 1992.
Wisconsin, 1992.
Alabama, 1993.
Alaska, 1993.
Arizona, 1993.
Colorado, 1993.
Iowa, 1993.
Kentucky, 1993.
New Jersey, 1993.
New Mexico, 1993.
New York, 1993.
Ohio, 1993.
Utah, 1993.
Vermont, 1993.
Hawaii, 1994.
Maine, 1994.
Missouri, 1994.
Pennsylvania, 1994.
Idaho, 1995.
Nebraska, 1995.

"FROM SEA TO SHINING SEA" SERIES; COAUTHOR WITH WIFE, JUDITH BLOOM FRADIN; PUBLISHED BY CHILDREN'S PRESS

Montana, 1992.
Arkansas, 1994.
Connecticut, 1994.
Indiana, 1994.
Maryland, 1994.
North Dakota, 1994.
Washington, 1994.
West Virginia, 1994.
Wyoming, 1994.
Delaware, 1994.
Kansas, 1995.
Louisiana, 1995.
Minnesota, 1995.
Mississippi, 1995.
Nevada, 1995.

Oklahoma, 1995.
Oregon, 1995.
Puerto Rico, 1995.
Rhode Island, 1995.
South Dakota, 1995.

*"ENCHANTMENT OF THE WORLD" SERIES; PUBLISHED
    BY CHILDREN'S PRESS*

The Netherlands, 1994.
The Republic of Ireland, 1984, revised edition, 1994.

FICTION FOR CHILDREN

Cara, illustrated by Joann Daley, Children's Press,
    1977.
Cave Painter, illustrated by John Maggard, Children's
    Press, 1978.
Bad Luck Tony, illustrated by Joanne Scribner, Pren-
    tice-Hall (Englewood Cliffs, NJ), 1978.
North Star, illustrated by William Neebe, Children's
    Press, 1978.
Beyond the Mountain, Beyond the Forest, illustrated by
    Maggard, Children's Press, 1978.
The New Spear, illustrated by Tom Dunnington, Chil-
    dren's Press, 1979.
How I Saved the World, Dillon (Minneapolis), 1986.
Is Anyone Out There?, Holt (New York City), 1997.

■ Work in Progress

The Planet Hunters; "Remarkable Children" picture
book series.

■ Sidelights

A prolific author of both fiction and nonfiction books
for children, Dennis Brindell Fradin is a man who loves

In *The Search for Extraterrestrial Intelligence,* **Fradin
discusses attempts to search for life beyond the earth,
which involve radio telescopes such as this one in
Socorro, New Mexico.**

**Fradin presents famous people and places, covering
history and geography in this informative 1993 book
about the Grand Canyon state.**

his work. As he explained to *SATA:* "I have the time of
my life as a children's author. Each day I take about five
steps from my bedroom into my office, where I spend
my time reading, writing, rewriting, and phoning people
for information. Often I travel to do in-person research.
Just in the past couple months, I interviewed Clyde
Tombaugh for my upcoming book *The Planet Hunters.*
Clyde is ninety years old now, and he is famous for
discovering the planet Pluto back in 1930. It's not every
day that you can talk to someone who did something
famous sixty-six years ago! What a thrill! I'd heard about
Tombaugh all my life, and I got to meet him and talk to
him.

"Then a couple weeks later I went down to Puerto Rico
where I saw the biggest radio telescope in the world.
That's for a book I'm doing on the search for extraterrestrial intelligence. I talked to a scientist there who
takes part in a program in which they listen for signals
that ETs may be sending us. Can you imagine getting to
visit places like that and actually making a living at it?
Every day I'm thrilled when I think that I became what I
dreamed of becoming: a children's author."

Fradin has written almost 150 books during his career.
"Each one I research extremely carefully and rewrite
about five to six times," he explained. "I also check over
all my facts line by line to make sure everything is
accurate. So all that keeps me pretty busy. I try not to let
a day of the year go by without working. Even when I fly

on a plane I'm sure to bring along a book to read, just so the day doesn't go by without me doing any work.

"Not everything always [goes] smoothly, though. I love colonial history—a topic not too many people seem concerned about today. For fun, I wrote a young people's biography of Samuel Adams, the man who planned the Boston Tea Party and over whom the British fought the first battle of the Revolution when they were trying to capture him. For a time, no publisher wanted it, although Clarion has now accepted it for publication. One thing about being a writer," Fradin cautioned, "you often have to keep trying to have success because manuscripts often get rejected."

As an author for children, Fradin is often asked for advice by young writers-to-be. "Once when young Thomas Jefferson wrote to Samuel Adams for advice, Adams told him that just because he was old, that didn't mean he had any wisdom to offer. I just turned fifty, and I don't have much wisdom to offer young authors, except an experience I had. When I was a freshman in high school, I wrote a science-fiction story that my English teacher said was the best story by a freshman he had ever seen. But then when I was a junior and showed my English teacher some of my stories, he advised me to forget about becoming an author. That was when I realized that if I wanted to become an author I couldn't live and die by other people's opinions but should do it out of my own desire and need to write."

■ For More Information See

PERIODICALS

Booklist, May 1, 1990, p. 1702; September 15, 1992, p. 143.
Horn Book, January, 1993, p. 97; September-October, 1996, p. 613.
Kirkus Reviews, August 15, 1992, p. 1060.
Publishers Weekly, August 31, 1992, p. 80.
School Library Journal, February, 1977, p. 56; September, 1977, p. 107; April, 1978, p. 68; September, 1978, p. 108; January, 1979, p. 41; September, 1979, p. 136; August, 1980, p. 50; March, 1981, p. 131; October, 1981, p. 128; April, 1983, p. 113; September, 1983, p. 122; October, 1983, p. 145; March, 1984, pp. 142, 144, 159; April, 1984, p. 101; November, 1984, p. 106; April, 1985, p. 78; February, 1986, p. 73; April, 1986, p. 70; January, 1987, pp. 74, 82; August, 1987, p. 82; December, 1987, p. 93; January, 1988, p. 72; February, 1988, p. 94; October, 1988, p. 132; November, 1988, p. 101; January, 1989, p. 70; March, 1989, p. 173; April, 1989, p. 111; September, 1989, p. 262; November, 1989, pp. 122, 134; February, 1990, pp. 81, 114; March, 1990, p. 206; April, 1990, p. 132; October, 1990, p. 108; February, 1991, p. 79; October, 1991, p. 138; January, 1992, pp. 124, 126; March, 1992, p. 246; August, 1992, p. 164; September, 1992, p. 216; April, 1993, p. 130; January, 1994, p. 121; February, 1994, p. 108; November, 1994, p. 114; August, 1995, p. 146.
Voice of Youth Advocates, August, 1996, p. 176.

FRADIN, Judith (Bernette) Bloom 1945-

■ Personal

Born January 8, 1945, in Chicago, IL; daughter of Harold J. (a postal supervisor) and Elsie R. (a secretary and homemaker) Bloom; married Dennis Brindell Fradin (a writer), March 19, 1967; children: Anthony, Diana, Michael. *Education:* Northwestern University, B.A., 1967; Northeastern Illinois University, M.A., 1975. *Politics:* "Local." *Religion:* Jewish. *Hobbies and other interests:* Trying to grow dahlias.

■ Addresses

Home and office—2121 Dobson, Evanston, IL 60202.

■ Career

High school English and history teacher, 1967-75, 1982-90; Northeastern Illinois University, Chicago, writing instructor, 1975-82; photo researcher, 1985—; researcher and writer, 1990—. President, Southwest Evanston Associated Residents (SWEAR).

■ Writings

"FROM SEA TO SHINING SEA" SERIES; COAUTHOR WITH HUSBAND, DENNIS B. FRADIN; PUBLISHED BY CHILDREN'S PRESS

Montana, 1992.
Arkansas, 1994.
Delaware, 1994.

JUDITH BLOOM FRADIN

Connecticut, 1994.
Indiana, 1994.
Maryland, 1994.
North Dakota, 1994.
Washington, 1994.
West Virginia, 1994.
Wyoming, 1994.
Minnesota, 1995.
Louisiana, 1995.
Kansas, 1995.
Mississippi, 1995.
Nevada, 1995.
Puerto Rico, 1995.
Oklahoma, 1995.
Oregon, 1995.
Rhode Island, 1995.
South Dakota, 1995.

OTHER

Writer and editorial board member, *Evanston's Beacon* (local monthly newspaper).

■ Sidelights

Judith Bloom Fradin told *SATA:* "When my husband Dennis and I started our state book series, 'From Sea to Shining Sea,' I researched the books and he wrote them. I spent hours each day in local and university libraries seeking information about recent events in each state. I also gathered biographical material for the 'Famous People' section of each book. Dennis and I often disagreed about which people and events should be included. Finally he said, 'If you think you could do better, why don't you write those sections?'

"In 1994 I began writing the 'Famous People' part of the state books. I also wrote what we called the 'modern stuff,' including events and issues since 1980. As we finished each state, I spent several days checking all facts in the book. We wrote one book every month for nearly five years. Our children, Tony, Diana, and Mike, and our neighbor, Sam Ali, helped with research once I started writing.

"While working on the state books I found many fascinating ideas for future books. I have a file drawer filled with clippings and ideas. I'm also a better-than-average photographer. In the future, I'd like to write and illustrate children's books on my own."

* * *

FRASER, Wynnette (McFaddin) 1925-

■ Personal

Born March 7, 1925, in Gable, SC; daughter of Henry Wheeler (a farmer and country plumber) and Bessie (a homemaker and bookkeeper; maiden name, Higgins) McFaddin; married Ladson Lawrence Fraser (a refrigeration technician and mechanic), April 30, 1946; children: Donna McRee, Beth (deceased), L. L. "Larry" Jr., Doug. *Education:* Brevard College, junior college diplo-

WYNNETTE FRASER

ma, 1943; attended Francis Marion University, Florence-Darlington Technical College, Anderson College, and Institute of Children's Literature. *Politics:* Republican. *Religion:* Presbyterian.

■ Addresses

Home—212 West Smith Ave., Darlington, SC 29532.

■ Career

Spent twelve years in secretarial positions, including work for Shaw Air Base in South Carolina, Crippled Children's Society of South Carolina, Presbyterian churches in Florence and Darlington, SC, and assistant librarian in a high school; spent nineteen years as a caseworker at Darlington County Department of Social Services. Public speaker at schools, colleges, and workshops. *Member:* Member of Presbyterian Church and Friends of the Library.

■ Awards, Honors

First place for juvenile fiction, Anderson College Writer's Conference, 1984 and 1985; honorable mention, *Writer's Digest* magazine poetry competition, 1986 and 1987.

■ Writings

CHILDREN'S MYSTERY-ADVENTURE BOOKS

Mystery on Mirror Mountain, Chariot Family Publishing/David Cook, 1989.

Courage on Mirror Mountain, Chariot Family Publishing/David Cook, 1989.

Mystery at Deepwood Bay, Chariot Family Publishing/David Cook, 1992.

Invasion on Mirror Mountain, Chariot Family Publishing/David Cook, 1994.

OTHER

Contributor to periodicals, including *Country Living* and *Pee Dee.*

■ Work in Progress

Belle—of Alabama, "a circa 1900 novel about a young girl growing up in the home of relatives in rural Alabama. It is fiction based on my mother's experiences and strives to give a picture of everyday life as it was then."

■ Sidelights

Wynnette Fraser told *SATA:* "When I was eleven, I discovered the joy of writing and wanted to be a journalist. But to survive the Big Depression, I took a business course and worked as a secretary-receptionist 'till World War II was over. Then I chose marriage and raising our family. We were rich in what matters most, so I have no regrets.

"In the mid-1980s, I realized that I would soon retire, and I took a correspondence course with the Institute of Children's Literature in West Redding, Connecticut. Soon after that, Church School Take-Home Papers began accepting my short stories. In June 1984, my daughter encouraged me to take some of my work to a Christian writer's conference at Anderson College, South Carolina. I was thrilled to win first place in juvenile fiction and place in three other award categories. One of the staff suggested that I make a book of a short story he had reviewed. I accepted the challenge, and a year passed before I decided *Mystery on Mirror Mountain* was ready to send to publishers. Just before retirement in 1988, I signed a contract for it and its sequel, *Courage on Mirror Mountain.*

"My idea for the series came from a newspaper article about some children who had missed several years of school because the bus couldn't risk travelling the terrible mountain road to their house. A judge ordered a four-wheel drive station wagon to transport the children, and their imagined conflicts in readjusting to school provided what ifs I had to address. I never dreamed the situation would spawn four mystery-adventure books that boys and girls would seem to enjoy."

Johnny Elbert Finley is the main character in each book of the series. He and his friends create a clubhouse from an old hermit's hut and care for an injured red-tailed hawk in *Courage on Mirror Mountain.* In *Mystery at Deepwood Bay,* Johnny and his sister visit their sick uncle and try to discover who vandalized a church in the area.

"Why do I write? I believe God put me here to do it, to show young readers the reality of His love," Fraser told *SATA.* "And I've always loved a good story. In 1990, I was invited to be juvenile consultant at the Anderson College Writer's Rally. I've had many opportunities to talk to school children and adult groups in both Carolinas and enjoyed this contact.

"The writer's dilemma is to find quiet time to write without losing touch with the reality of life around him or her. My husband and I belong to a weekly bowling league. The youngest of our four grandchildren is twelve, and they don't live in the area. I'm grateful for contact with children in my chosen work as church librarian. It's a good place for a writer to serve and keep in touch. So—I press on."

■ For More Information See

PERIODICALS

Messenger (NC), March 24, 1993.
Parents' Paper, Ink, July, 1992, p. 12.

*   *   *

FREEDMAN, Jeff 1953-

■ Personal

Born July 11, 1953, in Los Angeles, CA; son of Leonard (a manager of a men's clothing store) and Roberta (Cassileth) Freedman; married Deborah R. Cletsoway (a computer programmer), December 17, 1978; children: Rebecca, Shoshanna. *Education:* Massacusetts Institute of Technology, B.S. (mathematics), 1975; University of California at Los Angeles, Ph.D. (mathematics), 1979. *Politics:* Libertarian. *Religion:* Jewish. *Hobbies and other interests:* Woodworking, home renovation.

■ Addresses

Home—2865 Southeast Camwal Dr., Hillsboro, OR 97123. *Office*—Cypress Semiconductor, 8196 Southwest Hall, Suite 100, Beaverton, OR 97008.

■ Career

Intel, Hillsboro, OR, senior software engineer, 1988-90; Cypress Semiconductor, Beaverton, OR, senior software engineer, 1990—.

■ Writings

The Magic Dishpan of Oz, illustrated by Denis McFarling, Books of Wonder, 1995.

■ Work in Progress

A Cure for a Cat, a fantasy for children.

■ Sidelights

Jeff Freedman told *SATA:* "I had never cared much for writing nor considered myself very good at it. But as I approached forty, it became time to have a 'midlife crisis.' Since I couldn't afford a Porsche, I decided to write a book. I wrote *The Magic Dishpan of Oz* partly as a personal challenge but mainly to amuse my daughter, who has been a fan of the Oz books since she was three. That is why she and her sister are the main characters!

"My goal is to write novels for children that are exciting but not scary, and with young protagonists who prevail through cleverness and resourcefulness. Children often outsmart the adults in my stories, especially when the adults are misbehaving.

"Favorite authors: Charles Dickens, L. Frank Baum, E. Nesbit, Charles Kingsley—perhaps I'm a hundred years too late!"

G

GARDNER, Miriam
See BRADLEY, Marion Zimmer

*   *   *

GARFIELD, Leon 1921-1996

OBITUARY NOTICE—See index for *SATA* sketch: Born July 14, 1921, in Brighton, Sussex, England; died of complications following surgery, June 2, 1996, in London, England. Author. Garfield gained prominence as the prolific author of numerous children's stories. He began his writing career after serving in the British Army's Medical Corps during World War II, followed by twenty-three years as a biochemical technician for several London hospitals. In 1964, his first novel was published. *Jack Holborn,* a tale of a young boy's adventures on the high seas, earned him an award from the Boys Clubs of America. He followed this with numerous children's and young adult historical novels, novels for adults, and many adaptations of Shakespearean, Greek, and Biblical stories. In all, he wrote more than sixty stories, including *The House of Cards, The Valentine, The Apprentices, Mister Corbett's Ghost, and Other Stories, Smith,* and *The Saracen Maid.* He also completed *The Mystery of Edwin Drood,* Charles Dickens's unfinished novel.

OBITUARIES AND OTHER SOURCES:

BOOKS

Children's Literature Review, Vol. 21, Gale Research, 1990.
Twentieth-Century Young Adult Writers, St. James Press, 1994.

PERIODICALS

New York Times, June 9, 1996, Section 1, p. 44.
Times (London), June 4, 1996, p. 21.
Washington Post, June 7, 1996, p. B7.

GEORGE, Sally
See ORR, Wendy

*   *   *

GERRARD, Roy 1935-

■ Personal

Born January 25, 1935, in Atherton, Lancashire, England; son of Arthur (a miner) and Elsie (Hackett) Gerrard; married Jean Thatcher (a teacher), March 29, 1958; children: Sally Gerrard Turpie, Paul. *Education:* Attended Salford School of Art, 1950-54. *Politics:* "Nonexistent." *Religion:* "Barely visible." *Hobbies and other interests:* "My spare time is spent recuperating."

■ Addresses

Home—10 Maynestone Rd., Chinley, Stockport, Cheshire SK12 6AQ, England.

■ Career

Egerton Park County Secondary School, Denton, England, art teacher and department head, 1956-66; Hyde Grammar School, Hyde, England, art teacher and department head, 1966-80; painter, 1980—; author and illustrator of children's books, 1980—. *Exhibitions:* Annual one-man shows at SEEN Gallery, London, 1975-85. Illustrations have been exhibited at National Theatre, London, and in New York galleries.

■ Awards, Honors

Mother Goose Award runner-up, *Books for Your Children* Bookshop, 1982, for *Matilda Jane;* "Fiera di Bologna" Children's Graphic Art Prize, Bologna Children's Book Fair, Parents' Choice Award for Illustration in Children's Books, Parents' Choice Foundation, and Best Illustrated Children's Books of the Year, *New York Times,* all 1983, all for *The Favershams;* Best Illustrated

ROY GERRARD

Children's Books of the Year, *New York Times,* 1984, for *Sir Cedric,* and 1988, for *Sir Francis Drake: His Daring Deeds;* Parents' Choice Award for Picture Book, 1989, for *Rosie and the Rustlers.*

■ Writings

SELF-ILLUSTRATED CHILDREN'S BOOKS

The Favershams, Gollancz, 1982, Farrar, Straus, 1983.
Sir Cedric, Farrar, Straus, 1984.
Sir Cedric Rides Again, Farrar, Straus, 1986.
Sir Francis Drake: His Daring Deeds, Farrar, Straus, 1988.
Rosie and the Rustlers, Farrar, Straus, 1989.
Mik's Mammoth, Farrar, Straus, 1990.
A Pocketful of Posies, Farrar, Straus, 1991.
Jocasta Carr, Movie Star, Farrar, Straus, 1992.
Croco'nile, Farrar, Straus, 1994.
Wagons West!, Farrar, Straus, 1996.

ILLUSTRATOR

Jean Gerrard, *Matilda Jane,* Gollancz, 1981, Farrar, Straus, 1983.

■ Work in Progress

A children's book set in ancient Rome.

■ Sidelights

English author-illustrator Roy Gerrard is the creator of a number of award-winning picture books in verse for children that feature historical settings. His thumb-

shaped humans play out their adventures and misadventures amid a rich and varied backdrop of period detail, as Gerrard gently satirizes medieval life, the Victorian and Edwardian ages, and the American West with a fanciful affection. Gerrard's verse texts provide a light accompaniment to his highly decorative and slyly humorous illustrations. "My paintings express a sense of whimsy which owes much to Lewis Carroll and Edward Lear," Gerrard once told *SATA.* "I think this helped when I started to write children's books. I'm not really an author—I am more an amateur dabbler in light verse."

Gerrard's books have found a following on both sides of the Atlantic and with parents as well as children. Indeed, some critics have noted that Gerrard's satire and wit is directed more at adults than at young readers. Reviewing his first solo effort, *The Favershams,* in the *New York Times Book Review,* Janice Prindle commented that "an appreciation of the real humor here demands a grown-up sense of history and an ability to understand the irony that the point of the Favershams' story is its very pointlessness." But if children do not always understand the historical context of the story, they can surely empathize with Gerrard's curiously foreshortened characters and appreciate his playful ballads, such as this one that begins his 1989 romp set in the American West, *Rosie and the Rustlers:* "Where the mountains meet the prairie, where the men are wild and hairy / There's a little ranch where Rosie Jones is boss. / It's a place that's neat and cozy, and the boys employed by Rosie / Work extremely hard, to stop her getting cross."

The Wild West is a long way from the English Midlands, where Gerrard was born in 1935. "As a boy I was brought up 12 miles outside Manchester," Gerrard told Jean Russell in an interview for *Books for Your Children,* "and as a child always thought of it as a magical city, the streetlife, the trams, horses, and cobblestone." After studying at the Salford School of Art, Gerrard taught art at secondary and grammar schools for twenty-five years. At the same time he was a Sunday painter, working in oils, but at one point he decided to quit painting and destroyed all his works. "Then in 1972," he further related to Russell, "I was immobilized for several weeks after a climbing accident and started tinkering around with small watercolours." After three years of such tinkering, Gerrard had hit on his idiosyncratic style that he described for Russell as "small, highly-detailed watercolours, remorselessly whimsical and often [featuring] Victorian/Edwardian subjects."

There followed several one-man shows in London, and in 1980 Gerrard quit teaching to devote full time to painting. It was at one of his shows that someone suggested that his paintings would also make good book illustrations. Subsequently, he teamed up with his wife, who wrote the text for his first illustrated book, *Matilda Jane.* Light verse tells the story—set in Edwardian England—of little Matilda, who takes a seaside vacation with her parents and nanny and sees and experiences extraordinary things. Critics were quick to respond to

Gerrard's quirky illustrations. Margery Fisher, in *Growing Point,* called *Matilda Jane* a "delectable book," and drew special attention to the "meticulous details of the Edwardian scenes on the railway and at the seaside, with their picture-postcard colours." Writing in *School Library Journal,* Ruth K. MacDonald also commented favorably on Gerrard's watercolor illustrations for *Matilda Jane.* "The abundant detail of gingerbread trim on houses, wallpaper patterns and bathing costumes are whimsically pleasing," noted MacDonald.

With his next title, Gerrard also wrote the text, as he has done for each of his subsequent works. "*The Favershams* is a story in verse of a Victorian gentleman, soldier, and scholar," Gerrard told *SATA.* "Based on my childhood memories of my great-uncle Sam, who served in the British Army during Victoria's reign, it's an affectionately satirical look at nineteenth-century values and behavior." The verse story follows the life of one Charles Augustus Faversham from his birth, through school, the Army, love and marriage, a honeymoon, service in India, hunting big game, family life, and into retirement during which he becomes an author. All of this is told in low-key, humorous iambic tetrameter, as in this verse introducing the protagonist: "One day in eighteen fifty-one / These parents posed beside their son, / The son (that's him inside the pram) / Was Charles Augustus Faversham." Above this verse is a signature Gerrard watercolor with the proud parents in their garden and the family mansion behind with its acres of roof and solarium addition. The round-faced

baby sits in his pram, his head covered by a wide straw hat. A table is laid for tea; a cat peeks out from behind the table cloth. The rest of the story is told in similar verses with full-page illustrations, one even of the newly married Charles and his wife nude bathing.

"This is good fun, gentle satire, a relevant comment on a period of history, all in one happy book," commented Marcus Crouch in the *Junior Bookshelf.* Elaine Moss, in her *Picture Books for Young People 9-13,* called *The Favershams* "a loving satire on the life of the ruling class in Victorian England." Commenting especially on the illustrations, Ann A. Flowers in *Horn Book* described the details of fabrics, wallpaper, and other elements as "brilliantly rendered," while noting that the "dark, muted reds and browns are certainly Victorian in feeling." A reviewer for *Publishers Weekly* called Gerrard's watercolors for *The Favershams* "tender, affectionately satiric slants on the proper Victorian and astonishingly beautiful," and noted that the "story equals the paintings as humorous art." Donnarae Mac-Cann and Olga Richard, writing in the *Wilson Library Bulletin,* praised the technique which allowed Gerrard to infuse his illustrations with such a wealth of detail while suffering from neither "confusion or claustrophobic excess." MacCann and Richard added that there is "a haunting charm about [Gerrard's] static, posed figures, who look frozen in time while they are still living out an entire life span against changing backdrops." *The Favershams* won several international awards, including the "Fiera de Bologna" from the

The people he met on the long country road
passed him by with a smile and a wave
And said they'd not seen such a very fine knight,
so handsome and sturdy and brave.

A balding knight in search of adventure brings comedy and color to the age of chivalry in Gerrard's eye-catching, self-illustrated tale *Sir Cedric.*

Rollicking rhyme and Lawson-like detail relate how some wicked bandits get their comeuppance in Gerrard's self-illustrated *Rosie and the Rustlers.*

Bologna Children's Book Fair, and established Gerrard's reputation as an innovative and highly original illustrator and writer.

Gerrard furthered this reputation with his next effort, *Sir Cedric,* "a verse story of a medieval knight who is a do-gooder but also an all-round nice guy," as the author described the book to *SATA.* The story, Gerrard explained, "owes much to the derring-do books I used to read as a boy, such as Kipling, Conan Doyle, Sir Walter Scott, and the Arthurian legends. It's written in the style of the Victorian music-hall monologue—deliberately lugubrious. The setting of *Sir Cedric* is based on Beeston Castle, a thirteenth-century ruin set on a 300-foot rocky knoll which rises steeply and dramatically from a typical Cheshire landscape—sleepy village and rich agricultural land." This parody of a medieval knight's tale is a mock-biography of Sir Cedric, who rescues Princess Matilda from her evil jailor, Black Ned, and then marries her. Humor comes, as Fisher noted in *Growing Point,* from "Cedric's small size . . . and the satirical suggestions in such details as the cucumber sandwiches eaten on the journey." Roy Foster, writing in the *Times Literary Supplement,* commented that *Sir Cedric* "is crammed not only with jingling quatrains recounting stirring deeds, but also with pictures of breathtaking intricacy and verve." Foster concluded that the illustrations

might make *Sir Cedric* "a classic," but that the text also deserved praise as "tough-minded, funny and convincing," as in this description of Princess Matilda and her jailor: "Matilda, though fat, was a princess, you see, / and could have any man that she chose, / But Black Ned was badtempered, dirty and mean, / and had hairs growing out of his nose." Laurance Wieder, in the *New York Times Book Review,* found similarities to Pieter Breughel, Albrecht Duerer, William Blake, and William Morris in Gerrard's illustrations, and noted that such "lavish illustrations incorporate his verses in their design, and neither is complete without the other." Zena Sutherland in the *Bulletin of the Center for Children's Books* also commented favorably on Gerrard's illustrations for *Sir Cedric,* calling them "deft in technique and composition, humorous in effect, and often beautifully detailed and ornamented."

Sir Cedric Rides Again revisits the diminutive medieval knight who in this adventure finds that his daughter Edwina needs rescuing from Arab bandits. Her suitor, Hubert the Hopeless, turns into an instant hero when called upon, and all turns out well in this book which, according to Carolyn Phelan in *Booklist,* "pleases the ear, the eye, and the funny bone." A commentator in *Kirkus Reviews* also noted that *Sir Cedric Rides Again* was "a book to pore over, read aloud, and share with delight," while Zena Sutherland in *Bulletin of the Center for Children's Books* concluded that "this is lively, witty narrative poetry, and the paintings are of comparably high quality." Lachlan Mackinnon, however, writing in the *Times Literary Supplement,* called attention to "sexual and racial undertones [that] unsettle because they distract from the story and invite speculation and inquiry more mature than the likely readership." A reviewer for *Publishers Weekly* efficiently summed up the criticisms for and against *Sir Cedric Rides Again* by concluding that "those who side with Sir Cedric will hail his latest adventure; others may find his views too absolute."

Such absolute views seemingly inform Gerrard's next title, as well. *Sir Francis Drake: His Daring Deeds* tells the story of a man who was the first Englishman to circumnavigate the globe and who helped to destroy the Spanish Armada, but who was also a privateer for Queen Elizabeth I and not necessarily renowned for his tender mercies. Gerrard, however, manages to tell the main points of Drake's life in his usual tongue-in-cheek verse accompanied with his foreshortened people set against lushly detailed backgrounds. Kay E. Vandergrift, writing in *School Library Journal,* concludes that this is "a book that children will love to discover and explore," with its "majestic and detailed illustrations" and playful language, such as this from the final battle scene with the Armada: "The discombobulated foe / decided it was time to go." Ellen Mandel of *Booklist* declared that "rarely is history recalled with such verve or inspired liberty." Other critics, however, wondered at the subtext. John Cech in the *New York Times Book Review* noted that Gerrard's choice of scenes from Drake's ambiguous career put the privateer in the best possible light. "Alas, once one starts trying to make literal sense of the fragments Mr. Gerrard has chosen from Drake's life, the text quickly loses its credibility. Finally, as an American reader, one wonders if this is trying to pass for a fragment of unreconstructed history in Thatcher England." Cech also drew attention to Gerrard's strange little characters, "all head and torso on legs without thighs," and their odd juxtaposition with backgrounds which have normal proportions. Cech commented that this mannerism might work in other stories, but "here it limits rather than enriches the story, trivializing the very events Mr. Gerrard wishes to celebrate." Other commentators disagreed with such an appraisal, like Marcus Crouch in the *Junior Bookshelf* who warned that "we mustn't take [Gerrard's] account of the 'daring deeds' too literally: there is more artistic truth than sound fact in them." A *Publishers Weekly* reviewer also noted that "the irony of his plundering Spanish 'chaps' and other calculated word choices will not be lost on adults reading the story aloud.... This is diverting and sophisticated fare." *Sir Francis Drake: His Daring Adventures* was chosen as one of the ten best illustrated children's books of 1988 by the *New York Times.*

In a departure from English history, Gerrard's next book, *Rosie and the Rustlers,* tells the story of Rosie Jones and her band of hard-working cowboys in oversized ten-gallon hats and their battle with the rustlers led by Greasy Ben. Employing his usual blend of one or two quatrains per page along with detailed watercolors, Gerrard manages to reach "children with little details that will make them giggle and even explode into laughter," concluded Kay E. Vandergrift in *School Library Journal.* Gerrard had a new venue for his painting, creating something of a parody of a movie Western chase scene allowing for panoramic double-page spreads of mountains and canyons. Betsy Hearne, reviewing *Rosie and the Rustlers* for the *Bulletin of the Center for Children's Books,* asserted that "the patterned landscapes and detailed portraits make this one of Gerrard's best." Nancy Vasilakis, writing in *Horn Book,*

Two young Egyptian siblings narrowly escape disaster with the help of a remarkable crocodile in Gerrard's self-illustrated *Croco'nile.*

Gerrard's trademark thumb-shaped characters brave pioneer adventures on the Oregon Trail in *Wagons West!*, illustrated by the author.

commented that Gerrard's "solid, chunky" figures worked especially well in a Western setting, and concluded that this was a book that would "be enjoyed at story hours as much for its visual fun as for its word play."

More recent additions to Gerrard's playful menagerie have included *Mik's Mammoths,* in which a caveman proves that wit and intelligence can win out over brawn; *Jocasta Carr, Movie Star,* which combines images of Shirley Temple and Amelia Earhart with the young star Jocasta setting off in her plane to find her stolen dog; *Croco'nile,* set in ancient Egypt; and *Wagons West!,* a return to a frontier setting in the story of a wagon train's journey west. A reviewer for *Publishers Weekly* called *Mik's Mammoths* a "refreshingly original glimpse of prehistoric life," while Carolyn Phelan in *Booklist* concluded that "touches of droll humor in both artwork and verse will endear it to readers young and old." Reviewing *Jocasta Carr, Movie Star* for *Magpies,* Moira Robinson described the book as a "tongue in cheek

send-up" of early Hollywood movies with "dastardly villains" and "plucky heroines," and Eve Larkin in *School Library Journal* called it "a smashing adventuring," praising its illustrations as both fun and informative. A commentator for *Publishers Weekly* also noted Gerrard's illustrations in *Jocasta Carr,* asserting: "An abundance of fetching Art Deco motifs, from the array of geometric borders surrounding text and illustrations to furnishing and architectural details, give the book a bold, graphic look suggestive of its pre-World War II era." *Croco'nile* follows the adventures of a brother and sister and their pet crocodile in ancient Egypt, and the illustrations include ten hieroglyphic messages for which a key has been provided on the jacket flap. Phelan noted in *Booklist* that *Croco'nile* would be "an entertaining addition to any elementary unit on ancient Egypt," and a *Publishers Weekly* reviewer dubbed Gerrard's book "an innovative amalgam of ancient history lesson, introduction to hieroglyphics and fanciful story."

Wagons West! details the 1850s journey of a wagon train from Independence, Missouri to Oregon's Willamette Valley. Buckskin Dan leads this band of intrepid travelers until they reach "Oregon at last, with all hazards safely past." Such hazards include cattle bandits, rough terrain, and river crossings. "The rich, dramatic scenes are rendered in earth-tone watercolors," noted Wendy Lukehart in *School Library Journal.* Kay Weisman, writing in *Booklist,* pointed out that "primary classes studying the westward movement and young history buffs will find this a pleasing introduction to life on the Oregon Trail." A *Publishers Weekly* reviewer assessed *Wagons West!* in a manner that has become fairly common in analyses of Gerrard's works. While noting that the author's verse "rolls easily off the tongue," the reviewer concluded that the artwork provides the real flavor of the volume. "The stylized characters indicate not so much an artistic idiosyncracy as a fully realized imaginative vision just waiting to be shared with the reader."

■ Works Cited

Cech, John, review of *Sir Francis Drake: His Daring Deeds, New York Times Book Review,* April 10, 1988, p. 38.

Review of *Croco'nile, Publishers Weekly,* September 5, 1994, p. 109.

Crouch, Marcus, review of *The Favershams, Junior Bookshelf,* December, 1982, p. 220.

Crouch, Marcus, review of *Sir Francis Drake: His Daring Adventures, Junior Bookshelf,* June, 1988, p. 130.

Review of *The Favershams, Publishers Weekly,* April 15, 1983, p. 50.

Fisher, Margery, review of *Matilda Jane, Growing Point,* September, 1981, p. 3950.

Fisher, Margery, review of *Sir Cedric, Growing Point,* November, 1984, p. 4347.

Flowers, Ann A., review of *The Favershams, Horn Book,* October, 1983, p. 562.

Foster, Roy, "Costume Drama," *Times Literary Supplement,* October 5, 1984, p. 1139.

Gerrard, Roy, *The Favershams,* Gollancz, 1982, Farrar, Straus, 1983.

Gerrard, Roy, *Sir Cedric,* Farrar, Straus, 1984.

Gerrard, Roy, *Sir Francis Drake: His Daring Deeds,* Farrar, Straus, 1988.

Gerrard, Roy, *Rosie and the Rustlers,* Farrar, Straus, 1989.

Gerrard, Roy, *Wagons West!,* Farrar, Straus, 1996.

Hearne, Betsy, review of *Rosie and the Rustlers, Bulletin of the Center for Children's Books,* November, 1989, p. 55.

Review of *Jocasta Carr, Movie Star, Publishers Weekly,* October 26, 1992, p. 71.

Larkin, Eve, review of *Jocasta Carr, Movie Star, School Library Journal,* November, 1992, p. 70.

Lukehart, Wendy, review of *Wagons West!, School Library Journal,* March, 1996, p. 173.

MacCann, Donnarae, and Olga Richard, "Picture Books for Children," *Wilson Library Bulletin,* November, 1983, p. 210.

MacDonald, Ruth K., review of *Matilda Jane, School Library Journal,* April, 1982, p. 58.

Mackinnon, Lachlan, "Exotic Excursions," *Times Literary Supplement,* December 26, 1986, p. 1458.

Mandel, Ellen, review of *Sir Francis Drake: His Daring Deeds, Booklist,* August 8, 1988, p. 1924.

Review of *Mik's Mammoth, Publishers Weekly,* October 12, 1990, p. 63.

Moss, Elaine, review of *The Favershams, Picture Books for Young People 9-13,* Thimble Press, 1985, p. 43.

Phelan, Carolyn, review of *Sir Cedric Rides Again, Booklist,* January 1, 1987, p. 70.

Phelan, Carolyn, review of *Mik's Mammoths, Booklist,* December 1, 1990, p. 745.

Phelan, Carolyn, review of *Croco'nile, Booklist,* October 15, 1994, p. 435.

Prindle, Janice, review of *The Favershams, New York Times Book Review,* June 19, 1983, p. 26.

Robinson, Moira, review of *Jocasta Carr, Movie Star, Magpies,* July, 1993, p. 31.

Russell, Jean, "Cover Artist: Roy Gerrard," *Books for Your Children,* Summer, 1981, p. 4.

Review of *Sir Cedric Rides Again, Kirkus Reviews,* October 15, 1986, p. 1576.

Review of *Sir Cedric Rides Again, Publishers Weekly,* November 28, 1986, p. 71.

Review of *Sir Francis Drake: His Daring Deeds, Publishers Weekly,* April 29, 1988, p. 74.

Sutherland, Zena, review of *Sir Cedric, Bulletin of the Center for Children's Books,* January, 1985, p. 83.

Sutherland, Zena, review of *Sir Cedric Rides Again, Bulletin of the Center for Children's Books,* December, 1986, p. 66.

Vandergrift, Kay E., review of *Sir Francis Drake: His Daring Deeds, School Library Journal,* August 8, 1988, p. 81.

Vandergrift, Kay E., review of *Rosie and the Rustlers, School Library Journal,* February, 1990, p. 74.

Vasilakis, Nancy, review of *Rosie and the Rustlers, Horn Book,* March-April, 1990, pp. 188-89.

Review of *Wagons West!, Publishers Weekly,* March 18, 1996, p. 69.

Weisman, Kay, review of *Wagons West!, Booklist,* March 15, 1996, p. 1268.

Wieder, Laurance, review of *Sir Cedric, New York Times Book Review,* November 4, 1984, p. 23.

■ For More Information See

BOOKS

Children's Book Illustration and Design, edited by Julie Cummins, PBC International, 1992.

Children's Literature Review, Volume 23, Gale, 1991, pp. 118-23.

PERIODICALS

Books for Your Children, Autumn, 1986, p. 9; Spring, 1989, p. 7; Autumn, 1992, p. 51; Summer, 1995, p. 23.

Bulletin of the Center for Children's Books, July, 1988, p. 228; November, 1990, p. 59; January, 1995, p. 164.

Horn Book, January, 1989, p. 53.

Magpies, March, 1995, p. 27.

New York Times Book Review, August 13, 1995, p. 23.
Times Literary Supplement, April 1, 1988, p. 371.

—*Sketch by J. Sydney Jones*

*   *   *

GERSHATOR, Phillis 1942-

■ Personal

Born July 8, 1942, in New York, NY; daughter of
Morton Dimondstein (an artist) and Miriam Honixfeld
Green (an artist); married David Gershator (an author)
October 19, 1962; children: Yonah, Daniel. *Education:*
Attended University of California, Berkeley, 1959-63;
Douglass College, B.A., 1966; Pratt Institute, M.L.S.,
1975. *Hobbies and other interests:* Reading, gardening,
cooking.

■ Addresses

Home—P.O. Box 303353, St. Thomas, Virgin Islands
00803-3353.

■ Career

St. Thomas Public Library, St. Thomas, Virgin Islands,
librarian, 1974-75, 1988-89; Enid M. Baa and Leonard
Dober Elementary School libraries, Brooklyn, NY,
children's librarian, 1977-84; Department of Education,
St. Thomas, children's librarian, 1984-86. Has also
worked as a secretary and in library promotion for
various New York City publishers. Reading Is Fundamental volunteer in St. Thomas, 1984—; secretary of
Friends of the Library, St. Thomas, 1985-95. *Member:*
Society of Children's Book Writers and Illustrators,
Virgin Islands Library Association.

■ Awards, Honors

Cooperative Children's Book Center of the University
of Wisconsin choice book, Children's Book of the Year,
Bank Street's Child Study Children's Book Committee,
American Children's and Young Adult literature Award
commended title, Consortium of Latin American Stud-
ies Programs, and Blue Ribbon Book, *Bulletin of the
Center for Children's Books,* all 1994, all for *Tukama
Tootles the Flute: A Tale from the Antilles;* Children's
Book of the Year, Bank Street's Child Study Children's
Book Committee, 1994, for *The Iroko-man: A Yoruba
Folktale;* Junior Library Guild selection, National
Council of Teachers of English Notable Trade Book in
the Language Arts, 1995, and Best Black History for
Young People, *Booklist,* 1995, all for *Rata-pata-scata-
fata: A Caribbean Story.*

■ Writings

FOR CHILDREN

Honi and His Magic Circle, illustrated by Shay Rieger,
  Jewish Publications Society of America (Philadel-

PHILLIS GERSHATOR

  phia), 1979, revised edition published as *Honi's
  Circle of Trees,* illustrated by Mim Green, 1994.
Rata-pata-scata-fata: A Caribbean Story, illustrated by
  Holly Meade, Little, Brown, 1993.
(Reteller) *Tukama Tootles the Flute: A Tale from the
  Antilles,* illustrated by Synthia St. James, Orchard
  Books, 1994.
(Reteller) *The Iroko-man: A Yoruba Folktale,* illustrated
  by Holly Kim, Orchard Books, 1994.
Sambalena Show-off, illustrated by Leonard Jenkins,
  Macmillan Books for Young Readers, 1995.
(With husband, David Gershator) *Bread Is for Eating,*
  illustrated by Emma Shaw-Smith, Holt, 1995.
Sweet, Sweet Fig Banana, illustrated by Fritz Millevoix,
  Albert Whitman (Morton Grove, IL), 1996.

OTHER

*A Bibliographic Guide to the Literature of Contemporary
  American Poetry, 1970-1975,* Scarecrow Press (Me-
  tuchen, NJ), 1976.

Also author of poems and book reviews.

■ Work in Progress

Two picture books: *Palampam Day* (with David Gers-
hator) illustrated by Enrique O. Sanchez, for Cavendish/
Benchmark, and *Zzzng, Zzzng, Zzzng,* illustrated by
Greg Henry, for Orchard Books; a chapter book entitled

Junjun liked to daydream. He liked to night dream. And he liked to dream in between, when the birds sang and the lizards came out to bask in the morning sun.

But Junjun's dreams were often interrupted. There was always so much work to do!

Little dreamer Junjun hopes a magic chant will take care of his chores in Gershator's Caribbean story *Rata-pata-scata-fata*. (Illustration by Holly Meade.)

Sugar Cakes Cyril, illustrated by Cedric Lucas, for Mondo.

■ Sidelights

Phillis Gershator is the author of award-winning picture books often grounded in the folkloric traditions of such places as the Caribbean and Africa. Her stories have been either original works, like *Rata-pata-scata-fata: A Caribbean Story,* or retellings, such as *Tukama Tootles the Flute: A Tale from the Antilles.*

Having spent her entire life surrounded by books, it is not surprising that Gershator's career path eventually led her to become an author. "[My] family was in the book business in New York," she explained in a *Junior Library Guild* article, and she often received books as gifts. She read so much that her mother often had to force her to go outside to play and get some exercise. As a graduate student, Gershator majored in library science. Her first job as a librarian was on the island of St. Thomas, where her family had moved from New York City in 1969. The Caribbean eventually became the setting for *Rata-pata-scata-fata* and *Tukama Tootles the Flute.*

After working for several years at libraries and publishing companies in New York City, Gershator returned to St. Thomas in 1988. Gleaning much satisfaction through her library work and as a Reading Is Fundamental (RIF) volunteer, Gershator wanted to contribute

even more to children by writing her own stories. Career and family kept her from spending much time on her writing, though she published her first book, *Honi and His Magic Circle,* in 1979 and has been composing poems and short stories since the early 1970s. It was not until the mid-1990s that her career would really take off, however. In 1993 and 1994 she published three very successful books: *Rata-pata-scata-fata, Tukama Tootles the Flute,* and *The Iroko-Man: A Yoruba Tale,* all of which have won awards.

Rata-pata-scata-fata is about a young St. Thomas boy named Junjun who tries to avoid household chores by chanting "Caribbean gobbledygook" in the hope that his tasks will be completed by magic. Although luck, not magic, smiles on him to grant him all his wishes, Junjun attributes everything to his gobbledygook. A *Kirkus Reviews* critic called the tale "an engagingly cadenced story that will be just right for sharing aloud." "Gershator has a light and lively sense of language," declared *Bulletin of the Center for Children's Books* contributor Betsy Hearne, "along with a storytelling rhythm that shows experience with keeping young listeners involved."

In a similar vein to *Rata-pata-scata-fata, Tukama Tootles the Flute* is about another St. Thomas boy who is unreliable in his chores. In this yarn, young Tukama loves to play his flute so much that he does not help his grandmother like he should, although she warns him that his disobedient ways might one day cause him to wind up in the stomach of the local two-headed giant. Tukama's grandmother's words prove unsurprisingly prophetic when the boy is captured by the giant, but he manages to escape by playing his flute for the giant's wife. The frightening experience teaches Tukama a lesson, and thereafter he restricts his playing until after his chores are done. Pointing out the similarities between this story and "Jack and the Beanstalk," *School Library Journal* reviewer Lyn Miller-Lachman commented that *Tukama Tootles the Flute* "offers an opportunity to observe similarities and differences in folklore around the world." A *Publishers Weekly* critic favorably remarked that the "text pulses with the rhythms of island dialect and is laced with the casual asides of an oral storyteller."

Like the Caribbean children in these stories, Gershator considers herself to be very lucky. "Wishes do, once in a while, [come true]," she said in *Junior Library Guild,* "so I don't consider *Rata-pata-scata-fata* a fairy tale, and oddly enough, that little boy seems very familiar."

■ Works Cited

Gershator, Phillis, interview in *Junior Library Guild,* April-September, 1994, p. 14.

Hearne, Betsy, review of *Rata-pata-scata-fata: A Caribbean Story, Bulletin of the Center for Children's Books,* April, 1994, p. 257.

Miller-Lachman, Lyn, review of *Tukama Tootles the Flute: A Tale from the Antilles, School Library Journal,* April, 1994, p. 118.

Review of *Rata-pata-scata-fata: A Caribbean Story, Kirkus Reviews,* May 1, 1994, p. 629.

Review of *Tukama Tootles the Flute: A Tale from the Antilles, Publishers Weekly,* January 10, 1994, p. 60.

■ For More Information See

PERIODICALS

Booklist, April 15, 1994, p. 1541; May 1, 1994, p. 1603; May 15, 1994, p. 1676; February 15, 1995, p. 1094.
Horn Book Guide, fall, 1994, p. 340.
Kirkus Reviews, February 1, 1994, p. 142.
Publishers Weekly, April 4, 1994, p. 79.
School Librarian, November, 1994, p. 145.
School Library Journal, July, 1995, p. 27; September, 1995, p. 194.

*   *   *

GILBERT, Roby Goodale 1966-

■ Personal

Born February 4, 1966, in New York, NY; son of Thomas Franklyn Roby (an industrial psychologist) and Marilyn Ruth (a writer and teacher) Gilbert; married Juliette Gybelle (a graphic designer), June 24, 1995. *Education:* Attended Rutgers College; School of Visual Arts, B.F.A.

■ Addresses

Home—2526 Northwest 194th Pl., Seattle, WA 98177.

■ Career

Animator and designer for Broadcast Arts, NY, 1989-92; illustrator for Our House, NJ, 1992—; Livingbooks Software, San Francisco, CA, senior animator, 1994-95; Broderbund Software, Novato, CA, senior animator, 1994-95. Musician.

■ Awards, Honors

Master Eagle Award.

■ Writings

It's Raining, It's Pouring, Whispering Coyote Press, 1994.
Out of the Night, Whispering Coyote Press, 1995.

Also author of *Hey Diddle Diddle,* 1996.*

*   *   *

GLASS, Andrew

■ Personal

Education: Attended Temple University and School of Visual Arts, New York, NY.

■ Addresses

Home—New York, NY. *Office*—Doubleday & Co., Inc., 1540 Broadway, New York, NY, 10036-4094.

■ Career

Author and illustrator.

■ Awards, Honors

Newbery honor book, American Library Association (ALA), 1983, for *Graven Images: Three Stories,* written by Paul Fleischman and illustrated by Andrew Glass, and 1984, for *The Wish Giver: Three Tales of Coven Tree,* written by William Brittain and illustrated by Glass.

■ Writings

FOR CHILDREN; SELF-ILLUSTRATED

Jackson Makes His Move, Warne (New York City), 1982.
My Brother Tries to Make Me Laugh, Lothrop, 1984.
Chickpea and the Talking Cow, Lothrop, 1987.
Charles T. McBiddle, Doubleday, 1993.
Folks Call Me Appleseed John, Doubleday, 1995.
The Sweetwater Run: The Story of Buffalo Bill Cody and the Pony Express, Doubleday, 1996.

FOLKS CALL ME
APPLESEED JOHN
Andrew Glass

Glass tells of the legendary Johnny Appleseed and his citified half brother Nathaniel and their adventures in the wilds of Pennsylvania in this self-illustrated work.

ILLUSTRATOR

George E. Stanley, *Crime Lab*, Avon Books, 1980.
Nancy Etchemendy, *The Watchers of Space*, Avon, 1980.
Bill Brittain, *Devil's Donkey*, Harper, 1981.
Catherine E. Sadler, adapter, *The Adventures of Sherlock Holmes* (4 volumes), Avon, 1981.
Elizabeth Charlton, *Terrible Tyrannosaurus*, Elsevier/Nelson, 1981.
Theodore Taylor, *The Battle of Midway Island*, Avon, 1981.
Taylor, *H.M.S. Hood vs. Bismarck: The Battleship Battle*, Avon, 1982.
Robert Newton Peck, *Banjo*, Knopf, 1982.
Natalie Savage Carlson, *Spooky Night*, Lothrop, 1982.
Paul Fleischman, *Graven Images; Three Stories*, Harper, 1982.
Marilyn Singer, *The Fido Frame-Up*, Warne, 1983.
Taylor, *Battle in the English Channel*, Avon, 1983.
Joan Lowery Nixon, *The Gift*, Macmillan, 1983.
Brittain, *The Wish Giver: Three Tales of Coven Tree*, Harper, 1983.
Carlson, *The Ghost in the Lagoon*, Lothrop, 1984.
Singer, *A Nose for Trouble*, Holt, 1985.
Carlson, *Spooky and the Ghost Cat*, Lothrop, 1985.
Carlson, *Spooky and the Wizard's Bats*, Lothrop, 1986.
Singer, *Where There's a Will, There's a Wag*, Holt, 1986.
Brittain, *Dr. Dredd's Wagon of Wonders*, Harper, 1987.
Beverly Major, *Playing Sardines*, Scholastic, Inc., 1988.

Carlson, *Spooky and the Bad Luck Raven*, Lothrop, 1988.
Susan Beth Pfeffer, *Rewind to Yesterday*, Delacorte, 1988.
Pfeffer, *Future Forward*, Delacorte, 1989.
Carlson, *Spooky and the Witch's Goat*, Lothrop, 1989.
Robert D. San Souci, *Larger than Life: John Henry and Other Tall Tales*, Doubleday, 1991.
Brittain, *Professor Popkin's Prodigious Polish*, Harper-Collins, 1991.
David Gifaldi, *Gregory, Maw, and the Mean One*, Clarion, 1992.
Tom Birdseye, reteller, *Soap Soap Don't Forget the Soap: An Appalachian Folktale*, Holiday House, 1993.
Karen Hesse, *Lavender*, Holt, 1993.
Susan Whitcher, *Real Mummies Don't Bleed: Friendly Tales for October Nights*, Farrar, Straus, 1993.
Susan Mathias Smith, *The Booford Summer*, Clarion, 1994.
T. Birdseye and Debbie Holsclaw Birdseye, adapters, *She'll Be Comin' Round the Mountain*, Holiday House, 1994.
Al Carusone, *Don't Open the Door after the Sun Goes Down: Tales of the Real and Unreal*, Clarion, 1994.
Tololwa M. Mollel, reteller, *Ananse's Feast: An Ashanti Tale*, Clarion, 1996.
Whitcher, *The Key to the Cupboard*, Farrar, Straus, 1996.
Emily Herman, *Liza and the Fossil*, Hyperion, 1996.
Bethany Roberts, *Monster Manners: A Guide to Monster Etiquette*, Clarion, 1996.

Also illustrator of *The Glass Ring*, Mary Kennedy, Dandelion Press.

■ Sidelights

A talented artist, Andrew Glass illustrates his own stories as well as those of other authors. In fact, art is so much a part of his life that the first book he authored and illustrated, *Jackson Makes His Move*, features a raccoon artist, rendered by Glass in pencil and watercolor. When Jackson realizes that he is no longer inspired by the country around him, and when he tires of his realistic paintings, he heads for the busy, chaotic city. There, instead of painting what he sees, he paints what he feels. The resulting works are large and abstract. According to Kenneth Marantz of *School Library Journal*, Jackson "helps readers come to grips with some of the rationale of such movements as Abstract Expressionism."

My Brother Tries to Make Me Laugh provides an example of the author-illustrator's whimsical talent. In crayon-colored illustrations, Glass portrays a brother and sister traveling to planet Earth on their spaceship. Odeon, a bright purple alien with a snout and stalk-eyes, attempts to get his sister to laugh to break up the monotony of a long journey. "How could this miss?" asked a critic from the *Bulletin of the Center for Children's Books*.

Glass provided the illustrations for Natalie Savage Carlson's popular read-aloud *Spooky and the Wizard's Bats.*

Another of Glass's works recalls the classic children's story, "Tom Thumb." In *Chickpea and the Talking Cow,* a tiny boy named Chickpea is swallowed up by his father's cow. Despite his misfortune, the boy is determined to make his father rich by speaking from within the cow and tricking the Emperor into thinking that the cow can talk. According to Patricia Dooley in *School Library Journal,* "everyone should enjoy" the book's line and wash illustrations, which are "warm, fuzzy, and light-struck."

Glass adopts a cartoon style, with natural colors and bright blues, to create the illustrations for his retelling, *Folks Call Me Appleseed John.* Narrated by John Chapman (also known as Johnny Appleseed), the book tells of winter travels and adventures. A *Publishers Weekly* critic remarked that the text has a "rough-hewn tone," and that the "homespun, almost unfinished appearance" of the illustrations helps "express a variety of moods."

Glass has illustrated the stories of other authors, including those in the "Spooky" series by Natalie Savage Carlson. Ann F. Flowers in *Horn Book* commented on the variety of techniques that Glass incorporates into his illustrations, dubbing the art in *Spooky and the Ghost Cat* "vibrant" and "textured," while describing the illustrations for *Spooky Night* as "crosshatched" and "shadowy." In a review of *Spooky and the Wizard's Bats,* a *Kirkus Reviews* critic concluded that Glass captured the "essence of . . . Halloween without being trite." Susan H. Patron in *School Library Journal* found the illustrations for the same book to be "dramatic and colorful."

■ Works Cited

Dooley, Patricia, review of *Chickpea and the Talking Cow, School Library Journal,* October, 1987, pp. 111-12.

Flowers, Ann A., review of *Spooky Night, Horn Book,* October, 1982, pp. 508-09.

Flowers, Ann A., review of *Spooky and the Ghost Cat, Horn Book,* March/April, 1986, p. 190.

Review of *Folks Call Me Appleseed John, Publishers Weekly,* July 10, 1995, p. 58.

Marantz, Kenneth, review of *Jackson Makes His Move, School Library Journal,* May, 1982, pp. 52-53.

Review of *My Brother Tries to Make Me Laugh, Bulletin of the Center for Children's Books,* October, 1984, p. 25.

Patron, Susan H., review of *Spooky and the Wizard's Bats, School Library Journal,* December, 1986, p. 81.

Review of *Spooky and the Wizard's Bats, Kirkus Reviews,* September 15, 1986, p. 1443.

■ For More Information See

PERIODICALS

Kirkus Reviews, February 1, 1993, p. 146.
New York Times Book Review, June 5, 1983, p. 34.
Publishers Weekly, October 7, 1996, p.75.
School Library Journal, August, 1995, p. 134.

*   *   *

GOLDMAN, Elizabeth 1949-

■ Personal

Born June 22, 1949, in El Paso, TX; daughter of Allan Edgar (an engineer) and Ruth (a homemaker; maiden name, Farkas) Goldman; married Patrick Lon Clary, August 13, 1983; children: Gabriel Robert Clary, Jacob Ethan Clary. *Education:* Indiana University—Bloomington, B.A., 1971, M.A., 1978; Alliance Francaise (Paris), diploma, 1979; attended Indiana Writers Conference, 1977, 1978. *Politics:* Liberal. *Religion:* Reform Judaism. *Hobbies and other interests:* Gardening, hiking, canoeing.

■ Addresses

Home and office—41 Summer St., Dover, NH 03820.

■ Career

University of New Hampshire, Durham, lecturer, 1991-93; New England College, Portsmouth, NH, lecturer, 1994—; McIntosh College, Dover, NH, lecturer, 1994—; writer. Editor, 1974-78 and 1980-84; book publicist at Oxford University Press, 1984-88. Has also worked as an abstractor/indexer and a secretary; volunteer educator and conductor of poetry workshops; vice president, Temple Israel (Dover, NH), 1995.

■ Awards, Honors

D. J. Bowden Religion Essay Award, 1976; Academy of American Poets' Prize, 1976; *Carolina Quarterly* Poetry Award, 1977; New York State CAPS Poetry fellow, 1984; Seacoast Writers Fiction Prize, 1993.

■ Writings

Believers: Spiritual Leaders of the World, Oxford University Press, 1995.

Also contributor of articles to periodicals, including *Metropolis, Interior Design,* and *Women Artists News;* contributor of poems to *Carolina Quarterly, Hanging Loose Press,* and *Indiana Writes.*

■ Sidelights

Elizabeth Goldman told *SATA:* "I write—every day, if possible—in the converted attic of my house, under the sheltering arms of a giant beech tree. Because my room is at the top of the house, it's very quiet. I like that.

"When I was a child, my father told me that I had a 'guardian angel'—a filmy being who stood directly behind me in everything I did, every waking moment. For years I sat and lay down with a pang of conscience, knowing I was surely crushing an angel. My interest in religion may date to the first questions I asked myself about how angels avoided being squashed.

"I always liked to make things as a child, and when I was old enough to write, I especially loved making stories. When I went off to college, I studied English literature, which I enjoyed immensely. But that question of the angels still plagued me; in fact, I wanted to know not only how angels worked, but how the whole cosmic setup was arranged. I wanted to know the meaning of life. So I went back to school, this time to study religion. My courses didn't address the angel question, but they did show me how studying religion opens the door to the other pressing questions—what are we here for? How shall we live?

"For many years, I worked as a writer in offices in the midwest and New York City. In my free time, I wrote poetry and continued to wonder about the same questions that had always puzzled me. When I had children, I found they had the same questions I did: who are we? Why are we here?

"When the opportunity came my way to write about religion for young people, I jumped at the chance. In writing *Believers,* which is a collection of short biographies, I got to look at how forty-three different people grappled with the pressing questions of human existence. Studying for and writing this book was one of the most exciting times of my life: I felt as though I were in the company of some of the most extraordinary people on earth.

"It would be easy to say that in their company, writing and thinking about their lives, I finally answered my old questions. I didn't, really, though I came to see that I had been asking the wrong questions. The real question, it seems to me, is, why are *you* here—and what is *your* life about? Every religion eventually steers its followers toward that all-important question. I think I know now why our angels are not squashed when we sit or lie down: we *are* those angels.

"I hope that my next book takes me outdoors and into the woods—into my particular heaven. I plan to write about my local landscape, the Great Bay of southern New Hampshire. This is a network of tidal estuaries, rivers, and bays that thread through wetlands, forests, and fields. I want to write about how this landscape came into being and what's happening to it."

*   *   *

GRAVES, Valerie
See BRADLEY, Marion Zimmer

*   *   *

GRAY, Luli 1945-

■ Personal

Born March 4, 1945, in Buenos Aires, Argentina; daughter of George (a lawyer/economist) and Marceline (Gray) Eder. *Education:* Attended Boston University, 1977. *Politics:* None. *Religion:* "Heathen." *Hobbies and other interests:* Cooking, cartooning, travelling, swimming.

■ Addresses

Home and office—204-18 Melville Loop, Chapel Hill, NC 27514. *Agent*—Anne Elizabeth Suter, Gotham Literary Agency, 25 Tudor City Place, New York, NY 10017.

■ Career

Freelance recipe developer, 1987—; writer. Held a variety of jobs, including actress and singer, short order cook, barmaid, housemaid, chef, and caterer. *Member:* International Association of Culinary Professionals, Authors Guild, Authors League of America, North Carolina Writers Network, American Museum of Natural History, Smithsonian Institution.

■ Awards, Honors

American Library Association Notable Book, Best Children's Books of 1995 selection, *Publishers Weekly,* and 100 Titles for Reading and Sharing selection, New York Public Library, all 1995, all for *Falcon's Egg.*

■ Writings

Falcon's Egg, Houghton, 1995.

LULI GRAY

Contributor of articles and recipes to cookbooks and food magazines, including *Weight Watchers* and *Cooking Light.*

■ Work in Progress

Back to Yesterday, a time travel fantasy.

■ Sidelights

Luli Gray is the author of the highly acclaimed children's book *Falcon's Egg,* a tale that blends reality and fantasy while addressing parent-child relationships in a divorced family setting. Born into a family of successful writers, who "write the way that other people eat french fries," as Gray mentioned to Sally Lodge for *Publishers Weekly,* Gray found that facing her family's criticism proved to be more difficult than writing the book itself. "They are very stern critics," the author explained to Lodge, "and love doesn't get in the way."

In *Falcon's Egg,* Gray contrasts the caring and love that eleven-year-old Falcon offers a mysterious egg found in Central Park with the lack of caring and love Falcon receives from her self-absorbed, divorced parents. After the egg eventually hatches and produces a dragon, Falcon tries to keep the mythical creature as a pet. She soon realizes, however, that the dragon must live in its own world. Complimenting Gray's juxtaposition of two worlds, a reviewer in *School Library Journal* stated, "The real world blends well with the fantasy elements as tidbits of lore and locale are woven seamlessly." A critic in *Publishers Weekly* also hailed the author's first children's novel, calling it "an imaginative and meaningful tale, told with flair." The success of the author's debut has inspired her to begin a new novel dealing with time travel. She commented in *Publishers Weekly,* "Realizing that people really like my book is an incredible feeling."

Gray told *SATA:* "I come from a reading, writing, talking family, and have wanted to be a writer for as long as I can remember, but did not begin writing in a disciplined way until 1987. I have led a raggle-taggle life since leaving my husband in 1971, wandering all over Europe and Latin America, working as a barmaid, housemaid, short order cook, receptionist, waitress, actress and singer, restaurant chef, and caterer before settling into food writing. I have always preferred children's books to adult books, and am amazed and delighted to find myself writing them and getting published. I moved to North Carolina in 1995, after fifteen years in New York City, and now live rather quietly with two cats and a pepper plant."

■ Works Cited

Review of *Falcon's Egg, Publishers Weekly,* July 24, 1995, p. 65.
Review of *Falcon's Egg, School Library Journal,* September, 1995, pp. 199-200.
Lodge, Sally, "Flying Starts," *Publishers Weekly,* December 18, 1995, pp. 29-30.

*   *   *

GREENWOOD, Barbara 1940-

■ Personal

Born September 14, 1940, in Toronto, Ontario, Canada; daughter of George A. (a manufacturing jeweler) and Anne (Fisher) Auer; married Robert E. Greenwood (a physicist and professor), July 16, 1966; children: Edward, Martha, Adrienne, Michael. *Education:* Attended Toronto Teachers College, 1960-61; University of Toronto, B.A., 1971. *Religion:* United Church of Canada. *Hobbies and other interests:* Reading, choral singing.

■ Addresses

Home—59 Leacroft Crescent, Don Mills, Ontario, Canada M3B 2G5.

■ Career

Leaside Board of Education, Toronto, Ontario, Canada, classroom teacher, 1961-66; freelance teacher for the gifted, 1975-85; freelance writer, 1980—; freelance creative writing teacher, 1985—. Writer in residence,

BARBARA GREENWOOD

Markham Library System, 1989-90. Member of board of directors, Orpheus Choir of Toronto, 1989-94. *Member:* Writers' Union of Canada, Canadian Society of Children's Authors, Illustrators, and Performers (president, 1985-87).

■ Awards, Honors

Vicky Metcalf Short Story Award, Canadian Authors Association, 1982, for "A Major Resolution"; White Raven Award, International Youth Library, 1992, for *Spy in the Shadows;* Ruth Schwartz Children's Book Award, Ruth Schwartz Foundation, Mr. Christie's Book Award, Canadian Children's Book Centre and Communications Jeunesse, and Information Book Award, Children's Literature Roundtables of Canada, all 1995, all for *A Pioneer Story: The Daily Life of a Canadian Family in 1840; A Pioneer Sampler: The Daily Life of a Pioneer Family in 1840* was chosen a Notable Children's Trade Book in the Field of Social Studies by the Children's Book Council and the National Council for Social Studies, 1996, and named to the Utah Children's Informational Book Award Master List, 1996.

■ Writings

FICTION

A Question of Loyalty, Scholastic Canada, 1984.
Spy in the Shadows, Kids Can Press, 1990.
A Pioneer Story: The Daily Life of a Canadian Family in 1840, illustrated by Heather Collins, Kids Can Press, 1994, revised edition as *A Pioneer Sampler:*

The Daily Life of a Pioneer Family in 1840, Ticknor and Fields, 1995.

NONFICTION

(With Audrey McKim) *Her Special Vision: A Biography of Jean Little,* Irwin, 1987.

Jeanne Sauve, Fitzhenry & Whiteside, 1989.

Klondike Challenge: Rachel Hanna, Frontier Nurse, Grolier, 1990.

(With Patricia Hancock) *The Other Side of the Story,* Scholastic Canada, 1990.

(With husband, Bob Greenwood) *Speak Up! Speak Out!: A Kid's Guide to Public Speaking,* illustrated by Graham Pilsworth, Pembroke, 1994.

Canada: A Child's Guide to the Provinces and Territories, illustrated by Jock McRae, Kids Can Press, 1997.

Pioneer Crafts, illustrated by Heather Collins, Kids Can Press, 1997.

EDITOR

Presenting ... Children's Author's, Illustrators, and Performers, Pembroke Publishers, 1990.

The CANSCAIP Companion, Pembroke Publishers, 1994.

Behind the Story: The People Who Create Our Best Children's Books and How They Do It, Pembroke Publishers, 1995.

OTHER

Also author of articles and short stories appearing in educational anthologies, including *Contexts I,* Nelson Canada, 1981; editor of the *Canadian Society of Children's Authors, Illustrators, and Performers News;* contributor of a monthly column to *City Parent Magazine.*

■ Work in Progress

Books on the Underground Railroad and the Klondike Gold Rush.

■ Sidelights

Barbara Greenwood is the author of several children's books which explore the lives of Canadian settlers in the 1800s. As a child, Greenwood enjoyed reading books set in the past, yet by the time she was a teenager, as she once told *Canadian Children's Literature,* she realized that "one place I never found myself on these story-trips was in Canada's past." Hoping to expose young readers to the rich and varied experiences of Canada's past, Greenwood began searching for information about the lives of important historical figures about which children would be interested in reading. The result of that research was *A Question of Loyalty,* a book about the Mackenzie Rebellion in 1837 when an armed group of Canadian farmers and mechanics led by William Lyon Mackenzie began an unsuccessful rebellion against British colonial rule.

In her 1994 book, *A Pioneer Story: The Daily Life of a Canadian Family in 1840,* Greenwood continued to write about Canada's past, this time focusing on the everyday life of settlers in the mid-1800s. By following the events of a fictional pioneer family, Greenwood carefully recreates what life was like in a pioneer household and explains how settlers farmed, went to school, and made everything they needed, including butter, maple sugar, and candles. Calling it "an ideal book for all Canadian schools and libraries," Ken Setterington, writing in *Quill & Quire,* praised Greenwood for her skill in weaving factual information into her narrative.

In 1995 Greenwood modified *A Pioneer Story: The Daily Life of a Canadian Family in 1840* to fit an American audience, calling the new work *A Pioneer Sampler: The Daily Life of a Pioneer Family in 1840.* Again, Greenwood blends fictional narratives with historical information to illustrate how settlers lived in the mid-1800s, creating an engaging story about pioneer life. Greenwood covers a wide range of pioneer activities and daily chores, including making cheese, building a house, and dyeing wool, and then provides instructions for activities that readers can try on their own, like making ink, toys, and honey butter. A critic in *Publishers Weekly* applauded Greenwood's narrative passages, saying they "convey a lively sense of character and place." For schools and libraries in need of books about pioneer life, Elaine Fort Weischedel in *School Library Journal* recommended *A Pioneer Sampler,* saying it is "a welcome and useful addition" for children interested in the subject.

Greenwood told *SATA:* "I have always loved the feeling of sinking into a story, living in its world, becoming in my imagination each of the characters in turn. I was quite young when my voyages into stories also became voyages into the past. I traveled from the worlds of

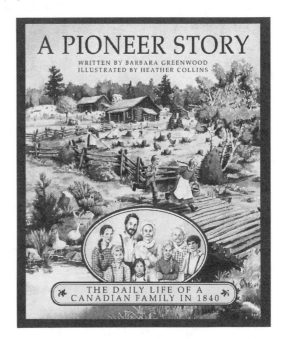

Greenwood blends historical fact with fiction, entertaining her readers while providing insight into the lives of Canada's early pioneers.

Heidi and *The Secret Garden* back through adventures in Elizabethan England, Roman England, and ancient Egypt. Through stories, those times became as real for me as my own home, neighborhood, and classroom. I was about twelve before I realized that I wanted to be in charge of the time travel ship—not just experience adventures in books but actually write my own. And although my earliest adventures in books were based on ones I'd read, I soon realized that I wanted to write about life as it was lived long ago in my neighborhood. That impulse led me to the reference library and many fascinating diaries and letter collections by early settlers. I have been intrigued by and writing about pioneer life ever since."

■ Works Cited

Greenwood, Barbara, remarks in *Canadian Children's Literature*, Number 48, 1987, pp. 66-68.
Review of *A Pioneer Sampler: The Daily Life of a Pioneer Family in 1840, Publishers Weekly,* January 16, 1995, p. 455.

Setterington, Ken, review of *A Pioneer Story: The Daily Life of a Canadian Family in 1840, Quill & Quire,* September, 1994, p. 74.
Weischedel, Elaine Fort, review of *A Pioneer Sampler: The Daily Life of a Pioneer Family in 1840, School Library Journal,* April, 1995, p. 142.

■ For More Information See

PERIODICALS

Booklist, April 1, 1995, p. 1390.
Books for Young People, April, 1988, p. 7.
Books in Canada, February, 1995, p. 50.
Canadian Children's Literature, number 63, 1991, p. 79; number 78, 1995, p. 83.
Children's Book Review Service, May, 1995, p. 117.
CM: A Reviewing Journal of Canadian Materials for Young People, July, 1988, p. 121; July, 1989, p. 167; November, 1990, p. 276; May, 1991, p. 163; November, 1994, p. 211.
Horn Book, May, 1995, p. 341.
Library Times, September, 1995, p. 48.
New York Times Book Review, June 4, 1995, p. 25.
Quill & Quire, October, 1990, p. 16; June, 1991, p. 27.

H

HARRILL, Ronald 1950-

■ Personal

Born August 31, 1950; married Denise D. Harrill, September, 1985; children: Kenyon, Aaron, Nathan. *Education:* North Carolina A & T State University, B.S., 1973; graduated from the BAI School for Bank Administration, University of Wisconsin, Madison, 1984. *Hobbies and other interests:* Coaching baseball and basketball.

■ Addresses

Office—2311 Holly Lane, Shelby, NC 28150.

■ Career

Author, lecturer, and storyteller. First Union National Bank, Charlotte, NC, began as systems analyst, became assistant vice president, 1978—. Chairman of Financial Committee, Shiloh Baptist Church, Shelby, NC. Has lectured at schools, colleges, universities, churches, and other organizations.

■ Writings

Makeda, Queen of Sheba, illustrated by Derek Shaw Anderson, Winston-Derek, 1994.

■ Work in Progress

A second book about an African queen; a book of fiction on black cowboys.

■ Sidelights

Ronald Harrill told *SATA:* "Why do I write? For the self-fulfillment of doing something that I can do and 'to be all I can be.' I write to provide information and stories for children and their parents about the true history of Africa and the African people; to secure a permanent place in history by having made a positive and notable contribution to the world; to make my children proud of me so that they can take my books to school, read them to their classmates, and say 'This is my dad.'

"How do I find time in my hectic schedule to write books? I believe that people usually find time to do the things that they really want to do in life. If it is important enough, the individual will find time to achieve their goal. When I am writing a book, I try to

RONALD HARRILL

reserve one hour per day to devote to writing. This then requires writing seven days a week, 365 days a year, when I am in a dedicated writing mode. This allows me to set an achievable goal that requires discipline. Some days I write for longer time periods, but the one hour requirement is the daily standard.

"How did I begin writing? I have been a researcher of African history for twenty years and also a lecturer for ten years. I have had the desire to write for a long time, but only after visiting public schools over the last eight years did I decide to write books for children. After so many requests from students to 'turn my stories into books for them,' I decided to write children's books. The students that I have visited with over the years are a major reason for my writing children's books. Their constant encouragement and feedback is very valuable to me.

"What other books or publications am I working on? I have completed my second children's book that also covers the life of another African queen. I do not have a predicted publishing date but I am very pleased with the manuscript. The research for my second book required traveling to West Africa, and that was a wonderful experience. My third book, which I am currently working on, will be my first attempt at fiction. This book involves the life and stories of black cowboys in the Old West. I finished the first draft of this book in 1984 and now I want to finish it for publication. Being a historian, I have a large inventory of stories that I would like to write on in the future. My only problem will be the selection of ones to write about from my inventory."*

* * *

HARRIS, Robie H. 1940-

■ Personal

Born April 3, 1940, in Buffalo, NY; daughter of Norman (a physician) and Evelyn (a biologist and homemaker; maiden name, Levy) Heilbrun; married William W. Harris (a lobbyist), September 7, 1968; children: Ben, David. *Education:* Wheaton College, B.A., 1962; Bank Street College of Education, M.A.T., 1970. *Politics:* Democrat. *Religion:* Jewish. *Hobbies and other interests:* Biking, hiking, reading, listening to jazz and rock and roll.

■ Addresses

Home—6 Longfellow Park, Cambridge, MA 02138. *Office*—80 Trowbridge St., Cambridge, MA 02138. *Agent*—Elaine Markson, Elaine Markson Agency, New York, NY 10011.

■ Career

Freelance writer, 1975—. Taught at Bank Street College of Education's School for Children and in public schools for several years; has also worked in film and television,

ROBIE H. HARRIS

designed parks for children, and served as a consultant to the Children's Museum in Boston. *Member:* Planned Parenthood Federation of America (member of board of advocates), Planned Parenthood League of Massachusetts (advisory board member), Boston City Hospital Reach Out & Read Program (advisory board member).

■ Awards, Honors

Outstanding Science Trade Book citation, National Science Teacher's Association and Children's Book Council, for *Before You Were Three: How You Began to Walk, Talk, Explore, and Have Feelings; Rosie's Double Dare* and *I Hate Kisses* were named Children's Choice books, International Reading Association and Children's Book Council; Notable Children's Book selection, American Library Association, Editor's Choice, *Booklist,* Blue Ribbon winner, *Bulletin of the Center for Children's Books,* Reading Magic Award, *Parenting* magazine, and *Boston Globe—Horn Book* Honor Award winner, all for *It's Perfectly Normal: Changing Bodies, Growing Up, Sex, and Sexual Health.*

■ Writings

NONFICTION

(With Elizabeth Levy) *Before You Were Three: How You Began to Walk, Talk, Explore, and Have Feelings,* photographs by Henry Gordillo, Delacorte, 1977.

It's Perfectly Normal: Changing Bodies, Growing Up, Sex, and Sexual Health, illustrated by Michael Emberley, Candlewick Press, 1994.
Let's Talk about Sex, illustrated by Michael Emberley, Walker, 1994.

FICTION

Don't Forget to Come Back, illustrated by Tony de Luna, Knopf, 1978.
Rosie's Double Dare, illustrated by Tony de Luna, Knopf, 1980.
I Hate Kisses, illustrated by Diane Paterson, Knopf, 1981.
Rosie's Razzle Dazzle Deal, Knopf, 1982.
Hot Henry, illustrated by Nicole Hollander, St. Martin's, 1987.
Messy Jessie, illustrated by Nicole Hollander, St. Martin's, 1987.
Rosie's Rock 'n' Roll Riot, Minstrel Books, 1990.
Rosie's Secret Spell, Minstrel Books, 1991.
Happy Birth Day!, illustrated by Michael Emberley, Candlewick Press, 1996.

■ Sidelights

In both her nonfiction books for young adults and her picture books for children, Robie H. Harris deals with the changes and challenges that concern young people in a realistic and understanding way. Her first published book was 1977's *Before You Were Three: How You Began to Walk, Talk, Explore, and Have Feelings,* which is intended to help middle-grade readers remember and appreciate how much they learned and how amazing they are—since the moment of birth and in the first years of life. The book follows two children, Tommy and Hillary, from the time that they first enter the world until they learn to walk and talk. It includes over one hundred black-and-white photographs depicting children at different stages of early development. Though one critic found *Before You Were Three* a bit too complex for its intended audience, a reviewer in *Appraisal* noted that "parents may find this a useful book to share with their children, especially to help explain behavior of a younger brother or sister."

Harris's first picture book, *Don't Forget to Come Back,* provides an honest and straightforward look at a problem common to children. Little Annie becomes terribly upset when her mother tells her that she is going out for the evening, so Annie will be staying at home with a babysitter. Because she does not want her parents to leave without her, Annie tries every conceivable tactic to disrupt their plans. For example, she packs up her things in order to go with them, pretends that she has an upset stomach, refuses to let her parents leave until they find her lost blanket, hides, and has a temper tantrum. But Annie's parents cope with her not wanting them to leave patiently and firmly, and she finally realizes that staying home with the babysitter will not be so bad after all. Writing in *School Library Journal,* Joan W. Blos stated that "reading this story aloud together might engender useful discussions" in families where leaving a child with a sitter has become a problem.

Harris presents another typical toddler in *Hot Henry.* On a cold and snowy day, Henry's parents bundle him up in warm clothes to take him to a party. Before long he feels too hot standing in the hallway in his winter clothes. Henry removes his snowsuit, hat, and other garments, throws them on the floor, and decides that he will dress himself. Though he ends up wearing his shirt like a pair of pants and puts his mittens on his feet, the result is just as warm as before. Since his parents do not have time to start all over again, they allow Henry to go to the party in his mixed-up attire. A contributor in *Kirkus Reviews* called *Hot Henry* "a lighthearted look at toddler life."

Harris's next picture book, *Messy Jessie,* also features a typical toddler. Jessie loves making a mess out of whatever she can find. When she sits at the kitchen table and draws a picture, for example, she ends up drawing all over the table and herself. Later she accidentally drops an egg from the refrigerator, and in characteristic toddler fashion she adds catsup, mustard, and milk to make an even bigger mess. After she has delighted in making messes throughout the house, Jessie's father finally cleans her up and puts her to bed. A critic in *Kirkus Reviews* noted that the story of *Messy Jessie* "will appeal to toddlers and preschoolers who are testing the limits of the adult world."

Harris returned to writing nonfiction in 1994 with the award-winning *It's Perfectly Normal: Changing Bodies, Growing Up, Sex, and Sexual Health.* In this work, Harris provides a straightforward, wide-ranging guide intended to help readers in their early teens understand the various aspects of their own sexuality. It includes seven sections on basic topics like the male and female anatomy, the changes that take place during puberty, and the specifics of sexual intercourse. It also provides a balanced viewpoint on issues like teen parenthood, abortion, sexually transmitted diseases, and homosexuality. The book maintains a lighthearted tone with the help of numerous cartoon-like diagrams by illustrator Michael Emberley. Two tiny cartoon characters—an open-minded, curious bird and a reluctant, embarrassed bee—appear frequently and add amusing commentary to the text.

"Naked human bodies appear throughout the book in a reassuring variety of sizes, shapes, colors, and sexes," according to Deborah Stevenson in *Bulletin of the Center for Children's Books,* helping to make *It's Perfectly Normal* "one of the most unintimidating and informative sex books to come along for this age group." Writing in *School Library Journal,* Virginia E. Jeschelnig noted that "what it offers in scope, currency, and a cheerfully engaging format is quite special" and should allow readers to gain "a healthy respect for their bodies and a better understanding of the role that sexuality plays in the human experience." A reviewer in *Horn Book* added that the book seemed likely to "raise eyebrows, produce giggles, and arm younger readers with all the information they need to understand their developing bodies and to stay healthy."

Harris and Emberley collaborated on a later work, *Happy Birth Day!*, which looks at the first day in the life of a newborn baby girl. Harris captures such moments as the baby's first cry, the cutting of the umbilical cord, and the mother nursing her child. In a *Booklist* interview with Stephanie Zvirin, Harris described how Emberley—who has no children—and she witnessed an actual birth while researching the book: "We were on call for three days at Boston City Hospital. After the birth, we spent time with the mother and her baby so Michael could see how alert and active and sleepy a baby is during the first day." *Happy Birth Day!* has received several positive reviews. A contributor in *Publishers Weekly* stated that "tenderness flows like a current throughout the warmhearted prose," and Zvirin, in her *Booklist* review, added that the story is "full of the universal wonder of new life and the quiet drama of family bonding."

Harris told *SATA:* "I am writing nonfiction again as exemplified by the recent publication of *It's Perfectly Normal* and *Happy Birth Day!* In writing both of these books, two techniques—consultations with and teaching from experts in the field, and close collaboration with the illustrator Michael Emberley—have been a major part of the writing process.

"One of the rewards of writing nonfiction is how much I've learned from others. During the writing of *It's Perfectly Normal,* I met with HIV and AIDS experts numerous times to learn as much as I could about the virus. After I had written the HIV and AIDS chapter, I again met with these experts and others to make sure that the science and my 'writing' of the science was as up-to-date and accurate as possible. I then met with parents, teens, teachers, librarians, pediatricians, and other health professionals to make sure that what I had to say was also psychologically appropriate and useful for kids and teens.

"I first began to work in a collaborative manner in the 1960s when I was a member of the Bank Street College of Education's Writing Laboratory. It was there I learned to work with other writers, to show my text to them, to 'grin and bear it' when I heard their criticism, and then make the tough decisions about what to do next. It was there I learned that 'the final word' was my decision and that I bore responsibility for my words. This is a model I have used throughout my writing career.

"So as I continue to create nonfiction books for children, I try to keep in mind, what do kids want to know, what do they need to know, what would be fascinating and fun to know—and what would be fun and fascination for me to learn and write about."

■ Works Cited

Review of *Before You Were Three: How You Began to Walk, Talk, Explore, and Have Feelings, Appraisal,* spring, 1978.

Blos, Joan W., review of *Don't Forget to Come Back, School Library Journal,* December, 1978, p. 44.
Review of *Happy Birth Day!, Publishers Weekly,* June 17, 1996.
Harris, Robie, interview with Stephanie Zvirin, *Booklist,* May 1, 1996, p. 1495.
Review of *Hot Henry* and *Messy Jessie, Kirkus Reviews,* December 1, 1987, p. 1674.
Review of *It's Perfectly Normal: Changing Bodies, Growing Up, Sex, and Sexual Health, Horn Book,* March, 1995, p. 214.
Jeschelnig, Virginia E., review of *It's Perfectly Normal, School Library Journal,* December, 1994, p. 123.
Stevenson, Deborah, "The Big Picture," *Bulletin of the Center for Children's Books,* October, 1994, p. 35.
Zvirin, Stephanie, review of *Happy Birth Day!, Booklist,* May 1, 1996, p. 1502.

■ For More Information See

PERIODICALS

Appraisal, spring, 1995, p. 28.
Bulletin of the Center for Children's Books, November, 1981, p. 46; July/August, 1996, pp. 374-75.
Kirkus Reviews, November 15, 1978, p. 1241; October 15, 1981, p. 1291.
Magpies, September, 1996, p. 28.
New York Times Book Review, June 12, 1977, p. 31; March 12, 1995, p. 20.
Publishers Weekly, October 23, 1978, p.61; October 30, 1987, p. 69; July 18, 1994.
School Library Journal, September, 1977, p.129; February, 1988, p. 61.

*   *   *

HATCH, Lynda S. 1950-

■ Personal

Born February 19, 1950, in Portland, OR; daughter of Marley E. (owner of a meat market) and Undine S. (a teacher; maiden name, Crockard) Sims. *Education:* Attended University of Oregon, 1968-70; Washington State University, B.A., 1972; Portland State University, M.S., 1975; Oregon State University, Ed.D., 1984. *Politics:* Democrat. *Religion:* Protestant. *Hobbies and other interests:* Photographing and researching emigrant trails, cross-country skiing, hiking, canoeing, crafts, gardening, traveling, cooking, reading.

■ Addresses

Office—Center for Excellence in Education, Northern Arizona University, P.O. Box 5774, Flagstaff, AZ 86011-5774. *Electronic mail*—Lynda.Hatch@nau.edu.

■ Career

Clover Park School District #400, Tacoma, WA, teacher, 1971-72; Hillsboro Elementary District #7, Hillsboro, OR, teacher, 1972-78; Bend-La Pine Public Schools, Bend, OR, teacher and elementary curriculum

LYNDA S. HATCH

specialist, 1978-90; Northern Arizona University, Flagstaff, associate professor and coordinator of elementary education, 1990—. Adjunct professor at Oregon State University, Portland State University, and the University of Oregon; served on the Committee on the Supervision of Science Teaching Education, National Science Teachers Association, 1995—; consultant in science, math, and language arts to schools around the United States. Selected as a GEMS (Great Explorations in Math and Science) Associate, Lawrence Hall of Science, University of California, Berkeley, 1994, and for international workshop presentations in Russia, Canada, Mexico, Jamaica, and the United States, National Science Teachers Association, 1991-95; presents workshops and lectures on education, the Oregon Trail, bookbinding, Russian culture, and other topics. Docent, Museum of Northern Arizona, Flagstaff; member of board of directors, Council for Elementary Science International, and at the Arboretum at Flagstaff; member of the Christian Education Commission, First Congregational Church, Flagstaff. *Member:* International Reading Association, Council for Elementary Science International (council member, 1995—), National State Teachers of the Year (national president, 1988-90; member, Past Presidents Council, 1995—), National Education Association, National Council for the Social Studies, National Science Teachers Association, National Council of Teachers of Mathematics, Phi Delta

Kappa, Kappa Delta Pi (National State Teachers of the Year chapter), Delta Kappa Gamma, Golden Key National Honor Society; also member of teacher-related organizations in Arizona and Oregon.

■ Awards, Honors

Oregon Teacher of the Year, 1982; Excellence in Teaching Awards, Bend Foundation, Bend, OR, 1985-87; U.S. Professor of the Year, Center for Excellence in Education and Northern Arizona University, 1994; Celebration of Teaching grants, Geraldine Rockefeller Dodge Foundation, 1989-94; grants from the Center for Excellence in Education, Office of Cultural Diversity in America, 1994-96.

■ Writings

"PATHWAYS OF AMERICA" SERIES

The Oregon Trail, illustrated by Ted Warren, Good Apple, 1994.
Lewis and Clark, illustrated by Ted Warren, Good Apple, 1994.
The California Gold Rush Trail, illustrated by Kathryn R. Marlin, Good Apple, 1994.
The Santa Fe Trail, Good Apple, 1995.

OTHER

Fifty States, Instructional Fair/T. S. Denison, 1996.
American Presidents, Instructional Fair/T. S. Denison, 1996.
Reading Maps, Instructional Fair/T. S. Denison, 1996.

Also author of *Tools for Teachers: Teaching Curriculum for Home and the Classroom* (nine guides), Northland, 1994-96, and contributing author for *Substitute Teaching Handbook,* Kappa Delta Pi; reviewer for *Science Books and Films, Teaching Children Mathematics,* and *Science in Our Parks* (curriculum developed for the Petrified Forest National Park); contributor of articles to *Teacher, Childhood Education, Elementary English, Science and Children, New Teacher Advocate,* and other teacher-related publications.

■ Work in Progress

The California Missions, a "Pathways of America" book; editing a collection of stories from the National State Teachers of the Year.

■ Sidelights

Lynda S. Hatch told *SATA:* "My 'Pathways of America' series grew out of my love of teaching history, of family stories, and from developing curriculum for my fourth grade students.

"When I was a third grade student in Eugene, Oregon, I was in a 'combination classroom' along with fourth graders. The most enjoyable part of the day was listening across the room to the fourth grade lessons on pioneers, their Oregon history social studies. Then when I was finally a fourth grader, the state of Oregon celebrated its centennial. The year was devoted to studying state history and was full of pageants, songs, and festivals. Eventually, I became a fourth grade teacher in Bend, Oregon, at Bear Creek School, where state history and geography was still the year-long social studies curriculum. This curriculum development provided the perfect 'excuse' to spend part of ten summers reading, photographing, and traveling the Oregon Trail from Missouri to Oregon. The curriculum I developed led to my first book, *Pathways to America: The Oregon Trail,* completed during 1993, the sesquicentennial of the Oregon Trail emigration. The fourth grade curriculum and travels also led to my second book, *Pathways of America: Lewis and Clark.*

"In addition to curriculum development, my interest in emigrant trails stemmed from family stories of relatives who made their way across the continent. On my father's side of the family, Nathaniel Green McDonald and Rebecca Jane Munkers traveled by covered wagon to Oregon's Willamette Valley on the Oregon Trail in 1846. We have a small booklet that tells the story of their travels and settlement. On my mother's side of the family, the Oldfields traveled from England to Utah, and then to California in 1855. This side of the family inspired my third book, *Pathways of America: The California Gold Rush Trail.* The fourth book, *Pathways of America: The Santa Fe Trail,* took a great deal of research. Since I had moved to the Southwest, it made travel to the routes and sites much more convenient. In addition, a fifth book on the California missions has also been written.

"Writing these books has been important to me because quality curriculum hasn't always been available to teachers and children. Historical topics often have conflicting 'facts,' unfortunate stereotypes, and unclear conclusions. Hopefully, my extensive research and travels have made the books as accurate and fair as possible. Also, curriculum activities should not belittle children, so I enjoyed choosing the activities that accompanied the information about the sites along the trail.

"In addition to studying and writing about emigrant trails, I teach in Flagstaff at Northern Arizona University's Center for Excellence in Education. I teach elementary science methods courses in a cohort team where we prepare future teachers to teach math, science, and social studies. Field work experiences are in Leupp, Arizona, on the Navajo Nation. I also work as a docent at the Museum of Northern Arizona and serve on the Board of Directors at the Arboretum at Flagstaff, the highest elevation botanic garden in the United States. I am active in many professional organizations and do consulting work across the country and in Canada, Mexico, Russia, and Jamaica."

HAUSMAN, Gerald 1945-
(Gerry Hausman)

■ Personal

Born October 3, 1945, in Baltimore, MD; son of Sidney (an engineer) and Dorothy (Little) Hausman; married Lorry Wright (a publicity director), June, 1968; children: Mariah Fox, Hannah. *Education:* New Mexico Highlands University, B.A., 1968. *Hobbies and other interests:* Swimming, jogging, reading, observing animals.

■ Addresses

Home—12699 Christi Way, Bokeelia, FL 33922. *Electronic Mail*—104053.747@compuserve.com.

■ Career

Writer, 1968—; poetry teacher in Lenox, MA, 1969-72; Bookstore Press, Lenox, editor, 1972-77; Sunstone Press, Santa Fe, NM, vice-president, 1979-83; Santa Fe Preparatory School, Santa Fe, teacher of English, 1983-87. Poet-in-residence in public schools, 1970-76, and at Central Connecticut State College, 1973. *Member:* Authors Guild, Authors League of America, Poets and Writers.

■ Awards, Honors

Wilderness was named a "Book for the Teen Age," New York City Public Librarians, 1995; Aesop Accolade

GERALD HAUSMAN

Award, American Folklore Society, 1995, for *Duppy Talk: West Indian Tales of Mystery and Magic.*

■ Writings

(With David Kherdian) *Eight Poems,* Giligia Press, 1968.

(Editor) *Shivurrus Plant of Mopant and Other Children's Poems,* Giligia Press, 1968.

New Marlboro Stage, Giligia Press, 1969.

(Editor with David Silverstein) *The Berkshire Anthology,* Bookstore Press, 1972.

Circle Meadow, illustrated by Bob Totten, Bookstore Press, 1972.

The Boy with the Sun Tree Bow, Berkshire Traveller Press, 1973.

Beth: The Little Girl of the Pine Knoll, Bookstore Press, 1974.

Sitting on the Blue-Eyed Bear: Navajo Myths and Legends, Lawrence Hill, 1975.

(Under name Gerry Hausman with wife, Lorry Hausman) *The Pancake Book,* Persea Books, 1976.

The Day the White Whales Came to Bangor, Cobblesmith Books, 1977.

(With Alice Winston) *The Atlantic Salmon,* Cobblesmith Books, 1977.

(Under name Gerry Hausman with wife, Lorry Hausman) *The Yogurt Book,* Persea Books, 1977.

Night Herding Song, Copper Canyon Press, 1979.

No Witness, Stackpole, 1980.

Runners, Sunstone Press, 1984.

Meditations with Animals: A Native American Bestiary ("Meditations With" series), illustrated by Liese J. Scott, Bear & Co., 1986.

Meditations with the Navajo: Prayer-Songs and Stories of Healing and Harmony ("Meditations With" series), Bear & Co., 1988.

Stargazer ("Stargazer Trilogy" series), Lotus Light, 1989.

Turtle Dream, Mariposa, 1989.

Ghost Walk: Native American Tales of the Spirit, illustrated by Sid Hausman, Mariposa, 1991.

Native American Animal Stories, Sunset Productions, 1992.

Navajo Nights, Sunset Productions, 1992.

The Sun Horse: Native Visions of the New World, Lotus Light, 1992.

Turtle Island Alphabet: A Lexicon of Native American Symbols and Culture, St. Martin's, 1992.

Coyote Walks on Two Legs, illustrated by Floyd Cooper, Philomel, 1993.

The Gift of the Gila Monster: Navajo Ceremonial Tales, Simon & Schuster, 1993.

Duppy Talk: West Indian Tales of Mystery and Magic, illustrated by Cheryl Taylor, Simon & Schuster, 1994.

Tunkashila: From the Birth of Turtle Island to the Blood of Wounded Knee, St. Martin's, 1994.

(With Roger Zelazny) *Wilderness,* Forge, 1994.

Turtle Island ABC: A Gathering of Native American Symbols, illustrated by Cara and Barry Moser, HarperCollins, 1994.

Doctor Moledinky's Castle: A Hometown Tale, Simon & Schuster, 1995.

How Chipmunk Got Tiny Feet: Native American Animal Origin Stories, illustrated by Ashley Wolff, HarperCollins, 1995.

(Editor) Edward S. Curtis, *Prayer to the Great Mystery: The Uncollected Writings and Photography of Edward S. Curtis,* St. Martin's, 1995.

(With Kevin Rodriques) *African-American Alphabet: A Celebration of African-American and West Indian Culture, Custom, Myth, and Symbol,* St. Martin's, 1996.

Eagle Boy: A Traditional Navajo Legend, illustrated by Barry and Cara Moser, HarperCollins, 1996.

Night Flight, Putnam, 1996.

(With wife, Loretta Hausman) *The Mythology of Dogs: The Legend and Lore of 75 Major Breeds,* St. Martin's, 1997.

Contributor to anthologies, including *Contemporaries: 28 New American Poets,* Viking; *Desert Review Anthology,* Desert Review Press; and *Poetry Here and Now,* edited by David Kherdian, Morrow. Some of Hausman's work has been recorded on audio cassette and released by Sunset Productions, including *Navajo Nights,* 1987, *Stargazer,* 1989, *Native American Animal Stories,* 1990, and *Ghost Walk,* 1991.

■ Work in Progress

Rastafarian Tales.

■ Sidelights

As a college student in New Mexico, author and poet Gerald Hausman became interested in Native American mythology while living and working with the Navajo. As a result of this close interaction with the Navajo and many other native peoples, Hausman began writing books about traditional Indian myths and customs, including *Turtle Island Alphabet: A Lexicon of Native American Symbols and Culture.*

Naming his book after the Indian term for the earth, "turtle island," Hausman presents the historical, cultural, and spiritual significance of over fifty Indian objects, artifacts, and rituals in *Turtle Island Alphabet.* In a series of essays, Hausman records how Native Americans passed on important sacred images in their culture, such as beads, arrows, and totem poles, through the art of storytelling. "Fascinating and poetically written" is how Pat Monaghan describes *Turtle Island Alphabet* in *Booklist.* Mongahan adds that Hausman, unlike many other writers, "avoids the inverse racism of romanticism" by mixing essays about ancient rituals with conversations with contemporary Native Americans. Writing in *Library Journal,* Bruce Alan Hanson calls the collection "a sensitive examination," while Margaret Tice, in *School Library Journal,* feels the book "is quite readable."

Not limiting his research of ancient myths to North America, Hausman also explored the Caribbean in search of legends and returned with *Duppy Talk: West Indian Tales of Mystery and Magic.* Hausman retells six Jamaican ghost stories whose roots trace back to Africa, carried by the men and women who arrived in slave ships. Winning an Aesop Accolade Award in 1995, *Duppy Talk* features spine-tingling tales of duppies, a Jamaican word for ghosts, who reward men and women for their good deeds but play tricks on those who are evil. Susan Scheps, writing in *School Library Journal,* applauds the "informative" notes and an expansive glossary which explains some of the unfamiliar Jamaican vocabulary and expressions.

Turtle Island ABC: A Gathering of Native American Symbols, a 1994 work, gives children an introduction to the alphabet while relating the letters to Native American life. Hausman goes through every letter of the alphabet and picks a term important to Indian culture, explaining why words like corn, buffalo, and wolf have special meaning among the native peoples. Lisa Mitten in *School Library Journal* commends Hausman's technique and notes that "the text flows like poetry." However, in the *Bulletin of the Center for Children's Books,* reviewer Roger Sutton criticizes Hausman's blending of many different Native American tribal beliefs into one book, asserting that Hausman thus

I am the KACHINA, made from the branch of a cottonwood tree. ❖ Long ago, The People lived in the underworld, which is the belly of the earth. The kachinas lived with them there and taught them many things. The kachinas taught The People how to live, how to be thankful for all that is good. And The People never forgot. That is why they still carve kachina dolls out of wood and give them to their children. ❖ I am the kachina, made from the branch of a cottonwood tree.

In Hausman's *Turtle Island ABC,* Cara and Barry Moser illustrate Native American symbols that represent the traditions of The People, the original inhabitants of North America.

implies that diverse tribes share all of the same traditions.

Continuing with his fascination and appreciation of American Indian culture, Hausman wrote *How Chipmunk Got Tiny Feet: Native American Origin Stories* to share with children some of the traditional animal tales of the Navajo, Koasati Creek, and Tsimshian tribes. In *How Chipmunk Got Tiny Feet,* Hausman retells Native American explanations of why crickets chirp, horses run fast, and skunks have long furry tails. In addition, each story offers children a lesson about human behavior and how to cooperate with others. Calling the picture book "a standout in an increasingly crowded genre," a critic writing in *Publishers Weekly* praises Hausman's "casual and unpretentious tone." In *School Library Journal,* Beth Tegart suggests that the attraction of *How the Chipmunk Got Tiny Feet* comes from the "light approach, humorous tone, and authentic style" Hausman takes in this work.

■ Works Cited

Hanson, Bruce Alan, review of *Turtle Island Alphabet: A Lexicon of Native American Symbols and Culture, Library Journal,* March 15, 1992, p. 94.

Review of *How Chipmunk Got Tiny Feet: Native American Animal Origin Stories, Publishers Weekly,* May 29, 1995, p. 84.

Mitten, Lisa, review of *Turtle Island ABC: A Gathering of Native American Symbols and Culture, School Library Journal,* July, 1994, p. 94.

Monaghan, Pat, review of *Turtle Island Alphabet: A Lexicon of Native American Symbols and Culture, Booklist,* March 15, 1992, p. 1320.

Scheps, Susan, review of *Duppy Talk: West Indian Tales of Mystery and Magic, School Library Journal,* January, 1995, p. 118.

Sutton, Roger, review of *Turtle Island ABC: A Gathering of Native American Symbols, Bulletin of the Center for Children's Books,* April, 1994, p. 260.

Tegart, Beth, review of *How the Chipmunk Got Tiny Feet: Native American Origin Stories, School Library Journal,* June, 1995, p. 102.

Tice, Margaret, review of *Turtle Island Alphabet: A Lexicon of Native American Symbols and Culture, School Library Journal,* November, 1992, p. 137.

■ For More Information See

PERIODICALS

Booklist, February 15, 1993, pp. 1014, 1044; September 15, 1993, pp. 118, 139; July, 1994, p. 1965; January 15, 1995, p. 918; April 1, 1995, p. 1421; September 1, 1995, p. 68.

Children's Book Review Service, April, 1995, p. 99.

Horn Book, fall, 1994, p. 400; spring, 1995, p. 106.

Library Journal, November 15, 1992, p. 120; October 15, 1993, p. 70; November, 1994, p. 37.

Locus, fall, 1989, p. 49.

New York Times Book Review, November 21, 1993, p. 26.

Publishers Weekly, December 8, 1989, p. 56; February
   10, 1992, p. 69; January 11, 1993, p. 57; April 5,
   1993, p. 73; August 2, 1993, p. 60; May 9, 1994, p.
   71.
School Library Journal, September, 1992, p. 188; June,
   1995, p. 102; August, 1995, p. 122.

*   *   *

HAUSMAN, Gerry
See HAUSMAN, Gerald

*   *   *

HAZEN, Barbara Shook 1930-

■ Personal

Born February 4, 1930, in Dayton, OH; daughter of
Charles Harmon (a contractor and engineer) and Eliza-
beth (Foster) Shook; married Freeman Brackett Hazen,
December 27, 1956 (divorced, 1960); children: Freeman
Brackett, Jr. *Education:* Smith College, B.A., 1951;
Columbia University, M.A., 1952. *Politics:* "Varying."
Religion: "Presbyterian and/or eclectic." *Hobbies and
other interests:* "I am a passionate swimmer, traveler,
pizza addict, and also a cat-aholic who is, alas, allergic
to cats"; also a winegrower with two vinerights in
Benmarl Vineyard, Marlboro, NY.

■ Addresses

Home and office—108 East 82nd St., New York, NY
10029; and Box 739, Otis, MA 01253 (summer).

■ Career

Ladies' Home Journal, New York City, editorial assistant in fiction/article department and poetry editor,
1952-56; Western Publishing Co., New York City,
children's book editor, 1956-60; freelance writer,
1960—. Writer on "Andy and the Petbots" and "Kingdom Chums" projects for American Broadcasting Co.
(ABC-TV), 1984-87. Board member of Drama League
of City of New York, 1976—. Consultant to Columbia
Broadcasting System (CBS) children's records, 1968-74,
and *Sesame Street* magazine, 1973-75. *Member:* American Society of Journalists and Authors, Authors League
of America, Authors Guild, Bank Street Writers Lab.

■ Awards, Honors

Christopher Award, 1981, for *Even If I Did Something
Awful;* Children's Choice Award, 1990, for *The Knight
Who Was Afraid of the Dark.*

■ Writings

FOR CHILDREN

Animal Alphabet from A to Z, illustrated by Adele
   Werber, Golden Press, 1958, reprinted, 1976.

BARBARA SHOOK HAZEN

(Adapter) Robert L. May, *Rudolph, the Red-Nosed
   Reindeer,* illustrated by Richard Scarry, Golden
   Press, 1958.
Mister Ed, the Talking Horse, Western Publishing, 1958.
The Lion's Nap, Western Publishing, 1958.
Animal Daddies and My Daddy, Western Publishing,
   1962.
A Visit to the Children's Zoo, illustrated by Mel Craw-
   ford, Golden Press, 1963.
Playful Puppy, illustrated by Jan Pfloog, Golden Press,
   1967.
*Please Pass the P's and Q's: The Barbara Hazen Book of
   Manners,* illustrated by Mell Lazarus, World Pub-
   lishing, 1967.
*Please Protect the Porcupine: The Barbara Hazen Book
   of Conservation,* illustrated by Lazarus, World Pub-
   lishing, 1967.
David and Goliath, illustrated by Robert J. Lee, Golden
   Press, 1968.
Ookpik in the City, illustrated by Irma Wilde, Golden
   Press, 1968.
What's Inside?, illustrated by Richard Erdoes, Lion
   Pres, 1968.
City Cats, Country Cats, illustrated by Ilse-Margret
   Vogel, Golden Press, 1969.
The Sorcerer's Apprentice, illustrated by Tomi Ungerer,
   Lancelot Press, 1969.
The Tiny, Tawny Kitten, Golden Press, 1969, new
   edition, illustrated by Pfloog, 1975.
Danny Dougal, the Wanting Boy, illustrated by Ken
   Longtemps, Lion Press, 1970.
If I Were, illustrated by Lee Ames, Golden Press, 1970.
Where Do Bears Sleep?, illustrated by Ian E. Staunton,
   Addison-Wesley, 1970.
Girls and Boys Book of Etiquette, illustrated by Nancy
   Sears, Grosset, 1971.

Happy, Sad, Silly, Mad: A Beginning Book about Emotions, illustrated by Elizabeth Dauber, Wonder-Treasure Books, 1971.

Raggedy Ann and the Cookie Snatcher, illustrated by June Goldsborough, Golden Press, 1972.

Frere Jacques, illustrated by Lilian Obligado, Lippincott, 1973.

A Nose for Trouble, illustrated by Tim Hildebrandt and Greg Hildebrandt, Golden Press, 1973.

Raggedy Ann and Andy and the Rainy Day Circus, Golden Press, 1973.

Animal Manners, illustrated by Leonard Shortall, Golden Press, 1974.

The Gorilla Did It, illustrated by Ray Cruz, Atheneum, 1974.

(Adapter) *Davy Crockett, Indian Fighter* (from the Walt Disney Production film based on the story by Tom Blackburn), illustrated by Joseph Guarino, Pyramid Communications, 1975.

Me and the Yellow-Eyed Monster, illustrated by Tony De Luna, Me-Books, 1975.

Noah's Ark, Golden Press, 1975.

To Be Me, illustrated by Frances Hook, Child's World, 1975, revised edition published as *I'm Glad to Be Me,* 1979.

Why Couldn't I Be an Only Kid Like You, Wigger, illustrated by Leigh Grant, Atheneum, 1975.

(Editor) *The Golden Happy Birthday Book: Poems, Riddles, Giggles, Magic, Stories, Presents, and Prizes to Make Your Special Day the Happiest Birthday Ever,* illustrated by Rosalyn Schanzer, Golden Press, 1976.

The Ups and Downs of Marvin, illustrated by Richard Cuffari, Atheneum, 1976.

World, World, What Can I Do?, illustrated by Margaret Leibold, Abingdon, 1976.

Amelia's Flying Machine, illustrated by Charles Robinson, Doubleday, 1977.

(Adapter) *Wonderful Wizard of Oz,* illustrated by Eleanor Mill, Golden Press, 1977.

Gorilla Wants to Be the Baby, illustrated by Jacqueline B. Smith, Atheneum, 1978.

The Me I See, illustrated by Ati Forberg, Abingdon, 1978.

Two Homes to Live In: A Child's-Eye View of Divorce, illustrated by Peggy Luks, Human Sciences, 1978.

If It Weren't for Benjamin, I'd Always Get to Lick the Icing Spoon, illustrated by Laura Hartman, Human Sciences, 1979.

Last, First, Middle, and Nick: All about Names, Prentice-Hall, 1979.

Tight Times, illustrated by Trina S. Hyman, Viking, 1979.

Step on It, Andrew, illustrated by Lisl Weil, Atheneum, 1980.

Even If I Did Something Awful, illustrated by Nancy Kincade, Atheneum, 1981.

Very Shy, Human Sciences, 1981.

It's a Shame about the Rain, illustrated by Bernadette Simmons, Human Sciences, 1981.

The Fat Cats, Cousin Scraggs and the Monster Mice, illustrated by Lonni Sue Johnson, Atheneum, 1985.

Learn about Living series (*Why Did Grandpa Die?, Why Are People Different?, Growing up Is Hard Sometimes, Why Can't You Stay Home with Me?, It Isn't Fair,* and *What's Mine Is Mine*), Western Publishing, 1985-86.

(Editor) *Little David's Adventure,* Word Publishing, 1986.

Just Say No, Western Publishing, 1987.

Fang, illustrated by Leslie Morrill, Atheneum, 1987.

Stay, Fang, illustrated by Morrill, Atheneum, 1989.

The Knight Who Was Afraid of the Dark, illustrated by Tony Ross, Dial, 1989.

Wally the Worry-Warthog, illustrated by Janet Stevens, Houghton Mifflin, 1990.

Hello, Gnu, How Are You?, Doubleday, 1990.

Mommy's Office, illustrated by David Soman, Atheneum, 1992.

Alone at Home, illustrated by Irene Trivas, Atheneum, 1992.

The Magic Stick, Newbridge Communications, 1992.

Who Lost a Shoe?, Newbridge Communications, 1992.

Turkey in the Straw, illustrated by Brad Sneed, Dial, 1993.

The Knight Who Was Afraid to Fight, illustrated by Toni Goffe, Dial, 1994.

Count on Bunnies, illustrated by Patrick Girouard, Newbridge Communications, 1994.

Let's Go, illustrated by Girouard, Newbridge Communications, 1994.

Goodbye/Hello (also published in Spanish as *Adios/Hola*), illustrated by Michael Bryant, Atheneum, 1995.

Santa Clues, illustrated by Simon Galkin, Longmeadow, 1995.

Please and Thank You, Western Publishing, 1996.

The New Dog, Dial, 1997.

FOR ADULTS

You and Your Lucky Stars: A Zodiac Guide to Dating, Compatibility, and Personal Characteristics, Golden Press, 1970.

(With others) *Baby's First Six Years,* Golden Press, 1972.

Your Wedding Your Way, Golden Press, 1973.

The Dell Encyclopedia of Cats, illustrated by Roy Wiltshire and Paul Singer, Delacorte, 1974, published as *The Concise Encyclopedia of Cats,* Octopus Books, 1974.

(Editor) *Mothers Are Marvelous,* C. R. Gibson, 1977.

(Editor) *To Be a Friend,* C. R. Gibson, 1977.

(Editor) *A Cat Lover's Cat Book: The Many Delights of Kittens and Cats,* illustrated by Roland Rodegast, C. R. Gibson, 1978.

(Editor) *You Can't Have Sunbeams without Little Specks of Dust: Household Hints, Quotes, and Humorous Anecdotes,* C. R. Gibson, 1980.

Have Yourself a Merry Little Christmas: Hints and Homilies for Happy Holidays, C. R. Gibson, 1980.

Pets, Pets: Hints, Tips, and Fascinating Facts, C. R. Gibson, 1980.

The Very Best Name for Baby, C. R. Gibson, 1986.

■ Work in Progress

A humorous book to help adults with bad backs; a new-viewpoint pet book; several children's books.

■ Sidelights

Barbara Shook Hazen is the author of over sixty books for children, in addition to a dozen adult nonfiction titles. Hazen's books for children are generally geared to the primary grade audience and cover a wide range of subject matter, from 'goodnight' picture books to pure fancy to family dynamics and problem books in the guise of fiction. "I always wanted to write as a way to find my voice, and also as a way of being heard when no one seemed to listen," Hazen once told *SATA*. "My first sale was a soulful four-line poem to *True Confessions* in the third grade, about 'After the sun the rain.' I kept at it, particularly the poetry, which I am getting back to, despite parental warnings that this was no way to make a living."

But Hazen has been making a living with her writing skills for more than four decades, beginning as a poetry and fiction editor at *Ladies' Homes Journal* and then working as a children's book editor at Western Publishing, which published many of her early books. Her first book was released in 1958 and since 1960 she has been a full-time freelance writer. Some of Hazen's early titles were reworkings of fairy tales and classic stories such as *David and Goliath* and *The Sorcerer's Apprentice*. Others looked at animals—especially cats: *The Tiny, Tawny Kitten, Playful Puppy,* and *City Cats, Country Cats*. The text in these books was straightforward and easy for children to follow.

Beginning with *Happy, Sad, Silly, Mad: A Beginning Book about Emotions*, published in 1971, Hazen took on the niggling problems of childhood. *The Gorilla Did It* tells the familiar story of the imaginary friend—in this case a gorilla—who is responsible for the mess in a preschooler's room. With the child's help, the imaginary gorilla is made to clean up the mess and earns a cookie for his troubles. "There will be instant appeal for the young reader," noted a reviewer in *Junior Bookshelf*. Hard economic times and their effect on a young child are examined in *Tight Times,* in which the father eventually loses his job, but the little boy is happy enough to make do with a stray cat in lieu of the dog he badly wanted. "The story has a sweet, sad poignancy," commented a reviewer in *Booklist,* and Zena Sutherland in the *Bulletin of the Center for Children's Books* noted that "the first-person monologue is convincingly that of a child." *Tight Times* was chosen as one of the first titles to be narrated on the Public Broadcasting System's *Reading Rainbow* television program.

The award-winning *Even If I Did Something Awful* explores a child's anxiety at losing her mother's love. While playing ball in the house, a little girl in pigtails breaks the vase her father gave to her mother. Frightened of the consequences, the girl asks for reassurance by inventing other worse offenses, and then finally tells the truth. The mother answers at this point: "I'd love you if it wasn't an accident. But I might also be mad ... and send you to your room ... and cry a little and pick up the pieces .... But I'd still love you." Kristi L. Thomas, writing in *School Library Journal,* concluded that the book was "a minor lesson for children and parents alike, in learning to rely on love." A *Publishers Weekly* reviewer called the work a "touching, funny, realistic happening," and noted that "readers will be as relieved as the naughty one when they discover how the loving but human mother handles the crisis." Zena Sutherland in *Bulletin of the Center for Children's Books*

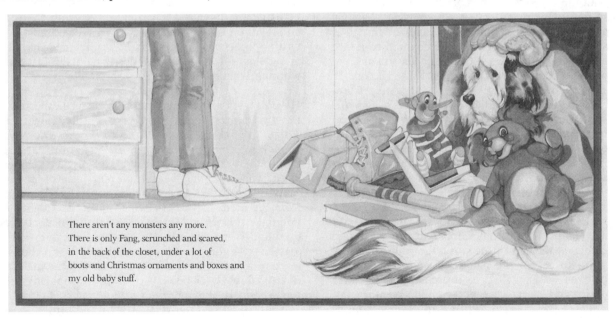

There aren't any monsters any more.
There is only Fang, scrunched and scared,
in the back of the closet, under a lot of
boots and Christmas ornaments and boxes and
my old baby stuff.

In her 1987 picture book *Fang,* Hazen tells about a large, ferocious-named dog who turns out to be more fearful than his timid young master. (Illustration by Leslie Holt Morrill.)

Little Emily accompanies her mother to work in Hazen's picture book *Mommy's Office.* (Illustration by David Soman.)

remarked that the book has "no tone of didacticism, but is more a clearing of the air."

Hazen also looked at the problem of a child's shyness in *Very Shy;* at the difficulty a child has in learning to handle disappointment in *It's a Shame about the Rain;* and at being different in *Why are People Different?* which deals with race relations and intercultural understanding. With *Fang,* Hazen examines a child's fears. The dog Fang is selected to help a young boy cope with his fears of monsters in his closet, of the bulldog next door, and the big kids on the corner. Fang, however, a big and fierce-looking animal, is a scaredy-cat, cringing at puppies and his own shadow. The tables are turned as the young master has to console the dog and convince his pet to overcome fears. "Comically portraying yet perceptively understanding childhood fears, Hazen ... [has] crafted an amusing and warm story of pet and child devotion," noted Ellen Mandel in a *Booklist* review. Writing in *School Library Journal,* Sharron McElmeel concluded that "this is a warm and memorable story that gently shows the love between a boy and his dog as well as a boy gaining self-assurance that helps him 'chase the monsters away.'" Hazen also used Fang to examine the emotions of being left behind or separated in *Stay, Fang.* In this story, Fang watches from the window lonely and miserable as his young master and playmate romps to and from school and play each day. In a parallel at the end of the story, the young narrator must learn to accept the babysitter and his mother's absence even as Fang had to overcome his constant whimpering and learn to accept the child's comings and goings. Pearl Herscovitch, writing in *School Library Journal,* considered this work a "disappointing sequel to Fang," contending that "the subtext of a child facing his own anxieties about staying behind is not effectively

integrated" with the plight of the dog. Ellen Mandel, writing in *Booklist,* offered another view of Hazen's second *Fang* title, noting that *Stay, Fang,* like its predecessor, "humorously relate[s] how a youngster, in trying to help his pet be brave, finds courage to overcome his own everyday qualms."

Hazen has also looked at a child's need for independence in *Alone at Home.* In this work, young Amy's wish to be home by herself is realized when her babysitter becomes ill with the flu and both of her parents have to work, agreeing to allow her to remain home alone for the day. However, Amy becomes lonely and then frightened by unfamiliar noises, and ends up hiding under the kitchen table until her parents return. *Alone at Home,* according to a review by Jacqueline Rose in *School Library Journal,* is an "entertaining story" that has "special relevance for today's latchkey children." Karen Hutt in *Booklist,* however, stated that Amy's "parents' arrival is a relief but an unsatisfactory one since Amy hasn't dealt successfully with being home alone."

Another major theme in Hazen's books for children is family dynamics and relationships. Divorce, sibling rivalry, and parental bonding have all found places in her stories. *Why Couldn't I Be an Only Kid Like You, Wigger* looks at a child's dream of being an only child rather than having to share with all one's brothers and sisters, though all the advantages of such a life are also looked at from Wigger's point of view and do not look so rosy. "The two differing views are presented in a brisk, running commentary," noted Mary M. Burns in a *Horn Book* review. In *Mommy's Office,* a little girl accompanies her mother to work and compares her mother's work with her own daily routine, growing closer to her in the process. Reviewing this work, Deborah Abbott in *Booklist* commented favorably on the "convincing" characterizations of mother and daughter, adding: "Hazen's details make the outing realistic: Emily calls her grandmother from the office and takes a rest while her mom works." Debra S. Gold, writing in *School Library Journal,* concluded that "this is a delightful story with a positive image of today's working woman."

Hazen's work also has a zanier side, as seen especially in her two books dealing with a cowardly knight: *The Knight Who Was Afraid of the Dark* and *The Knight Who Was Afraid to Fight.* In the first title, Sir Fred, though he has bashed monsters and rescued maidens, has a "knee-bumping, heart-thumping" fear of the dark. Melvin the Miffed, eager to win back Lady Wendylyn from Sir Fred, suggests that she invite the knight on a midnight tryst. But Melvin is defeated when both Sir Fred and Wendylyn admit to mutual fears and ride off together. "A romp with wit," Phillis Wilson called the work in a *Booklist* review, and a contributor in *Kirkus Reviews* dubbed the book "a treat for the sophisticated." *The Knight Who Was Afraid to Fight* again follows the adventures of Sir Fred when Melvin the Miffed, knowing the knight's aversion to the sight of blood, challenges Sir Fred to a duel. But again the knight outsmarts Melvin, defeating him without loss of blood from either

Sir Fred overcomes his fear of the dark in order to win the lovely Lady Wendylyn in Hazen's droll *The Knight Who Was Afraid of the Dark*. (Illustration by Tony Ross.)

In another tale about the gentle knight, Sir Fred, Melvin the Miffed challenges the hero to a duel with unexpected results.
(From *The Knight Who Was Afraid to Fight*, written by Barbara Shook Hazen and illustrated by Toni Goffe.)

party. "The contrast between two styles of masculinity is humorously portrayed in this medieval tale," wrote Merri Monks in *Booklist*. Virginia Opocensky, writing in *School Library Journal*, added: "This book calls for a bold, brave, dramatic reading for laughs all around."

As many critics have noted, Hazen's work consistently displays a concern with language and using words to convey meaning as simply and clearly as possible. Such messages touch children with their immediacy or fancifulness. "Words are friends, and writing gives second chances," Hazen told *SATA*. "It's also like traveling, a wonderful way to explore, learn things and get to know people—including oneself."

■ Works Cited

Abbott, Deborah, review of *Mommy's Office, Booklist,* March 1, 1992, p. 1287.

Burns, Mary M., review of *Why Couldn't I Be an Only Kid Like You, Wigger, Horn Book,* December, 1973, p. 585.

Review of *Even If I Did Something Awful, Publishers Weekly,* August 21, 1981, p. 55.

Gold, Debra S., review of *Mommy's Office, School Library Journal,* March, 1992, p. 215.

Review of *The Gorilla Did It, Junior Bookshelf,* December, 1976, p. 314.

Hazen, Barbara Shook, *Even If I Did Something Awful,* Atheneum, 1981.

Hazen, Barbara Shook, *The Knight Who Was Afraid of the Dark,* Dial, 1989.

Herscovitch, Pearl, review of *Stay, Fang, School Library Journal,* June, 1990, p. 100.

Hutt, Karen, review of *Alone at Home, Booklist,* February 1, 1992, p. 1040.

Review of *The Knight Who Was Afraid of the Dark, Kirkus Reviews,* January 1, 1989.

Mandel, Ellen, review of *Fang, Booklist,* December 1, 1987, p. 633.

Mandel, Ellen, review of *Stay, Fang, Booklist,* February 15, 1990, p. 1164.

McElmeel, Sharron, review of *Fang, School Library Journal,* December, 1987, p. 74.

Monks, Merri, review of *The Knight Who Was Afraid to Fight, Booklist,* May 15, 1994, p. 1682.

Opocensky, Virginia, review of *The Knight Who Was Afraid to Fight, School Library Journal,* June, 1994, p. 101.

Rose, Jacqueline, review of *Alone at Home, School Library Journal,* June, 1992, p. 115.

Sutherland, Zena, review of *Tight Times, Bulletin of the Center for Children's Books,* February, 1980, p. 110.

Sutherland, Zena, review of *Even If I Did Something Awful, Bulletin of the Center for Children's Books,* January, 1982, p. 86.

Thomas, Kristi L., review of *Even If I Did Something Awful, School Library Journal,* November, 1981, p. 76.

Review of *Tight Times, Booklist,* October 1, 1979, p. 276.

Wilson, Phillis, review of *The Knight Who Was Afraid of the Dark, Booklist,* May 15, 1989, p. 1649.

■ For More Information See

PERIODICALS

Bulletin of the Center for Children's Books, July, 1970, p. 178; October, 1972, p. 26; July, 1974, p. 178; September, 1976, p. 10; September, 1977, p. 16; May, 1983, p. 168; September, 1983, p. 9; September, 1985, p. 10; March, 1992, p. 181; June, 1992, p. 262.

Horn Book Guide, July, 1990, pp. 46, 127; fall, 1992, p. 233; fall, 1993, p. 332; spring, 1994, p. 361; spring, 1995, p. 114; fall, 1995, pp. 266, 337.

Los Angeles Times Book Review, September 8, 1985, p. 8.

New York Times Book Review, November 9, 1969, p. 64.

Publishers Weekly, February 5, 1973, p. 89; February 4, 1974, p. 73; July 25, 1977, p. 71; August 16, 1993, p. 103; May 9, 1994, p. 72.

Wilson Library Bulletin, October, 1989, p. 105.

—*Sketch by J. Sydney Jones*

*   *   *

HEILIGMAN, Deborah 1958-

◼ Personal

Born April 24, 1958, in Allentown, PA; daughter of Nathan (a physician) and Helen (maiden name, Rockmaker) Heiligman; married Jonathan Weiner (an author), May 29, 1982; children: Aaron, Benjamin. *Education:* Brown University, A.B., 1980. *Religion:* Jewish.

◼ Career

Author of children's books. Scholastic Inc., editor, 1981-85. *Member:* Authors Guild, Authors League of America, Society of Children's Book Writers and Illustrators.

◼ Awards, Honors

Distinguished alumnus award, Allen High School, 1993; *Barbara McClintock: Alone in Her Field* was named an outstanding science trade book for children, 1995.

◼ Writings

Into the Night, illustrated by Melissa Sweet, HarperCollins, 1990.

Barbara McClintock: Alone in Her Field, illustrated by Janet Hamlin, W. H. Freeman, 1994.

Deborah Heiligman's *From Caterpillar to Butterfly* explains metamorphosis simply and clearly to preschool and kindergarten children. (Illustration by Bari Weissman.)

Mary Leakey: In Search of Human Beginnings, illustrated by Janet Hamlin, W. H. Freeman, 1995.
On the Move, illustrated by Lizzy Rockwell, HarperCollins, 1996.
From Caterpillar to Butterfly, illustrated by Bari Weissman, HarperCollins, 1996.

■ Work in Progress

Three children's titles, *Pockets, Levin the Pig,* and *Mike Swan, Sink or Swim.*

■ Sidelights

"I remember so clearly the first time I checked a book out of the library," Deborah Heiligman told *SATA.* "I was in kindergarten. We went to the school library—I can still see the warm wood of the floor, the card catalogue, the heavy doors. I can still smell the books—they smelled warm and musky. I can still feel those first books I pulled off the shelf. They had hard covers, and soft, worn pages. The book I checked out was *What Is a Butterfly?*

"I brought it home; I felt as though I were carrying a real treasure. My mother read it to me, sitting on my bed. I was so small my legs did not reach to the side of the bed. But the world became larger and larger with each word she read. This book told me everything I wanted to know about how a caterpillar becomes a butterfly. I was in a whole new world.

"I took *Butterfly* back to the library and checked out *What Is a Tree?* Next came *What Is a Frog?* I was hooked! I now knew that books were my entry into the world, and I wanted to explore every nook and cranny. I kept reading nonfiction, and then branched out into fiction, longer books, encyclopedias, and magazines. While I was growing up, I had many friends and did all kinds of wonderful things. But the one anchor in my life was always my love of reading. Reading was like magic for me. I found, too, that I loved to write, and that I was pretty good at it. The magic came full circle a few years ago when an editor asked me to write a picture book on how a caterpillar turns into a butterfly! I had long been searching for my first butterfly book, but it was out of print. So I was able to write my own!

"I wrote the book the month after my mother died, and I poured into it memories of her, and all of my books, and the wonders of the world, and of life. From a funny-looking caterpillar comes a beautiful Painted Lady butterfly. And life comes full circle too, as I dedicated *From Caterpillar to Butterfly* to my first son, Aaron, who loves books even more than I do, if that is possible."

■ For More Information See

PERIODICALS

Booklist, November 15, 1994, p. 596.
Children's Book Review Service, January, 1991, p. 51.
Horn Book Guide, July, 1990, p. 38.

School Library Journal, January, 1991, p. 74; August, 1996, p. 138.

*   *   *

HOLINGER, William (Jacques) 1944- (Scott Eller, a joint pseudonym)

■ Personal

Born June 12, 1944, in Chicago, IL; son of Paul H. (a physician) and Julia C. (Drake) Holinger; married Dorothy Helen Powe (a classical psychologist), August 18, 1978; stepchildren: Gordon Ondis, Jr., Aleta T. Ondis. *Education:* Wesleyan University, A.B., 1966; Brown University, A.M., 1977.

■ Addresses

Home—20 Chapel St., Brookline, MA 02146. *Agent*—McIntosh & Otis, Inc., 310 Madison Ave., New York, NY 10017.

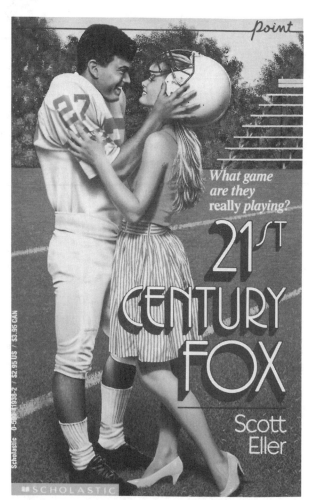

William Holinger, writing with Jim Shepard under the joint pseudonym Scott Eller, tells of two football-playing brothers, Brad and Dean, who both fall for the same visiting movie star, Fox Renard.

■ Career

University of Michigan, Ann Arbor, faculty member, 1978-90; Harvard University, Cambridge, MA, faculty member, 1990—. *Military service:* U.S. Army, 1966-69. *Member:* Authors Guild, Authors League of America.

■ Awards, Honors

Associated Writing Programs award in the novel, 1984, for *The Fence-walker;* Eyster Award for fiction, 1984, for short story, "Younker's Jump"; creative artist grant from Michigan Council for the Arts, 1984.

■ Writings

YOUNG ADULT NOVELS; WITH JIM SHEPARD, UNDER JOINT PSEUDONYM SCOTT ELLER

Short Season, Scholastic, 1985.
21st Century Fox, Scholastic, 1989.

"THE JOHNSON BOYS" SERIES FOR YOUNG ADULTS; WITH JIM SHEPARD, UNDER JOINT PSEUDONYM SCOTT ELLER

The Football Wars, Scholastic, 1992.
First Base, First Place, Scholastic, 1993.
That Soccer Season, Scholastic, 1993.
Jump Shot, Scholastic, 1994.

OTHER

The Fence-walker (adult novel), State University of New York Press, 1985.

Also author of short stories published in anthologies and periodicals, including *Delta Review, Texas Review,* and *Iowa Review.*

■ Sidelights

After English professor and author William Holinger published his first novel, *The Fence-walker,* which is based on his experiences as a soldier in Korea during the late 1960s, he teamed up with Jim Shepard to write stories for children under the name Scott Eller. All of the Scott Eller books involve sports in one way or another. The stories often blend game action with the personal struggles of their young protagonists. *Short Season,* for example, mixes play-by-play baseball action with twelve-year-old Brad Harris's problems with his developing sense of identity and his close relationship with his brother, Dean. Susan McCord, writing in *School Library Journal,* felt that the blend was a successful one. "Eller has woven a story of substance about growing up," she remarked. *21st Century Fox* continues the story of Brad and Dean, this time as players with the Adrian High School football team. When a teenage movie star named Christiana "Fox" Renard arrives in town to make a horror film, Brad is star-struck and begins to date her, while Dean is eager to get a part in the movie.

About his writing experiences, Holinger once commented in *The Writer:* "When writing fiction, try above all to tell a good story. Give your narrative a structure. If your material is based on experience, so much the better: The fiction will contain a loud ring of truth, and the passion you bring to it will infuse your work with energy and make it that much more powerful."

■ Works Cited

Holinger, William, "Turning Experience into a Novel," *The Writer,* May, 1986, pp. 7-9, 46.
McCord, Susan, review of *Short Season, School Library Journal,* October, 1985, p. 171.

■ For More Information See

PERIODICALS

Booklist, August, 1985, p. 1663.
Choice, February, 1986, p. 868.
Kliatt, November, 1992, p. 6.
Library Journal, July, 1985, p. 93.
New York Times Book Review, October 20, 1985.
Publishers Weekly, May 17, 1985, p. 98.
School Library Journal, October, 1985, p. 171; March, 1989, p. 198.
Sewanee Review, fall, 1986.
Voice of Youth Advocates, June, 1989, p. 100; October, 1990, p. 257.

*   *   *

HOON, Patricia Easterly 1954-

■ Personal

Born March 9, 1954, in Mount Holly, NJ; daughter of Nathan William (a college professor) and Marjorie Ellen (a volunteer; maiden name, Wood) Easterly; married Jeffrey Vincent Hoon (an insurance representative), June 13, 1976; children: Vincent, Matthew, Deborah, Juli. *Education:* Graduate in interior design from Bowling Green State University, 1976. *Politics:* Republican. *Religion:* Christian. *Hobbies and other interests:* "Reading, museum trips, classical music, and watching our children's events."

■ Addresses

Office—Matrix Lifeline, 1824 Maple St., Lafayette, IN 47904.

■ Career

Scholz Homes (luxury home manufacturer), draftsman, 1979; Poggemeyer Design Group (engineering and architectural firm), draftsman, 1980-83; self-employed artist and interior designer, 1985—; Matrix Lifeline (nonprofit agency), Lafayette, IN, office manager, 1993—, executive director, 1994—. Has also worked as a kitchen designer. Lafayette Adult Reading Academy, advisory board member; Mentor Mother program, advisory council; also actively involved in community network of social service agencies, volunteer for church outreach programs for needy families. *Member:* Tecumseh Area Literacy League.

PATRICIA EASTERLY HOON

■ Writings

(And illustrator) *Lollipop Lunch,* The Speech Bin, 1994.

Also author of story, "Robert's Friends," in *Rainy Day, Sunny Day, Any Day,* Concordia, 1994.

■ Work in Progress

The Secret Place, a physically challenged child's search for faith, expected 1996; a book about a genius toddler; research about women artists, such as Mary Cassatt.

■ Sidelights

Patricia Easterly Hoon told *SATA:* "I was first introduced to the fascinating world of children's literature by my grandmother. When I excitedly ripped open Christmas and birthday wrapping paper, I always discovered a beautifully illustrated book from Grandmother instead of the trendy toys I might have suggested. Many times, I listened intently as her gentle, quavery voice introduced me to literary characters. Grandmother's eyes shone as she read to me, whether it was a children's story or lyrical poetry. Her mountain home was built in a wild-flowered ravine where the natural beauty reinforced Grandmother's own appreciation of the arts, and each visit to this wonderland was engraved in my mind.

"Like many self-absorbed young people, I didn't fully value Grandmother's gifts until I had my own children. One day in the library, I discovered the book *When I was Young in the Mountains* (author Cynthia Rylant/ illustrator Diane Goode) and was transported back to the childhood wonderland of my grandparents' tender hospitality. I felt a fierce desire to write and illustrate a children's book. I didn't imagine I could ever improve upon such a beautiful combination of prose and art as this book, but I wanted to *try* to approach it. I surrounded myself with *Writer's Digest* books and a blissful cushion of naivete which enabled me to survive five years of rejections.

"The book which actually did get published began as a poem about our youngest daughter Juli's severe speech delay. I sent it to the Speech Bin, Inc., who asked me to compile a series of stories for speech-challenged children. I woke up every morning at 5 a.m. to work on it, carefully planning how much I needed to accomplish to complete *Lollipop Lunch* before the deadline. It was an enjoyable time spent with my characters, whose situations seemed as real to me as our four children's antics.

"Current children's literature seems to be overflowing with imaginative writing and illustration. It can be an intimidating field to enter, but I believe that persistence is an author's most valuable companion. It is satisfying to contribute even a teaspoonful to a vigorous stream of gifted children's authors whom I admire tremendously."*

*   *   *

HOWARD, Norman Barry 1949-

■ Personal

Born December 9, 1949, in Brooklyn, NY; son of Morris (a theatrical agent) and Rae (an executive financial secretary; maiden name, Magner) Litvack. *Education:* Long Island University, B.S., 1972. *Hobbies and other interests:* Walking, rowing, hiking, gardening.

■ Addresses

Home—1013 Indian Mountain Lakes, Albrightsville, PA 18210-3100.

■ Career

Marc Howard Productions, Brooklyn, NY, talent and booking agent, 1972-80; teacher in Brooklyn, NY, 1974-94. *Member:* Indian Mountain Lake Civic Association, Indian Mountain Lake Cliff Club.

■ Writings

Uncle Philip's Fickle Formula, Winston-Derek, 1996.

Also writer of country songs "Mike Hammer" and "Beowolf," produced by HillTop Records, 1996.

■ Work in Progress

The Dog from Biodesign, a short story for children and young adults.

■ Sidelights

Norman Barry Howard told *SATA:* "From the first time my mother took me to the East Flatbush branch of the Brooklyn Public Library, I've had great respect for the power of the written word. As a student I never fell short of words and ideas when it came to writing compositions, essays, and term papers. Although *Uncle Philip's Fickle Formula* is my first published work, I hope to be a regular contributor to the world of children's literature, creating short stories that have the impact and satisfaction of novellas, abounding with themes, devoid of violence and tragedy, that place young people in situations that become everlasting memories. Recently, I moved with my parents into a house of my own design in the Pocono Mountains."

*   *   *

HUDSON, Margaret
See SHUTER, Jane Margaret

I–J

IMAI, Miko 1963-

■ Personal

Born September 20, 1963, in Niigata, Japan; daughter of Atsushi (a teacher) and Michiko (a general practitioner) Imai; married Thomas Brais (a software engineer), May 15, 1993; children: Hanako. *Education:* Musashino Art University, B.F.A. (painting), 1986; Rhode Island School of Design, B.F.A. (textile design), 1989. *Hobbies and other interests:* Needlework.

■ Addresses

Office—2 Liberty Ave., Lexington, MA 02173.

■ Career

Studio Elizabeth Carpenter, Norton, MA, assistant designer, 1989; freelance textile designer and illustrator, 1990-91. *Member:* Society of Children's Book Writers and Illustrators, Authors Guild, Authors League of America.

■ Writings

SELF-ILLUSTRATED

Little Lumpty, Candlewick Press, 1994.
Lilly's Secret, Candlewick Press, 1994.
Sebastian's Trumpet, Candlewick Press, 1995.

ILLUSTRATOR

Robin and Helen Lester, *Wuzzy Takes Off,* Candlewick Press, 1995.

■ Work in Progress

Picture books.

■ Sidelights

Miko Imai told *SATA:* "I was an extremely sensitive child. I was always quiet, therefore I was able to observe. I was also a day-dreamer and thinker. I have an older sister who was a charmer and carefree when she was very young. I always wished I was as carefree and childlike as she was. I think I had a lot going through my mind as a young child, and I can still remember how I was feeling about things and how I reacted to things. Now I can view those events objectively and figure out why I felt the way I did. These emotions of my childhood memories help me write.

"I'm an illustrator with no one particular style. I switch the medium accordingly. For example, I used gouache for *Little Lumpty.* With gouache, I can paint bright and flat colors that helped me to make Lumpty look more like a cartoon character. He's a fun kid with a bright personality. For *Lilly's Secret* I used watercolor and pencil. The original dummy was done in pen and ink. It was very graphic. But during the process of making the book, I switched to watercolor in order to convey Lilly's shy and sensitive character.

MIKO IMAI

130

"*Sebastian's Trumpet* is done in gouache but is a little different from *Lumpty*. For *Lumpty* I painted like I was painting with oil paint, but *Sebastian* is done in a more straightforward way. This book is for a younger audience and therefore its clear, bright, and easy-to-understand pictures seemed more appropriate."

■ For More Information See

PERIODICALS

Booklist, May 15, 1994, p. 1683; December 15, 1994, p. 758.
Children's Book Review Service, spring, 1994, p. 136.
Kirkus Reviews, December 15, 1994, p. 1565.
Publishers Weekly, April 4, 1994, p. 79; November 28, 1994, p. 60.
School Library Journal, December, 1994, p. 76.

* * *

ISAACS, Anne 1949-

■ Personal

Born March 2, 1949, in Buffalo, NY; daughter of Samuel (a materials handling engineer) and Hope (an anthropologist; maiden name, Levy) Isaacs; married Samuel Koplowicz (a media producer), 1978; children: Jordan, Amy, Sarah. *Education:* University of Michigan, B.A., 1971, M.S., 1975; attended State University of New York, Buffalo, 1971-72. *Religion:* Jewish.

■ Addresses

Agent—Gail Hochman, Brandt & Brandt Literary Agents, 1501 Broadway, New York, NY 10036.

■ Career

Held numerous positions in environmental education from 1975 to 1990.

■ Awards, Honors

Swamp Angel, illustrated by Paul O. Zelinsky, was a Ralph Caldecott honor book and a Notable Books selection by the American Library Association, both 1994; other awards for *Swamp Angel* include: Best Illustrated Books citation, *New York Times,* Best Books, *School Library Journal,* and Best Books, *Publishers Weekly,* all 1994, and Honor Book, *Boston Globe-Horn Book,* Children's Book of the Year list, Child Study Children's Book Committee, and Notable Trade Book in Language Arts, National Council of Teachers of English, all 1995.

■ Writings

Swamp Angel, illustrated by Paul O. Zelinsky, Dutton Children's Books, 1994.
Treehouse Tales, illustrated by Lloyd Bloom, Dutton Children's Books, 1997.

ANNE ISAACS

A Bowl of Soup, illustrated by Jerry Pinkney, Scholastic, in press.
Cat up a Tree, Dutton Children's Books, in press.

■ Adaptations

Swamp Angel appeared on *Storytime,* PBS, 1995.

■ Work in Progress

A historical novel and poetry.

■ Sidelights

Anne Isaacs is best known for *Swamp Angel,* an imaginative historical tale spotlighting a young female heroine who sometimes appears larger than life. She is also the author of the fictional work *A Bowl of Soup,* which is based on the true story of a young girl imprisoned in a Nazi labor camp during World War II.

Written in a tongue-in-cheek style, *Swamp Angel* features Angelica Longrider, who, as an infant, is a bit taller than her mother, and who later accomplishes some amazing feats. In addition to building her first log cabin by the time she is two, Angelica rescues a wagon from Dejection Swamp and then defeats a bear, Thundering Tarnation, by throwing him up to the sky and creating a prairie from the bear's pelt. Commentators have compared Angelica to the legendary American hero Paul

Bunyan. A Caldecott honor book, *Swamp Angel* was declared "visually exciting, wonderful to read aloud ... a picture book to remember" by a *Horn Book* contributor. A reviewer in *Kirkus Reviews* exclaimed, "It is impossible to convey the sheer pleasure, the exaggerated loopiness, of newcomer Isaacs's wonderful story."

A more serious work is Isaacs's *A Bowl of Soup,* which, as Isaacs explained to *SATA,* "is a fictional account of the experiences of my mother-in-law, Eva Buchbinder Koplowicz, as a young woman in a Nazi labor camp in Czechoslovakia from 1943 to 1945. All of the incidents are either true or possible." To write this emotionally painful story, Isaacs researched a number of holocaust topics; read the testimony of other holocaust survivors; visited concentration camps, death camps, and former ghettos in Europe; and visited the labor camp and factory where Eva worked. About writing the story, Isaacs revealed to *SATA:* "It has been hard going. I have had to invent the most wonderful father I have ever known, then hand him over to the Nazis again and again during subsequent drafts of the book. I have had to experience repeatedly many unbearable realities. But at the end of each writing day, I have been fortunate to be able to return to the safe and loving world of my family."

About her own life, Isaacs told *SATA:* "I was born in 1949 in Buffalo, New York, and lived there until I left to attend the University of Michigan in 1967. As a child, I did a limited amount of creative writing on my own. I had two poems published at the age of ten in a city-wide magazine of writing by school children. I read constantly, selecting books haphazardly from my parents' and the public library shelves. In fifth grade, for example, along with *The Wind in the Willows,* I read Shakespeare's *Romeo and Juliet* and *The Tempest,* plus *Lorna Doone* and *The Caine Mutiny.* As now, poetry affected me more profoundly than any other genre. At age ten, I memorized Coleridge's 'Kubla Khan' while reading it for the first time.

"Probably the greatest childhood influence on my writing was reading and re-reading, over a period of years, *Little Women.* I would finish the last page and immediately start over at the first. The story became a kind of life plan for me, although I didn't realize that until a few years ago. Like Alcott's semi-autobiographical heroine, Jo, I grew up to marry a kindly, professorial man with an unpronounceable name, to raise a passel of kids in the country, and to combine careers in educational program development and children's book writing. This experience has taught me to respect the long-term influence a children's book may have on its readers.

"I studied English literature in my undergraduate years at the University of Michigan, and in a year of graduate study at the State University of New York, Buffalo. I also studied French, Russian, Latin, and American literature during these years. I have always been especially interested in nineteenth-century novels and poetry. Only as an adult have I begun to read extensively in children's literature, often experiencing a book for the first time while reading it to my children.

"As a result of reading children's and adult literature interchangeably throughout my life, I have never recognized a clear distinction between them, nor do I apply different standards."

■ **Works Cited**

Review of *Swamp Angels, Horn Book,* March/April, 1995, p. 184.
Review of *Swamp Angels, Kirkus Reviews,* October 15, 1994, p. 1408.

■ **For More Information See**

PERIODICALS

Booklist, October 15, 1994, p. 424; January 15, 1995, pp. 862, 907; April 15, 1995, p. 1412.
New York Times Book Review, November 13, 1994, p. 30.
Publishers Weekly, October 3, 1994, p. 69; November 7, 1994, p. 43.
School Library Journal, December, 1994, pp. 24, 76.
U.S. News & World Report, December 5, 1994, p. 95.

* * *

IVES, Morgan
See BRADLEY, Marion Zimmer

* * *

JOHNS, Janetta
See QUIN-HARKIN, Janet

* * *

JONES, Jennifer (Berry) 1947-

■ **Personal**

Born January 4, 1947, in Pomona, CA; daughter of Ferris M. (a U.S. Army officer) and Jean (Riley) Berry; married A. Wesley Jones (a professor of humanities), June 2, 1969; children: Elise Claire. *Education:* Radford College, B.S., 1969. *Religion:* Episcopalian. *Hobbies and other interests:* Reading, dolls, cats, history, travel.

■ **Addresses**

Home—920 North Washington St., Bismarck, ND 58501. *Office*—Bismarck Public Library, 515 North Fifth St., Bismarck, ND 58501.

■ **Career**

Bismarck Public Library, Bismarck, ND, head of technical services, 1976—. Member of Missouri Valley Montessori Board, 1982-84; active in Shade Tree Players Board children's theater, 1993-95; deputy systems ad-

JENNIFER JONES

ministrator for Central Dakota Library Network, 1993—. *Member:* Society of Children's Book Writers and Illustrators, North Dakota Library Association, Mountain-Plains Library Association.

■ Awards, Honors

■ Writings

(Reteller) *Heetunka's Harvest: A Tale of the Plains Indians,* illustrated by Shannon Keegan, Roberts Rinehart, 1994.

■ Work in Progress

A nonfiction picture book about animals who live under the snow in winter; a middle-grade novel, *The Little Cow,* about a lonely boy living at a North Dakota game preserve during the bitter winter of 1919; a novel about a frontier family living at Fort Abraham Lincoln, Dakota Territory, in 1876.

■ Sidelights

Jennifer Jones told *SATA:* "I've always loved books and writing, and I vividly remember the creative flood I felt writing my first mystery in fifth grade. By high school I'd graduated to purple-ink-only and churned out romance stories for my friends to read.

"After a hiatus of too many years, I began to write again, seriously, about twelve years ago. While doing research for an ongoing, yet unfinished, project about a frontier military family, I stumbled across a reference to Plains Indian legend that was unfamiliar to me. The early twentieth-century ethnobotanist Melvin Gilmore had collected a Dakota legend which concerned a custom common to a number of tribes. It was the cautionary story of Heetunka, the 'bean mouse,' and the selfish woman who stole all of the mouse's harvest. I was charmed by the idea of Indian women actually trading with the mice each fall.

"The story had many possible levels of meaning, and I set about turning it into a children's book. I did a lot of research about voles (the 'mouse' isn't really a mouse at all!), the earth bean, and, of course, Plains Indian culture. I was especially interested in enriching the story with details of daily life before white contact, since it seems to me that many retellings of legends merely gloss over details and leave the reader with only a broad, and sometimes misleading, sense of the culture.

"*Heetunka's Harvest* had many revisions, and after the usual rejections, finally found a home with Roberts Rinehart. The Council for Indian Education, a committee composed of representatives of several tribes, endorsed the book for inclusion in their series. I couldn't have been luckier in the selection of Shannon Keegan to do the illustrations. She researched details, too, and captured the essence of the Northern Plains during late fall.

"I am interested in writing accurate historical accounts, and I research my projects carefully—being a librarian has been a great help!"

■ For More Information See

PERIODICALS

Booklist, January 1, 1995, p. 824.
Kirkus Reviews, February 15, 1995, p. 221.
Publishers Weekly, December 19, 1994, p. 54.
School Library Journal, April, 1995, p. 126.

K

KAHN, Katherine Janus 1942-

■ Personal

Born December 2, 1942, in Washington, DC; daughter of Milton Harold (a labor lawyer) and Edmina (Benish) Janus; married David Fitch Kahn (a history teacher), June 15, 1970; children: Robert Milton. *Education:* University of Chicago, A.B., 1964; attended Bezalel School of Art, 1967-68; attended Corcoran School of Art, 1968; University of Iowa, M.A., 1970; attended Montgomery College, 1985-90. *Religion:* Jewish.

■ Addresses

Home—4401 Ferrara Dr., Wheaton, MD 20906.

■ Career

National Institutes of Health, Bethesda, MD, exhibits technician, 1962; U.S. Information Agency, Washington, DC, visual information specialist, 1964-67; Institute of Modern Languages, Washington, DC, art director, 1970-73; Maryland College of Art and Design, Silver Spring, instructor, 1986-87. Part-time and freelance positions include Center for Science in the Public Interest, illustrator, 1970-73; WETA-TV, illustrator of animated television programs, including "The Wizard of Earthsea," 1973-76, 1985-86; WTTG-TV, courtroom illustrator, 1977-78. *Exhibitions:* Exhibitor with a number of shows, including those sponsored by the Pan American Health Organization, Washington, DC, Montgomery College, Montgomery County, MD, and Rockville Civic Mansion, Rockville, MD. *Member:* Children's Book Guild, Woman's Honorary Society (University of Chicago), Nu Pi Sigma.

■ Awards, Honors

Golden Hugo Award, Chicago International Film Festival, 1975, for "The Wizard of Earthsea."

■ Writings

(And illustrator) *Alef Is One, An Alphabet Counting Book,* Kar-Ben Copies, 1989.

ILLUSTRATOR

Seymour Rossel, *Journey Through Jewish History,* edited by Neil Kozodoy, Behrman House (New York), Volume 1, 1981, Volume 2, 1983.

Miriam Schlein, *Hanukah,* Behrman House, 1983.

KATHERINE JANUS KAHN

Miriam Schlein, *Passover,* Behrman House, 1983.

Evelyn Zusman, *The Passover Parrot,* Kar-Ben Copies (Rockville, MD), 1983.

Eileen Bluestone Sherman, *The Odd Potato,* Kar-Ben Copies, 1984.

Ruth Esrig Brinn, *More Let's Celebrate,* Kar-Ben Copies, 1984.

Howard Cushnir, *The Secret Spinner,* Kar-Ben Copies, 1985.

Erwin and Agnes Herman, *The Yanov Torah,* Kar-Ben Copies, 1985.

Carol Levin, *A Rosh Hashanah Walk,* Kar-Ben Copies, 1987.

Ellie Gellman, *Tamar's Sukkah,* Kar-Ben Copies, 1988.

Rosalind Schilder, *Dayenu, or How Uncle Murray Saved the Seder,* Kar-Ben Copies, 1988.

My Play-a-Tune Book of Jewish Songs, JTG of Nashville (Tennessee), 1988.

Varda Cohen-Grauman, *Yesh Lanu Lamah,* Behrman House, Volume 1, 1989, Volume 2, 1993.

Shoshana Silberman, *The Whole Megilla (Almost),* Kar-Ben Copies, 1990.

Harriet K. Feder, *Judah Who Always Said, No!,* Kar-Ben Copies, 1990.

M. Lev, *The Magic Faucet,* Antroll Publishers (Burlington, VT), 1991.

Mindy Avra Portnoy, *Matzah Ball: a Passover Story,* Kar-Ben Copies, 1994.

Miriam Ramsfelder Levin, *In the Beginning,* Kar-Ben Copies, 1996.

Contributor of illustrations to various periodicals, including *Defenders of Wildlife, Smithsonian,* and the *Washington Post.*

BOARD BOOKS; PUBLISHED BY KAR-BEN COPIES

Ellie Gellman, *It's Chanukah!,* 1985.

Ellie Gellman, *It's Rosh-Hashanah!,* 1985.

Myra Shostak, *Rainbow Candles: A Chanukah Counting Book,* 1986.

Judye Groner and Madeline Wikler, *Let's Build a Succah,* 1986.

Judye Groner and Madeline Wikler, *The Purim Parade,* 1986.

Judye Groner and Madeline Wikler, *My First Sedar,* 1986.

Susan Remick Topek, *Israel Is . . . ,* 1988.

Judye Groner and Madeline Wikler, *The Shofar Calls to Us,* 1991.

"SAMMY SPIDER'S FIRST" SERIES; WRITTEN BY SYLVIA A. ROUSS; PUBLISHED BY KAR-BEN COPIES

Sammy Spider's First Hanukkah, 1993.
Sammy Spider's First Passover, 1995.
Sammy Spider's First Rosh Hashannah, 1996.

"FAMILY SERVICE" SERIES; PUBLISHED BY KAR-BEN COPIES

Shoshano Silberman, *A Family Haggadah,* 1987.
Judith Z. Abrams, *Selichot: A Family Service,* 1990.
Judith Z. Abrams, *Rosh Hashanah: A Family Service,* 1990.
Judith Z. Abrams, *Yom Kippur: A Family Service,* 1990.

Although Sammy Spider began as a mere spectator of the Shapiro family observing Hanukkah, he ultimately gets to join in the celebration. (From *Sammy Spider's First Hanukkah,* written by Sylvia A. Rouss and illustrated by Katherine Janus Kahn.)

Judith Z. Abrams, *Shabbat: A Family Service,* 1992.
Judith Z. Abrams, *Sukkot: A Family Sedar,* 1993.
Judith Z. Abrams, *Simchat Torah: A Family Service,* 1995.

ACTIVITY BOOKS; PUBLISHED BY KAR-BEN COPIES

Hanukkah Fun for Little Hands, 1991.
Passover Fun for Little Hands, 1991.
Shabbat Fun for Little Hands, 1992.
Ruth Esrig Brinn, with Judye Groner and Madeline Wikler, *Jewish Holiday Crafts for Little Hands,* 1993.
Purim Fun for Little Hands, 1994.

■ Work in Progress

Writing with Tommy Feldman and illustrating *The Hole Bagel.*

■ Sidelights

Katherine Janus Kahn told *SATA,* "In 1967 I was twenty-four years old and working in Washington, D.C., for the U.S. Information Agency in their exhibits division. Although I had always loved to make art, college had awakened other interests and I really wasn't doing much art, nor had I done any to speak of in college. Although I worked with designers in my job, I was actually doing photographic research. There was a vague, unconscious need eating at me.

"There was also a desire to reconnect with my Judaism, and indeed to find out more about it. In June 1967, sudden war broke out between Israel and her neighbors. My roommate was glued to the television set, but I hadn't made the connection for myself yet. In fact, I had begun to think about the Peace Corps, which was very much a part of the thinking of young people at the time. But the connection was there, and obvious; when a friend suggested that I should go to Israel as a volunteer, it immediately struck me as being right. The war was over in an amazing six days, but it wasn't until August that the first airplanes again began flying between the United States and Israel. In those three months, I had done the necessary paper work to leave my job in Washington and become a volunteer in Israel. I was on the plane without a word of Hebrew, and with one small suitcase which held what were to be the three most significant pencils I have ever bought, one eraser, and one table of drawing paper.

"There were many volunteers on that plane, and many more already there from all over the world. I was put with other English speakers and sent down to the Negev Desert to be a part of an archeological dig. We worked out under the hot desert sun all day for a month, and we didn't find any artifacts at all, but I loved it. Months later, I spent a few days digging at the Wailing Wall in Jerusalem, and we found Roman glass and coins.

"From the Negev we were moved to a kibbutz in the Galilee, where I helped harvest olives. That was a wonderful kind of work, out in the olive orchards, with gentle breezes and the shade of the olive trees as protection from the sun. It was quiet work and we talked a great deal. And after work, I drew and drew and didn't stop drawing—not the scenery, which was beautiful, but the other volunteers—portrait after portrait.

"When we had finished the olive harvest and the grapefruit harvest (harder, because it was already the beginning of the rainy season), they asked me if I would like to go to Bezalel, the art school in Jerusalem. I jumped at the opportunity. Jerusalem was a gorgeous, heady place to be. The city was finally united, and for the first time since 1948, Jews were allowed back into the Old City, where two mosques occupied the Temple Mount and the Wailing Wall itself. The student quarters for the school were overlooking a beautiful, but deserted, Arab village in the valley right below us. My friends and I wandered it endlessly, and I was slowly learning Hebrew. I shopped and cooked. And I was drawing and painting and sculpting. I even started illustrating for the *Volunteer.*

"To make this pivotal year complete, I met an American who was an Orthodox Jew, and he and his family took me in, teaching me the daily rituals of living as a Jew. This has informed my life from then until now. I draw most of my inspiration from the wealth of my religion, getting both subject matter and understanding from the Torah and the cycles of the Jewish year.

"I have built my life around what I learned in the year of August 1967 to August 1968."

■ For More Information See

PERIODICALS

Publishers Weekly, September 20, 1993, p. 32; March 20, 1995, p. 59.
School Library Journal, October 1993, p. 47; July 1995, p. 68.

*   *   *

KENT, Lisa 1942-

■ Personal

Born September 13, 1942; daughter of Francis (an insurance consultant) and Agnes Coutts Loughlin; married Edward Krones (divorced); married Larry Kent (National Football League Properties founder and past president), June 25, 1985; children: Leah Barr Becker, Mark Krones. *Education:* Attended Columbia University, New School, and University of California at Los Angeles; graduated from Finch Jr. College.

■ Addresses

Home—28315 Ridgehaven Court, Rancho Palos Verdes, CA 90275. *Literary Agent*—R. Noetzle, Char-

LISA KENT

lotte Sheedy Agency, 611 Broadway, New York, NY 10012. *Screen Agent*—Lew Weitzman, Preferred Artists.

■ Career

Model, actress, talk-show hostess; Astrologer; Writer.

■ Writings

Love Is Always There, illustrated by Mikki Machlin, Paulist Press, 1993.
Hilde Knows: Someone Cries for the Children, illustrated by Mikki Machlin, Jalmar Press, 1994.
The Thirteenth Sign, Skyline Publishing, 1997.

Kent has also written a screenplay, *Hot Dogs.*

■ Work in Progress

Grandma's An Angel Now, another "Hilde Knows" title; *Raggedy Royal of New York City; Sun Sign Angel: Astrology and Angels.*

* * *

KIESLER, Kate (A.) 1971-

■ Personal

Born August 25, 1971, in Keene, NH; daughter of Lew (in hotel management) and Gail Audette (a craftsperson) Kiesler. *Education:* Rhode Island School of Design, B.F.A., 1993. *Hobbies and other interests:* Hiking, rock climbing, gardening.

■ Addresses

Home and office—P.O. Box 2504, Ranchos de Taos, NM 87557.

■ Career

Illustrator. Studio assistant to illustrator Barry Moser, North Hatfield, MA, 1993-94.

■ Illustrator

Marc McCutcheon, *Grandfather's Christmas Camp* (picture book), Clarion, 1995.
Jim Murphy, *Into the Deep Forest: With Henry David Thoreau* (for young adults), Clarion, 1995.
Andrew Clements, *Temple Cat* (picture book), Clarion, 1996.
Andrew Clements, *Bright Christmas: An Angel Remembers* (picture book), Clarion, 1996.
Kristine George, *The Great Frog Race* (collection of poems), Clarion, 1997.
Russell Freedman, *Out of Darkness* (for young adults), Clarion, 1997.
Ralph Fletcher, *Twilight Comes Twice* (picture book), Clarion, in press.

KATE KIESLER

■ Sidelights

Kate Kiesler told *SATA:* "Illustrating books was a very natural direction for me. I grew up in an environment where I was surrounded by creativity (my mother is a craftsperson and always had some project going—usually they took over the dining room table), and where reading and books were highly regarded. For entertainment (and I suppose to keep me out from under her feet), my mother often set me up with my own project or sent me off with a book. Drawing soon became second nature to me and books became my companions. I read piles of them. Picture books were part of a ritual for me as a child and became a passion for me as an adult. Pictures and words. There was magic there. I think, originally, I wanted to be a fine artist—paint pictures to hang on the walls. But my style of drawing and painting is really more suited for children's books—which have become a reliable source of income and inspiration.

"After graduating from school I was lucky enough to work for Barry Moser for a year as his studio assistant. It was there that I really became familiar with the process of making books. It was there that I learned to *design*—not just to illustrate—and I think that will always be a huge influence on my work.

"*Into the Deep Forest* was my first book. I think it allowed me to express the part of me that always wanted to be a painter. It required a lot of landscapes. Not just landscapes, but forests and mountains and rivers—subjects I was very familiar with and fond of as well. Due to that familiarity, I think it really allowed me to make a comfortable transition into picture books. More importantly, the book helped me to discover that illustration could be an exciting avenue of expression.

"To be able to enhance a child's world, to bring fairies and trolls to life, to add interest and to spark imagination, to *educate* with pictures is an incredible challenge—one that somehow gets me to my desk every morning with a sense of purpose. There are days that I think that I might have scratched that surface. There are also days that I am reminded how far I have to go. Those days are sometimes better spent in the woods or reading with a cup of tea. All those experiences somehow edge themselves back into the work. And make it better. And perhaps allow me to feel as though I have scratched the surface again. And then, I catch myself wide-eyed at how satisfying illustrating can be."

* * *

KIMBALL, Gayle 1943-

■ Personal

Born June 12, 1943, in Los Angeles, CA; daughter of Thomas R. (in insurance sales) and Barbara S. (an artist; maiden name, Stamps) Kimball; children: Jed Kimball-Hait. *Education:* University of California, Berkeley, B.A., 1964; University of California, Los Angeles, M.A., 1967; University of California, Santa Barbara, M.A., 1971, Ph.D., 1976. *Politics:* Democrat. *Hobbies and other interests:* Ballroom dancing, jogging, skiing.

■ Addresses

Office—Department of Sociology, California State University—Chico-445, Chico, CA 95929.

■ Career

Los Angeles City Schools, Los Angeles, CA, history teacher, 1965-70; California State University, Northridge, CA, part-time instructor, beginning 1971; California State University, Chico, CA, professor of women's studies and sociology, 1972—. Producer of instructional videos. Has made numerous television and radio appearances. *Member:* California Family Action (founder of Butte chapter), California State University—Chico Women's Faculty Association (founder), Chico Professional Women (founder).

■ Writings

(Editor) *Women's Culture: The Women's Renaissance of the Seventies,* Scarecrow, 1981.
The Religious Ideas of Harriet Beecher Stowe: Her Gospel of Womanhood, Edward Mellen, 1982.
The 50/50 Marriage, Beacon Press, 1983.
50/50 Parenting: Sharing Family Rewards and Responsibilities, Lexington, 1988.
(Editor) *Everything You Need to Know to Succeed after College,* Equality Press (Chico, CA), 1993.
How to Survive Your Parents' Divorce: Kids' Advice to Kids (for young people), Equality Press, 1994.
The Teen Trip: Complete Resource Guide (for young adults), Equality Press, 1996.
Empowering Parents, Equality Press, 1997.

Also contributor to anthologies.

GAYLE KIMBALL

■ Sidelights

Gayle Kimball told *SATA:* "I started writing when I was required to write a Ph.D. dissertation and kept on going. My books reflect stages in my life when I've needed models and information; I write to learn from others. Since my son is a teenager, I'm currently interested in resources for teens."

■ For More Information See

PERIODICALS

Booklist, February 1, 1983, p. 705.
Kirkus Reviews, February 1, 1983, p. 160.
Library Journal, March 1, 1983, p. 504.

* * *

KRAMER, Remi (Thomas) 1935-

■ Personal

Born March 7, 1935, in Los Angeles, CA; son of George N. (an author and college professor) and Justina M. (a musician) Kramer; married, February 1, 1969; wife's name, Agnes Marie; children: Matthew, Christiana, Timothy, Ian, Vincent, Brigitte, Danika. *Education:* University of California, Los Angeles, A.B., 1956; California State University, Los Angeles, M.A., 1963. *Religion:* Catholic. *Hobbies and other interests:* Oil painting.

REMI KRAMER

■ Addresses

Home—800 Thompson Rd., Sandpoint, ID 83864.
Office—P.O. Box 637, Sandpoint, ID 83864.

■ Career

Graphic designer for a number of companies including The Rand Corp. and System Development Corp., 1956-63; art director for Dolyle Dane Bernbach, 1964-65; art director, producer, and broadcast supervisor for N. W. Ayer, 1964-66; film director for John Urie & Assoc., 1966-67, The Haboush Company, 1967-69, Columbia Screen Gems, 1969-75, 1978-81, First Asian Films, 1975-76, and The Petersen Company, 1977-78; free-lance film director, 1981-84; Founder and CEO, Oz International, 1985—. *Military service:* U.S. Army, 1958-60; became sergeant (E-5). *Member:* Directors Guild of America, Writers Guild of America.

■ Awards, Honors

Best Illustration Award, *Creativity '90,* and 100 Top Products of the Year Award, *Curriculum Product News,* 1990, both for "LoneStar Bear" books. Golden Teddy Awards, 1990, 1991, and Golden Teddy Award nomination, 1992, Toby Award nomination, 1992, Best 10 Activity Toys award, 1994, all for LoneStar Bear plush toys. Won a number of film awards, including the AAAA Sweepstakes, Clio, IBA, and Cine Golden Eagle.

■ Writings

SELF-ILLUSTRATED

The Ballad of Klondike Ike, Northwind Press, 1992.
The Gift, Northwind Press, 1992.

"HAPPY TALES AND ADVENTURES FROM THE LEGEND OF LONESTAR BEAR" SERIES; SELF-ILLUSTRATED

The Legend of LoneStar Bear, Book 1: How Lonestar Got His Name, Northwind Press, 1988.
The Legend of LoneStar Bear, Book 2: Soaring with Eagles, Northwind Press, 1989.
The Legend of LoneStar Bear, Book 3: The Mystery of the Walking Cactus, Northwind Press, 1990.

Kramer has created plush toys and audio cassette recordings based on his "LoneStar Bear" series, which are produced by his company, Oz International.

OTHER

(And director) *High Velocity,* First Asian Films, 1976.

■ Work in Progress

LoneStar in the Land of the Rising Sun, Griz (CD and book), *Where's the Bear, The Littlest Buffalo, Moose*

McGee, CD version of *The Legend of Lonestar Bear, Book 1* in English and Japanese.

■ Sidelights

Remi Kramer was an award-winning film director for many years before he abandoned Hollywood for the simpler life of rural Idaho. But his creative impulses could not be denied, and he turned his talents to writing books for children. Having a great love of nature, Kramer set his original, self-illustrated series, "Happy Tales and Adventures from the Legend of LoneStar Bear," in the Selkirk Mountains near his log cabin home. The ongoing series features Willy, a bear who loves fishing, and his raccoon friend Barney. In his first adventure, Willy goes to Texas and saves a community from the Green Critters—strange green cats from outer space. The grateful Texans make him an honorary Texas ranger and give him the name LoneStar; Willy soon becomes a very famous bear. The LoneStar books feature lots of adventure for young readers, as well as full-color illustrations that testify to the author's love of the outdoors.

■ For More Information See

PERIODICALS

School Library Journal, May, 1991, p. 89.

L

LEE, Elizabeth Rogers 1940-
(Liz Lee)

■ Personal

Born July 12, 1940; daughter of Winston Robert (a minister) and Mary Frances (Megchelsen) Rogers; married Thomas Roy Lee (an educational consultant), November 24, 1958; children: Thomas Michael, Walter Roy, Joanna Hope. *Education:* Southeastern Louisiana University, B.A., 1971; also attended Southern Theological Seminary. *Politics:* Republican. *Religion:* Southern Baptist.

■ Addresses

Home—105 Knoll Ln., Clinton, TN 37716. *Office*—Tennessee Baptist Convention, P.O. Box 728, Brentwood, TN 37024. *Agent*—Broadman and Holman Publishers, 127 Ninth Ave. N., Nashville, TN 37234.

■ Career

Ferriday Elementary, Ferriday, LA, second-grade teacher, 1972-73, kindergarten teacher, 1973-76; Sunday school department of the Tennessee Baptist Convention, program associate and director of children's work, 1983—. Writer; conference leader, speaker, and consultant in the United States, India, Hong Kong, and Brazil.

■ Awards, Honors

Teacher of the Year, Ferriday Elementary; Young Woman of the Year, Civic Club of Ferriday.

■ Writings

"SPENDING PRIME TIME WITH GOD" SERIES; UNDER NAME LIZ LEE

(With Susan W. Nally) *How to Feel Most Excellent about Who You Are (and Really Enjoy It)*, Broadman and Holman (Nashville, TN), 1994.
How to Have a Radical Attitude toward God (and Really Believe It), Broadman and Holman, 1995.

ELIZABETH ROGERS LEE

■ Work in Progress

Research on "children and parents interacting with vital issues, values, etc."

■ Sidelights

"All children have secrets," Elizabeth Rogers Lee told *SATA,* "many of the secrets deal with their 'living in life!' Through my teaching children both in school and in church, I realized they need a secret place to interact with their thoughts and feelings. When Susan Nally asked for such a book for fifth- to sixth-graders, she found none in print. She 'birthed' the first book in the series, then asked me to help her complete the series.... The journal approach allows the pre-adolescent child to read and compare Bible stories to present-day happenings [and] then decide for themselves their course of action, behavior, feeling, and/or attitude.

"Because children are so important, yet faced with major life skills which often do not expose children to a 'serving' attitude, I want always to be a part of all that children do. Writing allows both of us [adult and child] to express ourselves without confrontation. Reading and writing are ultimate gifts often overlooked. I write in a rambling, rolling style—'talking' to the individual—in sheer bliss of the moment and 'wordage' available. To write is freedom!"

*   *   *

LEE, Liz
See LEE, Elizabeth Rogers

*   *   *

LeMIEUX, A(nne) C(onnelly) 1954-

■ Personal

Born December 15, 1954 in Bridgeport, CT; daughter of John D., Sr. and Elizabeth (Magee) Connelly; married Charles P. LeMieux III, January 7, 1977; children: Sarah Elizabeth, Brendan Wolfe. *Education:* Simmons College, B.A., 1976; attended University of Bridgeport School of Music, 1976-78. *Politics:* Democrat. *Religion:* Roman Catholic. *Hobbies and other interests:* Music, acoustic fingerstyle guitar, sailing.

■ Addresses

Home—490 Pequot Ct., Southport CT 06490. *Electronic Mail*—Swan522@AOL.COM. *Agent*—Fran Lebowitz, Writer's House, 21 West 26th St., New York, NY 10010.

■ Career

Freelance journalist, 1982-87; author, 1987—. Co-founder and co-moderator of the Children's Writer's Chat on America Online. *Member:* Authors Guild, Authors League of America, Society of Children's Book Writers and Illustrators.

■ Awards, Honors

Best Book for Young Adults, American Library Association, 1994, for *The TV Guidance Counselor;* Children's choice, International Reading Association, 1994, for *Super Snoop Sam Snout: The Case of the Missing Marble;* Notable Book, Society of School Librarians International, and Silver Honors Award, Parents'

A. C. LeMIEUX

Choice, both 1995, both for *Do Angels Sing the Blues?; Fruit Flies, Fish and Fortune Cookies* was named to the Sequoya Young Adult Master List by the Oklahoma Library Association, 1996-97.

■ Writings

The TV Guidance Counselor, Tambourine, 1993.
Super Snoop Sam Snout: The Case of the Yogurt Poker, Avon, 1994.
Super Snoop Sam Snout: The Case of the Stolen Snowman, Avon, 1994.
Super Snoop Sam Snout: The Case of the Missing Marble, Avon, 1994.
Fruit Flies, Fish and Fortune Cookies, illustrated by Diane de Groat, Tambourine, 1994.
Do Angels Sing the Blues?, Tambourine, 1995.

Contributor to anthologies, including a poem to *Food Fight,* Harcourt, 1996, and a short story, "Just Say ...," to *New Year, New Love,* Avon, 1996. Author of unpublished screenplays, including *Music of the Sphere* and an untitled screenplay based on *The TV Guidance Counselor.*

■ Work in Progress

Dare to Be, M.E.!, a sequel to *Fruit Flies, Fish, and Fortune Cookies; Sea-Sar Salad,* a collection of juvenile poetry; *Cyber-Eyes,* a young adult trilogy.

■ Sidelights

A former freelance journalist, A. C. LeMieux is the author of several young adult books that deal with subjects which are often painful for teenagers, such as suicide attempts, divorced parents, and the death of close friends. Her first published work, *The TV Guidance Counselor,* deals with a depressed sixteen-year-old boy named Michael who tries to commit suicide after his parents divorce, his girlfriend leaves him, and his family moves into a small, rundown house. While in a mental hospital, Michael reflects on the events leading to his near-fatal jump off a bridge. A contributor in *Publishers Weekly* applauds LeMieux for her excellent handling of "adolescent anguish," saying "this first novel admirably explores a young man's injured soul." While criticizing LeMieux for having Michael recite "adult pop psychology," Kathy Piehl, in *School Library Journal,* nevertheless commends the author for creating a character with "an authentic teen voice" and "masterfully depict[ing] various aspects of depression."

Fruit Flies, Fish, and Fortune Cookies, a 1994 book, deals with teen issues of a less serious nature. One evening, Mary Ellen Bobowick has the misfortune of eating a fortune cookie which warns, "Reflect carefully, or your deeds will bring bad luck." Shrugging off the ominous prediction, Mary Ellen notices that suddenly nothing seems to go her way: she shatters her mother's antique mirror, gets sprayed by a skunk, and learns that her best friend is moving to France for a year. After she drops a jar of fruit flies at school on Career Day, Mary Ellen becomes convinced that the cookie was telling the truth. However, Mary Ellen's luck eventually improves, and she even finds a new boyfriend. Leslie Barban, in *School Library Journal,* calls *Fruit Flies, Fish, and Fortune Cookies* a "lighthearted, funny novel" and enjoys LeMieux's "believable, likable ... characters." Carolyn Phelan, writing in *Booklist,* maintains that some of the minor characters in the story are not well developed, but adds that Mary Ellen is an "easily identifiable" heroine for middle-grade readers.

With *Do Angels Sing the Blues?,* LeMieux returns to a world where teenagers must overcome more serious problems in their lives. During their senior year in high school, Theo and Boog, best friends since childhood, find their friendship strained when Theo falls in love with a mysterious, troubled, and withdrawn girl named Carey. As Theo spends more time with Carey instead of with Boog and their blues band, Boog begins to feel betrayed, especially when Carey is allowed to write lyrics for the band. Before the school year is over, Theo dies in a tragic highway accident, and Boog is torn between blaming Carey for Theo's death and forgiving her for fraying his friendship with Theo. Although criticizing the slightly heavy-handed foreshadowing of Theo's death, Renee Steinberg in *School Library Journal* believes that LeMieux creates teenagers who "can deal with unexpected tragedy" in a way that is neither condescending or unbelievable. Maeve Visser Knoth in *Horn Book Magazine* compliments LeMieux for the emotional depth of her characters, describing Boog and Theo as "sympathetic, richly drawn characters with human complexities."

LeMieux told *SATA:* "For me, stories are parallel universes. If the world a writer creates is vital enough, and populated by people who ring with authenticity, be it a fantasy world of mice, or realistic fiction, I'm living in it while I'm reading it. And with certain books, even

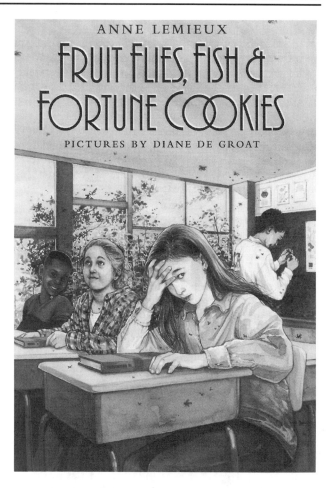

Young Mary Ellen's seemingly unending string of bad luck following the dire prediction of a fortune cookie is the focus of LeMieux's comical *Fruit Flies, Fish, & Fortune Cookies.* (Illustration by Diane de Groat.)

after I close the cover, part of me keeps living on in that other world—or it keeps living in me.

"I was born in 1954, and grew up in Fairfield, Connecticut, on a dead-end street, with lots of big old houses filled with big families. I'm the second oldest of seven, six boys and me. I used to steal my brothers' books when I ran out of fresh reading material of my own. Both of those things may have contributed to the fact that I often write from a boy's point of view. When I wasn't inside devouring books, I was outdoors, trespassing on country club property. Our street ran right up in the middle of a golf course, which all the neighborhoods used like a huge backyard, dodging golf balls and running away from Fudgebelly the greens-keeper in the warm weather, and sledding down the fairways and skating on the frozen water hazards in the winter.

"I wrote my first book in the seventh grade, a neighborhood saga called *From My Perch.* It was one of those tell-all exposes, written from the point of view of a crow who spied on all the neighborhood kids, and it got more than a few people mad at me when Sister Robert Ann read it out loud to the English classes at school. Without realizing it, I was following one of the cardinal writer's 'rules': write about what you know.

"I attended Simmons College in Boston, where I majored in writing, mostly nonfiction and journalism because creative writing intimidated me, and minored in illustration. I started keeping daily journals in college, which developed the habit of observing life, collecting details, data, musing on the meaning of it all. My first published piece, an article on the Arthurian legends, was an independent study paper I wrote while spending a semester in England during my junior year. I did a lot of research for that project, so I would add a footnote to that writer's rule: If you want to write about something you don't know about, learn about it.

"After I graduated from college, I felt that I didn't own an original thought or idea, so I decided to stop writing, and concentrate on living. I went back to school to study music—jazz, classical, and acoustic fingerstyle guitar. I also got married and had children, which kept me very much in touch with children's literature. Every once in a while, the urge to write would come over me like a spell, and I'd write an article about whatever I happened to be interested in at the time. Sailing has always been big in my family. Some of the pieces I wrote were about sailing, others were about music. Eventually a number

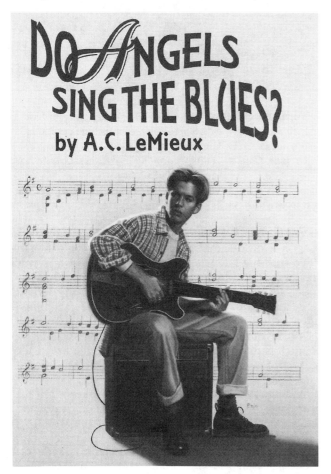

Although Boog and Theo are band partners as well as buddies, they break up when Theo falls in love with troubled Carey Harrigan in LeMieux's 1995 novel about loss and discovery. (Cover illustration by Eric Velasquez.)

of those were published. Doing freelance journalism, I also learned another important writing rule: writing is rewriting.

"After my son was born in 1987, I felt I had acquired enough experience, lived enough of life to accumulate some perhaps original thoughts on it. I signed up for a children's book writing course at Fairfield University. Five years and probably a dozen manuscripts later, I sold my first book.

"Especially in the early stages of a book, I often feel my way into a story with a pen—I see what it's about as it emerges on the page. I write all my drafts longhand, then edit them into the word processor. Using the computer actually seems to activate a different part of my 'writing brain'—a part that's as tuned into the sounds of language as the sense itself, and that thinks hypertextually, associatively. In fact, I write all my poetry directly on the computer.

"For me, writing is a process of finding connections. It's not only connecting words, but connecting ideas, symbols, events—and connecting them all to people. When I started writing *Do Angels Sing the Blues?*, I knew I wanted the book to be about the death of a best friend. My own best friend, who grew up across the street from me in my neighborhood, died when I was twenty-six. And I knew I wanted the book to be about music. I was listening to Stevie Ray Vaughan one day, singing "Life Without You," and that's when the connection clicked: I knew that the music in the book had to be the blues. When I was writing about King Arthur some twenty years ago, what captured me, what I identified with, was the theme of quest, of searching for something. That surfaced in the personality of the narrator in my first novel, *The TV Guidance Counselor*, which more than being about divorce or attempted suicide, is about my conviction that life is a process of searching, of formulating questions and seeking answers, through relationships and the self-discovery that accompanies creative endeavors.

"I find the act of writing to be a process of exploration and discovery. Much of the 'think-work' I do as a writer involves asking questions and postulating answers. When I sit down to write the first draft of the story, I consider two things: what is going to happen, a general plot, but even more important, to whom it is going to happen. I spend a lot of time getting to know my characters, who they are, what they're like, how they think, so that they really do take on a life of their own inside my head. Parts of me wind up in all my characters, both male and female, adult and young people.

"As a writer, I think of myself as a miner of life, digging for meaning, for raw ore to refine into characters of genuine metal, and forge into building blocks to create a world. My aim is to produce work that will be so genuinely evocative of and so true to life, that a reader will experience it as real."

■ Works Cited

Barban, Leslie, review of *Fruit Flies, Fish, & Fortune Cookies, School Library Journal,* October, 1994, p. 124.

Knoth, Maeve Visser, review of *Do Angels Sing the Blues?, Horn Book,* November/December, 1995, p. 746.

Phelan, Carolyn, review of *Fruit Flies, Fish, & Fortune Cookies, Booklist,* November 1, 1994, p. 497.

Piehl, Kathy, review of *The TV Guidance Counselor, School Library Journal,* October, 1993, p. 151.

Steinberg, Renee, review of *Do Angels Sing the Blues?, School Library Journal,* September, 1995, p. 219.

Review of *The TV Guidance Counselor, Publishers Weekly,* July 12, 1993, p. 81.

■ For More Information See

PERIODICALS

Booklist, December 15, 1993, p. 746; March 15, 1994, p. 1358; September 1, 1995, p. 66.

Bulletin of the Center for Children's Books, October, 1993, p. 50.

Kirkus Reviews, August 15, 1993, p. 1075; November 15, 1994, p. 1534.

Kliatt, January, 1995, p. 9.

Publishers Weekly, July 10, 1995, p. 58.

Voice of Youth Advocates, February, 1994, p. 370; August, 1995, p. 160.

* * *

LESTER, Alison 1952-

■ Personal

Born November 17, 1952, in Foster, Australia; daughter of Donald Robert (a grazier) and Jean Rosalind (a nurse; maiden name, Billings) Lester; married Edwin Hume (a solicitor), January 22, 1977; children: Will, Clair, Lachlan. *Education:* Melbourne State College, Higher Diploma of Teaching, 1975. *Hobbies and other interests:* Horses, basketball, the beach, gardening, music, skiing, cooking, travel, photography, shopping for clothes.

■ Addresses

Home—Dore Rd., Nar Nar Goon North, Victoria 3812, Australia.

■ Career

Victorian Education Department, high school art teacher in Alexandra, Australia, 1976-77, high school art teacher at correspondence school in Melbourne, Australia, 1977-78; writer and illustrator, 1978—. *Exhibitions:* Post Office Gallery, Mornington, Victoria, Australia, 1984; Gallery Art Navie, Melbourne, Australia, 1985; Seasons Gallery, Sydney, Australia, 1985, 1986.

■ Awards, Honors

Picture Book of the Year Award, Children's Book Council of Australia, 1983, for illustrating *Thing;* Picture Book of the Year honour book/commendation/shortlist, 1986, for *Clive Eats Alligators,* 1988, for *Birk the Berserker,* 1990, for *The Journey Home,* 1991, for *Magic Beach;* Australian Book Publishers Association design awards, 1989, for *Rosie Sips Spiders,* and 1990, for *Imagine.*

■ Writings

SELF-ILLUSTRATED CHILDREN'S BOOKS

Clive Eats Alligators, Oxford University Press, 1985, Houghton, 1986.

Ruby, Oxford University Press, 1987.

Rosie Sips Spiders, Oxford University Press, 1988, Houghton, 1989.

Bibs and Boots ("Australian Baby Books" series), Penguin, 1989.

Happy and Sad ("Australian Baby Books" series), Penguin, 1989.

Crashing and Splashing ("Australian Baby Books" series), Penguin, 1989.

Bumping and Bouncing ("Australian Baby Books" series), Penguin, 1989.

Imagine, Allen & Unwin, 1989, Houghton, 1990.

The Journey Home, Oxford University Press, 1989, Houghton, 1991.

Magic Beach, Allen & Unwin, 1990, Little, Brown, 1992.

Tessa Snaps Snakes, Oxford University Press, 1990, Houghton, 1991.

Isabella's Bed, Oxford University Press, 1991, Houghton, 1993.

My Farm, Allen & Unwin, 1992, Houghton, 1994.

I'm Green and I'm Grumpy, Penguin, 1993, Dutton, 1993.

Monsters Are Knocking, Penguin, 1993.

Yikes!, Allen & Unwin, 1993, Houghton, 1995.

When Frank Was Four, Hodder & Stoughton, 1994, Houghton, 1996.

Alice and Aldo, Allen & Unwin, 1996.

Celeste Sets Sail, Hodder Headline, 1996.

JUVENILE NOVEL

The Quicksand Pony, Allen & Unwin, 1996.

ILLUSTRATOR

June Epstein, *Big Dipper,* Oxford University Press, 1980.

June Epstein, *Big Dipper Rides Again,* Oxford University Press, 1982.

Robin Klein, *Thing,* Oxford University Press, 1982.

Clanty Collective, *Taught Not Caught,* Spiral, 1983.

Robin Klein, *Thingnapped,* Oxford University Press, 1984.

Robin Klein, *Ratbags and Rascals,* Dent, 1985.

June Epstein, *Big Dipper Returns,* Oxford University Press, 1985.

June Epstein, *Big Dipper Songs,* Oxford University Press, 1985.

Alison Lester and fans.

Morris Lurie, *Night-Night,* Oxford University Press, 1986.

June Factor, *Summer,* Penguin, 1987.

Robin Klein, *Birk the Berserker,* Omnibus Press, 1987.

Robin Klein, *Thinglets* (contains *Thingitis, Thing Gets a Job, Thing's Concert* and *Thing's Birthday*), Hodder & Stoughton, 1996.

ILLUSTRATOR OF "AUGUSTUS" SERIES; WRITTEN BY JUNE EPSTEIN

Augustus, T. Nelson, 1984.
Augustus Conducts the Band, T. Nelson, 1984.
Augustus Teaches the Children, T. Nelson, 1984.
Augustus Flies a Plane, T. Nelson, 1984.
Augustus Works in a Factory, T. Nelson, 1984.
Augustus Plays Football, T. Nelson, 1984.
Augustus the King, T. Nelson, 1984.
Augustus the Painter, T. Nelson, 1984.

■ Work in Progress

Running with the Horses, for Penguin, 1997.

■ Sidelights

Since the publication of her first self-illustrated picture book in 1985, Australian Alison Lester has become internationally renowned for works that celebrate the creativity and energy of childhood. "Few writers and illustrators can match Alison Lester's ability to depict the rich imagination of children," Kevin Steinberger writes in *Magpies,* and in works such as *Imagine, The Journey Home, Magic Beach,* and *Isabella's Bed* the author shows how a child's imagination can transform the ordinary into the fantastic. In addition, Lester has created books that explore the everyday lives of children in all their individuality. The popular series beginning with *Clive Eats Alligators,* for instance, demonstrates that "Lester's insights into the world of young children are wonderfully perceptive," according to Joan Zahnleiter in another *Magpies* article.

"I grew up on a beef farm in Southern Victoria—an area of hot summers, but blasting cold wet winters," Lester once told *SATA.* "It is beautiful farming country, rolling from windswept hills down to great sandy beaches and sparkling sea. Life *was* the farm and as kids we were constantly riding after cattle (we loved it), or doing some other project on the farm." After spending four years at a boarding school, the author added, "I finished my secondary education and, like many of my contemporaries, had no ambition other than to have a good time. Years of traveling, hiking, riding, and partying ensued. After I married Edwin, we traveled in South America for a year. I've also traveled in Australia and Southeast Asia."

Even after her marriage, Lester was not yet ready to develop her artistic interests into a career. "I'd always been fairly unambitious and lazy, I guess," she confessed to *SATA,* "until I was expecting my first child and saw a life as a housewife stretching out before me. I'd been illustrating class books at the correspondence school and loving it, so I took a folio to Oxford University Press and met Rosalind Price, then the children's editor at Oxford. My illustrating career took off from there." Lester illustrated several books by June Epstein and Robin Klein, including the latter's 1982 story *Thing,* which was named Picture Book of the Year by the Children's Book Council of Australia.

It was the publication of Lester's first self-illustrated book, however, that really gained her notice. *Clive Eats Alligators* follows a group of seven children as they participate in various everyday activities, such as playing or eating lunch, in their own unique style. The first six kids are featured in individual pictures over two pages; on the following double-page spread, the seventh is shown, usually acting in an unusual fashion (for instance, Clive eats alligator-shaped cereal for breakfast). Lester's watercolor illustrations are filled with detail but uncluttered; as a result, according to *Horn Book* contributor Ann A. Flowers, "the book is fun to look at, with lots to identify and lots to guess at." Lester uses the same format in *Rosie Sips Spiders,* which shows the children at home, gardening, and sleeping, among other activities. "The formula is brilliantly simple," Margery Fisher asserts in *Growing Point,* "and the wash and line pictures ... invite long and delighted study by children." As Marcus Crouch remarks in *Junior Bookshelf, Rosie Sips Spiders* shows "what the picturebook

can achieve without benefit of story-line if word and picture proceed in perfect harmony."

Youngsters who enjoy search-and-find games will also enjoy *Imagine,* which shows a boy and girl using their imaginations to transport themselves into exotic landscapes filled with animals. In combining illustrations of children "playing pretend" with the "real" settings they have imagined, Lester "offers a lively—and lovely—exercise in using one's creativity," a *Publishers Weekly* reviewer notes. Another game of make-believe results in *The Journey Home,* in which two children voyage from the sandpit where they are digging to the North Pole and back. Along the way, Wild and Woolly meet Father Christmas, the Good Fairy, Prince Charming, and other characters from traditional tales. In *Horn Book,* Carolyn K. Jenks hails Lester's "detailed, lighthearted watercolors," which are bordered with items corresponding to the characters, while a *Kirkus Reviews* critic comments that "the precise illustrations have an appealing blend of humor and charm." The combination of text and images in *The Journey Home,* a *Junior Bookshelf* reviewer concludes, "convey the movement of the journey and the possibilities that can be explored in dreams."

A summertime excursion is the inspiration for imaginary adventures in *Magic Beach,* as a sandcastle is transformed into a palace rescue and beachcombing leads to buried treasure. The illustrations, featuring Lester's trademark border details, "both suit the mood and reinforce the verse," Nancy Menaldi-Scanlan remarks in *School Library Journal,* while the "rhymed text reads aloud beautifully," according to *Booklist* contributor Chris Sherman. Lester takes a more serious approach to *Isabella's Bed,* as the world of the imagination serves to heal a family. When Anna and Luis visit their grandmother, they love to sleep in "Isabella's" room,

An invitation to live in contrasting places and meet the native animals introduces the young reader to the animal kingdom in Lester's lively self-illustrated picture book, *Imagine.*

Two Australian children fall through a hole to the North Pole and have adventures on the way home with such personalities as Father Christmas and the Good Fairy. (From *The Journey Home*, written and illustrated by Lester.)

which is full of unusual objects from South America. Their grandmother will answer few questions about the items, instead telling the story of how Isabella left her home after her husband drowned. "In fetching dreamscapes rendered in impressionistic brush strokes and intricate detailing," as a *Publishers Weekly* critic describes Lester's tale, the children imagine how the mysterious objects fit into the story, and their discovery that "Isabella" is their grandmother allows them to help her with her grief. "The quiet, poetic text, exotic journey, and warm conclusion make a pleasant unusual tale," states a *Kirkus Reviews* writer, adding praise for Lester's "serene, stylized illustrations." As a result, Steinberger concludes, *Isabella's Bed* is "a wonderful picture book to be savoured by readers of all ages."

Lester returned to the activities of the seven friends Clive, Rosie, Frank, Ernie, Celeste, Tessa, and Nicky in *Tessa Snaps Snakes*. This time the children are portrayed keeping secrets, expressing dislikes, laughing at jokes, and sneaking midnight snacks. Praising the detailed illustrations and "cheerful zaniness" of Lester's prose, Lori A. Janick notes in *School Library Journal* that the author "proves adept at capturing the idiosyncrasies of childhood." In *Frank Was Four* Lester adds the dimension of a counting book to her account of the children's accomplishments. "Children will recognise themselves and their own prowess in the doings of the seven friends," *Magpies* contributor Joan Zahnleiter explains, especially as they are shown from ages one to seven. The critic praises the framed pictures and border details in *Frank Was Four*, adding that the book's design "works as well and is as fresh and entertaining as is the book's predecessors."

Lester journeyed back into her own childhood to create *My Farm*, an account of a typical year on an Australian farm. "In Lester's hands," Mary Lou Burket writes in *Five Owls*, "the incidents of an unselfconscious childhood spent primarily out-of-doors, raising livestock and larking about, prove to have plenty of appeal." Illustrated with a combination of full-page paintings and miniature scenes, the book shows Lester's "particular knack" for inserting "lots of faithful, suggestive touches into the story," according to a *Kirkus Reviews* critic. *Bulletin of the Center for Children's Books* contributor Betsy Hearne likewise praises the "vigorously varied" format and illustrations "that manage to include funny details without appearing crowded." Although the subject matter is ordinary, the critic concludes, in *My Farm* "it's the lively narrative action and rampant visual humor that energize everyday events for current listeners."

"As my imagination increases, I can't think of any work I would rather be doing, unless it is droving cattle," Lester once commented. "Still, I'm not sure that I'll keep writing children's books forever. I'm full of ideas about fabric design, toys, gardens, et cetera, and I may choose to follow one of these follies. It is hard to find time to work on all these creative things.

"My own children and my childhood memories are my greatest sources of inspiration. I'm a country girl and still live in the bush, so the horses, dogs, cats, and garden also inspire me. I love to see the funny side of things. Kids are very funny and sharp, but it is difficult to communicate humor to them without being patronizing. I also love the exotic and strange.

"I have been doing more and more writing, progressing on to a junior novel to be published next year. Increasingly my time is taken up travelling around Australia and overseas talking about my work and running writing and illustrating workshops."

■ Works Cited

Burket, Mary Lou, review of *My Farm, Five Owls,* November/December, 1994, pp. 35-36.

Crouch, Marcus, review of *Rosie Sips Spiders, Junior Bookshelf,* October, 1989, pp. 216-17.

Fisher, Margery, review of *Rosie Sips Spiders, Growing Point,* November, 1989, p. 5253.

Flowers, Ann A., review of *Clive Eats Alligators, Horn Book,* July/August, 1986, pp. 442-43.

Hearne, Betsy, review of *My Farm, Bulletin of the Center for Children's Books,* July/August, 1994, p. 365.

Review of *Imagine, Publishers Weekly,* July 13, 1990, p. 54.

Review of *Isabella's Bed, Kirkus Reviews,* April 15, 1993, p. 532.

Review of *Isabella's Bed, Publishers Weekly,* April 19, 1993, p. 60.

Janick, Lori A., review of *Tessa Snaps Snakes, School Library Journal,* December, 1991, p. 96.

Jenks, Carolyn K., review of *The Journey Home, Horn Book,* July/August, 1991, p. 449.

Review of *The Journey Home, Junior Bookshelf,* December, 1990, p. 270.

Review of *The Journey Home, Kirkus Reviews,* April 15, 1991, p. 545.

Menaldi-Scanlan, Nancy, review of *Magic Beach, School Library Journal,* June, 1992, p. 97.

Review of *My Farm, Kirkus Reviews,* July 15, 1994, p. 988.

Sherman, Chris, review of *Magic Beach, Booklist,* April 1, 1992, p. 1457.

Steinberger, Kevin, review of *Isabella's Bed, Magpies,* September, 1992, p. 30.

Zahnleiter, Joan, review of *When Frank Was Four, Magpies,* November, 1994, p. 14.

■ For More Information See

PERIODICALS

Horn Book, November/December, 1990, p. 729.
Junior Bookshelf, April, 1990, p. 56.
Kirkus Reviews, March 15, 1992, p. 395.
School Library Journal, May, 1990, p. 88.

—*Sketch by Diane Telgen*

*　　*　　*

LEWIN, Betsy 1937-

■ Personal

Born May 12, 1937, in Clearfield, PA; daughter of John K. (in insurance sales) and Winifred (a teacher; maiden name, Dowler) Reilly; married Ted B. Lewin (a writer and illustrator), 1963. *Education:* Pratt Institute of Art, B.F.A., 1959. *Hobbies and other interests:* Traveling to wilderness areas throughout the world, hiking, canoeing, and observing wildlife.

■ Addresses

Home and office—152 Willoughby Ave., Brooklyn, NY 11025.

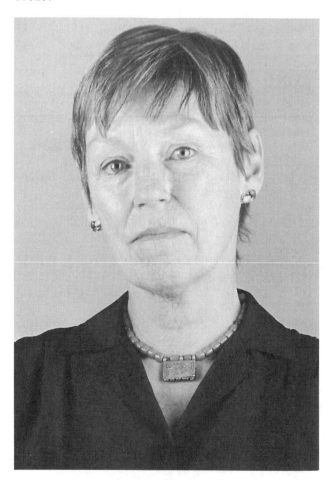

BETSY LEWIN

■ Career

Freelance writer and illustrator.

■ Awards, Honors

Pick of the List, American Booksellers, 1990, for *Araminta's Paintbox*, and 1993, for *Ho! Ho! Ho! The Complete Book of Christmas Words*, written by Lynda Graham Barber; Children's Choice, 1994, for *Yo! Hungry Wolf*, written by David Vozar, and *Somebody Catch My Homework*, written by David L. Harrison; Best Books, *School Library Journal*, 1995, for *Booby Hatch*.

■ Writings

SELF-ILLUSTRATED

Animal Snackers, Dodd, 1980.
Cat Count, Dodd, 1981.
Hip, Hippo, Hooray, Dodd, 1982.
Booby Hatch, Houghton, 1995.
Walk a Green Path, Lothrop, 1995.
Chubbo's Pool, Houghton, 1997.

ILLUSTRATOR

Helen Kronberg Olson, *The Strange Thing That Happened to Oliver Wendell Iscovitch*, Dodd, Mead, 1983.
Berniece Freschet, *Furlie Cat*, Lothrop, 1986.
Beatrice Schenk de Regniers, *Penny*, Lothrop, 1987.
Arnold Adoff, *Greens: Poems*, Lothrop, 1988.
Maria Polushkin, *Kitten in Trouble*, Bradbury Press, 1988.
Polushkin, *Here's That Kitten*, Bradbury Press, 1989.
Peter Limberg, *Weird: The Complete Book of Halloween Words*, Bradbury Press, 1989.
Karen Ackerman, *Araminta's Paintbox*, Atheneum, 1990.
Lynda Graham Barber, *Mushy: The Complete Book of Valentine's Words*, Bradbury Press, 1990.
Winifred Morris, *What If the Shark Wears Tennis Shoes?*, Atheneum, 1990.
Lynda Graham Barber, *Gobble: The Complete Book of Thanksgiving Words*, Bradbury Press, 1991.
Harry Allard, *The Hummingbirds' Day*, Houghton, 1991.
Patricia Reilly Giff, *The War Began at Supper: Letters to Miss Loria*, Dell, 1991.
Carolyn Haywood, *Eddie and the Fire Engine*, Beach Tree, 1992.
Grace Maccarone, *Itchy, Itchy Chicken Pox*, Scholastic, 1992.
Russell Hoban, *Jim Hedgehog and the Lonesome Tower*, Houghton, 1992.
Hoban, *Jim Hedgehog's Supernatural Christmas*, Houghton, 1992.
Lynda Graham Barber, *Doodle Dandy: The Complete Book of Independence Day Words*, Bradbury Press, 1993.
Joanne Ryder, *First Grade Elves*, Troll, 1993.
Ryder, *First Grade Ladybugs*, Troll, 1993.
Ryder, *First Grade Valentines*, Troll, 1993.
Stephen Krensky, *Fraidy Cats*, Scholastic, 1993.
Joanne Ryder, *Hello, First Grade*, Troll, 1993.
Lynda Graham Barber, *Ho! Ho! Ho! The Complete Book of Christmas Words*, Bradbury Press, 1993.
Ida Luttrell, *Mattie's Little Possum Pet*, Atheneum, 1993.
David L. Harrison, *Somebody Catch My Homework: Poems*, Boyds Mills, 1993.
David Vozar, *Yo! Hungry Wolf: A Nursery Rap*, Doubleday, 1993.
David L. Harrison, *The Boy Who Counted Stars: Poems*, Boyds Mills, 1994.
Caroline A. Levine, *The Detective Stars and the Case of the Super Soccer Team*, Dutton, 1994.
Steven Kroll, *I'm George Washington and You're Not!*, Hyperion, 1994.
Evan Levine, *What's Black and White and Came to Visit?*, Orchard Books, 1994.
Grace Maccarone, *The Classroom Pet*, Scholastic, 1995.
Maccarone, *The Lunch Box Surprise*, Scholastic, 1995.
Maccarone, *My Tooth Is about to Fall Out*, Scholastic, 1995.
David Vozar, *M. C. Turtle and the Hip Hop Hare: A Nursery Rap*, Doubleday, 1995.
Grace Maccarone, *The Gym Day Winner*, Scholastic, 1996.
Maccarone, *The Recess Mess*, Scholastic, 1996.
Maccarone, *Sharing Time Troubles*, Scholastic, 1996.

■ Sidelights

The lively and whimsical illustrations of Betsy Lewin have graced the pages of more than forty books for children, including several that she wrote herself. A born artist, Lewin grew up in Clearfield, Pennsylvania. "Drawing and painting have always been my main interests," she once told *SATA*, "and there was never a doubt in my mind when I was a child that I would be anything but an artist." Lewin completed her formal training in fine arts at the Pratt Institute in New York City. In 1963, she married fellow author and illustrator Ted Lewin. Though the couple have lived in a brownstone in Brooklyn, New York, for many years, they share a love of the outdoors that has led them to travel all over the world. For example, Lewin has observed animals in Africa, Australia, Brazil, and the Galapagos Islands. She has also hiked into a volcanic crater in Hawaii, canoed through the Everglades in Florida, and watched whales off the coast of Baja California in Mexico. Incidents from her vast travels have inspired many of her books for children. "My books combine my love of drawing, the sound of words, and the touching humor in much animal behavior," Lewin explained to *SATA*. "I observe and draw animals and wildlife and paint flowers in watercolors."

Booby Hatch, which Lewin both wrote and illustrated, grew out of her experience in the Galapagos Islands. It tells the story of Pepe, an unusual bird known as a blue-footed booby, who hatches from his egg to live along the rocky shore there. As Pepe grows up he learns how to fly, dive into the ocean and catch fish, and avoid being eaten by bigger animals. Before long, he meets a female bird and engages in a mating dance. The story ends with

The true story of the life cycle of a blue-footed booby in the Galapagos Islands, *Booby Hatch* was written and illustrated by Lewin from direct observation.

another egg nestled among the rocks, as the cycle of life begins again. Carolyn Phelan, writing in *Booklist*, praised the book as "a simple, appealing nature study for young children." In a review for *School Library Journal*, Ellen Fader called *Booby Hatch* "a lovely book that succeeds in every way," adding that "Lewin's watercolor landscapes are spare and evocative."

In her next book, *Walk a Green Path*, Lewin introduces young readers to many of the exotic places she has visited. The book consists of a series of large watercolor paintings, each depicting the types of plants native to a certain part of the world. For example, there are pictures of giant lily pads in the Amazon River, tiny mosses growing on a dead stump near a lake in upstate New York, the dense greenery of the Australian rain forest, and potted flowers on an iron staircase in New York City. Each spread is accompanied by a short statement describing the vegetation and a brief poem expressing Lewin's feelings about it. "Most of the writing is intensely, compactly personal," stated a writer for *Kirkus Reviews*, "giving readers the impression that they are tagging along Lewin's trail." In a review for *Booklist*, Mary Harris Veeder called the illustrations "the most memorable part of the book, beautifully conveying a sense of Lewin's affection for growing things." Kathy Piehl, writing in *School Library Journal*, added that

Walk a Green Path should "encourage readers to view their own surroundings with renewed attention."

Like her own books, many of the books that Lewin has illustrated for other authors feature animals as prominent characters. For example, in *Mattie's Little Possum Pet* by Ida Luttrell, a woman on her way to pick flowers finds a possum lying on its back with its tongue hanging out and its eyes rolled back in its head. Mattie feels sorry for the charming little creature, who was actually just playing dead, and takes it home with her. Her cat and dog do not trust the possum, however, and before long the possum proves them right by causing trouble and arranging for the pets to take the blame. Finally, Mattie realizes that the mischievous possum has fooled her and taken advantage of her generosity. "Excitement, action, and fun characterize Lewin's lively drawings, which seem to have been effortlessly and spontaneously executed," Anna Biagioni Hart wrote in a review for *School Library Journal*.

Another clever animal tale enhanced by Lewin's illustrations is *What's Black and White and Came to Visit*, by Evan Levine. The adventure begins when a young girl named Lily discovers a skunk in the drainpipe of her house. Her parents are not sure how to get the skunk to come out without causing it to create an odor. They call the fire department, but the firemen do not know how to handle the situation either. Before long the police department, the town's expert yodeler, and a variety of other characters have taken over Lily's lawn in a noisy disagreement about how to proceed. Finally, the skunk has to leave its hiding place in the drainpipe and run back into the woods for some peace and quiet. In a review for *School Library Journal*, Mary Lou Budd noted that "Lewin's pen-and-ink drawings, colored in with soft, watercolor pastels, deftly express the story's fun, action, and emotion."

■ Works Cited

Budd, Mary Lou, review of *What's Black and White and Came to Visit*, *School Library Journal*, September, 1994, p. 188.

Fader, Ellen, review of *Booby Hatch*, *School Library Journal*, May, 1995.

Hart, Anna Biagioni, review of *Mattie's Little Possum Pet*, *School Library Journal*, September, 1993, p. 210.

Phelan, Carolyn, review of *Booby Hatch*, *Booklist*, March 1, 1995, p. 1248.

Piehl, Kathy, review of *Walk a Green Path*, *School Library Journal*, April, 1995, p. 126.

Veeder, Mary Harris, review of *Walk a Green Path*, *Booklist*, June 1, 1995, p. 1778.

Review of *Walk a Green Path*, *Kirkus Reviews*, March 15, 1995.

■ For More Information See

PERIODICALS

Booklist, May 15, 1992, p. 1680; August 1993, p. 2071; October 15, 1994, p. 436; August 1996.

Bulletin of the Center for Children's Books, November 1982, p. 50.
Horn Book, June 1981, p. 294.
Publishers Weekly, March 16, 1990, p. 68; March 23, 1992, p. 72; July 19, 1993, p. 253; October 11, 1993, p. 88; August 8, 1994, p. 428.
School Library Journal, June 1990, p. 105; June 1992, p. 95.

*   *   *

LOOMANS, Diane 1955-

■ Personal

Born June 25, 1955, in Milwaukee, WI; daughter of James (a sales manager) and Marie (Nicholas) Fitzpatrick; children: Julia Loomans. *Education:* University of Wisconsin, degrees in community education and adult education.

■ Addresses

Office—P.O. Box 1203, Solana Beach, CA 92075.

■ Career

Author, public speaker, teacher, freelance journalist, and poet. Director of Global Learning, San Diego, CA, 1985—; college teacher, Milwaukee, WI, 1987-91. Consultant to colleges and corporations in creative thinking. *Member:* National Speakers Association, Writers Guild, Book Forum, Best Selling Authors of San Diego.

DIANE LOOMANS

■ Writings

The Lovables in the Kingdom of Self-Esteem, edited by Martha Weston, illustrated by Kim Howard, H. J. Kramer/Starseed Press, 1991.
(With Karen Kolberg and Julia Loomans) *Positively Mother Goose,* illustrated by Ronda E. Henrichsen, edited by Linda Kramer, H. J. Kramer, 1992.
(With Karen Kolberg) *The Laughing Classroom: Everyone's Guide to Teaching with Humor and Play,* illustrated by Martha Weston, foreword by Steve Allen, "backword" by Professor Oops, H. J. Kramer, 1993.
(With Julia Loomans) *Full Esteem Ahead: 100 Ways to Build Self-Esteem in Children and Adults,* edited by Nancy Carleton, foreword by Jack Canfield, introduction by Sky Schultz, H. J. Kramer, 1994.
The Lovables (board book), illustrated by Kim Howard, H. J. Kramer, 1994.
Today I Am Lovable! 365 Positive Activities for Kids, H. J. Kramer, 1996.

Also author of inspirational poetry books, *If I Had My Child to Raise Over Again* and *The Soulful Life.*

■ Adaptations

The Lovables in the Kingdom of Self-Esteem is currently being adapted into an animated series.

■ Work in Progress

Global Blessings: A Child's First Book of Prayers from Around the World.

*   *   *

LUCCARELLI, Vincent 1923-

■ Personal

Born December 6, 1923, in Volturara, Italy; son of Luigi (a baker) and Antonietta (a homemaker; maiden name, Parziale); married Phyllis Clara (a homemaker; maiden name, Shaffer) Luccarelli; children: Vincent, Philip, Donna, Paula. *Education:* Attended University of Maryland. *Politics:* Independent. *Religion:* "Free Spirit." *Hobbies and other interests:* Music appreciation, choral singing, opera, animal rights.

■ Addresses

Home—4312 Robertson Blvd., Alexandria, VA 22309.

■ Career

Comsat Corporation, Washington, DC, internship, 1967-68; Don Norman, Transportation Consultants, Washington, DC, public relations director, 1968-71. *Northern Virginia News,* Fairfax, VA, freelance reporter; freelance consultant to writers on religious topics. Worked variously as a customer service manager and an event planner and director. *Military service:* U.S. Ma-

VINCENT LUCCARELLI

rine Corps, 1942-45, Pacific theater; attained rank of corporal, awarded Purple Heart Medal. *Member:* Washington Independent Writers/Writers Group Association.

■ Writings

Job Revisited, Winston-Derek Publishers, 1994.

■ Work in Progress

"The Wedding," a long poem based on the "Song of Solomon" of the Bible, 1997; a novel; research on the "Song of Solomon" and the Poetics of Shakespeare and Milton.

■ Sidelights

Vincent Luccarelli told *SATA* that he spent the early years of his childhood in "a small hill town in the Appenine Mountains which form the lower spine of the Italian peninsula." Luccarelli's father, a baker, came to America "in order to escape Mussolini's oppressive government, and to regain economic stability for his family." Luccarelli's mother, "a deeply religious person and a devout Catholic, infused [me] with the 'love of Christ.'"

Luccarelli was just a teenager when he immigrated to America with one of his brothers. He lived through the Great Depression, and served the United States in the Second Marine Division in the Pacific theater during World War II. Luccarelli was wounded at Tarawa and received the Purple Heart. The fact that he survived combat led Luccarelli to conclude that "God spared me

in the war" for a specific purpose, "and so I made a vow." Luccarelli pledged to "write for the Lord."

Luccarelli's "passion for Christianity" and ambition to "evangelize through the written word" inspired him to study at the University of Maryland, and to research the King James Bible. "The Book of Job, with its dramatic monologues, fired [my] imagination and desire to create a poem defining Christianity dramatically." As Luccarelli explained to *SATA*, he "had at last found the perfect vehicle ... for the publication of ... a destined undertaking." The resulting work, *Job Revisited,* tells of an "inner venture to salvation" in the "rhythm of Hebrew Verse."

*   *   *

LUTHER, Rebekah (Lyn) S(tiles) 1960-

■ Personal

Born July 20, 1960, in Muskogee, OK; daughter of Arthur Boyd (a minister and salesman) and Myrlita J. (an accountant; maiden name, Franklin) Stiles; married Euil E. "Marty" Luther (a medical doctor), May 25, 1985 (divorced 1996); children: Clifton E., Katharin E. *Education:* Attended Northeastern State College, 1978-79, and Connors State College, 1982, 1992; presently attending Northeast Louisiana University. *Politics:* Registered Republican. *Religion:* Non-denominational. *Hobbies and other interests:* Singing, cooking, gardening, going to movies and plays, writing.

REBEKAH S. LUTHER

■ Addresses

Home and office—4439 Churchill Circle, Monroe, Louisiana 71203.

■ Career

Cave & McKay Law Firm, Baton Rouge, LA, receptionist, 1991; Professional Specialties, Baton Rouge, office manager, 1995; Department of Liberal Arts, Northeast Louisiana University, office clerk, 1996—. *Member:* National Registry of Authors and Unity.

■ Writings

The Yoda Family, Dorrance Publishing, 1994.

Also the author of poetry collected in anthologies and reviews, including "Desire," in *Golden Dreams: An Anthology of Modern Poetry,* Dover Beach Poetry Press, 1994; "Special Moments," in *Perspective,* The Poet's Guild, 1994; "Memories," in *Memories,* JMW Publishing Co., 1994; "You Make My Day," in *Perceptions,* Iliad Press, 1994; "If You Were Here," in *Arcadia Poetry Anthology,* Arcadia Poetry Press, 1994; "These Arms," in *Dusting Off Dreams,* Quill Books, 1994; "Let Us Follow" and "Father," in *Mirrors of the Mind,* Poetry Press, 1994; "Books," in *Dark Side of the Moon,* National Library of Poetry, 1994; "Windows of the Poet," in *Windows of the Poet,* JMW Publishing Co., 1995; "Faith in Me" and "What is a Friend?" in *Love Poems,* Poetry Press, 1996.

■ Sidelights

"I began taking writing seriously during my junior high school years, when writing term papers," Rebekah S. Luther told *SATA.* "However, it wasn't until years later when I began keeping my poems in a journal and continued adding to the collection as the years passed and life events took place.

"In 1985, I moved to Louisiana, where I live with my two children, Clifton, nine years, and Katharin, eight years. With the encouragement of my mother and my best friends I sent several short stories to publishers. Almost a year later I received an invitation to publish *The Yoda Family,* a children's short story. Since this book's release in May 1994, I have been published in several poetry anthologies and plan to have my own book of poetry published in the near future.

"I am a full-time mom and student at Northeast Louisiana University, continually working on a degree in English education. When time allows my hobbies include singing, cooking, gardening, going to movies and plays, and writing.

"Poetry is a window of the soul."

M

SUSAN A. MADSEN

MADSEN, Susan A(rrington) 1954-

■ Personal

Born August 25, 1954, in Logan, UT; daughter of Leonard J. (a historian) and Grace F. (a homemaker) Arrington; married Dean Madsen (a music professor), August 20, 1974; children: Emily, Rebecca, Sarah, Rachel. *Education:* Utah State University, B.S., 1975. *Religion:* Latter-day Saint. *Hobbies and other interests:*

"Horseback riding, snow skiing, genealogy, being with my husband and children."

■ Addresses

Home—401 North 400 E., Hyde Park, Utah 84318.

■ Career

Writer and homemaker. Hyde Park Board of Adjustments, chairperson, 1985-94; adjunct faculty member, Logan Latter-day Saints Institute of Religion, 1991-95.

■ Awards, Honors

Honored at Utah State University National Women's History Week, 1985; National Society Daughters of the Utah Pioneers Community Service Award, 1990.

■ Writings

Christmas: A Joyful Heritage, illustrated by Glen Edwards, Deseret (Salt Lake City, UT), 1984.
(With father, Leonard J. Arrington) *Sunbonnet Sisters: True Stories of Mormon Women and Frontier Life,* Bookcraft (Salt Lake City, UT), 1984.
(With father, Leonard J. Arrington) *Mothers of the Prophets,* Deseret, 1987.
The Lord Needed a Prophet, Deseret, 1990.
I Walked to Zion: True Stories of Young Pioneers on the Mormon Trail, Deseret, 1994.
Growing Up in Zion: True Stories of Young Pioneers Building the Kingdom, Deseret, 1996.

Contributor of more than thirty articles to *Collier's Encyclopedia Yearbooks.*

■ Sidelights

"I have a special love for the history of The Church of Jesus Christ of Latter-day Saints (the Mormons)," Susan A. Madsen told *SATA.* "I especially admire the women and children who played a significant role in the western migration of the early Mormon pioneers and the settling of their Zion in the West, and yet have received little credit and attention for their accomplishments.

"I have written two books focusing on early Mormon pioneer women and I grew to love their grit and commitment. *I Walked to Zion: True Stories of Young Pioneers on the Mormon Trail* taught me of the courage and strength of the children and teenagers who crossed the Great Plains between 1847 and 1869 on the Mormon Trail. These youngsters had some amazing experiences: humorous and tragic, exciting and devastating. They were a remarkable group of young people. They played an important role in the westward journey of the early Latter-day Saints (LDS), which is often referred to as one of the greatest epics in American history.

"My most recent book, *Growing Up in Zion: True Stories of Young Pioneers Building the Kingdom,* uses first-person accounts to tell what it was like to be a child growing up in the Utah Territory, an area that encompassed parts of what are now seven western states. I was amazed at the amount of back-breaking work performed by these sturdy young pioneers. Their stories tell of Indians, grasshoppers, fearsome school teachers, hunger, and a multitude of life-threatening experiences.

"I do most of my historical research in the LDS Church archives in Salt Lake City, the Utah State Historical Society, and the special collections of the major universities of Utah. I especially love reading first-person accounts of historical events, found in journals, diaries, and life histories.

"I write at home and enjoy the freedom of choosing my own schedule. I hope my writings will bring history alive for the average American reader, including young people, interested in learning about people whose lives were guided by their commitment to the principles they believed in, not just by the desire for material wealth or capital gain. These good people were guided by their hearts, their beliefs, and accomplished seemingly impossible tasks along the way."

■ For More Information See

PERIODICALS

Bulletin of the Center for Children's Books, October, 1994, p. 57.
Horn Book Guide, spring, 1995, p. 164.

*   *   *

A MAN WITHOUT A SPLEEN
See CHEKHOV, Anton (Pavlovich)

MARNEY, Dean 1952-

■ Personal

Born December 30, 1952, in Waterville, WA; son of Keith S. (a realtor) and Alice (a musician; maiden name, Osborne) Marney; married Susan Carr (a psychiatric nurse practitioner), July 12, 1975; children: Blythe, Dylan, Luke. *Education:* University of Washington, B.A., 1975; University of Oregon, M.L.S., 1977. *Politics:* "Diverse." *Religion:* Christian/ Episcopalian. *Hobbies and other interests:* His children and their interests.

■ Addresses

Home—2996 Riviera Blvd., Malaga, WA 98828. *Office*—North Central Regional Library, 238 Olds Station Rd., Wenatchee, WA 98801.

■ Career

North Central Regional Library, Wenatchee, WA, began as request clerk, 1972, became director, 1990—. Organist and choirmaster of St. Luke's Episcopal Church in Wenatchee, WA. President of the board of a nonprofit gallery, 1984-87. *Member:* Allied Arts group (vice president, 1980-82).

DEAN MARNEY

■ Writings

Just Good Friends, Addison Wesley, 1982.
The Computer That Ate My Brother, Houghton, 1985.
The Trouble with Jake's Double, Scholastic, Inc., 1988.
You, Me, and Gracie Makes Three, Scholastic, Inc., 1989.
The Christmas Tree That Ate My Mother, Scholastic, Inc., 1992.
Dirty Socks Don't Win Games, Scholastic, Inc., 1992.
The Jack-o'-Lantern That Ate My Brother, Scholastic, Inc., 1994.
The Turkey That Ate My Father, Scholastic, Inc., 1995.
The Easter Bunny That Ate My Sister, Scholastic, Inc., 1996.

■ Work in Progress

Pet-rified and *The Valentine That Ate My Teacher.*

■ Sidelights

Dean Marney told *SATA:* "I think at times that I write to discover who I was as a kid and who I am now. I'm always surprised by the parts of myself that I encounter through my characters that I had ignored or never knew. There is always an element of shock at what comes out from me onto the page.

"I love to build imaginary worlds and temporarily move in. I did it all the time as a kid, building forts and towns that had whole histories and were populated by all sorts of strange people. I discovered that through some authors' books I could also be a guest, transported to another place—that author's world. Luckily, I also found out how much fun it was to share your imaginary worlds and situations by writing them down.

"People ask me where I get my weird ideas. They say 'creative' but they mean weird. Since I can remember, I've always tried to live pretty close to the edge of my imagination, whether it's been through make-believe play, or music, or art, or theater, or dance—because I like how it feels. Living close to my imagination also seems to allow me to stay connected to that big sea of ideas and possibilities out there (or in there) that can be, at times, mysteriously available to us. I have a great dream life.

"I tend to find a lot in life that I think is funny and I tend to laugh easily. My characters laugh easily too. Finding things funny has gotten me into trouble. If someone sticks their finger up their nose, I have to laugh no matter where I am. People ask me why I've written a series of books about something eating a member of a family. I always tell them that they've never met my family.

"I've found that I like writing for the paperback market. I like it that my books are easily affordable and can be carried anywhere. I write for kids because I love them. I'm grateful that I don't love snakes that much or I'd have to write for them too."

MARRIN, Albert 1936-

■ Personal

Born July 24, 1936, in New York, NY; son of Louis and Frieda (Funt) Marrin; married Yvette Rappaport, November 22, 1959. *Education:* City College (now City College of the City University of New York), B.A., 1958; Yeshiva University, M.Ed., 1959; Columbia University, M.A., 1961, Ph.D., 1968. *Hobbies and other interests:* Travel in Europe.

■ Addresses

Home—750 Kappock St., Bronx, NY 10463. *Office*—Department of History, Yeshiva University, 500 West 185th St., New York, NY 10033. *Agent*—Toni Mendez, Inc., 141 East 56th St., New York, NY 10022.

■ Career

William Howard Taft High School, New York City, social studies teacher, 1959-68; Yeshiva University, New York City, assistant professor of history, 1968-78, professor and chairman of history department, 1978—; writer, 1968—. Visiting professor, Yeshiva University, 1967-68, and Touro College, 1972-74. *Member:* Western Writers of America, American Association of University Professors.

ALBERT MARRIN

■ Awards, Honors

Notable Children's Trade Book selection, National Council for Social Studies and Children's Book Council, and *Boston Globe/Horn Book* Honor Book, both 1985, both for *1812: The War Nobody Won;* Western Heritage Award for best juvenile nonfiction book, National Cowboy Hall of Fame, and Spur Award, Western Writers of America, both 1993, both for *Cowboys, Indians, and Gunfighters: The Story of the Cattle Kingdom; Boston Globe/Horn Book* Honor Book, 1994, Dorothy Canfield Fisher Children's Book Award, 1995, and Association of Christian Public School Teachers and Administrators Honor Award, 1995, all for *"Unconditional Surrender": U. S. Grant and the Civil War;* Best Books, *School Library Journal,* 1995, for *The Sea King: Sir Francis Drake;* Children's Book Guild and *Washington Post* Nonfiction Award for contribution to children's literature, 1995.

■ Writings

JUVENILE NONFICTION

Overlord: D-Day and the Invasion of Europe, Atheneum (New York City), 1982.
The Airman's War: World War II in the Sky, Atheneum, 1982.
Victory in the Pacific, Atheneum, 1983.
War Clouds in the West: Indians and Cavalrymen, 1860-1890, Atheneum, 1984.
The Sea Rovers: Pirates, Privateers, and Buccaneers, Atheneum, 1984.
The Secret Armies: Spies, Counterspies, and Saboteurs in World War II, Atheneum, 1985.
1812: The War Nobody Won, Atheneum, 1985.
The Yanks Are Coming: The United States in the First World War, Atheneum, 1986.
Aztecs and Spaniards: Cortes and the Conquest of Mexico, Atheneum, 1986.
Struggle for a Continent: The French and Indian Wars, 1690-1760, Atheneum, 1987.
Hitler, Viking (New York City), 1987.
The War for Independence: The Story of the American Revolution, Atheneum, 1988.
Stalin: Russia's Man of Steel, Viking, 1988.
Inca and Spaniard: Pizarro and the Conquest of Peru, Atheneum, 1989.
Mao Tse-tung and His China, Viking, 1989.
Napoleon and the Napoleonic Wars, Viking, 1990.
The Spanish-American War, Atheneum, 1991.
America and Vietnam: The Elephant and the Tiger, Viking, 1992.
Cowboys, Indians, and Gunfighters: The Story of the Cattle Kingdom, Atheneum, 1993.
"Unconditional Surrender": U. S. Grant and the Civil War, Atheneum, 1993.
Virginia's General: Robert E. Lee and the Civil War, Atheneum, 1994.
The Sea King: Sir Francis Drake, Atheneum, 1995.
Plains Warrior: Chief Quanah Parker and the Comanches, Atheneum, 1996.
Empires Lost and Won: The Spanish Heritage in the Southwest, Atheneum, 1996.

ADULT NONFICTION

War and the Christian Conscience: Augustine to Martin Luther King Jr., Gateway (Chicago), 1971.
The Last Crusade: The Church of England in the First World War, Duke University Press (Durham, NC), 1974.
Nicholas Murray Butler: An Intellectual Portrait, Twayne (Boston), 1976.
Sir Norman Angell, Twayne, 1979.

■ Work in Progress

Commander in Chief: Abraham Lincoln and the Civil War.

■ Sidelights

Albert Marrin is a professor of history who, in more than twenty juvenile nonfiction books, has attempted to make the past accessible to young readers. In award-winning books such as *1812: The War Nobody Won, Cowboys, Indians, and Gunfighters: The Story of the Cattle Kingdom,* and *"Unconditional Surrender": U. S. Grant and the Civil War,* he has created a tapestry of United States history by focusing on dramatic moments

Adolf Hitler is the subject of the first of Marrin's well-received biographies of prominent world leaders. (Cover illustration by Viqui Maggio.)

and famous personalities. With biographies of leaders and tyrants from Napoleon to Hitler, Marrin has also interpreted the events of a larger world stage for juvenile readers. Additionally, his several books on the First and Second World Wars provide well-organized introductions to many aspects of those struggles.

Chairman of the history department at New York's Yeshiva University, Marrin's books for young readers complement his academic duties and writings. One of his earliest such books, *Victory in the Pacific,* is indicative of Marrin's thorough, no-nonsense approach to history. A critic in *Voice of Youth Advocates* commented on his "straightforward account," with "lucid capsule descriptions of selected topics" that were interspersed in the otherwise chronologically organized narrative, which follows the war through major battles, from Pearl Harbor to Midway and Guadalcanal and the bombing of Japan. Marrin's treatment, anecdotal rather than detailed, would appeal, the reviewer noted, to "hi/lo readers." A *Booklist* reviewer particularly noted Marrin's ability to get his information across to young readers "in a highly readable manner." And Kate M. Flanagan, writing in *Horn Book,* pointed out Marrin's "fast-paced" accounts of various battles and his balanced narration, looking at history from both sides of the conflict to "provide an understanding of the warrior heritage that made the Japanese such a formidable enemy."

Marrin has dealt with various other aspects of World War II, from the invasion of Europe by the Allies to a history of spies and a study of the air war. With his *The Yanks Are Coming,* he also examined United States involvement in World War I. His concentration on military subjects involved a more domestic topic in his *War Clouds in the West: Indians and Cavalrymen, 1860-1890,* which chronicles battle by battle the thirty-year war of destruction of the Plains Indians and Apache by the U.S. Cavalry. "The breadth of coverage," along with detailed diagrams and photos "all recommend this book for general readers," noted George Gleason in a *School Library Journal* review. Nancy C. Hammond in *Horn Book* found Marrin's book to be a "dramatic readable account," with enlightening cultural and historical perspectives on the struggle, such as the pressures ensuing from demands for buffalo brought on by a new hide-tanning process.

The Great Plains also figured in two more recent titles by Marrin: *Cowboys, Indians, and Gunfighters: The Story of the Cattle Kingdom* and *Plains Warrior: Chief Quanah Parker and the Comanches.* The award-winning *Cowboys, Indians, and Gunfighters* is a history of the Old West, from the earliest Spanish settlers who introduced horses and cattle to the region to the struggle between buffalo and cattle for the open range. Divided into six chronological chapters, the book includes "minority viewpoints," according to Julie Halverstadt in *School Library Journal,* in its listing of contributions of African American and Mexican cowboys. "A dynamic look at one of the most exciting and dangerous periods in U.S. history," Halverstadt concluded. With his *Plains*

Warrior, Marrin focused on the Comanche and their losing battle in the nineteenth century for their traditional life on the Great Plains. Providing at once an overview of Comanche history as well as a dramatic representation of the last tragic years of fighting under Chief Quanah Parker, son of a kidnapped settler, *Plains Warrior* "brings the period to life," according to a reviewer in *Bulletin of the Center for Children's Books.* The reviewer also praised Marrin for his even-handed treatment of both parties in the battle.

Marrin also investigated an earlier conflict between Europeans and Native Americans in the New World—the wars between the British and French and their Indian allies. *Struggle for a Continent: The French and Indian Wars, 1690-1760,* once again demonstrates Marrin's use of not only accurate research but the telling anecdote to create a "retelling of history that young people find accessible and appealing," according to Elizabeth S. Watson in *Horn Book.* Paula Nespeca Deal, writing in *Voice of Youth Advocates,* called *Struggle for a Continent* a "fascinating, easy to read overview," and noted that Marrin brought this little understood battle for power alive with "vivid details of the cultural and social background." Deal also pointed out that Marrin included the accomplishments of women in the struggle.

A logical chronological companion piece to *Struggle for a Continent* was *The War for Independence: The Story of the American Revolution,* which provides a "detailed account" of the American war for independence, according to Anne Frost in *Voice of Youth Advocates.* "This engrossing narrative gives the reader rare insight," Frost wrote. "Highly recommended." Marrin divided his narrative into eight chapters dealing with various topics such as causes, spies, naval battles, and the front-line skirmishes along the frontier. A contributor in *Kirkus Reviews* remarked particularly on Marrin's use of details that "engage the reader's senses," and a *Bulletin of the Center for Children's Books* reviewer called the work a "spirited and thoughtful account."

Marrin turned to the American Civil War with titles profiling generals on opposing sides. *"Unconditional Surrender": U. S. Grant and the Civil War* uses Union General Ulysses S. Grant to focus on the war years, though it also includes information about the general before and after that conflict. Marrin confines his chronicle to battles and strategies that Grant was personally involved in. Thus Gettysburg and Bull Run are not included, but detailed accounts of Shiloh and Petersburg are, along with a plethora of facts and anecdotes that combine to become a "history of living men and women who are complete with faults and contradictions," according to Deborah Stevenson in *Bulletin of the Center for Children's Books.* Stevenson called the book an "evocation as well as a description of war" that also shows the power of the "quiet intimacy of written words," as compared to television and film. Neither Grant's racism nor his drinking are glossed over in this account, and the extensive bibliography appended "will be much appreciated by both history students and Civil War buffs," noted Elizabeth M. Reardon in *School Library Journal.*

A view from the other side of the battle lines is provided in *Virginia's General: Robert E. Lee and the Civil War.* Again, the book provides a brief account of the subject's life before and after the Civil War, focusing on the war years through the Confederate general's eyes as well as through the eyes of a score of other witnesses. The extensive use of quotations from Lee and his generals, as well as plentiful detail, provides a "vivid picture of the war, its participants, and its effects," according to Deborah Stevenson in *Bulletin of the Center for Children's Books.* Carolyn Phelan, writing in *Booklist,* concluded that *Virginia's General* was "well researched and readable," and Connie Allerton in *Voice of Youth Advocates* noted that Marrin tells "an exciting story." Allerton, though, was somewhat critical of what she felt was a too "flattering" history of Lee, which did not take into account recent scholarship on the general. Marrin is

Marrin's history examines Napoleon's life in the context of his times, tracing his rise from soldier to military dictator and conqueror of Europe. (Cover illustration by Pamela Patrick.)

extending his series on the Civil War with a volume focusing on Abraham Lincoln.

With *The Spanish-American War* and *America and Vietnam: The Elephant and the Tiger,* Marrin tackled two bloody chapters in U.S. history. In *The Spanish-American War* he creates "a fine sense of intimacy in his text," according to Margaret A. Bush in *Horn Book,* as he details the events that led up to the war which President McKinley did not want, but that in many ways was thrust upon him by the power of the press. From the sinking of the *Maine* to the barbarities of the Philippine conflict, Marrin follows the course of what one American diplomat called "a splendid little war." Raymond E. Houser in *Voice of Youth Advocates* called *The Spanish-American War* "a good YA history," and a contributor in *Kirkus Reviews* labelled it "fresh (and timely)."

Marrin's history of America's longest war, *America and Vietnam,* was both praised for even-handedness and criticized for bias, demonstrating the deep rifts still apparent in U.S. society as a result of that conflict. Initially, Marrin provides an overview of Vietnamese history as one of struggle, beginning with Chinese control of the nation and continuing through the French colonial system, occupation by the Japanese, renewed conflict with the French, and U.S. involvement in the region. He also provides a lengthy account of the early life of the leader, Ho Chi Minh, who established Communism in the northern regions of the country following World War II. But the centerpiece of the book is the U.S. presence and the ensuing war. "Marrin covers the Vietnam Conflict in a sweeping fashion," according to Raymond E. Houser in *Voice of Youth Advocates.* "This is an excellent history book.... If a YA reader had but one book to read on this subject, this should be the one." Margaret A. Bush in *Horn Book* also found Marrin's account "remarkably even-handed." However, while noting that the book was "powerfully written" and "emotion-packed," a *Kirkus Reviews* critic called it a "highly biased account," viewing the Vietnamese as the villains and the American troops in a more positive light.

Marrin has also written a quartet of biographies on world leaders, including portraits of Hitler, Stalin, Mao Tse-tung, and Napoleon, as well as books on the influence of the Spanish in the Americas. A *Kirkus Reviews* critic deemed Marrin's *Hitler* "a dramatic account," and drew attention to the author's inclusion of various topics of recent interest, such as the White Rose resistance group and the fate of Josef Mengele. Mary A. Burns, writing in *Horn Book,* termed the work a "riveting account that is informative, illuminating, and inescapably painful." Marrin continued the series on world leaders with *Stalin,* dubbed "another fine biography" by Elizabeth S. Watson in *Horn Book,* and with *Mao Tse-tung and His China.* With the latter book, Marrin interweaves Mao's life with the history of China from 1911 to his death. From Mao's troubled childhood through the Long March and the days of the Cultural Revolution, Marrin traces the major turning points in the life of one of China's greatest and most controversial leaders. "A vivid but inconsistent account," noted Marsha L. Wagner in the *New York Times Book Review.* "This book is actually less a biography than a highly readable historical overview of modern China.... Sadly, Mao himself never emerges as a clear historical personalty," Wagner concluded. With *Napoleon and the Napoleonic Wars,* Marrin took on a project that has already been attempted by literally tens of thousands of other biographers. What distinguishes Marrin's book is that he put Napoleon's life into the context of his times, and also has the "particular talent for selecting an incident or anecdote" that sums up an individual, according to Margaret Miles in *Voice of Youth Advocates.* "The text is readable, dramatic, and well documented," noted Elizabeth S. Watson in *Horn Book.*

With *Inca and Spaniard: Pizarro and the Conquest of Peru, Aztecs and Spaniards: Cortes and the Conquest of Mexico,* and *Empires Lost and Won: The Spanish Heritage in the Southwest,* Marrin examined Spanish incursions in the New World and the clash of cultures such incursions brought about. Zena Sutherland in *Bulletin of the Center for Children's Books* commented particularly on Marrin's novelistic treatment of *Inca and Spaniard,* which might limit the research value of his book, "but has probably enhanced its appeal," while another reviewer in *Bulletin of the Center for Children's Books* described his *Aztecs and Spaniards* "as dramatic as fiction but well-grounded in fact."

As more than one reviewer has pointed out, Marrin has managed to bring history alive for young readers with his talent for the telling detail and anecdote. By focusing on personalities and the most significant moments in U.S. and world history, he lends a dramatic appeal to his works. If he has sometimes been criticized for oversimplification or heightened dramatic effects, more often he has been praised for his well-documented research and his readable texts.

■ Works Cited

Allerton, Connie, review of *Virginia's General: Robert E. Lee and the Civil War, Voice of Youth Advocates,* April, 1995, p. 50.

Review of *America and Vietnam: The Elephant and the Tiger, Kirkus Reviews,* April 1, 1992, p. 463.

Review of *Aztecs and Spaniards: Cortes and the Conquest of Mexico, Bulletin of the Center for Children's Books,* April, 1986, p. 153.

Burns, Mary A., review of *Hitler, Horn Book,* September-October, 1987, p. 630.

Bush, Margaret A., review of *The Spanish-American War, Horn Book,* July-August, 1991, p. 481.

Bush, Margaret A., review of *America and Vietnam: The Elephant and the Tiger, Horn Book,* September-October, 1992, pp. 600-601.

Deal, Paula Nespeca, review of *Struggle for a Continent: The French and Indian Wars, 1690-1760, Voice of Youth Advocates,* October, 1987, p. 189.

Flanagan, Kate M., review of *Victory in the Pacific, Horn Book,* April, 1983, p. 184.

Frost, Anne, review of *The War for Independence: The Story of the American Revolution, Voice of Youth Advocates,* June, 1988, p. 103.

Gleason, George, review of *War Clouds in the West: Indians and Cavalrymen, 1860-1890, School Library Journal,* March, 1985, p. 180.

Halverstadt, Julie, review of *Cowboys, Indians, and Gunfighters: The Story of the Cattle Kingdom, School Library Journal,* August, 1993, p. 199.

Hammond, Nancy C., review of *War Clouds in the West: Indians and Cavalrymen, 1860-1890, Horn Book,* March-April, 1985, pp. 195-96.

Review of *Hitler, Kirkus Reviews,* May 15, 1987, pp. 796-97.

Houser, Raymond E., review of *The Spanish-American War, Voice of Youth Advocates,* June, 1991, p. 127.

Houser, Raymond E., review of *America and Vietnam: The Elephant and the Tiger, Voice of Youth Advocates,* June, 1992, p. 130.

Miles, Margaret, review of *Napoleon and the Napoleonic Wars, Voice of Youth Advocates,* October, 1991, p. 265.

Phelan, Carolyn, review of *Virginia's General: Robert E. Lee and the Civil War, Booklist,* December 15, 1994, p. 746.

Review of *Plains Warrior: Chief Quanah Parker and the Comanches, Bulletin of the Center for Children's Books,* May, 1996, p. 308.

Reardon, Elizabeth M., review of *"Unconditional Surrender": U. S. Grant and the Civil War, School Library Journal,* July, 1994, p. 1122.

Review of *The Spanish-American War, Kirkus Reviews,* February 15, 1991, p. 250.

Stevenson, Deborah, review of *"Unconditional Surrender": U. S. Grant and the Civil War, Bulletin of the Center for Children's Books,* March, 1994, p. 227.

Stevenson, Deborah, review of *Virginia's General: Robert E. Lee and the Civil War, Bulletin of the Center for Children's Books,* January, 1995, p. 173.

Sutherland, Zena, review of *Inca and Spaniard: Pizarro and the Conquest of Peru, Bulletin of the Center for Children's Books,* February, 1990, p. 142.

Review of *Victory in the Pacific, Booklist,* June 15, 1983, p. 1340.

Review of *Victory in the Pacific, Voice of Youth Advocates,* October, 1983, p. 226.

Wagner, Marsha L., review of *Mao Tse-tung and His China, New York Times Book Review,* February 25, 1990, p. 33.

Review of *The War for Independence: The Story of the American Revolution, Bulletin of the Center for Children's Books,* April, 1988, p. 161.

Review of *The War for Independence: The Story of the American Revolution, Kirkus Reviews,* April 15, 1988, p. 621.

Watson, Elizabeth S., review of *Struggle for a Continent: The French and Indian Wars, 1690-1760, Horn Book,* January-February, 1988, p. 87.

Watson, Elizabeth S., review of *Stalin, Horn Book,* March-April, 1989, p. 234.

Watson, Elizabeth S., review of *Napoleon and the Napoleonic Wars, Horn Book,* September-October, 1991, p. 617.

■ For More Information See

PERIODICALS

Booklist, December 15, 1982, p. 565; February 1, 1983, p. 725; September 1, 1984, p. 68; August, 1985, p. 1668; May 1, 1986, p. 1322; July, 1987, p. 1681; December 15, 1988, p. 700; October 15, 1989, p. 460; December 15, 1989, p. 823; July, 1991, p. 2039; March 1, 1992, p. 1269; August, 1993, p. 2046; April 1, 1994, p. 1440.
Horn Book, June, 1984, p. 349; September, 1986, p. 610; January, 1990, p. 89; September, 1993, p. 625; July, 1994, p. 473; September-October, 1996, pp. 621-22.
School Library Journal, November, 1982, p. 88; April, 1983, p. 126; August, 1984, p. 76; August, 1986, p. 104; June, 1987, p. 110; December, 1987, p. 108; June, 1988, p. 124; November, 1989, p. 132; February, 1990, p. 116; May, 1991, p. 192; June, 1992, p. 146; December, 1994, p. 25.
Voice of Youth Advocates, August, 1996, p. 181.

—Sketch by J. Sydney Jones

* * *

McDONNELL, Flora (Mary) 1963-

■ Personal

Born July 11, 1963, in London, England; daughter of Alexander, Earl of Antrim (a picture restorer) and Sarah (an artist; maiden name, Harmsworth) Gates. *Education:* Attended Exeter College, Oxford, 1982-84; City and Guilds of London Art School, diploma (with distinction; illustrative arts), 1989. *Politics:* "Left of Centre." *Religion:* "Lapsed R-C."

■ Addresses

Home—The Mill House, Glenarm, County Antrim BT440BQ, Northern Ireland.

■ Career

Self-employed painter and illustrator, 1989—. *Exhibitions:* "Sheepsales; The Sheep and Their Farmers," Kerlin Gallery, Belfast, 1991; "Traffic Snarls and Street Life," St. Martin's Gallery, London, 1991; "Trawling for Prawns from Ardglass," Cadogan Gallery, London, 1992; "Familiar Faces and Favorite Places," No. 1 Oxford St., Belfast, 1993; Mixed Paintings, Cadogan Contemporary Gallery, 1995. Commissions include paintings of chefs for the Savoy Hotel, 1989, and studies of news crews at work for Ulster Television, 1992.

■ Awards, Honors

Mother Goose Award for most exciting newcomer to British children's book illustration, 1995, for *I Love Animals.*

■ Writings

SELF-ILLUSTRATED

I Love Animals, Candlewick (New York City), 1994.
I Love Boats, Candlewick, 1995.

Author's works have been translated into foreign languages, including Danish, Spanish and Japanese.

■ Work in Progress

Flora McDonnell's ABC (children's picture book), expected 1996 or 1997.

■ Sidelights

Artist and author Flora McDonnell, the winner of the 1995 Mother Goose award for the most exciting newcomer to British children's book illustration, told *SATA* that when she was just thirteen she lost an argument about "whether to study chemistry or art." As a result, she began to study art seriously only at university level. Once at art school McDonnell spent most of her time drawing and painting to escape from the strictures of an illustration course that did not appeal to her. She explained to *SATA* that her pictures have evolved from the time she spent observing in a life class. "I try to capture something of my delight in the colour, movement, and humor that I have enjoyed. Without this initial period of intense life observation, my work would be wooden, I wouldn't have much to say."

Encouragement from publishers helped initiate McDonnell's career as a picture-book creator. As she told *SATA,* "Lucy Ingrams from Walker Books came to my degree show and asked me to bring my work into Walker Books. By which time the dreaded word 'illustration' was ringing alarm bells and I froze. After about eighteen months and gentle encouragement ... I felt I was never

FLORA McDONNELL

going to make children's book illustrator, and said so." The people at Walker Books were not about to take "No" for an answer; McDonnell was told by an editor there, "It's quite obvious you've got to do a book about animals called *I Love Animals,* and I want to see the first picture next week." That was the beginning of McDonnell's career as a children's writer and illustrator.

McDonnell's book *I Love Animals,* which features large, full-spread illustrations of her favorite animals (and frequently their young), became an immediate success. As a critic for *Kirkus Reviews* noted, the text of the book is "minimal," and the pictures provide "visual exuberance." A *Publishers Weekly* critic described McDonnell's technique on her acrylic and gouache paintings as "primitive folk-art." Charlotte Voake, one of the judges for the Mother Goose Award, wrote in *Books for Keeps* that she found the paintings "lovely, bold and thrilling." "It was an almost overwhelming moment when *I Love Animals* won the Mother Goose Award for the most exciting newcomer to British Illustration," McDonnell told *SATA.*

I Love Boats, in the words of a *Publishers Weekly* critic, is "[a]wash with color," an "exuberant paean to all things afloat." The work showcases a variety of boats within large acrylic and gouache paintings. Houseboats, racing boats, fishing boats, and sailboats are all depicted. At the end of the book, readers find that all the boats are toys, floating in a happy little girl's bathtub. A *Horn Book* critic concluded of *I Love Boats,* "boat lovers young and old will want to share it with friends."

McDonnell told *SATA* that her favorite children's book illustrators include John Burningham, Helen Oxenbury, Ludwig Bemelmans, and Maurice Sendak. She advises aspiring illustrators "to express what you enjoy and make small compromises but keep the essence of what you want to say." Indeed, McDonnell's own compromise—from painter to illustrator—was painless. "Luckily for me," she notes, "what I want to express about what I see falls quite naturally into children's book illustration."

■ Works Cited

Review of *I Love Animals, Kirkus Reviews,* July 15, 1994, p. 989.
Review of *I Love Animals, Publishers Weekly,* August 1, 1994, p. 77.
Review of *I Love Boats, Horn Book,* July/August, 1995, p. 452.
Review of *I Love Boats, Publisher's Weekly,* May 22, 1995, p. 58.
Voake, Charlotte, "I Love Animals," *Books for Keeps,* July, 1995, p. 8.

■ For More Information See

PERIODICALS

Australian Book Review, September, 1994, p. 69.
Booklist, October 15, 1994, p. 438.
School Library Journal, August, 1995, p. 126.

McLEAN, Virginia Overton 1946-

■ Personal

Born May 17, 1946; daughter of John (in business) and Mary Elizabeth (Bell) Overton; married George Hite McLean, Jr. (a lawyer); children: Mathilde, Hite. *Education:* Vanderbilt University, B.A.; University of Virginia, M.A. *Religion:* Presbyterian.

■ Addresses

Office—P.O. Box 11441, Memphis, TN 38111.

■ Career

Writer. Worked as a journalist for *Commercial Appeal,* Memphis, TN and *Newsday.*

■ Writings

The Memphis Guide, Redbird Press, 1982.
Chasing the Moon to China, illustrated by Nancy Cheairs, with photographs by Peggy Crump Brown and others, Redbird Press, 1987.
(With Katherine Perrow Klyce) *Kenya, Jambo!* (book with cassette), Redbird Press, 1989.
Pastatively Italy, Redbird Press, 1996.

■ Sidelights

Virginia Overton McLean told *SATA:* "I write to see clearly, to challenge children, and to stress what is positive, and I hope that my writing makes learning fun."

■ For More Information See

PERIODICALS

Booklist, August, 1987, p. 1749.
Children's Literature in Education, Volume 25, number 3, 1994, p. 180.
School Library Journal, December, 1987, p. 82.

*   *   *

MORA, Francisco X(avier) 1952-

■ Personal

Born February 3, 1952, in Mexico City, Mexico; immigrated to the United States in 1979; son of Luis (an art teacher) and Luz (Paz) Mora; married Jennifer L. Salsbury (divorced). *Education:* Attended Superior School for Painting and Sculpture ("La Esmeralda"), Mexico City, Mexico; University of Morelia, Michoacan, Mexico; School of Crafts and Design INBA, Mexico City, Ed.A.; National Center for Conservation of Fine Arts INBA; University of Wisconsin-Milwaukee. *Religion:* Roman Catholic.

FRANCISCO X. MORA

■ Career

Artist and art teacher. Milwaukee Institute of Art and Design, Milwaukee, WI, instructor for continuing education, 1993-94. Has also given numerous workshops and classes at libraries and schools in the Milwaukee area. *Exhibitions:* Galleries in Milwaukee, WI, La Jolla, CA, Santa Fe, NM, Scottsdale, AZ, Jackson, WY, Madison, WI, Kenosha, WI, and Naples, FL. Work exhibited in permanent collections in Kellogg Center, Michigan State University, McDonald's Corporation, Miller Brewing Company, University of Wisconsin Hospital, and many others.

■ Awards, Honors

Hispanic Festival of the Arts awards, 1989 and 1990; Racine Addy Award, 1991; "Latino Horizons" award, 1993.

■ Writings

SELF-ILLUSTRATED

The Legend of the Two Moons, Highsmith Press, 1992.
La Gran Fiesta de Navidad, Highsmith Press, 1993.
Juan Tuza and the Magic Pouch, Highsmith Press, 1994.

ILLUSTRATOR

The Tiger and the Rabbit: A Puerto Rican Folk Tale, Children's Press, 1991.

The Coyote Rings the Wrong Bell: A Mexican Folktale, Children's Press, 1991.
Las Vacas de Tio Conejo, Houghton, 1992.
Nuestras Cosas Favoritas, Houghton, 1992.
El Gato de Mi Casa, Houghton, 1992.
Cuando Cuentes Cuentos, Houghton, 1992.
Senora Hen, Scott, Foresman, 1992.
Pat Mora, *Listen to the Desert/Que Dice el Desierto?* (poetry), Clarion, 1994.
Roald Dahl, *James and the Giant Peach,* Harcourt, 1994.
Ruth M. Covault, *Pablo and Pimienta,* Northland, 1994.
Craig Kee Strete and Michelle Netten Chacon, *How the Indians Bought the Farm,* Greenwillow, 1995.
Shirley Climo, *The Little Red Ant and the Great Big Crumb,* Clarion, 1995.
How to Make Salsa, Mondo, 1995.
Carlos Rubalcava, *La Mariposa Bailarina,* Santillana, 1995.
Abuela's Big Bed: A Puerto Rican Folk Tale, Hampton Brown, 1995.
Jane Yolen, *The Wild Hunt,* Harcourt, 1995.

Also illustrator for numerous posters, cards, and book covers.

■ Sidelights

Francisco X. Mora told *SATA:* "What I paint is the mirror image, the reflection of the daily life of my own people, and the results are surreal imagery. There was a time when I had very grandiose dreams, but then I didn't have a language for my own expression. When I found that language, I knew that I could be speaking forever.

"I had a very happy childhood and a wonderful family. Although my father died when I was very young, as an art teacher he was able to leave me the ability to enjoy life through art. My mother, a wonderful storyteller who was always willing to tell me a tale, made me part of the tradition. I, too, became a storyteller.

"My paintings are to be enjoyed," Mora concluded. "They talk about friendship, joy, and the beauty of nature and life. I've learned how to express myself to people by translating my dreams and memories into something visual. After years of searching, I find my work giving extraordinary results. I am very pleased with what I am doing."

*   *   *

MORRISON, Meighan 1966-

■ Personal

Born May 22, 1966, in Chicago, IL; daughter of John (an advertising executive) and Susan (an actress) Morrison; married Ross Carmichael (divorced); children: Benjamin. *Education:* Attended Boston University and Parsons School of Design.

■ Addresses

Office—134 Rowayton Ave., Rowayton, CT 06853.

■ Career

Bloomcraft, division of P. Kaufman Home Furnishings, fabric designer, 1995—. *Exhibitions:* Illustrations exhibited at Drankeen Children's Museum in Melbourne, Australia, 1993-94.

■ Writings

FOR CHILDREN; SELF-ILLUSTRATED

Long Live Earth, Scholastic, 1993.
Linda Lou, Scholastic, 1995.

■ Work in Progress

Two adult fiction novels; several children's books, including a novelty series.

■ Sidelights

Meighan Morrison told *SATA,* "My mother has a drawing that I did when I was three while driving in our car. It's on the back of an envelope, and it's a picture of a little stone house with a shingled roof complete with car and garage. It's elaborately framed and on display in my mother's living room, and on occasion she's been known to exclaim to her various guests, 'Look, look what my daughter did!' I always hope she remembers to tell them that it's not one of my more recent endeavors.

"So after high school I went to college for a year before getting my way and switching to design school, where I studied fine art and illustration. Not long after that, I found myself on a remote farm in rural New Zealand with a new baby in tow. Trust me, it's a very long, strange story and I haven't quite worked it all out myself! Being there had two big effects on me. First, living in the countryside really let me appreciate the beauty and fragility of our natural world, especially after having just brought a new life into it. And second, I had a whole lot of free time that no amount of gardening could fill.

"Because I couldn't find for my son a simple, colorful book addressing the environment, I decided to try to write one myself. That's how my first book, *Long Live Earth,* started. And, as an added bonus, it gave me something to illustrate! After writing the text, which was a lot more work and a lot more fun than I'd anticipated, I decided on the quilted illustrative style because I've always loved fabric and collage and because to me it represents an early form of recycling. Maybe it was cabin fever, but I really loved stitching every one of those illustrations!

"After that was accepted for publication, I wrote several books that my publisher was not interested in. I was starting to think that I would be the one-book wonder when finally *Linda Lou* was accepted for publication.

Meighan Morrison, with son Benjamin.

She is hand-stitched too, but in a bigger and fancier style than *Long Live Earth.* She has feathers and sequins and pearls and was really fun to create. As of yet, *Linda Lou* has no U.S. publisher, though I hope to find one for her. I even made a doll prototype for her, but it was recently abducted by the granddaughter of a friend of mine!

"I am now living back in the States with my son, Benjamin, and I'm waiting for my new textile design job to settle down a bit so that I can focus again on my books. My current fear is that I'll be a two-book wonder! Actually, I've recently finished designing a novelty ABC, 1,2,3, etc. series, which was more a construction than a creation. Lots of cutting and pasting—my favorite pastime."

*   *   *

MOSENG, Elisabeth 1967-

■ Personal

Born April 12, 1967, in Oslo, Norway; daughter of John-Arne (an art director) and Anna Elisabeth (Wormdal) Moseng. *Education:* Attended Westerdals Reklameskole, 1988-90; Kingston University, B.A. (with honors), 1993. *Religion:* Protestant.

■ Addresses

Home—Normannsgt. 28, 0655 Oslo, Norway. *Office*—Pilestredet 27, 0164 Oslo, Norway. *Agent*—Eunice McMullen, 38 Clewer Hill Rd., Windsor, Berkshire SL4 4BW, England.

■ Career

Illustrator. *Member:* Grafill (Organization for Illustrators and Graphic Designers in Norway).

■ Awards, Honors

Commendation, Kingston University, 1993; special prize and grant, Gullblyanten (national Norwegian competition), 1994, for best newcomer; Visuelt (annual national competition), Gold prize, 1994, two awards, 1995.

■ Illustrator

Adrienne Geoghegan, *Six Perfectly Different Pigs,* Hazar, 1993.
Francesca Simon, *Higgledy Piggledy: The Hen Who Loved to Dance,* HarperCollins, 1995.
Diana Bentley, reteller, *The Little Red Hen,* Heinemann Educational, 1995.
Margaret Nash, reteller, *The Ugly Duckling,* Heinemann Educational, 1996.
Francesca Simon, *Fuzzy Frieda and the Gourmet Goat,* Levinson Children's Books, 1997.

■ Sidelights

Elisabeth Moseng shares one of Norway's best-known graphics studios, Illustratorene, with eight other independent illustrators. In addition to her work on children's books, she does freelance work for design studios and advertising agencies.

Moseng's work on *Six Perfectly Different Pigs,* which was written by fellow Kingston University student and close friend Adrienne Geoghegan, was the result of a HarperCollins competition in which she participated. "The competition was followed by an exhibition of entered work, at which I first made contact with Eunice McMullen, who became my agent," Moseng told *SATA.* Since that time Moseng and McMullen have developed

ELISABETH MOSENG

a strong overseas relationship (McMullen is British), and a number of "perfectly different" animals have been created on Moseng's drawing table.

Moseng's work has received critical acclaim in the United States, Great Britain, and Ireland, and she has earned a number of awards from the Norwegian Annual National Illustration exhibitions. Although she lives and works in Oslo, she has a particular interest in children's books published in other countries. "Not only do I enjoy my animals," she told *SATA,* "but doing the illustrations for children's books keeps me in close contact with British and American publishing companies."

*   *   *

MY BROTHER'S BROTHER
See CHEKHOV, Anton (Pavlovich)

N

SUSAN W. NALLY

NALLY, Susan W. 1947-

■ Personal

Born August 4, 1947, in Louisville, KY; daughter of Henry N. (a salesman) and Marguerite T. Ward; married William Doug Nally (a dentist), August 16, 1969; children: Melissa Diane, Kristen Michelle. *Education:* Western Kentucky University, B.S., 1969. *Politics:* Republican. *Religion:* Southern Baptist.

■ Addresses

Home—713 Shenandoah Dr., Brentwood, TN 37027.

■ Career

Public school teacher in Kentucky, 1969-74; substitute teacher in Tennessee for eight years; currently children's division director for Crievewood Baptist Church and part-time receptionist. Has done contract work for the Tennessee Baptist Convention and Baptist Sunday School Board, leading conferences on how to teach children. *Member:* Williamson County (Tennessee) Literary Society, Fraternity Alumni Club, Alpha Omicron Pi.

■ Writings

"SPENDING PRIME TIME WITH GOD" SERIES; FOR CHILDREN

How to Say Yes to All the Best Choices (and Really Mean It), Broadman and Holman (Nashville, TN), 1994.
(With Liz Lee) *How to Feel Most Excellent about Who You Are (and Really Enjoy It),* Broadman and Holman, 1994.
How to Stay Way Cool When Things Are Tough (and Really Like It), Broadman and Holman, 1994.

■ Work in Progress

"Working on a possible parent/child workshop to be held in churches."

■ Sidelights

Susan W. Nally told *SATA:* "After years of teaching both in public schools and in Sunday School, I discovered that children need to understand and believe that for every choice they make there is a consequence, whether good or bad. As a college student, I had the good fortune to learn from a Christian psychology professor that consistent, loving discipline was the best way to guide a child. How could I best help children learn these truths?

"While searching unsuccessfully for a devotion book for one of my Sunday school children, my mother suggested that I could write such a book. I kind of laughed at the idea and kept on looking. Like most mothers she didn't give up on this idea. Finally, I began to pray about the possibility—me writing a book? Then I met with my friend, Liz Lee, and we began to seriously explore some ideas. Thus the first book, *How to Say Yes to All the Best Choices (and Really Mean It)* was born. This began the series 'Spending Prime Time with God' that Liz Lee and I co-authored.... We decided that a journal was the best way to accomplish our objectives, which were to help children explore possible choices and to think through possible consequences because of their choices.

"After four years of working with the publisher, doing research, writing, rewriting, reading each other's manuscripts, editing, and proofing, I saw my mother's suggestion and this dream of an idea become a reality. The books were finally in print. The greatest reward would come from children that found the books, used them, and then would in some way let me know how helpful the books had been. I am so thankful that I listened to a simple suggestion from a mother who believed that I could do something I had never even thought about before. I am so glad I took a risk, and if I have learned nothing else from this experience, I know that God used me to do something greater than I believed possible."

*   *   *

NEWMAN, Shirlee P(etkin) 1924-

■ Personal

Born February 16, 1924, in Brookline, MA; married Jackson J. Newman (an automotive dealer), June 25, 1946; children: Paul, Jeffrey. *Education:* Attended high schools in Massachusetts and California; also studied at Boston Center for Adult Education and Cambridge Centre for Adult Education. *Hobbies and other interests:* Yoga, bird-watching, nature study, guitar, folk singing, bike riding.

■ Addresses

Home—58B Charles River Rd., Waltham, MA 02154.

■ Career

Freelance writer; copywriter for advertising agencies in Los Angeles, 1941-45, and New York City, 1945-46; *Child Life Magazine,* associate editor, 1962-63; teacher of writing for children, Cambridge Center for Adult Education, Cambridge, MA, 1975-76, Lesley College, 1978-79, and Brandeis University, 1980-85.

SHIRLEE P. NEWMAN

■ Writings

Liliuokalani, Young Queen of Hawaii, Bobbs-Merrill (New York City), 1960.
Yellow Silk for May Lee, Bobbs-Merrill, 1961.
(Adaptor) *Folk Tales of Latin America,* Bobbs-Merrill, 1962.
(Adaptor) *Folk Tales of Japan,* Bobbs-Merrill, 1963.
The Shipwrecked Dog, Bobbs-Merrill, 1963.
(With Diane Sherman) *About the People Who Run Your City,* illustrated by James David Johnson, Melmont (Chicago), 1963.
(With Sherman) *About Canals,* Melmont, 1964.
Marian Anderson: Lady from Philadelphia, Westminster (Philadelphia), 1966.
Ethel Barrymore: Girl Actress, Bobbs-Merrill, 1966.
The Story of Lyndon B. Johnson, Westminster, 1967.
Mary Martin on Stage, Westminster, 1969.
Tell Me, Grandma, Tell Me, Grandpa (picture book), illustrated by Joan Drescher, Houghton (Boston), 1979.
The Incas, F. Watts (Danbury, Connecticut), 1992.
The Inuits, F. Watts, 1993.
The Creek, F. Watts, 1996.
The Pequots, F. Watts, in press.

Contributor of fiction and nonfiction to periodicals, including *American Girl, Book News, Calling All Girls, Good Housekeeping, Grade Teacher, Highlights for Chil-*

dren, Instructor, Jack and Jill, Saturday Evening Post, Scholastic, and *Weekly Reader.*

■ Sidelights

Shirlee P. Newman has channelled a lifelong curiosity and enthusiasm into a series of books for young readers. The author of nonfictional accounts of everything from the workings of local government to Hawaiian princesses to the ancient peoples of the Americas, she has also published a highly acclaimed picture book for the preschool set. *Tell Me, Grandma, Tell Me, Grandpa,* for example, is a humorous depiction of an imaginative little girl's idea of her parents as children.

Newman was born and raised in Brookline, a suburb of Boston, Massachusetts. At the age of thirteen her father died, and the family moved to California. "Transplanted, I returned from whence I came...," Newman once explained to *SATA,* "the public library. Almost my whole life has been spent in libraries, especially boys' and girls' sections. My favorite reading has always been books for young people, from picture books to young adults'. Some say I've never grown up. 'You're just a big kid,' they say. Perhaps. Know what? Hope I never do."

In high school Newman joined the staff of her school newspaper and caught the writing bug; during her senior year she started a gossip column called "Campus Chatter" in a neighborhood weekly newspaper, which earned her a reputation as a budding journalist at her high school. After graduation Newman worked at various jobs, including copywriting at advertising agencies in both Los Angeles and New York City, before getting married and moving back to Brookline.

As a busy wife and mother, Newman still did some writing in her spare time. When her daughter began to tackle the articles in children's magazines as a beginning reader, Newman began to think that she might attempt to do the same—as a writer. She attended several classes in writing for children and then sat down to work. "After many long hours, days, weeks, months, of writing, re-writing, re-writing, re-writing, my work began to sell," she told *SATA.* From a successful article writer, it was on to books and, in 1962, the associate editorship of *Child Life* magazine.

All of Newman's books have involved live research of one type or another: "From going through old houses, to windjamming on a high-masted schooner along the New England seacoast," explained Newman. Set in San Francisco Chinatown, her 1961 novel *Yellow Silk for May Lee* made use of the author's own memories of living in the area as a young woman. "When I wrote the book many years later, I still read every scrap I could about Chinatown," she adds. *"The Shipwrecked Dog* started by watching a freighter being towed off a sandbar one summer, but involved research about Portuguese people here [in the United States], and much looking into how rescue operations are carried out." The live research? "[G]etting a puppy and bringing it up!"

One of Newman's popular children's titles exploring different cultures.

The Incas, which Newman published in 1992, is a study of this ancient South American civilization geared towards upper elementary and middle school students. Describing both the history of the culture and the lifestyle of the Incas' modern-day descendants, Newman also reveals the culture's advanced road system, counting system, and calendar in a book that Merlyn Miller in *Voice of Youth Advocates* called "a springboard to future study."

In *The Inuits,* Newman turns her attention to the indigenous people of Alaska, northern Canada, and Greenland. From a discussion of such basic essentials as clothing, shelter, and transportation, she expands the reader's understanding of the development of Inuit culture by examining family life, the influence of contact with early explorers and missionaries, and the transformations that have come about in the Inuit lifestyle with the advent of modern technology and changing resources. Patricia Fry deemed the book "very readable, interesting and informative" in *CM: A Reviewing Journal of Canadian Materials for Young People.*

While Newman enjoys the investigations—both in libraries and in real life—that form the basis for her stories and nonfiction works, they don't compare to the satisfaction she gets from her readers. "The most fun of all my work is receiving letters from boys and girls ... knowing they're out there, reading my books."

Works Cited

Fry, Patricia, review of *The Inuits, CM: A Reviewing Journal of Canadian Materials for Young People,* September, 1992, p. 128.

Miller, Merlyn, review of *The Incas, Voice of Youth Advocates,* August, 1992, p. 187.

For More Information See

PERIODICALS

Booklist, December 1, 1993, p. 688.

Bulletin of the Center for Children's Books, September, 1979.

Multicultural Review, March, 1993, p. 29.

School Library Journal, March, 1979, p. 128; August, 1992, p. 164.

* * *

NUMEROFF, Laura Joffe 1953-

Personal

Born July 14, 1953, in Brooklyn, NY; daughter of William (an artist) and Florence (a teacher; maiden name, Joffe) Numeroff. *Education:* Pratt Institute, B.F.A. (with honors), 1975; attended Parsons College, 1975. *Religion:* Jewish. *Hobbies and other interests:* Collecting children's books, watching movies.

Addresses

Home—San Francisco, CA.

Career

Author and illustrator of children's books. Lecturer at schools in California; has worked at jobs including running a merry-go-round and doing private investigation.

Awards, Honors

California Young Reader award, Colorado Children's Book Award, and Georgia Children's Picture Storybook award, all 1988, and Buckeye medal, 1989, all for *If You Give a Mouse a Cookie;* Parents' Choice award, 1991, for *If You Give a Moose a Muffin.*

Writings

FOR CHILDREN; AND ILLUSTRATOR, EXCEPT WHERE INDICATED

Amy for Short, Macmillan, 1976.

Phoebe Dexter Has Harriet Peterson's Sniffles, Greenwillow, 1977.

Walter, Macmillan, 1978.

(With Alice Richter) *Emily's Bunch,* Macmillan, 1978.

(With Alice Richter) *You Can't Put Braces on Spaces,* Greenwillow, 1979.

The Ugliest Sweater, F. Watts, 1980.

LAURA JOFFE NUMEROFF

Doesn't Grandma Have an Elmo Elephant Jungle Kit?, Greenwillow, 1980.

Beatrice Doesn't Want To, F. Watts, 1981.

Digger, Dutton, 1983.

If You Give a Mouse a Cookie, illustrated by Felicia Bond, Harper, 1985.

If You Give a Moose a Muffin, illustrated by Felicia Bond, HarperCollins, 1991.

Dogs Don't Wear Sneakers, illustrated by Joseph Mathieu, Simon & Schuster, 1993.

Why a Disguise?, illustrated by David McPhail, Simon & Schuster, 1994.

Chimps Don't Wear Glasses, illustrated by Joseph Mathieu, Simon & Schuster, 1995.

Mouse Cookies: Ten Easy-to-Make Cookie Recipes, illustrated by Felicia Bond, HarperCollins, 1995.

(With Barney Saltzberg) *Two for Stew,* illustrated by Sal Murdocca, Simon & Schuster, 1996.

■ Adaptations

You Can't Put Braces on Spaces and *The Ugliest Sweater* have been made into educational filmstrips by Westport Communications Group; *If You Give a Mouse a Cookie* has been adapted into an interactive CD-ROM book, HarperCollins, 1995, and has been recorded as an audiotape cassette. Numeroff's works have been translated into Spanish.

■ Sidelights

The popularity of her 1985 children's story, *If You Give a Mouse a Cookie,* has made Laura Joffe Numeroff well-known among the read-aloud set. With a wry humor that has become characteristic of her writing for children, Numeroff depicts the relationship between a helpful young boy and a demanding young mouse in an engaging, lyrical manner. Her stories about spunky female characters and unusual childhood situations continue to engage nonsense lovers of all ages.

"I grew up in a world of books, music, and art," Numeroff once told *SATA*. "I was a voracious reader and read six books every week. I've also been drawing pictures since I was old enough to hold a crayon, and writing came soon after. Doing children's books combines the two things I love the most." While a student at New York's Pratt Institute, Numeroff took a class taught by Barbara Bottner called "Writing and Illustrating for Children's Books." Her first book, *Amy for Short,* was one of her homework assignments.

With illustrations by the author, *Amy for Short* describes the friendship between Mark and Amy, who are brought together because they stand out from the rest of their classmates due to their height. As the tallest kid in the class, Amy is destined to have the coveted role of a tree in her school play and act the part of Abraham Lincoln in a summer camp performance. When Amy suddenly shoots past Mark in stature, she worries that he will no longer be her pal, but he proves his friendship by bowing out of the most important Little League game of the year to show at her birthday party.

Emily's Bunch introduces readers to a determined young girl who wants to find the most original Halloween costume ever to wear to the annual Halloween party. She remains undaunted by her older brother's insistence that one person cannot appear in costume as a bunch of grapes. When her friends arrive at the Halloween party and gather around her, each with purple sacks over their heads, Emily proves her cleverness.

A brother and sister who butt heads is again the focus of *Beatrice Doesn't Want To.* When Henry has to take his stubborn little sister to the library while he does his homework, she makes studying impossible until he drags her into the children's room where a story hour is in progress. Resistant at first, she soon becomes caught up in the magic of reading. By the end of Numeroff's humorous easy reader, stubborn Beatrice has to be dragged out of the library through the same door she didn't want to enter in the first place.

1983's *Digger* provides a new twist to the story of a child who wants a pet. Described by a *Kirkus Reviews* critic as "agreeably off-track without being all that far-fetched," the story features a young boy who tries to help his dad find a solution to the man's wish for a pet. Their landlord won't allow animals though, and a book of dog pictures just can't replace Digger, the dog Daddy had when he was a boy. Fortunately for father and son, the pro-pet policy of a new landlady affords the answer to their dilemma.

If You Give a Mouse a Cookie has become a childhood favorite, appearing in an interactive CD-ROM version and in several book editions since it was first published in 1985. A "what if" story about an insistent young mouse and the increasingly bewildered young boy who tries to help him out, Numeroff's tale lets its readers

Numeroff wryly explains the consequences of catering to a demanding mouse in her popular nonsense picture book *If You Give a Mouse a Cookie*, illustrated by Felicia Bond.

follow the chain of numerous activities, until they leave their polite young protagonist fast asleep. "If you give a mouse a cookie, he's going to ask for a glass of milk," the tale begins, winding its way to a close with light-hearted humor; "The similarities between mouse and child won't be lost on observant youngsters," noted a *Booklist* reviewer. *If You Give a Moose a Muffin* provided a humorous sequel, as "the complexities that can follow a simple act of kindness are played out with the same rampant silliness," according to a reviewer in *Publishers Weekly.* From jam to go on top, to more muffins, to a trip to the store, the demands of a moose on the loose add an even greater element of absurdity to Numeroff's circular plot.

Numeroff has continued to provide youngsters with stories that showcase her wacky inventiveness. In *Dogs Don't Wear Sneakers,* as well as its sequel, *Chimps Don't Wear Glasses,* the title gives readers a hint of what is to come, as the book serves up a full plate of nonsense rhymes. "Dogs don't wear sneakers/And pigs don't wear hats/And dresses look silly/On Siamese cats" the poem goes, while illustrations by Joe Mathieu show exactly the opposite: dapper hounds and lavishly costumed cats and pigs add to the general lunacy. A *Kirkus Reviews* critic deemed that the "deliciously silly text" is presented in "a spirited, comical style."

The 1996 publication, *Two for Stew,* features a matronly woman who simply will not believe her waiter at Chez

Nous when he claims the restaurant is out of its specialty, stew. The story is told through a conversation between the woman and the waiter; a critic in *Publishers Weekly* applauded the "lilting stanzas" created by Numeroff and co-author Barney Saltzberg, calling the work a "giddy and sometimes campy salute to stew."

As well as possessing an offbeat sense of humor, Numeroff has always been an avid reader. "I prefer biographies, nonfiction, and stories dealing with 'real-life' dramas—never did like fairy tales all that much. I guess that's why my children's stories tend to be based on things kids actually go through, like wearing braces, being too tall for your age, being a daydreamer, having to wear something your grandmother gave you even though you think it's hideous. The best reviews come from kids who write me—that makes it all worth it!"

Numeroff collects children's books and can usually be found in the library or bookstore. To supplement her income from writing children's books, she's taken on an array of unusual side jobs, including running a merry-go-round and working as a private investigator. "My work is my life," she once commented to *SATA.* "I can draw no distinction between the words 'work' and 'spare time.' I love what I'm doing and the only time it becomes work is when there's re-writing." While she plans to attempt screenplays and adult fiction, "I'll always have a first love for children's books. I hope to be writing until my last days."

■ Works Cited

Review of *Digger, Kirkus Reviews,* February 15, 1983, p. 182.

Review of *Dogs Don't Wear Sneakers, Kirkus Reviews,* July 1, 1993, p. 864.

Review of *If You Give a Moose a Muffin, Publishers Weekly,* June 28, 1991, p. 100.

Review of *If You Give a Mouse a Cookie, Booklist,* June 1, 1985, p. 1404.

Numeroff, Laura Joffe, *If You Give a Mouse a Cookie,* Harper, 1985.

Numeroff, Laura Joffe, *Dogs Don't Wear Sneakers,* Simon & Schuster, 1993.

Review of *Two for Stew, Publishers Weekly,* July 29, 1996, p. 87.

■ For More Information See

PERIODICALS

Bulletin of the Center for Children's Books, June, 1978, p. 165; January, 1979, p. 85; January, 1982; September, 1991, p. 17.

Publishers Weekly, September 18, 1978, p. 167; August 30, 1993, p. 94.

School Library Journal, December, 1978, p. 45; May, 1983, p. 65; May, 1985, p. 80; January, 1994, p. 96.*

O

FRANCINE M. O'CONNOR

O'CONNOR, Francine M(arie) 1930-

■ Personal

Born April 8, 1930, in Springfield, MA; daughter of Wallace H. (a machinist) and Celestine (Morrison) Provost; married John F. O'Connor (an accountant), December 29, 1951; children: Margaret Anne, Kathryn Mary O'Connor Boswell, Timothy John. *Education:* Attended Washington University. *Religion:* Catholic.

■ Addresses

Home—157 Crest Manor, House Springs, MO 63051. *Office*—Liguori Publications, One Liguori Dr., Liguori, MO 63057.

■ Career

Freelance writer, 1967-70; *St. Louis-Post Dispatch,* St. Louis, MO, book reviewer, 1970-75; *Liguorian* magazine, Liguori, MO, managing editor, 1975-93; Liguori Parish Educational Products, Liguori, associate editor, 1993—. Coordinator of children's church and communications director, parish council, Sts. Peter and Paul Parish. *Member:* Professed Secular Franciscan.

■ Awards, Honors

Catholic Book Award, Catholic Press Association, 1992, for *ABC's Lessons of Love: Sermon on the Mount for Children;* Angel Award of Merit, 1995, for *ABC's of Christmas.*

■ Writings

"THE ABC'S OF FAITH" SERIES

ABC's of the Ten Commandments, illustrated by daughter, Kathryn Boswell, Liguori Publications (Liguori, MO), 1980, revised, 1989.
ABC's of the Sacraments ... for Children, illustrated by Larry Nolte, Liguori Publications, 1981, revised, 1989.
ABC's of the Old Testament ... for Children, illustrated by Kathryn Boswell, 1984, Liguori Publications, revised, 1989.
(With Kathryn Boswell) *ABC's of the Rosary,* Liguori Publications, 1984.
ABC's of the Mass ... for Children, illustrated by Kathryn Boswell, Liguori Publications, 1988.
ABC's of Prayer ... for Children, illustrated by Kathryn Boswell, Liguori Publications, 1989.

ABC's Lessons of Love: Sermon on the Mount for Children, illustrated by Kathryn Boswell, Liguori Publications, 1991.

ABC's of Christmas, illustrated by Bartholomew, Liguori Publications, 1994.

ABC's of Our Church, Liguori Publications, 1996.

OTHER

Stories of Jesus, Liguori Publications, 1982.

Special Friends of Jesus, Liguori Publications, 1986.

Wait and Wonder, Liguori Publications, 1991.

My Lenten Walk with Jesus, Liguori Publications, 1992.

You and God: Friends Forever—A Faith Book for Catholic Children, Liguori Publications, 1993.

ABC's for Teaching the Faith: Old Testament Program for Preschool/Kindergarten, Liguori Publications, 1995.

ABC's for Teaching the Faith: Meeting Jesus Program for Preschool/Kindergarten, Liguori Publications, 1996.

Questions and Answers for Children: Handing on the Faith, Regina Press, 1996.

Also author of "ABC's of Faith" column, *Liguorian* magazine, 1976—. Recorded the audio cassette "Joysongs," Liguori Publications, 1995, and wrote lyrics for the audio cassette "The ABC's in Song," music by Curtis Bell, Liguori Publications, 1996.

■ Adaptations

Several books from the "ABC's of Faith" series have been recorded as audio cassettes by Liguori Publications, including *ABC's of the Ten Commandments,* 1990, *ABC's of the Sacraments,* 1990, *ABC's of Prayer,* 1990, *ABC's of the Old Testament,* 1993, *ABC's of the Mass,* 1993, and *ABC's Lessons of Love,* 1993.

■ Work in Progress

A book for teaching the faith for children ages nine to twelve based on the new catechism of the Catholic Church, for Regina Press, expected in 1997.

■ Sidelights

"I began my writing career in the 1960s, when I moved to the midwest from New England. Twelve hundred miles from home, friends, and family, I needed an outlet for the thoughts and feelings trapped inside my head," Francine M. O'Connor told *SATA.* "At that time, I did not think of myself as a children's writer. In 1975, I was invited by the editor of *Liguorian* magazine to consider an editorial position with Liguori Publications. Soon after, it was decided that the magazine needed a children's column. Since the entire editorial staff at that time was made up of celibate clergy, I was given the assignment. My first "ABC's of Faith" column appeared in January 1976 and has run in every issue since. In 1979, in response to reader requests, the column was published in book form. Suddenly I became the resident children's author. For me, it was a perfect fit. While the learned clergy and theologians passed on the faith to our more sophisticated readers, I relished the opportunity to share my own simple faith with the little ones. Later books were written on assignment for Liguori Publications and other publishers. As for my inspiration, I did not have to look far from my home. My ten grandchildren have been my primary resource and major wellspring of inspiration through the years."

*　　*　　*

OKOMFO, Amasewa
See COUSINS, Linda

*　　*　　*

ORR, Wendy 1953-
(Sally George)

■ Personal

Born November 19, 1953, in Edmonton, Alberta, Canada; daughter of Anthony M. (a Royal Canadian Air Force pilot) and Elizabeth Ann (a teacher and homemaker; maiden name, Jenkins) Burridge; married Thomas H. Orr (a farmer), January 11, 1975; children: James Anthony, Susan Elizabeth. *Education:* London School of Occupational Therapy, diploma, 1975; La-Trobe University, B.Sc., 1982. *Hobbies and other interests:* Animals, reading, gardening, people, travel.

WENDY ORR

■ Addresses

Home and office—R.M.B. 1257, Cobram, Victoria 3644, Australia. *Agent*—Debbie Golvan, Golvan Arts Management, P.O. Box 766, Kew, Victoria 3101, Australia.

■ Career

Albury Community Health, Albury, Australia, occupational therapist, 1975-80; Language and Development Clinic, Shepparton, Australia, occupational therapist, 1982-91; author, 1988—. *Member:* Australian Society of Authors, Australian Children's Book Council, Cobram Book Club (secretary).

■ Awards, Honors

First place award (with others), Ashton Scholastic Picture Book Awards, 1987, for *Amanda's Dinosaur;* Book of the Year: Junior Readers, Australian Children's Book Council, and Australian Family Therapy Association recommendation, both 1995, both for *Ark in the Park.*

■ Writings

Amanda's Dinosaur, illustrated by Gillian Campbell, Ashton Scholastic (Australia), 1988.
The Tin Can Puppy (picture book), illustrated by Brian Kogler, HarperCollins Australia/Angus & Robertson, 1990.
Bad Martha, illustrated by Carol McLean Carr, Angus & Robertson, 1991.
Aa-Choo! (picture book), illustrated by Ruth Ohi, Annick Press (Toronto), 1992.
Leaving It to You, Angus & Robertson, 1992.
The Great Yackandandah Billy Cart Race, illustrated by Neil Curtis, HarperCollins Australia, 1993.
Mindblowing! (middle-grade reader), illustrated by Ruth Ohi, Allen & Unwin Australia, 1994, published as *A Light in Space,* Annick Press, 1994.
Ark in the Park, illustrated by Kerry Millard, HarperCollins Australia/Angus & Robertson, 1994.
The Laziest Boy in the World, illustrated by Farbio Nardo, HarperCollins Australia/Angus & Robertson, 1994.
Yasou Nikki, illustrated by Kim Gamble, HarperCollins Australia, 1995.
Dirtbikes, HarperCollins Australia, 1995.
The Bully Biscuit Gang, HarperCollins Australia, 1995.
Jessica Joan, illustrated by Ann James, Reed Books (Australia), 1995.
Grandfather Martin, illustrated by Kate Ellis, Houghton Mifflin (Boston), 1996.
Alroy's Very Nearly Clean Bedroom, illustrated by Bettina Guthridge, Longman & Cheshire, 1996, Sundance Publishing, 1997.
Peeling the Onion (young adult), Allen & Unwin Australia, 1996, Holiday House, 1997.

"MICKI AND DANIEL" PICTURE BOOK SERIES

Micki Moon and Daniel Day, illustrated by Mike Spoor, Allen & Unwin Australia, 1993.
Pegasus and Ooloo Mooloo, illustrated by Ruth Ohi, Annick Press, 1993.
A Train to the City, illustrated by Ohi, Annick Press, 1993.
The Wedding, illustrated by Ohi, Annick Press, 1993.

UNDER PSEUDONYM SALLY GEORGE

Bad Dog George, Thomas Nelson Australia, 1994.
Breakfast in Bed, Thomas Nelson Australia, 1994.
George at the Zoo, Thomas Nelson Australia, 1994.

■ Sidelights

Australian author Wendy Orr has written books for children and young adults that are noted for their elements of fantasy and humor. Born in Edmonton, Canada, in 1953, Orr was lucky enough to have a father who worked for the Royal Canadian Air Force. She spent her childhood in locations all across Canada, travelling to France, and living for a time in Colorado. Her broad experiences were put to good use later, when she began her career as a writer.

"My parents instilled a love of language early," Orr recalled for *SATA,* "with books at bedtime and my father's stories of our dog's Great Great Great Grandfather, in the car. My own first 'book' was written when I was eight. 'Glossy the Horse' was a full four pages long and bore a striking resemblance to *Black Beauty,* which my mother had just read to us. Dramatic poems followed; how delighted my grandmother must have been to receive a 'Poem on Death' for her sixtieth birthday!

Young Megan wakes up too sick for daycare and must accompany her mother to work in Orr's humorous picture book *Aa-Choo!* (Illustration by Ruth Ohi.)

"On leaving high school," she added, "I spent a year studying animal care in Kingston, Ontario, went to England for a holiday, and stayed for three years to complete a diploma at the London School of Occupational Therapy. In my final year, 1975, I met and married an Australian farmer holidaying in the U.K., and returned to New South Wales with him after graduation.

"The business of growing up, and starting a career and family ... took over ... and except for an article on 'Living in Wheelchairs' when I was a student, my writing was limited to patient records and weekly epistles to my parents. At the end of 1985, however, when I had completed a Bachelor of Applied Science and another post graduate certificate, I decided that it was time to do what I had always wanted. In December 1986 I entered the Ashton Scholastic competition for a picture book manuscript. *Amanda's Dinosaur,* which shared the first place, was published in 1988 and subsequently had rights sold to Canada, New Zealand, and the U.S." Orr—who was disabled after a car accident in 1991—and her husband now live with their two children, two dogs, and a cat on a dairy farm in the southeast of Australia.

Orr's picture-book series "Micki and Daniel" centers on the friendship between two young children and their pets, Pegasus, a miniature horse, and Ooloo Mooloo, a parrot. Although some critics have found these stories somewhat constrained by the author's attempt to be "politically correct," others have considered their adventures amusing and appealing to children. "It is refreshing to see stories of friendship featuring human children instead of the more usual animal quasi-adults," remarked Sarah Ellis in her *Quill & Quire* review of *The Wedding* and *A Train to the City.* Reviews were mixed for the first book in the series, *Pegasus and Ooloo Mooloo,* in which Micki and Daniel find the animals that accompany them throughout the rest of the series. The four encounter evil circus-owners who want to steal Pegasus, the miniature horse, but Ooloo Mooloo the parrot saves the day when he makes a noise like a police siren and scares the bad guys away. Although critics faulted what they considered a lack of focus in the story, noting that the parrot rather than one of the children saves the day, some praised both the set-up for the series and the intrinsic interest of the characters. *The Wedding,* the second book in the series, was found to be more successful in its rendering of the story of a wedding ceremony in which Micki and Daniel are invited to take part, but their pets are not. Ooloo Mooloo and Pegasus insist on joining in nonetheless, "and it all adds up to a satisfying slapstick climax," according to Ellis. *A Train to the City,* however, in which the four sneak onto a train to the city because their parents won't take them, "lacks oomph," Ellis declared.

Orr's science fiction adventure *Mindblowing!,* published outside Australia under the title *A Light in Space,* was widely praised as a fast-paced, compelling story of a boy who meets a being from outer space who, though friendly to him, intends to capture the earth's oxygen for her own planet. "This is top-quality science fiction," a reviewer for *Books in Canada* enthused. Critics applauded the skillful way in which the author contrasts the viewpoints of the human boy and the alien girl who intends to mine the earth's oxygen for her own planet, despite the deadly effect this would have on the earth's inhabitants. "The plot of this light book is entertaining and fast paced, while the characters are well drawn," remarked J. R. Wytenbroek in *Quill & Quire.* Although Wytenbroek faulted Orr for failing to dramatize the resolution to her story, Anne Connor, reviewing *A Light in Space* for *School Library Journal,* praised Orr's character development and suspenseful plot, dubbing the novel "unusual and fun."

Orr's picture books for pre-schoolers and first readers include *The Tin Can Puppy,* in which Dylan, who has been told he is too young to take care of the pet he so badly wants, finds a puppy in a tin can in the dump while he is looking for wheels for his cart. Dylan takes the puppy home and hides him, and when his parents discover the puppy, Dylan is allowed to keep him. This is "a slight story," according to Joyce Banks in a review for *School Librarian,* "but told in an amusing, percipient and economical way." Similarly, Orr's *Aa-Choo!* in which Megan wakes up one morning too sick to go to daycare, presents a common problem critics felt would be appreciated by the pre-school audience for whom the book is intended. When no one can take the day off of work to stay home with her, Megan goes to work with her mother, camps out under her mother's desk during an important meeting, and has a few adventures while exploring the office looking for the bathroom. "The delicate dilemma of what to do when a young child is ill and parents have to work is treated gently and humorously," stated Theo Hersh in *CM: A Reviewing Journal of Canadian Materials for Young People.* Although Phyllis Simon found the story "rather contrived" in her review in *Quill & Quire,* Hersh called *Aa-Choo!* "a book working parents will want to share with their children."

Orr's books for pre-schoolers and young readers share a humorous approach to the common and uncommon dilemmas faced by her young heroes. Often employing elements of fantasy or science fiction, the author is noted for blending realistic human characters and their animal or alien counterparts in a way that illuminates the hearts and minds of each. While Orr is occasionally faulted for creating slim plots or both showing and telling readers about her characters, her most successful books are ones in which critics find a solid blend of character development, swift pacing, and humorous viewpoint.

"I tend to carry an idea for a story in my head for a year or so before I start writing," Orr told *SATA;* "the characters develop further as I redraft and the plot usually changes considerably from my first ideas. Although much of my work verges on fantasy, it has also of course been influenced by my own life. My childhood in a French village gave me the emotional background for *Ark in the Park*—like Sophie, I not only longed for the normalcy of nearby grandparents, but was lucky enough to find some. Similarly, *Yasou Nikki* was loosely based on my own first day of school, when a little girl named Jacqueline took me under her wing, taught me to speak French, and remained a close friend ever after. And *Leaving It to You,* while not drawn on any particular situation, was of course influenced by my first job as a community based occupational therapist in Albury—both by my memories of the people that I met, and of myself, as an idealistic young therapist coming to terms with life.

"In fact, once I'd finished *A Light in Space* (*Mindblowing* in Australia) I realised that despite being science fiction, it had also been influenced by my own life and concerns at the time of writing. It was actually started the week before [the car accident that dramatically curtailed my mobility], and was written in the two years following—I am sure that some of the issues of control versus independence in the story must have been influenced by my own disabilities and fight to regain independence."

Orr's *Peeling the Onion,* a novel for young adults, centers on a similar theme. In this work, seventeen-year-old protagonist Anna is tragically disabled in a car accident. While learning to make physical adjustments in order to function independently, Anna must also cope with the reactions of her family and friends, recognizing the inevitable strains that are put upon these relationships. Reviewing *Peeling the Onion* for *Australian Bookseller & Publisher,* Olivia Craze writes that Orr "mixes the spicy ingredients of authentic characters and relationships with a compelling plot to produce a novel full of power and honesty, touched with humour." Anne Briggs, writing in *Magpies,* adds that in *Peeling the Onion* Orr "displays yet again her precise observation of family relationships and her flair for creating original and richly individual characters of all ages."

■ **Works Cited**

Banks, Joyce, review of *The Tin Can Puppy, School Librarian,* November, 1993, p. 156.

Briggs, Anne, review of *Peeling the Onion, Magpies,* September, 1996, p. 38.

Connor, Anne, review of *A Light in Space, School Library Journal,* February, 1995, p. 100.

Craze, Olivia, review of *Peeling the Onion, Australian Bookseller & Publisher,* July, 1996, p. 78.

Ellis, Sarah, review of *The Wedding* and *A Train to the City, Quill & Quire,* July, 1993, pp. 55-56.

Hersh, Theo, review of *Aa-Choo!, CM: A Reviewing Journal of Canadian Materials for Young People,* May, 1992, p. 161.

Review of *A Light in Space, Books in Canada,* February, 1995, p. 50.

Simon, Phyllis, review of *Aa-Choo!, Quill & Quire,* March, 1992, p. 66.

Wytenbroek, J. R., review of *A Light in Space, Quill & Quire,* December, 1994, pp. 33-34.

The safety of the entire world rests on young Andrew's shoulders when he learns that the space alien he has befriended, a girl named Ysdran, seeks his help in order to rob the earth of its oxygen. (From *A Light in Space,* written by Wendy Orr and illustrated by Ruth Ohi.)

■ **For More Information See**

PERIODICALS

Books in Canada, May, 1993, pp. 30-31.
Quill & Quire, March, 1992, p. 66.

*   *   *

OXENDINE, Bess Holland 1933-

■ **Personal**

Born July 12, 1933, in Hazelton, PA; daughter of Raleigh L. (a coal miner) and Pearl (a homemaker; maiden name, Shook) Holland; married Denford Harold Oxendine (a pharmacist), December 1, 1956; children: Denford, Laura. *Education:* Mars Hill College, A.A.; Berea College, B.A.; University of North Carolina at Chapel Hill, M.A., C.A.S.; special studies at other schools, including Duke University, Davidson College, University of North Carolina at Greensboro, College of Charleston, and Western Carolina University. *Politics:* "Registered Democrat (vote for occasional other)."

■ Addresses

Home and office—1193 Daybrook Dr., Kannapolis, NC 28081.

■ Career

Teacher in South Carolina, 1957-60; Kannapolis City Schools, Kannapolis, NC, teacher and literary adviser, 1961-90; North Carolina Governor's School for Gifted, Laurinburg, NC, philosophy teacher, summers, 1979-80; Rowan-Cabarrus Community College, Salisbury and Kannapolis, NC, English teacher, 1989—. Good Writing Contest judge, National Council of Teachers of English; Charlotte Writers' Club writing contest judge; K-2000 community program member; church deacon; Sunday school director and teacher; speaker and reader at local schools. *Member:* American Field Service (adviser, Al Brown High School).

■ Awards, Honors

Outstanding Young Educator Award; Outstanding English Teacher Award, 1988; Outstanding Educator Award, 1990; awards from North Carolina Poetry Council, 1992, 1994, 1995.

■ Writings

Miriam, Winston-Derek Publication Group, 1994.

Also author of individual poems and essays published in journals, including *Bay Leaves.*

■ Work in Progress

Samuel (second in a children's series); a novel; a book of essays; researching other children of the Bible.

■ Sidelights

"I can't remember when I wasn't expressing myself on paper—first, by drawing and then, by writing," Bess Holland Oxendine told *SATA.* "While still young, I had my first poem published in *Wee Wisdom* and became a classroom celebrity!

"I was the daughter of a coal miner who had fathered six sons before I came along, followed soon by a baby sister. Following his death in California, where he had taken us in his early thirties for his health, Mother brought us to the mountains of North Carolina to live near her parents. Although we had no material wealth, I shall be eternally grateful for kind grandparents, for a small, rural Methodist church, and for the privilege of growing up in the unspoiled beauty of Appalachia.

"Eventually, the three youngest children became the first college graduates in our family—working our way through—and we are now art teacher, minister, and English teacher.

"Since my early twenties, I have been a 'liberated woman,' later with a supportive husband and family.

A young Hebrew girl in ancient Egypt helps save the life of her baby brother in this Biblical tale told from a unique perspective. (From *Miriam,* written by Bess Holland Oxendine and illustrated by June Steckler.)

After college, I determined that I would continue to experiment, to grow, and to develop my potential. Reading, writing, and photography became my chief hobbies.

"While reading, I am often moved by profound insight, and I marvel at how connected our hearts and minds really are. Sometimes, I see in the words of others what I have felt deeply but never expressed, and I hope that my own words can sound a familiar note for another person, who will also become aware of the commonalty of us all. Concerning my writing, I share the sentiments of Thoreau: 'To affect the quality of the day, that is the highest of arts.'

"Since childhood, I have wanted to know more about children of the Bible, little folks who seem so much like adults. Now, I am trying in my series of books to make them more like children of today—universal children, I believe—while holding on to their essentially spiritual natures. I dedicated *Miriam* to our first grandchild, Daniel, and will dedicate the second one to his baby sister, Hannah.

"I am currently watching the political landscape, troubled by the naivete of many 'Christians,' by their ready acceptance of harsh, mean-spirited would-be leaders. To me, loving actions and intercessory prayer are necessary for a sane and healthy life—of the individual and of society."

P

PACKARD, Edward 1931-

■ Personal

Born February 16, 1931, in Huntington, NY; children: Caroline, Andrea, Wells. *Education:* Princeton University, B.A., 1953; Columbia Law School, LL.B., 1959.

■ Addresses

Home—Box 720, Wainscott, NY 11975. *Agent*—Amy Berkower, Writers House, 21 West 26th St., New York, NY 10010.

■ Career

Lawyer, 1959-78. Author of children's books, 1975—. *Military Service:* U.S. Navy, 1953-56.

■ Awards, Honors

Jeremiah Ludington Award, 1986. Many of Packard's books have been Junior Library Guild selections.

■ Writings

"CHOOSE YOUR OWN ADVENTURE" SERIES

Sugarcane Island, illustrated by Barbara Carter, Vermont Crossroads Press, 1976.
Deadwood City, illustrated by Carter, Lippincott, 1978.
The Cave of Time, illustrated by Paul Granger, Bantam, 1979.
The Mystery of Chimney Rock, illustrated by Granger, Bantam, 1979, published as *The Curse of the Haunted Mansion,* 1989.
Third Planet from Altair, illustrated by Barbara Carter, Lippincott, 1979, published as *Exploration Infinity,* Magnet, 1982, published as *Message from Space,* Bantam, 1989.
Your Code Name is Jonah, illustrated by Paul Granger, Bantam, 1980.
The Circus, illustrated by Granger, Bantam, 1981.
Who Killed Harlowe Thrombey?, Bantam, 1981.
The Forbidden Castle, Bantam, 1982.

EDWARD PACKARD

Gorga, the Space Monster, Bantam, 1982.
Inside UFO 54-40, illustrated by Granger, Bantam, 1982.
Sunken Treasure, illustrated by Granger, Bantam, 1982.
Survival at Sea, illustrated by Granger, Bantam, 1982.
Jungle Safari, illustrated by Lorna Tomei, Bantam, 1983.
Help Your Shrinking, Bantam, 1983.
Underground Kingdom, Bantam, 1983.
Hyperspace, Bantam, 1983.
The Polar Bear Express, Bantam, 1984.

Mountain Survival, Bantam, 1984.
Supercomputer, Bantam, 1984.
You Are a Shark, Bantam, 1985.
Return to the Cave of Time, Bantam, 1985.
Ghost Hunter, Bantam, 1986.
The Great Easter Bunny Adventure, illustrated by Vincent Bell, Bantam, 1987.
Journey to the Year 3000, Bantam, 1987.
Space Vampire, Bantam, 1987.
A Day with the Dinosaurs, Bantam, 1988.
You Are a Monster, Bantam, 1988.
The Perfect Planet, Bantam, 1988.
Mutiny in Space, Bantam, 1989.
You Are a Superstar, Bantam, 1989.
You Are a Genius, Bantam, 1989.
The Worst Day of Your Life, Bantam, 1990.
Through the Black Hole, Bantam, 1990.
The Power Dome, Bantam, 1991, published as *Invaders from Within,* illustrated by Frank Bolle, Gareth Stevens Publishers, 1995.
Skateboard Champion, Bantam, 1991.
Faster Than Light, Bantam, 1991.
Vampire Invaders, Bantam, 1991.
Kidnapped, Bantam, 1991.
Magic Master, Bantam, 1992.
Superbike, Bantam, 1992.
Viking Raiders, Bantam, 1992.
You Are Microscopic, Bantam, 1992.
The Luckiest Day of Your Life, Bantam, 1993.
Secret of the Dolphins, Bantam, 1993.
Roller Star, Bantam, 1993.
Dinosaur Island, Bantam, 1993.
Horror House, Bantam, 1993.
Reality Machine, Bantam, 1993.
Comet Crash, Bantam, 1994.
Soccer Star, Bantam, 1994.
Who Are You?, Bantam, 1994.
War with Mutant Spider Ants, Bantam, 1994.
Cyberspace Warrior, Bantam, 1994.
You Are an Alien, Bantam, 1995.
Sky Jam, Bantam, 1995.
Hostage!, Bantam, 1995.
Fright Night, Bantam, 1995.
Greed, Guns and Gold, Bantam, 1996.

"ESCAPE FROM TENOPIA" SERIES

Tenopia Island, Bantam, 1986.
Castle of Frome, Bantam, 1986.

"EARTH INSPECTORS" SERIES

America: Why Is There an Eye on the Pyramid of the One-Dollar Bill?, illustrated by Barbara Carter, McGraw Hill, 1988.
Africa: Where Do Elephants Live Underground?, illustrated by Carter, McGraw Hill, 1988.
Olympus: What Is the Secret of the Oracle?, McGraw Hill, 1988.
Russia: What Is the Golden Horde?, illustrated by Carter, McGraw Hill, 1989.

"SPACE HAWKS" SERIES

The Comet Masters, Bantam, 1991.
Space Fortress, Bantam, 1991.

OTHER

E.S.P. McGee, Avon, 1983.
Imagining the Universe: A Visual Journey (nonfiction), Berkley, 1994.
Night of the Werewolf, Bantam, 1995.

Packard's books have been translated into several foreign languages.

■ Adaptations

Deadwood City and *Third Planet from Altair* have been adapted for videocassette, Positive Image, 1982.

■ Sidelights

At volume number 170 and counting, Edward Packard's "Choose Your Own Adventure" series has been one of the most popular children's series in publishing history. Dubbed interactive fiction, such books pioneered the path that CD-ROM has followed, and have been called both a boon for reluctant readers and intellectual junk food no better than video games. Such books involve the reader directly in choosing options through the course of the book about where to go next, which plot twist they desire to follow, and which action would be most logical for them, and thus provide upwards of forty possible endings in some of Packard's most creative titles. It is, however, with this very structure of multiple plots that some critics take exception. Packard himself is aware of such criticisms. In an article on interactive fiction he wrote for *School Library Journal,* Packard conceded that branching multiple plots tended to be short, and therefore left less chance for character development and complex dramatic development. "Fast-paced action is the norm," he explained. "On the other hand, multiple plots afford the author the opportunity to depict alternative consequences and realities. Complexity may inhere in breadth rather than in length."

But whatever critics and educators may or may not say about interactive fiction, young readers have enthusiastically given the concept a thumbs up, and every major juvenile publisher has established its own series. As Packard pointed out in *School Library Journal,* however, such products are not interchangeable. There is a big difference between choosing to go through door one or two, or whether to entrust your safety to a character for which adequate development has not been reached. "If these books are to be exercises in decision-making ... there should be motivation for each choice offered," so that readers have to weigh factors in favor of each choice. And there need to be consequences that are "consistent and plausible." Packard's subjects in his "Choose Your Own Adventure" series range from science to science fiction, from detective stories to detecting historical and natural truths, and reflect his own range of interests.

Born on Long Island, Packard wrote his first book at age twelve, an introduction to astronomy that was never published. From astronomy, his interest turned to meteorology, and he spent another year reading everything he could lay his hands on about that subject. "I read quite a bit as a kid," Packard once told *SATA*, "but I wasn't what you'd call a bookworm. My favorite was *The Book of Knowledge,* an out-of-date ... encyclopedia that was kept in the attic. It was wonderful. It had a marvelous section called 'Things to Make and Do,' lots of interesting puzzles and games, and lots of scientific material." It is exactly that sort of eclectic and playful knowledge that would later inform Packard's own books. At age fourteen he and some neighborhood kids made a movie, *Revenge on the Range,* which Packard shot with an eight millimeter camera. "Later on I often wondered why I didn't become more seriously interested in film and moviemaking," Packard told *SATA*. "I think it was because I didn't see any relationship between what I had done and the films I'd seen in the theater."

But such youthful explorations stopped when Packard was sent off to boarding school at Andover, and from there to Princeton. "Princeton was not a good experience for me. I didn't have any clear goals. I fell into the Princeton social life.... Later on I regretted not having studied a simple discipline in depth. If I had it to do over again, I would probably major in literature." After graduation, Packard went into the Navy for three years, having gone to Princeton on a Navy scholarship. Commissioned a Naval officer, Packard's job was in public relations, most of which was spent trying "to get the captain promoted to admiral," according to Packard in *SATA*. "The one good thing about the Navy for me was that I did a lot of my own reading. I read more literature there than during college." He also invented a board game, to keep boredom at bay. Once out of the Navy, Packard attended law school at Columbia and then practiced law for about the next twenty years, working during part of this time as counsel for RCA records.

Yet all the while there was a desire for something different in the back of his mind. Married with three children, Packard would read bedtime stories to his kids and often make up stories for them. And that is how he developed the idea for interactive stories. "If I were a better storyteller I wouldn't have come up with this idea," he recalled for *SATA*. "I'd have been able to devise the endings by myself. Sometimes while telling my kids stories, I'd get stuck or feel too tired to go on. I would ask the kids, 'What do you think Pete would do now?' To some extent I was introducing the Socratic method of questioning for which law school training is famous. The kids loved it. The storytelling became lively and, of course, bedtime was often delayed while we worked out all the adventures the hero might have enjoyed or suffered if he/she had made a different decision."

In this manner, Packard wrote his first interactive work, *Sugarcane Island.* He then gave it to a literary agent to place for him, but after a year of trying there were no takers. Packard filed the story away in a drawer until one day five years later when he was feeling "moderately unconsciously unhappy" as a lawyer. He read an article

CHOOSE YOUR OWN ADVENTURE® 124

SUPERBIKE
BY EDWARD PACKARD

One of Packard's popular "Choose Your Own Adventure" titles, this tale of a specially powered racing bike features a dozen possible endings. (Cover illustration by Catherine Huerta.)

about a new children's book publisher, Vermont Crossroads Press, whose co-owner, Ray Montgomery, was looking for innovative material. Packard sent along *Sugarcane Island,* which Vermont Crossroads subsequently published, and the rest is history. After the successful publication of this initial title, Bantam contracted for six more works, a contract that has since extended into the hundreds with sub-series included. Soon Packard was able to quit his law practice to devote his time to writing. The demand for his work was so high that he and Montgomery had to sub-contract writing to other authors.

Sugarcane Island, the first book in the popular series, finds the reader aboard a boat headed for the Galapagos Islands. The ship is wrecked and the 'you' in the narrative is then marooned on Sugarcane Island. "Now the excitement starts," a critic in *Publishers Weekly* noted in reviewing the book. On each page the reader has to make a choice that affects the possible ending. "Packard has an original idea," the *Publishers Weekly* reviewer added, concluding that readers could hardly resist trying out all the options and thus receiving "an exercise in thinking." Rex Benedict, writing in the *New York Times Book Review,* commented that the usual rule is to get the child "to turn the pages, preferably in the right direction, 1-2-3 and so on." But the first words of Packard's books are: "Do not read this book straight through from beginning to end." Benedict found that, in following the directions to turn to various pages as he made different choices, sometimes the reader found fortune, sometimes death. "Dead or alive," Benedict wrote, "you keep turning the pages. You become addicted."

Deadwood City has the reader as a stranger riding into town and faced with three initial choices: check out the saloon, the hotel, or the sheriff's office. Each selection will send the reader to a different page and from there more choices must be made. "Each choice has consequences," noted a *Publishers Weekly* commentator, "leading to further ramifications, so that the book can be a different adventure at each reading." Janet Mura, writing in *Voice of Youth Advocates,* remarked that such books as *Deadwood City* may "be helpful with unwilling readers." Reviewing Packard's third book, *The Cave of Time,* a critic for *Publishers Weekly* stated that Packard had come up with a "gimmicky but intriguing device" in

Imagining the Universe
A Visual Journey

From inside the atom to the ends of space and time, the whole cosmos scaled to the human eye...

Edward Packard

Packard offers a unique appreciation of space, time, and the intricacies of molecular structure in this 1994 nonfiction.

allowing the reader to create her own story. "The brisk, inventive writing will undoubtedly lure kids ... into making up dozens of different stories," the reviewer concluded. Other critics began to wonder about the negative aspects of the books, however. Writing in *School Library Journal,* Susan Cain declared that the format, "by definition, eliminates any chance for development of either character or plot line." As a result, Cain noted, the stories are "tedious the first time around, and if reread with the alternate options, they only get more so." A contributor in *Kirkus Reviews,* in a review of *Deadwood City,* found such books to be no more creative than video games, and concluded that there was another choice to be made: "Go along with Packard's gag or save your game-playing for the ones you plug into your TV set? Your move."

Many critics agree, however, that the best of such interactive books are not without value. They are, as Drew Stevens wrote in a *School Library Journal* review of *The Mystery of Chimney Rock,* "gimmicky maybe, fun definitely." Beyond that they could "be used in programming, book talks, creative writing and encouraging reluctant readers," concluded Carolyn Caywood in a *School Library Journal* review of *Inside UFO 54-40.* And Susan Williamson, writing in *Voice of Youth Advocates,* observed that the books have "appeal for readers of all ability levels" because of their emphasis on participation and concluded that "readers' choices and the resulting consequences are fertile ground for developing students' ability to predict outcomes or for group work on values clarification." Packard has created several sub-series to "Choose Your Own Adventure," including "Escape from Tenopia," which a *School Library Journal* critic described as a collective "chronicle of your attempt to escape after crash-landing on 'one of the most forbidding planets in the galaxy.'" Twenty years after the publication of his first "Choose Your Own Adventure," Packard continues to write for the series he created.

A non-series book for young readers and adults alike was *Imagining the Universe: A Visual Journey,* in which he brings distance and size in the universe down to comparisons with familiar objects. For example, he uses the dimensions of a baseball stadium to lay out the solar system. "This rather elegant pictorial method works just as well when Packard creates time lines that equate time and distance on different scales," stated Donna Seaman in *Sci-Tech Books for Adults.* "The idea behind this book is a very good one," commented Gloria Levine in a *Kliatt* review.

In all his books Packard has employed the techniques and playfulness he learned while perusing *The Book of Knowledge* in his childhood attic, or while shooting an adolescent movie on the local golf course—the closest he could find to the open range on Long Island. His books are visual, told in scenes rather than chapters, and full of information of all sorts. There is also very often a message in his interactive books. "I think there is a very strong moral element in my books," Packard once remarked to *SATA,* "but it's not tied up with the choices you make for endings, with rewards and things like that. Just because you choose the wise option in my book doesn't necessarily mean that things will go well from that point on. Choice operates in my books as it does in life: usually good judgement is rewarded, but not always.... The basic moral element in my books is the assumption that you, the reader, are a decent and caring person. 'You' never kill or assault anyone or act cruelly in my books. You may be guilty of a transgression—say, of not keeping a promise, or joining up in a dubious scheme to make some quick money—but these are things a weak person might do, a point made to the reader."

■ Works Cited

Benedict, Rex, "Trust a Dying Pirate," *New York Times Book Review,* April 30, 1978, p. 43.

Cain, Susan, review of *The Cave of Time, School Library Journal,* November, 1979, p. 68.

Review of *The Cave of Time, Publishers Weekly,* June 18, 1979, p. 94.

Caywood, Carolyn, review of *Inside UFO 54-40, School Library Journal,* August, 1982, p. 120.

Review of *Deadwood City, Kirkus Reviews,* April 1, 1978, p. 375.

Review of *Deadwood City, Publishers Weekly,* May 22, 1978, p. 233.

Levine, Gloria, review of *Imagining the Universe: A Visual Journey, Kliatt,* March, 1995, p. 39.

Mura, Janet, review of *Deadwood City, Voice of Youth Advocates,* April, 1982, p. 52.

Packard, Edward, *Sugarcane Island,* Vermont Crossroads Press, 1976.

Packard, Edward, "Interactive Fiction: Boon or Bane?," *School Library Journal,* October, 1987, pp. 40-1.

Seaman, Donna, review of *Imagining the Universe: A Visual Journey, Sci-Tech Books for Adults,* December 1, 1994, p. 643.

Stevens, Drew, review of *The Mystery of Chimney Rock, School Library Journal,* September, 1980, p. 76.

Review of *Sugarcane Island, Publishers Weekly,* April 18, 1977, p. 62.

Review of *Tenopia Island, School Library Journal,* September, 1986, p. 152.

Williamson, Susan, review of *Inside UFO 54-40, Voice of Youth Advocates,* June, 1982, p. 40.

■ For More Information See

BOOKS

Science Fiction and Fantasy Literature, 1975-1991, Gale, 1992, pp. 739-40.

PERIODICALS

Booklist, January 15, 1982, p. 651; July, 1982, p. 1438; December 1, 1994, p. 643.

Children's Book Watch, May, 1995, p. 2.

New York Times, August 25, 1981.

New York Times Book Review, January 25, 1981, p. 32.

School Library Journal, September, 1978, p. 145; March, 1983, p. 183; December, 1983, p. 31; May, 1984, p. 101; September, 1985, p. 153; January,

1986, p. 82; September, 1986, p. 152; October, 1987, p. 152; March, 1989, p. 177; August, 1990, p. 146.
Times Educational Supplement, April 4, 1980, p. 29; July 11, 1980, p. 28; October 1, 1981, p. 31.
Voice of Youth Advocates, August, 1986, p. 170; February, 1987, p. 295; June, 1987, p. 94; October, 1988, p. 185; June, 1989, p. 110; August, 1995, p. 146.*

—Sketch by J. Sydney Jones

* * *

PAGNUCCI, Susan 1944-

■ Personal

Born November 19, 1944, in Elgin, IL; daughter of John and Florence Howell; married Franco Pagnucci (a university English professor), August 20, 1966; children: Gian, Rob, Anna, Stefan. *Education:* University of Illinois, B.S.; University of Wisconsin-Platteville, M.S. *Religion:* Catholic. *Hobbies and other interests:* Swimming, walking, drawing.

■ Addresses

Home and office—8717 Mockingbird Rd., Platteville, WI 53818.

■ Career

Professional storyteller; Bur Oak Press, Platteville, WI, editor and publisher, 1979—.

■ Writings

WITH HUSBAND, FRANCO PAGNUCCI

Paul Revere and Other Story Hours, Bur Oak Press, 1988.
Story-Start Dinosaurs, Fearon Teacher Aids, 1990.
Story-Start Animals, Fearon Teacher Aids, 1990.
Story-Start Monsters, Fearon Teacher Aids, 1990.
Mother Goose Favorites, Bur Oak Press, 1991.
Storytelling Patterns, Bur Oak Press, 1991.
Storytelling Magic, Bur Oak Press, 1991.
Do Me! Stories, Bur Oak Press, 1993.
The 3 Little Pigs: And Other Great Stories with Masks, Bur Oak Press, 1994.
I Can! Folktales: Stories from Around the World for Young Children, Bur Oak Press, 1995.
The 3 Bears: And Other Great Stories with Hats, Bur Oak Press, 1995.
Hansel and Gretel and Grimm and More, Bur Oak Press, 1996.

OTHER

Games to Cut, Bur Oak Press, 1978.
Number Chomp, Bur Oak Press, 1984.

SUSAN PAGNUCCI

(Illustrator) Franco Pagnucci, *I Never Had a Pet,* edited by Gian Pagnucci, Bur Oak Press, 1992.
Shortcuts for Librarians and Teachers, Bur Oak Press, 1993.

■ Work in Progress

A children's picture book based on a classic folktale.

■ Sidelights

Susan Pagnucci told *SATA:* "I'm a professional storyteller and like to tell all kinds of folktales using puppets and props. I've done this in seventeen states and even abroad. But sometimes people would call me and ask how I had done this or where I got that. So it seemed that I needed a book with storytelling directions and patterns.

"My husband said he'd work with me, which was fun. Because I was working with a two-foot bear, a wolf, a rabbit, etc., which children would wear, I went into a kindergarten to try out our patterns. One little boy came running up crying out, 'Do me. Do me.' So we named this first book *Do Me! Stories.*

"But I also had a simple construction-paper story puppet which kids like to make. And I wanted to do another book using stories which would go well with these puppets. So my husband and I put together *I Can! Folktales: Stories from Around the World for Young Children* for kids, teachers, children's librarians, and parents to use. It has creative stories, plus step-by-step puppet construction techniques.

"Then I had more ideas for hat stories, mask stories, and flannel board pattern stories. Thus we wrote three more books. We also did three books for Fearon Teacher Aids, a division of Simon and Schuster. They bought those within a week of sending off our ideas and sample pages. Teacher book clubs picked up those three titles as book-of-the-month alternate selections. So we called the clubs with our other titles and they took four of these as book-of-the-month selections, too.

"I've had so much fun doing these books that I'm now working on illustrations to try my hand at a children's picture book. I started working at my husband's basement workbench, but now I have a studio with beautiful woods and big windows with natural light. And I'm having such a good time!"

*   *   *

PATIENCE, John 1949-

■ Personal

Born January 19, 1949, in Lancashire, England; son of Alexander McLeman and Beatrice (Sutton) Patience; married; wife's name, Jane; children: Kerry, Joseph. *Education:* Studied graphics and book design at Harris School of Art, Preston, Lancashire, England. *Hobbies and other interests:* Chess, snooker, playing the flute.

■ Addresses

Home—Sibford Ferris, Main St., West Witton, Leyburn, North Yorkshire DL8 4LP, England.

■ Career

Children's author and illustrator. Has worked as an in-house designer for publishing houses in London, England.

■ Writings

SELF-ILLUSTRATED

Adventures in Fern Hollow, Random House, 1985.
The Land of Nursery Rhymes, Random House, 1985.
Baked in a Pie, Macdonald Purnell, 1986.
Monty's Dragon, Macdonald Purnell, 1986.
The Sailing Race, Macdonald Purnell, 1986.
Magical Mr. Willowbank, Macdonald Purnell, 1986.
(Reteller) *Little Red Riding Hood,* Random House, 1992.
Little Merlin's Book of Magic Pets: A Pop-Up Book, Price, Stern, 1994.

JOHN PATIENCE

Roarasaurus: A Pop-Up Book, Price, Stern, 1994.
Who's Afraid of Tigers? (pop-up book), Price, Stern, 1994.

"HAPPY ENDING STORIES" SERIES; PUBLISHED BY RANDOM HOUSE

Hubble Bubble, 1991.
The Little People, 1991.
Tall Stories, 1991.

"PETRIFYING POP-UPS" SERIES; PUBLISHED BY PETER HADDOCK (ENGLAND)

Witches Spell Trouble, 1996.
Party on Spooky Street, 1996.
Dracula and the Dentist, 1996.
Monsters Don't Eat Pizza, 1996.

ILLUSTRATOR

Jane Patience, *Toby Claypot's Wishing Well,* Derrydale Books, 1987.
Jane Patience, *The Winter Warming,* Derrydale Books, 1987.

OTHER

Illustrator and author of over one hundred stories, pop-up books, and retellings of fairy tales, including *Cinderella, Parson Dimly's Treasure Hunt, Muddles at the Manor,* and *The Seasons in Fern Hollow.* Creator of *The Dumpies, Lost in Space,* an animated film based on his book, *The Dumpies.*

■ Work in Progress

Two pop-up books: a follow-up book to *Who's Afraid of Tigers?* entitled *Who's Afraid of Sharks?* and *Professor Mainspring's Mechanimal Zoo.*

■ Sidelights

English author and illustrator John Patience began his career working as a book designer for a number of publishers in London, but his real interest has always been in children's literature. His dream to write and illustrate stories for children came to fruition when he published his first book at the age of thirty. Since that time, he has published almost one hundred original stories, pop-up books, and retellings of classic fairy tales by Hans Christian Andersen and the Brothers Grimm. Originally influenced by turn-of-the-century English illustrators like Arthur Rackham, William Heath, and Charles Robinson, his more recent work bears evidence of a more individual style.

Now living with his wife and two children in a small Wensleydale village, Patience often gets his ideas from his children, who help him keep "in touch with what a child wants from a picture book," as he told *SATA.*

■ For More Information See

PERIODICALS

School Library Journal, February, 1985, p. 88; April, 1985, p. 104.

Q–R

JANET QUIN-HARKIN

QUIN-HARKIN, Janet 1941-
(Janetta Johns)

■ Personal

Born September 24, 1941, in Bath, England; immigrated to the United States in 1966; daughter of Frank Newcombe (an engineer) and Margery (a teacher; maiden name, Rees) Lee; married John Quin-Harkin (a retired sales manager), November 26, 1966; children: Clare, Anne, Jane, Dominic. *Education:* University of London,

B.A. (with honors), 1963; graduate study at University of Kiel and University of Freiburg. *Religion:* Roman Catholic. *Hobbies and other interests:* Tennis, travel, drama, music, sketching, and hiking.

■ Addresses

Home and office—31 Tralee Way, San Rafael, CA 94903. *Agent*—Amy Berkower, Writers House, Inc., 21 West 26th St., New York, NY 10010.

■ Career

British Broadcasting Corp. (BBC), London, England, studio manager in drama department, 1963-66; writer, 1971—; teacher of dance and drama, 1971-76. Founder and former director of San Raphael's Children's Little Theater. Writing teacher at Dominican College, San Rafael, 1988-95. *Member:* Society of Children's Book Writers and Illustrators, Associated Authors of Children's Literature.

■ Awards, Honors

Children's Book Showcase selection, Children's Book Council, Outstanding Books of the Year citation, *New York Times,* American Institute of Graphic Arts Children's Book Show citation, and Best Books of the year citation, *School Library Journal, Washington Post,* and *Saturday Review,* all 1976, all for *Peter Penny's Dance;* Children's Choice citation, 1985, for *Wanted: Date for Saturday Night.*

■ Writings

CHILDREN'S BOOKS

Peter Penny's Dance, illustrated by Anita Lobel, Dial, 1976.
Benjamin's Balloon, Parents Magazine Press, 1979.
Septimus Bean and His Amazing Machine, illustrated by Art Cumings, Parents Magazine Press, 1980.
Magic Growing Powder, illustrated by Art Cumings, Parents Magazine Press, 1981.

Helpful Hattie, illustrated by Susanna Natti, Harcourt, 1983.
Three Impossible Things, Parents Magazine Press, 1991.
Billy and Ben: The Terrible Two, illustrated by Carol Newsom, Bantam, 1992.

YOUNG ADULT NOVELS

Write Every Day, Scholastic, 1982.
(Under pseudonym Janetta Johns) *The Truth about Me and Bobby V.*, Bantam, 1983.
Tommy Loves Tina, Berkley/Ace, 1984.
Winner Takes All, Berkley/Ace, 1984.
Wanted: Date for Saturday Night, Putnam, 1985.
Summer Heat, Fawcett, 1990.
My Phantom Love ("Changes Romance" series), HarperCollins, 1992.
On My Own ("Changes Romance" series), HarperCollins, 1992.
Getting Personal: Becky, Silhouette Books, 1994.
The Apartment, HarperCollins, 1994.
The Sutcliffe Diamonds, HarperCollins, 1994.
The Boy Next Door ("Love Stories" series), Bantam, 1995.

"SWEET DREAMS" SERIES; PUBLISHED BY BANTAM

California Girl, 1981.
Love Match, 1982.
Ten-Boy Summer, 1982.
Daydreamer, 1983.
The Two of Us, 1984.
Exchange of Hearts, 1984.
Ghost of a Chance, 1984.
Lovebirds, 1984.
101 Ways to Meet Mr. Right, 1985.
The Great Boy Chase, 1985.
Follow That Boy, 1985.
My Secret Love, 1986.
My Best Enemy, 1987.
Never Say Goodbye, 1987.

"ON OUR OWN" SERIES; PUBLISHED BY BANTAM

On Our Own, 1986.
The Graduates, 1986.
The Trouble with Toni, 1986.
Out of Love, 1986.
Old Friends, New Friends, 1986.
Best Friends Forever, 1986.

"SUGAR AND SPICE" SERIES; PUBLISHED BY BALLANTINE

Flip Side, 1987.
Tug of War, 1987.
Surf's Up, 1987.
The Last Dance, 1987.
Nothing in Common, 1987.
Dear Cousin, 1987.
Two Girls, One Boy, 1987.
Trading Places, 1987.
Double Take, 1988.
Make Me a Star, 1988.
Big Sister, 1988.
Out in the Cold, 1988.
Blind Date, 1988.

It's My Turn, 1988.

"HEARTBREAK CAFE" SERIES; PUBLISHED BY FAWCETT

No Experience Required, 1990.
The Main Attraction, 1990.
At Your Service, 1990.
Catch of the Day, 1990.
Love to Go, 1990.
Just Desserts, 1990.

"FRIENDS" SERIES; PUBLISHED BY HARPERCOLLINS

Starring Tess and Ali, 1991.
Tess and Ali and the Teeny Bikini, 1991.
Boy Trouble for Tess and Ali, 1991.
Tess and Ali, Going on Fifteen, 1991.

"SENIOR YEAR" SERIES; PUBLISHED BY HARPERCOLLINS

Homecoming Dance, 1991.
New Year's Eve, 1991.
Night of the Prom, 1992.
Graduation Day, 1992.

"BOYFRIEND CLUB" SERIES; PUBLISHED BY TROLL COMMUNICATIONS

Ginger's First Kiss, 1994.
Roni's Dream Boy, 1994.
Karen's Perfect Match, 1994.
Ginger's New Crush, 1994.
Queen Justine, 1995.
Roni's Two-Boy Trouble, 1995.
No More Boys, 1995.
Karen's Lesson in Love, 1995.
Roni's Sweet Fifteen, 1995.
Justine's Babysitting, 1995.
The Boyfriend Wars, 1995.

"TGIF!" SERIES; PUBLISHED BY POCKET BOOKS

Sleepover Madness, 1995.
Friday Night Fright, 1995.
Four's a Crowd, 1995.
Forever Friday, 1995.
Toe-Shoe Trouble, 1996.
Secret Valentine, 1996.

SISTER, SISTER SERIES; POCKET BOOKS

Cool in School, 1996.
You Read My Mind, 1996.
One Crazy Christmas and 5 to Come

OTHER

(Contributor) *Chandler Reading Program*, five volumes, edited by Lawrence Carillo and Dorothy McKinley, Noble & Noble, 1967-72.
Madam Sarah (adult historical novel), Fawcett, 1990.
Fool's Gold (adult historical novel), HarperCollins, 1991.
Amazing Grace (adult historical fiction), HarperCollins, 1993.
The Secrets of Lake Success (based on the NBC miniseries, created by David Stenn), Tor Books, 1993.

Trade Winds (based on the NBC mini-series, created by Hugh Bush), Schoolfield/Caribbean Productions, 1993.

Also author of several documentaries and four radio plays and scripts, including "Dandelion Hours," for the BBC, 1966. Many of Quin-Harkin's young adult novels, including *California Girl, Love Match, Ten-Boy Summer,* and *Daydreamer,* have been translated into other languages. Contributor to periodicals, including *Scholastic* and *Mother's Journal.*

■ Sidelights

Janet Quin-Harkin is the popular author of more than one hundred books, most of which are geared for teen readers. Quin-Harkin's series include "Sweet Dreams," "Sugar and Spice," "Heartbreak Cafe," and "On Our Own," among others, comprising books of standard length with a fixed group of characters involved in "the sort of lives that Middle America leads," as Quin-Harkin once said in describing her work. According to the author, the "Sweet Dreams" series opened up a new direction in publishing, providing books that were cheap enough for the readers themselves to purchase and thus making teen readers independent from the choices of parents and librarians. These were also books that were more upbeat than previous YA contributions, which dealt primarily, according to Quin-Harkin, with "the darker side of reality."

Criticized by some as lacking in substance, and praised by others as an encouragement to reading, teen books such as those Quin-Harkin has built a career on are an important part of juvenile publishing, accounting for hundreds of thousands of sales annually. Quin-Harkin's books tell what happens when a teen and her best friend break up, when a family moves or parents are divorced. And most often there are young men involved: guys a girl wants to date, or loves from afar, or beats at tennis. Quin-Harkin writes about the concerns of teenage girls of the 1980s and 1990s; relevance is her watchword. And she has built an enormous and faithful readership as a result.

Born in Bath, England, Quin-Harkin began writing for fun at an early age; she had published her first short story by sixteen. Her own teen years were quite placid, as she attended an all-girls school where academics rather than sports or romance were emphasized. The usual emotional upheavals of a young woman were thus largely postponed until Quin-Harkin attended college, earning a B.A. with honors from the University of London. For the first few years after graduation, Quin-Harkin worked for the British Broadcasting Corporation, as a studio manager and also a writer of radio and television plays. Such writings were "fairly highbrow," as the author described them. She then moved to Australia, where she met her husband while working for the Australian Broadcasting Company. The couple married in 1966 and moved to the United States. Settling in the San Francisco Bay area, Quin-Harkin balanced the role of mother and writer. She worked

This popular tale of shy Julie and her efforts to find a date for the Freshman Formal earned Quin-Harkin a Children's Choice citation in 1985.

initially for a textbook company and helped develop new primary reading texts more relevant for contemporary urban children than the traditional primer stories of Dick and Jane.

Work on textbooks set Quin-Harkin to writing for herself again, and her first book was published in 1976. It was a long way from teen romance. *Peter Penny's Dance* was a picture book for children, inspired by the lyrics from an old English folk song: "I've come to claim a silver pound because I've danced the world around." Peter is a sailor who would rather dance a reel than scrub the decks, and sets off to dance around the world; he comes back in five years to claim the hand of his beloved Lavinia, the captain's daughter. Adventures greet him in France, Africa, China, and America, but Peter finally dances to the church to take Lavinia's hand. Everything about this first title was easy for Quin-Harkin: the story seemed to come of itself and the manuscript found a home on the second try. Zena Sutherland of the *Bulletin of the Center for Children's Books* called the tale "a bouncy, bonny book," and many critics praised the illustrations of Anita Lobel. Of the book's exciting conclusion, *Horn Book* reviewer Ethel L. Heins wrote: "In a splendid finale, reminiscent of *Around the World in Eighty Days,* Peter arrived back in England in the nick of time and skipped his way straight to the church and into the arms of his overjoyed bride." *Peter Penny's Dance* went on to win numerous awards. This early successful start, however, was followed by several years without sales as Quin-Harkin continued to raise her family while struggling to work at her craft. Then several early titles were sold to Parents Magazine Press: *Benjamin's Balloon, Septimus Bean and His Amazing Machine,* and *Magic Growing Powder.* Quin-Harkin was establishing a name as a picture book author.

In 1981 came a turning point in the author's career, when her agent called to ask if she could do a teen novel in a hurry. A trip to the local bookstore provided the author with a bundle of similar books which she studied carefully, and then she sat down to turn out sample chapters of her own teen fiction. These samples evolved into *California Girl,* the first in Bantam's "Sweet Dreams" series. In *California Girl,* Jenny is a sixteen-year-old swimmer with Olympic aspirations. When her coach moves to Texas, Jenny's family follows so that she can continue training. But Texas is a far cry from Jenny's former home state; here she is regarded as strange because of her devotion to her athletic dreams. She soon finds a friend, however: Mark is an injured football player who supports her swimming, helping her train, and the finale comes with Jenny competing in the Nationals for a berth in the Olympics. Along the way there is a crew of supporting characters: the scheming cheerleader who now wants her former boyfriend Mark back, Jenny's rather unsympathetic mother, and an empty-headed girl friend. Ella B. Fossum, writing in *School Library Journal,* thought the book was "a cut above the usual teenage love story" because of the added complications and insightful details of Jenny's Olympic aspirations, and Becky Johnson in *Voice of Youth Advocates* noted that "the story is fast-moving and the main character is serious-minded and independent." Johnson also felt, however, that the supporting cast of characters lacked meaningful depth: "This gets high marks for readability but could have had more realistic character development."

The second book in the series, *Love Match,* also involves an athletic theme, when Joanna refuses to try to ensure Rick's affection by allowing him to beat her at tennis. While *Bulletin of the Center for Children's Books* concluded that the book had "little substance" because of its formulaic plot—girl meets boy, loses boy, wins boy in the end—other reviewers, including Joe McKenzie in *School Library Journal,* commented that "readers will figure it all out early too, but many of them won't care," because of the sympathetic nature of the leading character, Joanna. This blend of sympathetic and generally well-drawn and independent main character along with a formula plot has formed the heart of much of Quin-Harkin's teen writing. Most of the titles fall into the category of escapist reading, "predictable but palatable," as Ilene Cooper of *Booklist* noted in a review of *Daydreamer,* a further title in the "Sweet Dreams" series. Maureen Ritter, however, writing in *Voice of*

Youth Advocates about *Daydreamer,* emphasized the readability factor and noted that the book was "perfect for a hi/lo reader," and that aside from divorced parents, the main character, Lisa, "does not suffer from the traumas that most YA novel characters do; only the necessary conflicts needed for growth."

Other titles in the series have also earned mixed praise: formula plots that have just that twist of originality or individuality to set them apart. Kathy Fritts in *School Library Journal* noted that "funny scenes and a fast pace" set *101 Ways to Meet Mr. Right* "a notch above average," and Elaine Patterson, reviewing the same book in *Kliatt,* commented that "girls of all ages" would identify with the main character's "fears, fantasies, and flops" as she searches for the true love that is under her nose all the time. Critics may disagree about the relative merits of such books, but readers have pronounced them successes. One book in the "Sweet Dreams" series, *Ten-Boy Summer,* sold over half a million copies. In this work, central characters Jill and Toni determine to liven up their junior-year summer by breaking up with their respective boyfriends, betting on who will be the first to have dated ten boys. Sally Estes of *Booklist* found the book's premise "a bit farfetched, perhaps, but light and lively enough to attract nondemanding readers of teenage romances." Similarly, Susan Levine wrote in *Voice of Youth Advocates* that *Ten-Boy Summer* "satisfies its requirements of a fast, uncomplicated, lightly romantic story with a happy ending."

Series writing has its pitfalls, according to Quin-Harkin, the largest of which is slipping into cliche. The author becomes so familiar with the set of characters that it is easy to use stock dialogue or responses instead of always being on guard to search for the most appropriate wording. Quin-Harkin generally writes a 200-page book every two months, and many of these are told in the first person. "On the whole, first person is very effective because it doesn't ever become overly dramatic," Quin-Harkin has noted, adding: "And of course, when you're first person, you're right there with the character and it's very immediate." Her experience in radio and television also informs her work, making for strong dialogue and pictorial writing. Quin-Harkin has said that she thinks in terms of scenes rather than chapters, a technique that gives her books a fast pace. Reaching back to her own feelings as a teenager for inspiration, Quin-Harkin has also used the experiences of her four children and their friends as they went through the teen years.

If cliche is one pitfall in series books, boredom for the writer can be another. According to Quin-Harkin, the "Sugar and Spice" series went on far longer than she wanted. The adventures of the two cousins, Chrissy and Cara, became somewhat stale after several books, but the series was so popular that Quin-Harkin was forced to go on with it, writing some twenty installments. Bouncy Chrissy is the cheerleader type from a small town in Iowa who has come to live in San Francisco with her serious, ballet-studying cousin, Caroline or Cara. *Flip Side* inaugurated the series and introduced the city cousin and country cousin in a situation in

Karen—
in love?

Karen's Perfect Match
Janet Quin-Harkin

In this installment of Quin-Harkin's popular "Boyfriend Club" series, Karen must cope with very different views among classmates and her Vietnamese parents regarding her seemingly "perfect match." (Cover illustration by Charles Tang.)

which they both yearn for the other's boyfriend but are too nice to do anything about it. *School Library Journal* contributor Kathy Fritts called the book "a winner," while Laurel Ibey, writing in *Voice of Youth Advocates,* concluded that everyone who read *Flip Side* would "find it full of fun!" Other adventures in the "Sugar and Spice" series take urban Cara to Chrissy's Iowa farm in *Nothing in Common,* about which Kathy Fritts asserted that a "fast pace, wonderful scenes of family and farm life, lots of action, and plenty of boy-girl mix and match make it a sure hit"; or have Cara finally decide to give up dancing in *The Last Dance,* which Juli Lund in *Voice of Youth Advocates* praised for the fact that it "did not have a perfect 'happy ending,' but instead realistically portrayed not-so-perfect actual life."

Other series books from Quin-Harkin include those from "On Our Own" and "Heartbreak Cafe," and do not suffer from claustrophobia as do the later titles of the "Sugar and Spice" series. "Heartbreak Cafe," for example, contains only six books and each is told from a different point of view of one of the people involved with the rundown cafe which is a hangout for teens with problems. With *No Experience Required,* Quin-Harkin

featured heroine Debbie Leslie, whose parents have just divorced. Debbie manages to get a position at the Heartbreak Cafe, but Joe, the grandson of the owner, figures the wealthy kid won't last a month. Debbie sets out to prove him wrong and turns out to be one of Quin-Harkin's archetypal feisty and headstrong female characters. A *Publishers Weekly* reviewer, commenting on *No Experience Required,* noted that "Quin-Harkin's skilled storytelling effectively blends wry humor with universal concerns." The "On Our Own" series is a spin-off from "Sweet Dreams," following some of those main characters on their way into college. Jill has been accepted to an exclusive out-of-state school but Toni has to defer college plans because of her father's heart attack. Plagued by a miserable roommate, Jill is finally rescued by a visit from Toni, who tells the girl off. First-time college experiences inaugurated this mini-series, and a *Publishers Weekly* reviewer noted that such experiences "ring true." Other commentators found problems with the series: "Although worthwhile for the exposure of so many real problems of college freshmen, it is unfortunate that the shallow dialogue and narrative read so very quickly," concluded Sandra Dayton in a *Voice of Youth Advocates* review of *The Graduates.* Another *Voice of Youth Advocates* reviewer, Kaye Grabbe, objected to what she considered "little character development," noting that central character Jill "never seems like much of a real person."

A series geared at pre-teens is "Friends," which follows the relationship between two girls, Alison and Tess, over the four summers they spend together in a small resort town. Tess is newly arrived in the town in the first book of the series, *Starring Tess and Ali,* and Alison forms a quick friendship with her. Trouble arises, however, with remarks Tess makes about how overprotective Ali's mother is. Ali is upset by such remarks until she learns the root of them: Tess's mother has recently deserted the family and envy and spite are undoubtedly contributing to the girl's behavior. A *Publishers Weekly* reviewer noted in a review of *Starring Tess and Ali* that younger readers might resent the "juvenile tone" of the book, but that Quin-Harkin had created a "compassionate protagonist whose heretofore compliant ways are undergoing thoughtful reevaluation."

Quin-Harkin has also written many non-series teen books, perhaps the best known being *Wanted: Date for Saturday Night,* in which the central problem is finding a date for shy Julie for the Freshman Formal. Along the way, Julie manages to join the "in" crowd, only to discover they are shallow and no fun. Reviews again were mixed. Carolyn Gabbard Fugate in *School Library Journal* found that "the characterizations of Julie and the minor characters are excellent," and concluded the book "a good, solid addition to a junior or senior high-school library." Zena Sutherland of *Bulletin of the Center for Children's Books,* however, concluded that the book had "a formula plot and cardboard characters," while Kaye Grabbe in *Voice of Youth Advocates* commented on the book's "improbable story" and "shallow characterizations." *Wanted: Date for Saturday*

Night went on to win a Children's Choice award as well as a large readership.

Another standalone book from Quin-Harkin is *Summer Heat,* in which teen protagonist Laurie Beth, on the verge of graduating from high school, must choose between two suitors and two completely different lifestyles. A *Publishers Weekly* reviewer commented favorably on this title, noting that "love certainly plays an important role in [Laurie Beth's] decision—but so does her new-found sense of self-worth—and that's what makes this story so refreshing." Other of Quin-Harkin's non-series efforts include *The Sutcliffe Diamonds,* which romance readers "will devour," according to Elaine M. McGuire in *Voice of Youth Advocates;* and *The Apartment,* which a *Voice of Youth Advocates* contributor describes as a story of "three girls from very different backgrounds [who] share an apartment during a pivotal period in their lives."

A new direction for Quin-Harkin has been adult fiction dealing with historical settings: the California Gold Rush or Australia in the 1920s. Perhaps her teen readership will follow her on to a different level of writing, as well. But for now, each new series brings in a new generation of teen readers, as "Boyfriend Club" and "TGIF!," Quin-Harkin's most recent series contributions, hope to do. "I enjoy writing for children because it is a very positive medium," Quin-Harkin once told *SATA.* "You can be optimistic, indulge in fantasy and have a happy ending. What's more, you don't have to introduce sex and violence to make it sell. Also, in common with many writers for children, I don't think I ever grew up." And there are thousands of teen readers hoping Quin-Harkin never does.

■ Works Cited

Review of *The Apartment, Voice of Youth Advocates,* October, 1994, p. 215.
Cooper, Ilene, review of *Daydreamer, Booklist,* May 15, 1983, p. 1221.
Dayton, Sandra, review of *The Graduate, Voice of Youth Advocates,* December, 1986, p. 231.
Estes, Sally, review of *Ten-Boy Summer, Booklist,* September 1, 1982, p. 37.
Fossum, Ella B., review of *California Girl, School Library Journal,* November, 1981, p. 110.
Fritts, Kathy, review of *101 Ways to Meet Mr. Right, School Library Journal,* September, 1985, p. 180.
Fritts, Kathy, review of *Flip Side* and *Nothing in Common, School Library Journal,* January, 1988, p. 95.
Fugate, Carolyn Gabbard, review of *Wanted: Date for Saturday Night, School Library Journal,* March, 1985, p. 181.
Grabbe, Kaye, review of *Wanted: Date for Saturday Night, Voice of Youth Advocates,* June, 1985, p. 134.
Grabbe, Kaye, review of *The Graduates, Voice of Youth Advocates,* August-October, 1986, p. 156.
Review of *The Graduate, Publishers Weekly,* July 25, 1986, pp. 192-93.

Heins, Ethel L., review of *Peter Penny's Dance, Horn Book,* June, 1976, p. 281.
Ibey, Laurel, review of *Flip Side, Voice of Youth Advocates,* April, 1988. p. 35.
Johnson, Becky, review of *California Girl, Voice of Youth Advocates,* December, 1981, p. 34.
Levine, Susan, review of *Ten-Boy Summer, Voice of Youth Advocates,* December, 1982, p. 35.
Review of *Love Match, Bulletin of the Center for Children's Books,* March, 1982, p. 136.
Lund, Juli, review of *The Last Dance, Voice of Youth Advocates,* April, 1988, p. 35.
McGuire, Elaine M., review of *The Sutcliffe Diamonds, Voice of Youth Advocates,* December, 1994, p. 279.
McKenzie, Joe, review of *Love Match, School Library Journal,* March, 1982, p. 160.
Review of *No Experience Required, Publishers Weekly,* December 22, 1989, p. 57.
Patterson, Elaine, review of *101 Ways to Meet Mr. Right, Kliatt,* Fall, 1985, p. 16.
Ritter, Maureen, review of *Daydreamer, Voice of Youth Advocates,* December, 1983, p. 281.
Review of *Starring Tess and Ali, Publishers Weekly,* May 24, 1991, p. 58.
Review of *Summer Heat, Publishers Weekly,* June 29, 1990, p. 103.
Sutherland, Zena, review of *Peter Penny's Dance, Bulletin of the Center for Children's Books,* October, 1976, p. 30.
Sutherland, Zena, review of *Wanted: Date for Saturday Night, Bulletin of the Center for Children's Books,* June, 1985, p. 192.

■ For More Information See

BOOKS

Authors and Artists for Young Adults, Volume 6, Gale, 1991, pp. 181-87.

PERIODICALS

Booklist, May 1, 1976, p. 1270; October 1, 1981, p. 189; January 15, 1982, p. 644; February 1, 1984, p. 810; February 15, 1984, p. 862; June 15, 1984, p. 1474.
Kliatt, Spring, 1982, p. 10; Spring, 1983, p. 5.
New York Times Book Review, May 9, 1976, p. 12; November 14, 1976, p. 53; April 1, 1979, p. 37.
Times Educational Supplement, April 21, 1995, p. 16.
Wilson Library Bulletin, October, 1991, p. 102.

—Sketch by J. Sydney Jones

*   *   *

RAGAN-REID, Gale 1956-

■ Personal

Born April 5, 1956, in Miami, FL; daughter of Jerry and Mae (a schoolteacher; maiden name, Calhoun) Ragan; children: Melvin, David. *Education:* University of Miami, B.A., 1978, M.S.Ed., 1986, post-graduate courses, 1985-93. *Politics:* Democratic. *Religion:* Catholic.

■ Career

Burdines, Miami Beach, FL, department manager, assistant buyer, 1980-82; Black Business Association of Dade County, FL, president and secretary, 1982-84; Dade County Public Schools, Miami, FL, math curriculum specialist teacher, 1984—; Miami-Dade Community College, Miami, college professor, 1990—; Educational Games for Learning, Inc., founder, 1991—. Member of the board of directors, University of Miami Alumni Association, College of Arts and Sciences, 1992—. *Member:* National Council of Teachers of Math, Florida Council of Teachers of Mathematics, Book Review Club Between Friends, Alpha Kappa Alpha.

■ Awards, Honors

Fulbright Scholar, 1988; selected for Teachers for Africa Program, International Fellows for Education and Self-help, 1994; "Early Morning" selected for *Poetry Today,* National Poetry Radio Network, 1995.

■ Writings

Divine, Winston-Derek, 1996.
Teardrops and Lemonade, Dorrance Publishing, 1996.
In My Room, a Book of Poems, Watermark Press, 1996.

Also author of poems published by the National Library of Poetry and creator of songs produced for the America Album project, Hill Top Records.

■ Sidelights

"I enjoy writing and creating educational materials for children. I have been influenced by my mother, a country school teacher," Gale Ragan-Reid told *SATA.* Ragan related that her books, *Divine* and *Teardrops and Lemonade,* were simply a delight to create. "I look forward to the production of my children's board game, *Game of Hearts,* and the continuation of my writing career."*

*   *   *

RAY, Mary Lyn 1946-

■ Personal

Born in 1946, in Monroe, LA. *Education:* Smith College, A.B. in American studies, 1968; University of Delaware (Winterthur fellow), M.A. in Early American arts and culture, 1970.

■ Addresses

Home—Box 174, South Danbury, NH 03230.

MARY LYN RAY

■ Career

Writer and conservationist. Worked in museums for fifteen years; has also worked as a professional consultant in land protection and historic preservation.

■ Awards, Honors

New Hampshire Conservationist of the Year, 1989; Calder Award finalist, Conservation Fund, 1991; Citizen of the Year, Danbury Grange and New Hampshire State Grange, both 1995; Fiera di Bologna, Menzione d'Onore, for *Pumpkins;* American Bookseller Pick of the Lists citation, for *A Rumbly Tumbly Glittery Gritty Place;* Notable Children's Trade Book in the Field of Social Studies citation, National Council of Social Studies-Children's Book Council, for *Shaker Boy.*

■ Writings

PICTURE BOOKS

Angel Baskets: A Little Story about the Shakers, illustrated by Jean Colquhoun, Martha Wetherbee Books, 1987.
Pumpkins, illustrated by Barry Root, Gulliver Green/ Harcourt, 1992.
A Rumbly Tumbly Glittery Gritty Place, illustrated by Douglas Florian, Harcourt, 1993.
Alvah and Arvilla, illustrated by Barry Root, Harcourt, 1994.

Pianna, illustrated by Bobbie Henba, Harcourt, 1994.
Shaker Boy, illustrated by Jeanette Winter, Browndeer/
    Harcourt, 1994.
Mud, illustrated by Lauren Stringer, Harcourt, 1996.

■ Work in Progress

Picture books.

■ Sidelights

Mary Lyn Ray—a conservationist and author of books for children—was born in Louisiana and grew up in Little Rock, Arkansas. "But I never felt identity there," she told *SATA*. "When I was very young, one of my favorite books was about an old farm in New Hampshire. If the idea was not already planted in me when I was born, the book—Tasha Tudor's *Snow Before Christmas*—planted it." Ray has lived in New England since 1964, when she first came east to attend college. In 1973 she began living in New Hampshire. In 1984 she came to South Danbury, the place she feels she has "always been coming to."

"I came here, to South Danbury, because I saw and felt a poetry in this place. A kind of scenery," Ray recalled

for *SATA*. "Everything I write is in some way informed by the memory and poetry I've found here. But I'm not just taking stories from this place. As it has become a part of me, I have had to risk opening myself to it. Everything I write is, in some way, from my life. And much comes directly from this old New Hampshire farm where I live."

When Ray bought her farmhouse, which is about 150 years old, it "hadn't been lived in for forty years before that," she told *SATA*. "It had never had electricity or plumbing or running water, and squirrels and raccoons and foxes had taken it over." Room by room, she has restored plaster and painted, but has been careful to leave it "still an old house with old memories in it." A few years after she moved in, 160 acres of farmland surrounding her house were put up for sale. "I knew that I would buy the land to protect it from development," Ray said. "What I didn't know was how I would pay for it."

When Ray's sister jokingly suggested that she could plant pumpkins in the fields and sell them to come up with the necessary money, the idea came to Ray for her 1992 picture book, *Pumpkins*. In this story, a man worries that the field across from his home will be sold

An elderly woman reflects on her best memories—those centering on her beloved piano—in Ray's picture book *Pianna,* **set in the early 1900s.** (Illustration by Bobbie Henba.)

Last of all Alvah brought the horses—Horace and Albert—and hitched them to pull. Arvilla climbed onto the little front porch. Alvah took the reins. And when he called "Giddyup," they rolled out of the yard.

After a while they came to a wide river. Horace stopped and looked around with a look that meant "Are we there yet?" Arvilla shook her head "No." So they crossed the river and continued.

Anxious to realize her dream of seeing the Pacific Ocean after thirty-one years on a New England farm, Arvilla convinces her husband that it *is* possible to both have a farm and travel in Ray's humorous picture book *Alvah and Arvilla*, illustrated by Barry Root.

to developers. He sells almost everything he owns to try to raise money to buy the land himself, but he still does not have enough. So he plants pumpkin seeds. "The rain came and wet them, the sun came and warmed them. Soon the field was covered in pumpkins. And they grew and they grew and they grew." In the fall the man harvests 461,212 pumpkins—so many that he has to ship them around the world to sell them. Now he is able to buy the land, but he keeps one pumpkin for seeds. Pumpkins, he knows, would make him rich. But he chooses to give the seeds away, "because somewhere, someone might love another field pumpkins could save."

Ray herself didn't plant pumpkins. "Books have become my pumpkins," she told *SATA*. She did, however, buy the land and protect it. "My commitment to saving this farm has encouraged neighbors to protect their land also—some 6,000 acres are now conservation land—and has sparked a larger project to create a greenway linking nine towns and three mountains in a preserve of thousands and thousands of acres. These numbers are dramatic; it's not everywhere that so much contiguous land can be protected. But everywhere something is possible, and that's what *Pumpkins* speaks to."

Ray has received several conservation awards for her work protecting New Hampshire's natural areas, but "it has had a cost," she explained to *SATA*. Because she wasn't planting pumpkins, she had to borrow all of the

money from a bank, planning to repay the loan by allowing excavation of a lapsed gravel pit. The deposit of gravel turned out to be shallow. "Suddenly I held a loan I couldn't expect to pay. It hasn't been easy," she told *SATA*. "But accepting the scar of the gravel pit was no easier. It was hard to walk there and look at it. Until a small story came that helped me see it differently." In *A Rumbly Tumbly Glittery Gritty Place* a child explores a gravel pit. For her it becomes "a place to watch machines in," "a beach without an ocean," "an album crossed with tracks of deer and bear who come at night." Ray noted to *SATA* that the story has reminded her "of what children know, but we outgrow childhood and forget."

Other books by Ray also center around the people and places she's come to know in New Hampshire. For example, Ray was inspired to write *Alvah and Arvilla* after she attended the wedding of two of her neighbors. Since the couple ran a dairy farm, their honeymoon only lasted one night because they had to be home the following morning to milk the cows. In the story that grew from this, Alvah and Arvilla, who are farmers too, have been married for thirty-one years. But they've never taken a vacation due to the daily demands of running their farm. To achieve her dream of seeing the Pacific Ocean, Arvilla convinces her husband to pack up their belongings and all their animals to make the journey to California. After the unusual assortment of characters spends several days relaxing on the beach, they return home, where they spread sand they collected to make their own miniature beach. "And here Arvilla and Alvah and sometimes a cow or a cat or a dog lie and remember the ocean."

Pianna was also inspired by one of Ray's neighbors. Set in the early 1900s, Ray's book introduces an elderly woman named Anna as she looks back on her long life. Many of her best memories center around her beloved piano, which her parents bought for her when she was seven years old. Because no one else in town had a piano then, Anna had to ride the train 215 miles to Boston every week for a music lesson. As a young girl, she practiced so much that her brothers and sisters nicknamed her "Pianna." Over the years she got married and played for her husband and children, as well as at church and at social functions. "But mostly she played for herself." After her husband dies, her children move away, and times change, the piano continues to keep her company. "This is a story," Ray told *SATA,* "about what endures. And finding it."

Despite her success as a writer for children, Ray grew up believing that she couldn't write. "I thought stories and characters and plots were something authors made up in their heads. I thought I wasn't smart enough—or, as it was called then, creative enough. I looked at blank paper and turned in blank paper," she recalled for *SATA.* In graduate school, where she studied the history of American art and architecture, "something changed," she said. "Suddenly I began to see with my eyes, and to write what I saw. Becoming a writer was that simple." Still, she never thought that she could make up stories.

"Fiction, I thought, required a talent for invention which I didn't have," Ray told *SATA.* "For another twenty years, I remained occupied with other work. Until stories, of themselves, began to come. I found out stories aren't something authors make up in their heads. Stories come to us, asking to be told. Like fish, maybe, they swim out of mystery and return to mystery. The responsibility of the writer is to receive them and give them voice, then let them go. I believe stories choose us. And because they choose us, they are very particular to us. We must each hear and tell our own."

■ Works Cited

Ray, Mary Lyn, *Pumpkins,* Gulliver Green/Harcourt, 1992.
Ray, Mary Lyn, *A Rumbly Tumbly Glittery Gritty Place,* Harcourt, 1993.
Ray, Mary Lyn, *Alvah and Arvilla,* Harcourt, 1994.
Ray, Mary Lyn, *Pianna,* Harcourt, 1994.

■ For More Information See

PERIODICALS

Booklist, October 15, 1992; December 1, 1993, p. 701; March 15, 1994, p. 1375; November, 1994.
Bulletin of the Center for Children's Books, July/August, 1994, p. 371; November, 1994, p. 101.

Christian Science Monitor, September 16, 1994; November 4, 1994.
Five Owls, November, 1994.
Horn Book, November/December, 1992, p. 719; November, 1994, p. 725; January, 1995, p. 55.
Kirkus Reviews, March 1, 1994, p. 309; September 15, 1994, p. 1279; October 15, 1994; March 1, 1996.
National Geographic, April, 1995, pp. 122-28.
New York Times Book Review, October 25, 1992.
Publishers Weekly, September 7, 1992, p. 93; October 25, 1993, p. 60; March 7, 1994; September 5, 1994, p. 110; October 17, 1994; May 6, 1996.
School Library Journal, March, 1993, p. 184; January, 1994, p. 97; May, 1994; November, 1994, p. 89; January, 1995; June, 1996.

*   *   *

RHOADES, Diane 1952-

■ Personal

Born January 20, 1952, in Brooklyn, NY; daughter of Benjamin (a police officer and brokerage firm executive) and Mildred (King) Rhoades; children: Casey Rhoades. *Education:* Attended Brooklyn College for one year and Hunter College for two years; Swedish Institute of Massage, received massage therapist license. *Politics:* "Random." *Religion:* Quaker. *Hobbies and other interests:* Sustainable agriculture, tennis, vermicomposting.

DIANE RHOADES

Addresses

Home—RD 3 Box 95, Walnut Cove Rd., Hendersonville, NC 28739.

Career

Massage therapist. Has also worked as a gardener, Bridgehampton, NY, 1978-80; as a temporary typist for Jacques Cousteau; and as director of the Farm School, Bridgehampton. Directs a middle-school compost and gardening project.

■ Writings

(Self-illustrated) *Garden Crafts for Kids: 50 Reasons to Get Your Hands Dirty,* Sterling, 1995.

Contributed a weekly column to *What's Happening* magazine, summer, 1994; has illustrated a number of booklets.

Work in Progress

A sequel to *Garden Crafts for Kids;* research on further application of composting/vermicomposting.

Sidelights

Diane Rhoades told *SATA:* "It's raining hard on this tinny attic roof. I wrote my book *Garden Crafts for Kids* up here in this space and I can see out the window to my garden and to the chickens and stray dogs that come shopping for my chickens, at which point the dogs that live here go nuts.

"I was born in Brooklyn, New York, and I have always been sure that I wanted to live on a farm when I grew up. Now that I am grown and here, I see that I was quite insightful at an early age. This 'farm' that I live on is teeming with animals, garden spaces, fruit trees, and lots of cooperation. For seven years now I have been adding organic matter and cover cropping and paying attention to the fertility and health of this land.

"My garden is alive for me year 'round now that I am becoming as aware of the activity that appears on the top of the soil as I am of the activity and divination going on below. I feel tremendous love and play regarding my garden and it is with this wholeheartedness that I wrote my book. What a gift for any person, young or old, to have a relationship based on joy, discovery, and hard work.

"Worms have played a central part in this cooperative adventure. My family has been composting our household scraps with the help of redworms, or vermicomposting. It is a quick way to produce very fertile soil. We have also added lots of leaves and manure to the garden beds to encourage the earthworms to stick around. I am impressed with the worms' physiology and anatomy. They have three hundred kidneys, five sets of hearts, they are both male and female, and their mating practices seem a whole lot more dynamic than those of humans. When was the last time you spent three hours in an intimate embrace under the stars on a soft, moonlit night?

"Having lived in Brooklyn Heights (New York City); Sag Harbor, NY; St. John in the U.S. Virgin Islands; and in France and England, I am amazed that this sleepy little North Carolina mountain community could suit me so well. I recreate the same whizzened pace that I once complained about and moved to this retiree community to get away from. There are people here that I can hike, canoe, sing, camp out, and be inspired with. I sing with a group of women friends. We could sing with men as well but none are inclined to sing with us. For each engagement, we change our name, depending on the nature of the gathering. For a United Way benefit, we were The Out to Lunch Bunch (very corny—not my choice). For the summer solstice celebration at the local community college we were Women with Wings. At private parties, we have been Psychic Lingerie (my name choice).

"At present, I am working with the Hendersonville Middle School, grades six through eight, building raised beds and working up a gardening program. They loved my worms. On any given week day, I massage two to four people (which is what I do for a living), haul manure, feed children and hundreds of worms, pack lunch boxes, write to someone about something, breathe deeply, and enjoy the light of day or the slinkiness of night. Lately, in my single status, I'm beginning to feel envious of the worms."

*   *   *

RIVERS, Elfrida
See BRADLEY, Marion Zimmer

*   *   *

ROSENBLATT, Lily 1956-

■ Personal

Born June 17, 1956, in Israel; daughter of Irving (a jeweler) and Fani (a homemaker; maiden name, Iwanir) Teichman; married Joseph Rosenblatt (a physician), July 26, 1977; children: Aliza, Eliana, Joshua. *Education:* University of California, Los Angeles, B.A.. *Hobbies and other interests:* Children, writing.

■ Addresses

Home—Rochester, NY.

■ Career

Hot Stuff, Los Angeles, CA, owner, 1989-93; Maimonedes Academy, Los Angeles, preschool teacher, 1993-94; Chabad School, Los Angeles, elementary school teacher, 1994-95. Youth group advisor for Bnei Akiva, Los Angeles; fund raiser for the Israel Cancer Research

LILY ROSENBLATT

Fund. *Member:* Society of Children's Book Writers and Illustrators.

■ Awards, Honors

Magazine Merit Award, 1993.

■ Writings

Fire Diary (picture book), illustrated by Judith Friedman, Albert Whitman, 1994.

Contributor to *Highlights for Children;* poetry included in anthologies.

■ Sidelights

Lily Rosenblatt told *SATA,* "People often ask me why I, a person who never experienced a personal catastrophe, would choose to write about a fire survivor. Part of the reason was because of a fire tragedy I read about in a newspaper series. I was very moved by the tale of a father and daughter who survived a fire that killed the rest of the family. But perhaps it is my own background that made this story resonate for me. I am a child of Holocaust survivors whose families were wiped out in concentration camps. For me, this story is about tragedy and trauma, the pain that follows, and the path toward healing. My finest moment came after I finished writing the book, even before it was published. The story was presented to a burn survivors group and received with overwhelming enthusiasm. If only one person could find comfort in the pages of *Fire Diary,* then I have done it right."

■ For More Information See

PERIODICALS

Children's Book Review Service, December, 1994, p. 44.
Horn Book Guide, spring, 1995, p. 70.
Publishers Weekly, October 10, 1994, p. 71.
School Library Journal, January, 1995, p. 110.

*   *   *

ROWH, Mark 1952-

■ Personal

Born March 12, 1952, in South Charleston, WV; son of C. A. and Evelyn I. Rowh; married Linda Kabulski (an educator), November 11, 1972; children: Lisa, David, Jennifer. *Education:* West Virginia State College, B.A., 1973; Marshall University, M.A., 1975; Clemson University, Ed.D., 1988; additional studies completed at West Virginia University and University of South Carolina-Spartanburg. *Religion:* United Methodist.

■ Addresses

Home—341 Zeigler Ave., Dublin, VA 24084. *Office*—New River Community College, Box 1127, Dublin, VA 24084.

■ Career

Parkersburg Community College, Parkersburg, WV, assistant to the president, 1975-78; Bluefield State College, Bluefield, WV, assistant to the president and director of community relations, 1978-82, director of continuing education, 1979-85, executive assistant to the president, 1982-85; Greenville Technical College, Greenville, SC, director of planning and grants, 1985-88, associate vice president for institutional development, 1988-89; New River Community College, Dublin, VA, director of institutional advancement, 1989—. Consultant on grant proposal development; Tazewell (Virginia) High School, writer in residence, 1983. Active in community groups such as the chamber of commerce, parent-teacher associations, United Methodist Church committees and activities, Junior Achievement, Rotary International, and other civic associations. *Member:* National Council for Resource Development, National Council for Marketing and Public Relations, Virginia Organization for Resource Development, College News Association of Virginia, South Carolina Development Officers Peer Group (past chair), South Carolina Council for Resource Development (past vice-president), Alpha Kappa Mu National Honorary Society, Lambda Iota Tau National Literary Society.

■ Awards, Honors

Outstanding Young Man of America, 1978, 1981; Outstanding Service Award, West Virginia Community College Association, 1984.

Welding Careers, NTC Publishing Group, 1994.
Opportunities in Electronic Careers, NTC Publishing Group, 1994.
Careers for Crafty People and Other Dexterous Types, NTC Publishing Group, 1994.
How to Improve Your Grammar and Usage, Franklin Watts, 1994.
Opportunities in Drafting Careers, NTC Publishing Group, 1994.
Opportunities in Metal Working Careers, NTC Publishing Group, 1994.
Opportunities in Installation and Repair Careers, NTC Publishing Group, 1995.
Career Portraits: Crafts, NTC Publishing Group, 1996.

OTHER

(With M. Hartman) The One Person Manager, Learning Resources Network, 1984.
The Small Shop in Resource Development, National Council for Resource Development, 1985.
Coping with Stress in College, College Board Books, 1989.
Winning Government Grants and Contracts for Your Small Business, McGraw-Hill, 1992.
How to Write Dynamic Business Proposals, American Management Association, 1994.

Has also published numerous magazine articles, including some for younger readers, in periodicals such as Reader's Digest, Writer's Digest, Circle K, The Rotarian, Careers and Colleges, Career World, and others.

■ Work in Progress

Articles.

■ Sidelights

Mark Rowh told SATA: "I've always enjoyed writing and encourage others to write, even if not for publication. One of the nicest aspects of being a writer is that anyone can qualify. You don't need a specific degree or credential (although studying the writing of others certainly helps). What you *do* need is the willingness to try and the tenacity to keep at it."

Mark Rowh's book offers guidance for young people who wish to pursue a career utilizing their skills in arts and crafts.

■ Writings

FOR YOUNG ADULTS

Drafting Careers, NTC Publishing Group, 1991.
Opportunities in Warehousing Careers, NTC Publishing Group, 1994.
Opportunities in Waste Management Careers, NTC Publishing Group, 1994.

S

SANDERS, Nancy I. 1960-

■ Personal

Born May 17, 1960, in Everett, PA; daughter of Richard J. (a dairy farmer) and Phyllis (a homemaker; maiden name, Harden) Hershberger; married Jeffrey L. Sanders (an elementary school teacher), May 23, 1982; children: Daniel M., Benjamin L. *Religion:* Christian (interdenominational).

■ Addresses

Home—15212 Mariposa Ave., Chino Hills, CA 91709.

■ Career

Freelance writer, 1985—. Editor, TCC Manuscript Critique Service. *Member:* Society of Children's Book Writers and Illustrators.

■ Writings

FOR CHILDREN

Favorite Bible Heroes: Activities for Ages 4 and 5, Rainbow Publishers, 1993.

Bible Crafts on a Shoestring Budget for Grades 3 and 4, Rainbow Publishers, 1993.

Amazing Bible Puzzles: Old Testament, Concordia, 1993.

Amazing Bible Puzzles: New Testament, Concordia, 1993.

Jumbo Bible Bulletin Boards: More Bible Stories for Preschool and Primary, Christian Education Publishers, 1994.

Jumbo Bible Bulletin Boards: Fall and Winter, Preschool and Primary, Christian Education Publishers, 1994.

Jonah: Six Fun Surprises, illustrated by Bill Stroble, Tyndale House (Wheaton, IL), 1994.

Moses: Six Fun Surprises, illustrated by Bill Stroble, Tyndale House, 1994.

My Book about Ben and Me, Concordia, 1994.

My Book about Sara and Me, Concordia, 1994.

Cents-ible Bible Crafts, Concordia, 1995.

The Fall into Sin, Concordia, 1995.

Jesus Walks on the Water, Concordia, 1995.

WA-A-AY COOL Bible Puzzles, Concordia, 1996.

Red Hot Bible Puzzles, Concordia, 1996.

Marshal Matt and the Gummy Worm Mystery, Concordia, 1996.

Marshal Matt and the Case of the Secret Code, Concordia, 1996.

Marshal Matt and the Topsy-Turvy Trail Mystery, Concordia, 1996.

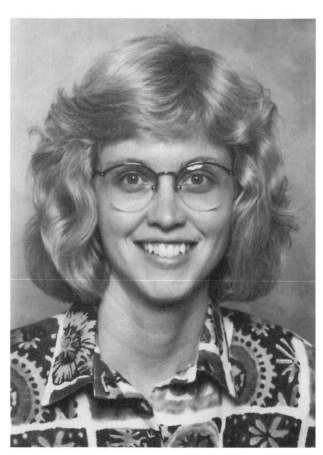

NANCY I. SANDERS

Marshal Matt and the Puzzling Prints Mystery, Concordia, 1996.
Marshal Matt and the Case of the Freezing Fingers, Concordia, 1997.

OTHER

Contributor to *The Complete Handbook for Christian Writing and Speaking,* Promise Publishers, 1994; contributing editor, *The Christian Communicator.* Contributor to periodicals, including *Better Homes and Gardens, Today's Christian Woman, Virtue, Helping Hand, R-A-D-A-R, Pockets, Clubhouse Jr., Discoveries, Power and Light, On the Line, My Friend,* and *Society of Children's Book Writers and Illustrators Bulletin.*

■ Work in Progress

The Mandate of the State, a fiction work for adults about adopting an AIDS curriculum in the community; *Meeting the First Christians* (for eight to twelve year olds), an in-depth look at the early church from Christ to Constantine.

■ Sidelights

"'Relationship' is the key word in my writing career," Nancy I. Sanders told *SATA.* "My main love is for the picture book because of the relationship this type of book builds between the reader and the child. I want to write picture books that unite the adult with the child as they experience the books together—fostering communication, encouraging time together, and developing a common bond of love for the story and thus for life.

"I write for both the mainstream and Christian market. One of the reasons I write for the Christian market is because I believe that a relationship with Jesus is integral to all other relationships in life. I write curriculum and teacher resource materials to help create a positive relationship between the teacher and student. I write books for beginner readers to provide positive models for relationships with peers. I write books in general to help nurture the relationship of the readers with their own identities to increase their self-esteem.

"One of the highlights of my career thus far was when a woman approached me at a writer's conference. She said that *Jonah* is her granddaughter's favorite book. 'Every evening we have to snuggle together and read this book from beginning to end before I tuck her into bed.'

"My desire is for the words I write to be bridges connecting people to build positive relationships in life."

*   *   *

SANDERS, Winston P.
See ANDERSON, Poul (William)

MARY SAWICKI

SAWICKI, Mary 1950-

■ Personal

Born January 25, 1950, in Toledo, OH; daughter of Albert (a corporate executive) and Genevieve (a homemaker; maiden name, Elendt) Sawicki; married Karl Hostetler (a professor), 1978; children: Jacob, Jesse. *Education:* Attended Ohio University, Athens; University of Wisconsin—Madison, B.A., 1973; Northwestern University, M.A.T., 1977. *Hobbies and other interests:* Running, biking, swimming, reading.

■ Addresses

Home—8136 South Hazelwood Dr., Lincoln, NE 68510. *Office*—Pioneers Park Nature Center, 2740 A St., Lincoln, NE 68502.

■ Career

Art teacher in various schools in the Chicago area, 1976-80; Colegio Internacional de Carabobo, Valencia, Venezuela, elementary and art teacher, 1980-81; Spec Graphics, New York City, graphic artist, 1985-86; Pioneers Park Nature Center, Lincoln, NE, naturalist and artist, 1993—.

■ Writings

(Self-illustrated) *My Backyard Giant,* Barron's, 1994.

■ Work in Progress

"Many."

■ Sidelights

Mary Sawicki told *SATA:* "When I was about three years old my family moved into a new house. My parents planted sunflowers in the backyard by the wood pile. I loved those giant yellow flowers. So when my four-year-old son, Jacob, was moved into our first house I planted sunflowers for him. He too enjoyed watching the sunflowers grow into giants. At school he wrote a poem about the sunflowers. Jacob's poem was the inspiration for my first book, *My Backyard Giant.*

"The other books that I am working on all find their source in family events or memories. I find a wealth of inspiration in the people around me. My parents lived their childhood on family farms in Ohio. Their love of plants and animals has always been a part of my life. I find that not only sunflowers but many things in nature are a wonderful source for children's books.

"In addition to writing and illustrating books and parenting two sons, I am a naturalist and staff artist at Pioneers Park Nature Center in Nebraska. In the spring I can't wait to watch the baby goslings, all soft and warm. In summer the wildflowers and butterflies color the prairie. And there is nothing finer than a warm, sunny golden afternoon on the prairie in the fall. Helping children experience these wonders is my job as a naturalist.

"I am also the staff artist at the nature center. I help create and produce exhibits. The most recent exhibit is titled 'Fly Away.' This exhibit has child-sized butterfly and moth costumes. The children can make their own antennae, put on the wings, and 'fly away.' The exhibit also has pictorial and written information about the caterpillars and their life stages, cocoons and chrysalises. There are even live caterpillars to watch as they eat, spin, and emerge to fly away.

"My art, like my writing, finds its source in the people around me. To illustrate *My Backyard Giant* I used my younger son, Jesse, as a model. I had him balance on fences and jump off of our picnic table so that I could draw the characters for the book. My husband served as the source for the giant. He willingly glowered fiercely to help me create the bumpy-faced giant."

*   *   *

SCARRY, Richard (McClure) 1919-1994

OBITUARY NOTICE—See Index for *SATA* sketch: Born June 5, 1919, in Boston, MA; died of a heart attack, April 30, 1994, in Gstaad, Switzerland. Illustrator and author of children's books. One of the most successful creative talents in the children's book industry, Scarry penned and illustrated more than 250 titles; according to estimates, over one hundred million volumes of his assorted works have been published worldwide. Scarry started drawing professionally in the late 1940s, providing illustrations for such books as Kathryn Jackson's *Let's Go Fishing,* which appeared in 1949. By 1951, with *The Great Big Car and Truck Book,* he was rendering pictures for his own stories. Many of Scarry's books are populated by cute, anthropomorphic animals—the popular characters Lowly Worm and Mr. Frumble the Pig, for example—and contain a great deal of visual detail. Among his most popular titles are *Richard Scarry's Best Word Book Ever, Richard Scarry's Please and Thank You,* and *Richard Scarry's Find Your ABC's.* In 1994, an animated television series produced for cable, *The Busy World of Richard Scarry,* premiered on the Showtime channel.

OBITUARIES AND OTHER SOURCES:

BOOKS

Children's Literature Review, Vol. 40, Gale Research, 1996.
Twentieth-Century Children's Writers, Fourth edition, St. James Press, 1995.

PERIODICALS

Chicago Tribune, May 3, 1994, p. 13.
Los Angeles Times, May 4, 1994, p. A16.
New York Times, May 3, 1994, p. B10.
Washington Post, May 4, 1994, p. B8.

*   *   *

SCHERTLE, Alice 1941-

■ Personal

Surname rhymes with "turtle"; born April 7, 1941, in Los Angeles, CA; daughter of Floyd C. (a real estate investor) and Marguerite (a teacher; maiden name, Soucie) Sanger; married Richard Schertle (a general contractor), December 21, 1963; children: Jennifer, Katherine, John. *Education:* University of Southern California, B.S. (cum laude), 1963.

ALICE SCHERTLE

■ Addresses

Home—La Habra Heights, CA.

■ Career

Highland School, Inglewood, CA, elementary school teacher, 1963-65; writer, 1965—.

■ Awards, Honors

Parents' Choice Picture Book award, 1989, and Christopher Award, 1990, both for *William and Grandpa;* Parents' Choice Picture Book award, 1991, for *Witch Hazel;* Best Books citation, *School Library Journal,* 1995, for *Advice for a Frog and Other Poems;* Notable Children's Books citations, American Library Association, 1996, for both *Advice for a Frog and Other Poems* and *Down the Road.*

■ Writings

FOR CHILDREN

The Gorilla in the Hall, illustrated by Paul Galdone, Lothrop, 1977.
The April Fool, illustrated by Emily Arnold McCully, Lothrop, 1981.
Hob Goblin and the Skeleton, illustrated by Katherine Coville, Lothrop, 1982.
In My Treehouse, illustrated by Meredith Dunham, Lothrop, 1983.
Bim Dooley Makes His Move, Lothrop, 1984.
Goodnight Hattie, My Dearie, My Love, Lothrop, 1985.
My Two Feet, Lothrop, 1985.
That Olive!, Lothrop, 1986.
Jeremy Bean's St. Patrick's Day, illustrated by Linda Shute, Lothrop, 1987.
Bill and the Google-Eyed Goblins, Lothrop, 1987.
Gus Wanders Off, illustrated by Cheryl Harness, Lothrop, 1988.
That's What I Thought, illustrated by John Wallner, Harper, 1988.
William and Grandpa, Lothrop, 1989.
Witch Hazel, illustrated by Margot Tomes, Harper, 1991.
Little Frog's Song, illustrated by Leonard Everett Fisher, HarperCollins, 1992.
How Now, Brown Cow? Poems, illustrated by Amanda Schaffer, Browndeer Press (San Diego), 1994.
Down the Road, illustrated by Margot Tomes, Harper-Collins, 1994, illustrated by E. B. Lewis, Browndeer Press, 1995.
Maisie, illustrated by Lydia Dabcovich, Lothrop, 1995.
Advice for a Frog and Other Poems, illustrated by Norman Green, Lothrop, 1995.
Keepers, illustrated by Ted Rand, Lothrop, 1996.

"CATHY AND COMPANY" SERIES; ILLUSTRATED BY CATHY PAVIA

Cathy and Company and Mean Mr. Meeker, Children's Press, 1980.
Cathy and Company and Bumper the Bully, Children's Press, 1980.
Cathy and Company and the Green Ghost, Children's Press, 1980.
Cathy and Company and the Nosy Neighbor, Children's Press, 1980.
Cathy and Company and the Double Dare, Children's Press, 1980.
Cathy and Company and Hank the Horse, Children's Press, 1980.

■ Sidelights

Alice Schertle is the author of a long list of engaging books for the read-aloud set. "I write children's books because I love them—always have," Schertle has stated. "The various seasons of my childhood are identified in my memory with the books that were important to me then. There was the year Mary Poppins floated into the lives of Jane and Michael Banks and me. And my sixth grade year I think I spent with the *Black Stallion* and *King of the Wind.*" As an adult helping to provide such moments to new generations of children, Schertle takes her work seriously; she asserted before the audience of the 1986 Writer's Conference in Children's Literature that "we who write for young children share the considerable responsibility and the wonderful opportunity of showing them that words can paint pictures too."

Schertle was born and raised in Los Angeles, California. "As a child, I could usually be found folded into some unlikely position (as often as not I was in a tree) either reading a story or trying to write one," she once told *SATA.* "My writing was always very much influenced by the book I was reading at the moment. *The Wizard of Oz* and *Mary Poppins* inspired me to try my hand at fantasy. *The Black Stallion* led to a rash of horse stories. And after a summer of reading Nancy Drew books, I churned out mysteries peppered with words like 'sleuth' and 'chum.'

"My early stories did have one thing in common: each got off to a roaring good start and ended abruptly somewhere in the middle. Those beginnings were always fun to write, but when it came to developing the plot and bringing it along to a logical conclusion, the whole thing began to smack of work. It still does, sometimes, but I've found it to be a very satisfying kind of work when the tale is told."

After graduating from the University of Southern California in 1963, Schertle married and began teaching elementary school students in Inglewood, California. Following the birth of her first child two years later, she left her teaching job to devote herself full time to raising what would soon be three children. It wasn't until 1975, when her kids had grown old enough to allow her some free time, that she began writing again. Her first book for children, *The Gorilla in the Hall,* a story about a young boy's vivid imagination, was published in 1975.

While her first read-aloud book received only mixed reviews from critics, Schertle's next book, *The April Fool,* was a winner. An amusing story about a curmudgeonly king's search for a pair of shoes that will not hurt

In Schertle's tender story *Witch Hazel*—about a boy, the lady scarecrow he made, and his one pumpkin that grew—strange and wonderful things happen on the night of the harvest moon. (Illustration by Margot Tomes.)

his feet, *The April Fool* was described by *School Library Journal* reviewer Patt Hays as "a satisfying story." For Schertle, the story "almost seem[ed] to write itself, from beginning to end.... I started with 'Once there was a king whose feet hurt,' and wrote through to 'the end' with scarcely a hitch along the way."

Schertle has often gotten ideas for stories by keeping track of the activities of her three children. "*In My Treehouse* was inspired by my son's adventures in his own treehouse," she told *SATA*. "As a child, I spent a good deal of time in trees, so I took John up on his invitation to join him in his house in a big fruitless mulberry. In fact, I did a lot of writing up there, though I find they're not making treehouses as big as they used to be." With *In My Treehouse*, Schertle translated the experience of being in her son's tree fort into a book about a young boy's love of being apart from the hustle and bustle of the world at large, and about gaining independence. And living with cats as well as children certainly provided Schertle the inspiration for *That Olive!*, a picture book about a mischievous kitty that Lucy Young Clem described in *School Library Journal* as "a hall-of-fame cat story." Andy spends a lot of time looking for his cat, Olive, and Olive spends a lot of time playing hide-and-seek with Andy. Only the lure of tuna fish sandwiches brings the elusive Olive out into the open and into Andy's arms.

A book about making friends, *Jeremy Bean's St. Patrick's Day* features a first-grader whose excitement about his school's St. Patrick's Day party withers when he arrives at school and realizes that he has forgotten to put on the green sweater he so excitedly planned to wear the night before. The only one without green on, Jeremy is taunted by his classmates and finally hides in a closet, until the school principal discovers him there and loans him the use of his green bow tie for the party. Describing the book's "clear prose and sympathetic observation of small children and their concerns," a *Kirkus Reviews* critic praised *Jeremy Bean's St. Patrick's Day* as a good book about making friends, even with school principals.

The award-winning *William and Grandpa* is another book about the relationship between children and adults, and the friendships that can develop. When Willie comes to stay with his lonely grandfather, the two share a host of simple activities—singing songs, catching shadows, making shaving cream moustaches, and telling old stories about Willie's father—that bond them into a close and loving relationship. "The continuity of generations and the warm relationship between children and the elderly are communicated equally through story and pictures," noted Carolyn Caywood in *School Library Journal*.

Schertle's 1991 book, *Witch Hazel*, tells the story of Johnny, a young boy who is raised by his two grown brothers, Bill and Bart, after the death of his parents. Bill and Bart are farmers who can do without the young boy's help as they work their small farm. But they give their young brother some pumpkin seed and a branch of

How Now, Brown Cow? is Schertle's collection of poems about cows—some pensive, some droll—aptly illustrated with Amanda Schaffer's affectionate and humorous paintings.

witch hazel; Johnny plants the seeds and makes a scarecrow lady out of the tree branch, dressing "her" in one of his mother's old dresses. When Bill and Bart leave Johnny and take their crop to market after the fall harvest, Johnny dreams that the scarecrow, "Witch Hazel," has tossed his huge orange pumpkin up into the sky, where it has remained, a full, round harvest moon. "Schertle's style combines poetic prose, terse dialogue, and the tight construction of the folk tale," explains Donnarae MacCann and Olga Richard in *Wilson Library Bulletin.* "You hurry along the plot line, but you stop to wonder at how unobtrusively Schertle turns a drama about an underdog into a poetic experience."

Sensitively capturing the many emotions common to a young read-aloud audience, Schertle continues to write books that are praised by reviewers for their sensitivity and perception. *Little Frog's Song* tells of the adventures and fears of a young frog who is washed from his lily pad during a fierce rain shower and must now find his way home. "The text ... is a song, rich with images and the rhythm of repetition reminiscent of the writing of Margaret Wise Brown," commented Katie Cerra in *Five Owls.* Equally lyrical is Schertle's *How Now, Brown Cow?,* a collection of poetry. Everything from milking time to a cow's longing to jump the moon is covered in verses that a *Publishers Weekly* reviewer described as "by turns funny and tender, cheeky and thoughtful."

"When I talk to classes of children and tell them about the unfinished stories I used to write, they usually laugh and say they do the same thing," Schertle explained to

SATA. "Sometimes I suggest they try writing the last half of a story first, and then go back and write the beginning. That's something I occasionally do now with my books. Sometimes a funny, or exciting, or ridiculous situation will pop into my head, an idea that would make a good middle of a story. So I'll sit down and write about some characters who find themselves in that situation, though I haven't yet any idea how they got there or what will finally happen to them. Then comes the hard part—writing the beginning and the ending, and making the parts fit together smoothly and logically.

"One of the nicest things about being an author is that it gives me the opportunity to talk to classes of children about books and writing. I always tell them that the best way to learn to write is to read and read and read. It's advice I take myself. There's a tall stack of books precariously balanced on my bedside table, and a good many of them are children's books. One lifetime will never be long enough for me to read all the books I want to read, but it'll be fun to try."

Schertle makes her home on two acres of land in La Habra, California, along with her husband, three children, and "two dogs, four cats, eight chickens, two hives of bees, and assorted birds and butterflies. When I'm not feeding anybody or writing anything, I like to spend my time in my vegetable garden, where I spend a good deal of time trying to persuade the gophers and moles to live somewhere else. I find the garden quiet and peaceful, a good place to germinate seeds and ideas for stories."

■ **Works Cited**

Caywood, Carolyn, review of *William and Grandpa, School Library Journal,* August, 1989, p. 132.

Cerra, Katie, review of *Little Frog's Song, Five Owls,* April, 1992, pp. 76-77.

Clem, Lucy Young, review of *That Olive!, School Library Journal,* August, 1986, p. 87.

Hays, Patt, review of *The April Fool, School Library Journal,* October, 1981, p. 135.

Review of *How Now, Brown Cow?, Publishers Weekly,* September 5, 1994, pp. 110-11.

Review of *Jeremy Bean's St. Patrick's Day, Kirkus Reviews,* January 15, 1987, p. 132.

MacCann, Donnarae, and Richard, Olga, review of *Witch Hazel, Wilson Library Bulletin,* March, 1992, p. 93.

■ **For More Information See**

PERIODICALS

Booklist, September 15, 1994, p. 133.

Bulletin of the Center for Children's Books, June, 1977, p. 165; May, 1986.

Horn Book, September/October, 1991, p. 589.

Los Angeles Times Book Review, April, 3, 1983.

New York Times Book Review, May 1, 1977, p. 42.

Publishers Weekly, June 27, 1986, p. 85; January 16, 1987, p. 73; May, 19, 1989, p. 82.

School Library Journal, July, 1992, p. 64; April, 1995, p. 129.*

*   *   *

SCHRECKER, Judie 1954-

■ **Personal**

Born January 8, 1954, in Sunbury, PA; daughter of Russell and Faye (Pope) Funk; married Paul Schrecker (an F.B.I. special agent), July 27, 1977; children: Greg, Terry. *Education:* Lord Fairfax Community College, A.A.S. in Education, 1995; currently attending Mary Washington College to complete a bachelor's degree in science writing. *Hobbies and other interests:* Scuba diving, racquetball, horseback riding.

■ **Addresses**

Home—7332 Fox Call Lane, Warrenton, VA 20186. *Office*—Highland School, 597 Broadview Ave., Warrenton, VA 20186.

■ **Career**

Federal Bureau of Investigation (F.B.I.), Washington, DC, personnel assistant and research analyst, 1972-79; homemaker and part-time aerobics and racquetball teacher, 1979-89; Highland School, Warrenton, VA,

JUDIE SCHRECKER

teacher assistant, 1989—. Emergency medical technician with Laurel Rescue Squad, Laurel, MD; Earthwatch scholarship program for teachers, member of Michigan research team for "Saving Bald Eagles" program, summer, 1991; teacher/leader scholarship, "Black Bears" program, North Carolina research team, summer, 1993; teacher/leader scholarship, member of "End of the Dinosaurs" research team, summer, 1996, Glasgow, MT. *Member:* Phi Theta Kappa.

■ Writings

FOR CHILDREN

The Pet Shop Mouse, Winston-Derek, 1995.
Santa's New Reindeer, E. M. Press, 1996.

■ Sidelights

Judie Schrecker told *SATA:* "I've always loved adventure, travel, and animals, so most of my stories are centered on these themes or sometimes teach certain facts about animals. *The Pet Shop Mouse* was written for my son when he was six years old. It had always been a dream of mine to be a children's author. After the kindergarten class with which I worked convinced me it would make a good book, I decided I would try to get it published.

"Earthwatch offers me a chance to travel, have adventurous experiences, and work with scientists and/or biologists on their field research. I think it's very important to do whatever we can to help endangered or threatened animals and their habitats. The knowledge and experience gained from this hands-on research are so important, and students can learn so much from teachers who participate in these expeditions."

■ For More Information See

PERIODICALS

Publishers Weekly, September 30, 1996, p. 89.

* * *

SCOTT, Elaine 1940-

■ Personal

Born June 20, 1940, in Philadelphia, PA; daughter of George Jobling (a banker) and Ethel (a homemaker; maiden name, Smith) Watts; married Parker Scott (a geophysical engineer), May 16, 1959; children: Cynthia Ellen, Susan Elizabeth. *Education:* Attended Southern Methodist University, 1957-59, 1979-81, and University of Houston, 1979-81. *Religion:* Methodist. *Hobbies and other interests:* Reading, traveling, sailing.

■ Addresses

Home—13042 Taylorcrest Rd., Houston, TX 77079.
Agent—Jean V. Naggar, 216 East 75th St., New York, NY 10021.

ELAINE SCOTT

■ Career

Writer, 1975—. Teacher of workshops for Texas Conference of the United Methodist Church, 1978; teacher of writing workshops at Southwest Writer's Conference, Houston, TX, 1979, and at Trinity University, San Antonio, TX, 1980. Volunteer teacher of leadership workshops at United Methodist Church, Houston, 1959-77; volunteer publicity director for Camp Fire Girls of America, 1973-74. Board member and chair of committee on international adoptions, Homes of St. Mark (a private non-profit adoption agency), Houston, 1980-89. *Member:* Authors Guild, Authors League of America, Society of Children's Book Writers and Illustrators.

■ Awards, Honors

Reading Magic Award, *Parenting Magazine,* and American Library Association Notable Book citation, 1988, both for *Ramona: Behind the Scenes of a Television Show;* "Best Books of 1995" citation, *School Library Journal,* and *Voice of Youth Advocates* nonfiction honor list citation, 1995, both for *Adventure in Space: The Flight to Fix the Hubble.*

■ Writings

FOR CHILDREN; NONFICTION

Adoption, F. Watts, 1980.
The Banking Book, illustrated by Kathie Abrams, Warne, 1981.

Doodlebugging for Oil: The Treasure Hunt for Oil, Warne, 1982.

Oil! Getting It, Finding It, Selling It, Warne, 1984.

Stocks and Bonds, Profits and Losses, F. Watts, 1985.

Ramona: Behind the Scenes of a Television Show, photographs by Margaret Miller, Morrow, 1987.

Could You Be Kidnapped?, F. Watts, 1988.

Safe in the Spotlight: The Dawn Animal Agency and the Sanctuary for Animals, photographs by Margaret Miller, Morrow Junior Books, 1991.

Look Alive: Behind the Scenes of an Animated Film, photographs by Richard Hewett, Morrow Junior Books, 1992.

Funny Papers: Behind the Scenes of the Comics, photographs by Margaret Miller, Morrow Junior Books, 1993.

From Microchips to Movie Stars: The Making of Super Mario Brothers, Hyperion, 1995.

Movie Magic: Behind the Scenes with Special Effects (photo essay), Morrow Junior Books, 1995.

Adventure in Space: The Flight to Fix the Hubble, photographs by Margaret Miller, Hyperion, 1995.

Twins, Atheneum, 1997.

Close Encounters with the Universe: What the Hubble Saw, Hyperion, 1997.

OTHER

Choices (young adult novel), Morrow, 1988.

■ Work in Progress

Becoming an Astronaut, publication expected by Hyperion in 1998; *Outpost in Space: Building Space Station Alpha; Mamma's Getting Married.*

■ Sidelights

Elaine Scott is the author of several children's books which reveal the behind-the-scenes story about how things work. After she realized that the questions her children were asking her were the same ones that she had asked as a child, Scott decided to investigate and write books that explain the process behind products in which kids are interested, like comics, movies, and television. Scott's first book, *Adoption,* tells children what happens when a family takes in a child, a process her own adopted daughter wanted to know more about. She then went on to write more investigational books, including *The Banking Book, Oil! Getting It, Finding It, Selling It,* and *Stocks and Bonds, Profits and Losses,* before her name was suggested by Beverly Cleary to write a book that would demonstrate to readers how a television show is made.

The true story of how animals for hire on stage and screen help support animals in need, Scott's *Safe in the Spotlight: The Dawn Animal Agency and the Sanctuary for Animals* is enhanced by Margaret Miller's photographs.

Scott and photographer Margaret Miller team again to create *Funny Papers: Behind the Scenes of the Comics,* an engaging tour of a fascinating world.

In *Ramona: Behind the Scenes of a Television Show,* Scott explains to children how *Ramona,* the television series based on Cleary's books about Ramona Quimby, is put together. Illustrated with black and white photographs, *Ramona: Behind the Scenes of a Television Show* covers all aspects of the production cycle, from deciding on a plot and auditioning actors to filming each episode and making all of the actor's costumes. Commending the way Scott broke the complicated, technical world of television production into simple, digestible text, a critic in *Kirkus Reviews* called the book "attractive and engagingly written." Elizabeth S. Watson, writing in *Horn Book,* remarked on how well the text and pictures complemented one another, and said the book was "rich in information about . . . television series production." In the *Bulletin of the Center for Children's Books,* Zena Sutherland called Scott's text "direct, clear, sequential, and informative."

After *Ramona: Behind the Scenes of a Television Show,* Scott shifted to an older audience and wrote *Choices,* a young adult novel about a popular high school senior named Beth who faces reform school. Just before an important football game, the students at Millington High School discover that their team's mascot has been stolen. Immediately, Beth and her classmates suspect that students from their rival high school are to blame, and they decide to settle the score by vandalizing Woodrow Wilson High. A minor participant in the destruction, Beth is caught by the police and made a scapegoat by the school administration. Placed in a juvenile detention center for six weeks, Beth must suffer the consequences of an unfair punishment. Aldor L. Matta, in *Voice of Youth Advocates,* highly recommended the novel and stated that Scott "has packed many messages into her short novel."

In her 1991 work, *Safe in the Spotlight: The Dawn Animal Agency and the Sanctuary for Animals,* Scott tells readers about the farm of Leonard and Bunny Brook, a couple who rescue abandoned, abused, and neglected animals. After their farm grew to over seven hundred animals, among them camels, elephants, and lions, the Brooks discovered that private funds alone could not support their growing operation. To make up the shortfall, the couple founded the Dawn Animal Agency, a company which provides animals for use in commercials, television, and movies. Taking special care that the animals are treated properly, the Brooks allow professionals to film the animals, and all the money earned by the animals goes to support the farm. In *Horn Book,* reviewer Ellen Fader found the photographs "engaging" and said that "Scott's lively reporting is packed with details." Calling the book "enticingly formatted," Betsy Hearne, writing in the *Bulletin of the Center for Children's Books,* applauded Scott's ability to clearly emphasize the importance "of human respect and responsibility for animal life."

Funny Papers: Behind the Scenes of the Comics, the author's 1993 work, explores the world of comics and includes a brief history of comic strips and books. Scott explains how comics are syndicated, printed, and published, and even offers commentary about some of the most popular names in cartoons, like Charles Schultz and Hank Ketcham. Kathryn Jennings, writing in the *Bulletin of the Center for Children's Books,* claimed that Scott's text read at times like a "well-written but under-researched college research paper," but she admitted the second half of the book describes the printing and distributing process extremely well. "Very readable and lively" was how Carol Schene described *Funny Papers* in *School Library Journal,* adding that the book provides "an entertaining and well-organized introduction" to comics.

The details of the space shuttle mission to repair the Hubble telescope are the focus of Scott's *Adventure in Space: The Flight to Fix the Hubble.* Here Scott explains the problems with the space telescope and how the seven astronauts corrected the defective lens. In *Adventure in Space,* Scott also provides interesting insight into the personal lives of the men and women involved in the mission, including interviews with the astronauts' families. According to a reviewer in *Voice of Youth Advocates,* this additional information about the astronauts' life on earth "enhance[s] a vivid, fact-filled portrayal of an important space mission." Appreciating the "lively text which holds the interest of the reader," a critic in a *Reading Time* review applauded Scott's ability to capture the excitement of the mission and recommended the book for children interested in space.

Scott once told *SATA:* "When I write a book it is important to me to tell all the facts about the subject, but it is equally important to tell these facts in a way that is not boring. After all, a book that bores people usually isn't finished, and every writer wants his books to be read. So I try and include anecdotes about real people and real events in my work. Often boys and girls will ask me if everything in my books is true, and I delight in being able to answer, 'Yes. Everything happened just as I said.'

"I write about subjects I know and care about. I believe that without caring about the subject, the writer is in real danger of becoming nothing but a flesh and blood word processor—spitting out facts and nothing more. I think a writer should share himself, as well as his information, with his reader. It should be his voice that says to the reader, 'Come with me and together we'll explore sensitive issues like adoption, or complicated subjects like banking. Together you and I will visit the remote corners of the world, searching for oil with the doodlebuggers.' For me that is the essence of writing—

it's really a dialogue between me and my reader. I'm grateful for the reader, and out of that gratitude comes a willingness to share myself and my experience of life with him."

■ Works Cited

Review of *Adventure in Space: The Flight to Fix the Hubble, Reading Time,* May, 1996, pp. 43-44.

Review of *Adventure in Space: The Flight to Fix the Hubble, Voice of Youth Advocates,* August, 1996, p. 151.

Fader, Ellen, review of *Safe in the Spotlight: The Dawn Animal Agency and the Sanctuary for Animals, Horn Book,* September/October, 1991, p. 615.

Hearne, Betsy, review of *Safe in the Spotlight: The Dawn Animal Agency and the Sanctuary for Animals, Bulletin of the Center for Children's Books,* July-August, 1991, pp. 274-75.

Jennings, Kathryn, review of *Funny Papers: Behind the Scenes of the Comics, Bulletin of the Center for Children's Books,* January, 1994, p. 167.

Matta, Aldor L., review of *Choices, Voice of Youth Advocates,* June, 1989, p. 107.

Review of *Ramona: Behind the Scenes of a Television Show, Kirkus Reviews,* July, 15, 1988, p. 1065.

Schene, Carol, review of *Funny Papers: Behind the Scenes of the Comics, School Library Journal,* November, 1993, pp. 119-20.

Sutherland, Zena, review of *Ramona: Behind the Scenes of a Television Show, Bulletin of the Center for Children's Books,* October, 1988, pp. 52-53.

Watson, Elizabeth S., review of *Ramona: Behind the Scenes of a Television Show, Horn Book,* January/February, 1989, pp. 92-93.

■ For More Information See

PERIODICALS

Booklist, December 15, 1981, p. 552; December 15, 1982, p. 568; June 15, 1985, p. 1447; September 15, 1988, p. 165; April 15, 1989, p. 1456; August, 1991, p. 2146; May 1, 1992, p. 1612; September 1, 1992, p. 51; November 15, 1993, p. 621; July, 1995, p. 1897.

Children's Book Review Service, May, 1989, p. 116; July, 1989, p. 152.

Horn Book Guide, fall, 1991, p. 299; fall, 1992, p. 315; spring, 1994, p. 141.

Kirkus Reviews, May 15, 1989, p. 770.

New Advocate, spring, 1994, p. 149.

Publishers Weekly, December 11, 1981, p. 63; July 29, 1988, p. 233; May 19, 1989, p. 86; November 9, 1990, p. 59; June 15, 1992, p. 105.

School Library Journal, May, 1981, p. 68; January, 1982, p. 81; January, 1983, p. 79; August, 1985, p. 81; October, 1988, p. 158; April, 1989, pp. 120, 150; August, 1991, p. 194; April, 1995, p. 146.

Voice of Youth Advocates, December, 1985, p. 335.

—Sketch by Sheryl A. Ciccarelli

SHARMA, Rashmi
See SINGH, Rashmi Sharma

* * *

SHEPARD, Jim 1956-
(Scott Eller, a joint pseudonym)

■ Personal

Born December 29, 1956, in Bridgeport, CT; son of Albert R. and Ida (Picarazzi) Shepard. *Education:* Trinity College (Hartford, CT), B.A., 1978; Brown University, A.M., 1980.

■ Addresses

Home—132 White Oaks Rd., Williamstown, MA 01267. *Office*—Department of English, Williams College, Williamstown, MA 01267. *Agent*—Liz Darhansoff, 1220 Park Ave., New York, NY 10028.

■ Career

University of Michigan, Ann Arbor, lecturer in creative writing, 1980-83; Williams College, Williamstown, MA, assistant professor, 1983-90, associate professor of English, 1990—; writer. *Member:* Phi Beta Kappa.

■ Awards, Honors

Transatlantic Review Award, Henfield Foundation, 1979, for "Eustace."

■ Writings

NOVELS FOR YOUNG ADULTS AND ADULTS

Flights, Knopf, 1983.
Paper Doll, Knopf, 1987.
Lights out in the Reptile House, Norton, 1990.
Kiss of the Wolf, Harcourt, 1994.

YOUNG ADULT NOVELS; WITH WILLIAM HOLINGER UNDER JOINT PSEUDONYM, SCOTT ELLER

Short Season, Scholastic, 1985.
21st Century Fox, Scholastic, 1989.

"THE JOHNSON BOYS" SERIES FOR YOUNG ADULTS; UNDER JOINT PSEUDONYM, SCOTT ELLER

The Football Wars, Scholastic, 1992.
First Base, First Place, Scholastic, 1993.
That Soccer Season, Scholastic, 1993.
Jump Shot, Scholastic, 1994.

OTHER

(Editor with Ron Hansen) *You've Got to Read This: Contemporary American Writers Introduce Stories That Held Them in Awe,* HarperPerennial, 1994, also published as *Spellbound: Contemporary American Writers Introduce Stories That Held Them in Awe.*

JIM SHEPARD

(Editor with Amy Hempel) *Unleashed: Poems by Writer's Dogs,* Crown Publishers, 1995.

Also author of *Battling against Castro,* Random House; author of story, "Eustace." Contributor to periodicals, including *Atlantic Monthly, Esquire, Harper's, New Yorker,* and *Redbook.*

■ Sidelights

Jim Shepard is the author of several teen sports stories, which he has cowritten with William Holinger under the joint pseudonym Scott Eller, but much of his critical acclaim has been received for the novels he has penned solo. *Flights,* his first published work, is the story of a luckless adolescent boy, Biddy Siebert, who lives in Connecticut. Biddy's life is lonely and unpleasant. He seems to have no lasting relationships, and the few friendships he does maintain are undone when families move away. Biddy's home life is hardly more fulfilling, for his parents are given to tormenting each other. Judy, Biddy's mother, is weak and submissive to her husband, the domineering Walt. It is Biddy's father who becomes the catalyst for the boy's great adventure, for he encourages the youth's interest in airplanes. Walt Siebert brings his son books on aircraft and even takes Biddy along when his friend offers a ride. Biddy, who sees himself as a failure, is inspired by the books and his flight, so he determines to steal the friend's plane and fly. For Biddy the theft and flight seem an opportunity for redemption. *Flights* was praised as a distinguished debut for its author. *Washington Post Book World* critic Tom Paulin deemed Shepard's work "subtle, brilliant, beautifully-wrought fiction." Another reviewer, Frederick Busch, described the novel in the *New York Times Book Review* as "well-made, well-written and splendidly imagined."

Shepard's second novel, *Paper Doll,* is about an American B-17 crew flying dangerous missions over Germany during World War II; it is told from the viewpoint of one of the plane's crew. The author returned to a more young-adult-oriented novel with *Lights out in the Reptile House,* a story about a youth's experiences in a country increasingly dominated by fascism. The novel's hero is fifteen-year-old Karel Roeder, who finds that his school work is becoming more and more devoted to subjects extolling the virtues of fascism and the fascist state. The meek, socially withdrawn Karel, who works at a zoo's reptile house, is in love with the rebellious Leda, who defies the state in its institutionalization and impending execution of her dyslexic brother. While Leda's family is subjected to scrutiny by local authorities, Karel finds that his own home life—he lives with a shiftless father—is disrupted by the state's presence. After Karel's father disappears, a soldier moves into his family's house. This menacing figure, Kehr, soon becomes Karel's personal tormentor, whereupon the hapless hero conspires to flee. As fear and suspicion spread throughout the community, so too does the presence of the fearful Civil Guard. It is this group, which counts the cruel Kehr among its members, that brings about the novel's key episode, the torching of the reptile house.

Since he began writing in the early 1980s, Shepard has been alternating between his solo ventures and his Scott Eller sport stories, which he writes because of his interest in athletics, an interest shared with his coauthor. The sports novels, which feature teens facing typical coming-of-age problems in plots generously peppered with play-by-play game action, are written with a more breezy approach that appeals to teen audiences looking for a light read. The novels Shepard writes under his own name, however, are much more intense, his more recent work, the highly praised *Kiss of the Wolf,* being no exception.

Kiss of the Wolf mixes the terror and intrigue of the thriller novel with the psychological drama of the strained relationship between a boy and his mother. Eleven-year-old Todd and his mother, Joanie, are deeply upset when Todd's father, Gary, abandons them and moves out west. Trying to fill the gap in her life, Joanie begins to see a man named Bruno, a used car salesman and suspicious character who seems to have connections with some pretty shady customers. The real trouble begins, however, on the night of Todd's confirmation party. Speeding off down a parkway after the festivities, Joanie does not see a pedestrian in time and hits him with her car. Horrified by what she has done, Joanie panics and drives off without reporting the incident to the police. Unwilling to confess her crime, she tries to persuade Todd to be quiet about what he has seen, too. "Altar boy Todd is deeply shocked by his mom's behavior and subsequent coverup," related a *Kirkus Reviews* contributor; "their rift is the heart of the

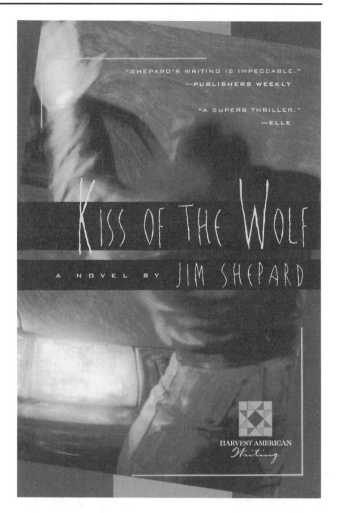

Eleven-year-old Todd and his mother become involved in a suspenseful drama of crime and guilt in this 1995 novel set in a blue-collar Italian neighborhood.

novel." This isn't the end of their troubles, however, for it turns out that the dead man was an associate of Bruno's, and that he was supposed to be carrying money that is now missing. Bruno begins to suspect Joanie, and he goes after her with a vengeance. Richard Bausch contended in the *New York Times Book Review* that *Kiss of the Wolf* succeeds not only as a thriller, but on other levels as well: "We go through all the stages of Joanie's guilt, we are privy to all the nuances of feeling between her and the boy as their understanding of what has happened changes them, and we come to see the story as a parable of responsibility and absolution."

■ Works Cited

Bausch, Richard, "Death in the Headlights," *New York Times Book Review,* February 12, 1995, p. 36.

Busch, Frederick, review of *Flights, New York Times Book Review,* October 9, 1983, pp. 15, 33.

Review of *Kiss of the Wolf, Kirkus Reviews,* November 15, 1993, p. 1419.

Paulin, Tom, review of *Flights, Washington Post Book World,* September 25, 1983, p. 4.

■ For More Information See

BOOKS

Contemporary Literary Criticism, Volume 36, Gale, 1986, pp. 405-407.

PERIODICALS

America, December 3, 1983, p. 360.
Booklist, August, 1985, p. 1663.
Choice, February, 1986, p. 868.
Detroit News, February 1, 1987.
Kliatt, November, 1992, p. 6.
Library Journal, July, 1985, p. 93; December, 1993, p. 177.
Newsday, February 18, 1990.
New York Times Book Review, October 20, 1985; February 25, 1990, p. 27; February 20, 1994, p. 34; December 4, 1994, p. 71.
Publishers Weekly, May 17, 1985, p. 98; November 15, 1993, p. 69.
School Library Journal, October, 1985, p. 171; March, 1989, p. 198; August, 1994, p. 184.
Sewanee Review, fall, 1986.
Voice of Youth Advocates, June, 1989, p. 100; October, 1990, p. 257.
Washington Post Book World, February 11, 1990, p. 4.*

*   *   *

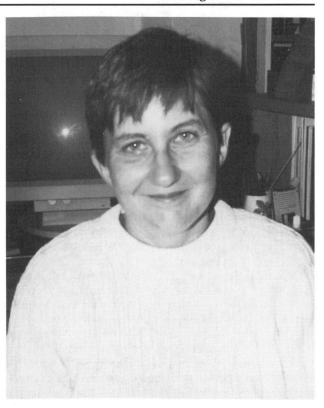

JANE MARGARET SHUTER

SHUTER, Jane Margaret 1955-
(Margaret Hudson)

■ Personal

Born June 21, 1955, in Broken Hill, Zambia, Africa; daughter of William Andrew Mortimer (a technical designer) and Ivy Louise Gross; married Paul Derek Shuter (a publisher), April 16, 1977; children: Joseph. *Education:* Lancaster University, B.A. (honors), 1976; teacher training, Madeley College of Education. *Hobbies and other interests:* Gardening herbs and vegetables, cooking, spinning and weaving wool.

■ Addresses

Home—30, Portland Rd., Oxford OX2 7EY, England.

■ Career

Teacher at various schools in England, 1977-83; freelance editor and layout person, 1987—; writer, 1989—; educational advisor for Hamlyn.

■ Writings

The Ancient Egyptians, Heinemann Educational Books, 1990.
(With Pat Taylor) *Invaders and Settlers,* Heinemann Educational Books, 1991.
(With Fiona Reynoldson) *Sunshine History Readers* (36 titles), Heinemann Educational Books, 1991.
(With Judith Maguire) *Tudor and Stuart Times,* Heinemann Educational Books, 1992.

Victorian Britain, Heinemann Educational Books, 1992.
Tudor Times, Heinemann Educational Books, 1995.
Shakespeare and the Theatre, Heinemann Educational Books, 1995.
The Poor in Tudor England, Heinemann Educational Books, 1995.
Life in a Tudor Town, Heinemann Educational Books, 1995.
Victorian Children, Hamlyn, 1995.
Tudor Children, Hamlyn, 1996.
Tudor Explorations, Heinemann Educational Books, 1996.
The Tudor Countryside, Heinemann Educational Books, 1996.

EYEWITNESS, SECOND SERIES (EDITOR AND NOTE WRITER)

Exquemlin and the Pirates of the Caribbean, Heinemann Library, 1993, Raintree Steck-Vaughn, 1995.
Charles Ball and American Slavery, Heinemann Library, 1993, Raintree Steck-Vaughn, 1995.
Parkman and the Plains Indians, Heinemann Library, 1993, Raintree Steck-Vaughn, 1995.

EYEWITNESS, FIRST SERIES (EDITOR AND NOTE WRITER)

Edmund Ludlow and the English Civil War, Heinemann Library, 1994.
Helen Williams and the French Revolution, Heinemann Library, 1994, Raintree Steck-Vaughn, 1996.
Sarah Royce and the American West, Heinemann Library, 1994, Raintree Steck-Vaughn, 1996.
Christabel Bielenberg and Nazi Germany, Heinemann Library, 1994, Raintree Steck-Vaughn, 1996.

■ Work in Progress

"World Focus," a series of books for six to eight year-olds, focusing on jobs around the world; "The Russian Revolution," a book for less able thirteen to fourteen year-olds.

■ Sidelights

Jane Margaret Shuter told *SATA*, "As a teacher, I always enjoyed teaching history, and was saddened by the lack of history teaching at the primary level in many schools. Most of the teachers I worked with set their own curriculum, and rejected history as 'too difficult' or 'too boring,' doubtless as result of unfortunate personal experience!

"The advent of the National Curriculum in this country led to a period of upheaval and change in teaching. It dictated that children had to be taught a variety of subjects, including history and geography. This led, in turn, to a need for books on historical topics that were written for children PTA under the age of eleven. Not only were these books needed, but they were needed fast and I was lucky enough to be well placed to help provide some. I was, at the time, working as an editor from home, so I understood book production. I had a history degree. I had also worked as a primary school teacher. So I was in the right place at the right time with just the sort of qualifications that my publisher needed. I've been writing ever since.

"I think it is vital for young children to be provided with reference books that are accurate, informative and well designed. I also think that it is very important that these books are written so that young children can read them for themselves. We are lucky that the days of reference books for six and seven year olds that consist of dense text, an almost adult vocabulary and the odd black and white photo or line drawing are now behind us."

*　　*　　*

SINGH, Rashmi Sharma 1952-
(Rashmi Sharma)

■ Personal

Born in September, 1952, in New Delhi, India; daughter of S. D. and S. Sharma; married R. P. Singh (a scientist); children: Anjali, Shalini, Arjun. *Education:* Delhi University, India, B.A. (with honors), 1972, M.A., 1974.

■ Addresses

Office—P.O. Box 7788, Berkeley, CA 94707-0788.

■ Career

Author and publisher in Berkeley, CA, 1991—. Founder and president, Education about South Asia-Vidya, Inc., 1995—. Former PTA president; former managing editor for a nonprofit newspaper.

RASHMI SHARMA SINGH

■ Writings

FOR CHILDREN; UNDER NAME RASHMI SHARMA

(Self-illustrated) *The Blue Jackal,* Vidya Books (Berkeley, CA), 1992.
(Self-illustrated) *A Brahmin's Castles in the Air,* Vidya Books, 1994.

Also author of numerous teacher's guides, educational booklets, and lesson plans; contributor of introduction and poetry to *Living in America,* Westview Press, 1995.

■ Work in Progress

A young adult novel; a collection of children's folktales from India; adult fiction; an historical novel; educational materials.

■ Sidelights

"As a parent in the U.S., I found very few books to share with my children which reflected the stories that I had grown up listening to in India," Rashmi Sharma Singh told *SATA.* "My dad used to tell me wonderful bedtime stories, all verbatim. I wish I had written some of these down before I forgot some of the details. I find it easier to remember things when I write them down, so that is what I started to do with these stories I had heard as a child.

"India has an ancient oral tradition of storytelling, as well as oral history and record keeping. Since I was born into a brahmin family, I guess I had always grown up with the notion that I needed to continue my family's tradition! In fact, when I researched The Punchtuntra, I found that this ancient collection of stories, more than two thousand years old, was attributed to a brahmin named Vishnu Sharma (in those days, called Sharman in Sanskrit), some predecessor of my birth family, which was also named Sharma! This made me decide that I would make an effort to keep alive these popular fables in some form, for my children, who have grown up in our adopted homeland of the United States.

"These fables are also excellent stories—a good reason why they have remained alive, and even popular, after so many years. In *A Brahmin's Castles in the Air,* for instance, although the story is set in India of the old days, it could be true of any young person, anywhere in the world, and even today. No matter what different languages we speak, what different foods we eat, what different clothes we wear, or what we look like, underneath all these differences, there is so much that is common to people all over the world. I wanted my children, and others, to understand and appreciate this fact—not through a lecture, but via a funny story, without their realizing they were being taught something! Which is precisely what Vishnu Sharman did brilliantly with these stories, two thousand years ago, for three princes who refused formal schooling.

"The illustrations of this book were a lot of fun, too. I have always loved drawing and painting. I did these illustrations in watercolor, in actual size, although with *The Blue Jackal* I did many of the illustrations twice the actual size so I would be able to get in a lot more details . . . .

"When I first sent out manuscripts of such books to publishers in the late 1980s, I got one rejection slip after another. Many of the rejection slips said that although the stories were good, these Indian stories would not have an appeal in the American market—therefore, the bottom line dictated that they were not worth publishing. The nicest rejection said that I was ahead of my time! I did not think that this was such a bad thing, so I started a niche company to reflect my heritage through such stories. Although most of the things we publish are instructional materials dealing with school curriculum in portraying South Asia (the historic region, not just the modern nation of India), some of these, such as *A Brahmin's Castles in the Air,* can have a place in trade markets as well.

"The majority of most publishers' titles go out of print within a calendar year, but to me the bottom line of quarterly and annual financial statements, while it makes sense to my bank and accountant, is not conducive to preserving my culture or heritage. Stories that have been around for thousands of years cannot be forced to have a life of just a few months! *The Blue Jackal* was published in 1992, and *A Brahmin's Castles in the Air,* the second in the series, in 1994. Slowly, but surely, other titles will follow, in keeping alive the heritage of South Asian Americans as they themselves retell stories from their ancient heritage."

*   *   *

SMITH, Jenny 1963-

■ Personal

Born February 6, 1963, in Washington, DC; daughter of Hedrick (an author and news correspondent) and Ann (a teacher; maiden name, Bickford) Smith. *Education:* Boston College, B.A., 1986; John F. Kennedy University, M.A., 1991.

■ Addresses

Home—P.O. Box 590, Tahoe City, CA 96145.

■ Career

Placer County Mental Health, Carnelian Bay, CA, peer counselor coordinator, 1990—; Organizational Services, Tahoe City, CA, consultant, 1990-91; Tahoe Truckee Unified School District, Kings Beach, CA, special friends aide, 1991-92; University of Nevada at Reno, Women's Center, program coordinator, 1992-93.

■ Writings

(With Richard Tichnor) *A Spark in the Dark* (for children), illustrated by Tichnor, Dawn Publications, 1994.

■ Adaptations

Michael Pinder (from the band *Moody Blues*) included *A Spark in the Dark* in his recording *A Planet with One Mind—Stories from around the World for the Child within Us All* (compact disc and audio cassette), which is a collection of creation myths with narration and music by Pinder and illustrations by Richard Tichnor, One Step Records, 1995. This work won the Benjamin Franklin Award silver medal for children's audio, 1996.

■ Work in Progress

Two books to join with *A Spark in the Dark* in a picture-book trilogy: *The Little Blue Ball,* a work "inspired by the second half of many creation stories," in which "the point of view shifts away from the source and the unfolding of creation" to that which has been created; and *Tumble and Play,* a book "based on the mythic motif of the 'hero's journey,'" in which "the point of view is that of the individual looking within." All three stories in the trilogy will be included in Michael Pinder's series of recordings, *A Planet with One Mind, A People with One Heart,* and *An Earth with One Spirit.*

■ Sidelights

Jenny Smith and her coauthor and illustrator, Richard Tichnor, told *SATA:* "*A Spark in the Dark* is the first in a series of three rhyming picture books that we've written and illustrated. The trilogy is about a star in the sky and a light that we share in our hearts. The stories and illustrations are based on mythological motifs found in cultures throughout time.

"In *A Spark in the Dark,* there is a flash—a *spark in the dark*—that grows into a star in the sky. The star gets lonely and so it makes a blue ball ... and then puts mountains and trees on the ball. The star is still lonely so it creates children ... and the star is lonely no more! Then the star gets a surprise. The children all have lights inside of them that shine up into the sky at night, filling it with stars!

"This book has common elements of creation stories from around the world. In these myths everything that is, appears. The universe unfolds and the stage is set upon which all life will be experienced. The point of view in these stories is usually that of the source of creation, a single consciousness that exists somewhere 'out there' (the star in our story)."

The other two books comprising Tichnor's and Smith's trilogy, tentatively entitled *The Little Blue Ball* and *Tumble and Play,* have not yet been published. "*The Little Blue Ball* is a story about two people who are so close that they think they are one. But when they look into a pool and see their reflection they realize that they are two! And not only that, they are different! So they start to argue about who is better. Then from deep in the pool there appears a fish who reminds them of the star that they came from and the planets of magical dust that make everyone different and special, which is what makes life fun. And even though everyone may look different, we all share the same light inside!

"*Tumble and Play* is a story about a time when the world grows cold and dark. Spark, the protagonist, sets off on a journey to find out why. With the help of a wise one, Spark is pointed up a mountain to talk to ... a star! The star tells Spark: 'The answer's not here, it's inside of you ... the meaning of things and the point of it all is in how you live life on the little blue ball.' And the world grows a little bit warmer and a little bit brighter!

"Together these stories comprise a complete mythological cycle. The cycle begins at the macrocosmic scale with the creation of everything, the unfolding of the universe.

Jenny Smith, with coauthor and illustrator Richard Tichnor.

A unique creation story, the poetic picture book *A Spark in the Dark* was written and illustrated jointly by Jenny Smith and Richard Tichnor.

The point of view or consciousness is that of the source of creation. Then the point of view moves to what has been created, which becomes conscious of itself. Finally the perspective shifts to that of the individual looking within. And the cycle culminates with the realization that the star which has created everything is inside all of us.''

Commenting on what inspired their first picture book, Smith and Tichnor told *SATA:* "We wrote *A Spark in the Dark* as a Christmas gift for family members. It grew out of a conversation we had about giving more personal and meaningful gifts, particularly to Richard's father and stepmother, both of whom had been diagnosed with cancer. We decided to write a story showing that each person is special and that we are all connected

to one another. When we finished, we realized that we had written a story that could be shared with everyone. The book is dedicated to Richard's stepmother, Connie.

"We wrote the story together. It is an expression of our combined interests and experiences. We were influenced by Dr. Seuss' books—by their rhymes and messages—which of course we both read as children. This wasn't something that we were consciously aware of when we were writing, but it's clear from the rhythm and feel of our book that his influence is there. One reviewer of our book says that *A Spark in the Dark* is where 'Joseph Campbell meets Dr. Seuss.'

"Richard is an architect. When we wrote the book he was designing a museum to house a collection of Native

American baskets. His research of Native American symbolism in conjunction with his personal interest in mythology inspired the use of the creation theme as the basis for *A Spark in the Dark.* Jenny was working at a local elementary school providing play therapy to children with emotional and behavioral problems. She found that the most important thing to communicate to these kids was that they were valued and that they were each special.

"Richard created the illustrations out of cut and ripped construction paper. He wanted the pictures to be elemental and symbolic like the story and he also wanted to make them in a way that kids might have done them, so construction paper seemed to be the perfect medium. The cut-paper artwork of Matisse and Ivan Chermayeff were primary sources of inspiration. The designs and forms are also reflective of Richard's architectural work.

"Creation stories are a type of myth. They are not just fanciful tales from the past, they are also allegories for the present. Myths are told symbolically so that each person can interpret the meaning in their own way. For example, the star in our story may represent God to some, or to others it may symbolize the explosion out of which our universe grew. On a more personal level the star may symbolize any act of creation: a new life, a new burst of growth, or the creative spark within us. There are as many possible interpretations as there are readers.

"*A Spark in the Dark* is our own creation story. It expresses archetypal motifs and themes of creation stories from around the world. Creation stories have been told by people everywhere, throughout time. From the Aborigines to the Zulus, these colorful tales explain not only how the world began but people's relationship to it. The details of each creation story are different, reflecting the culture from which they came. But if you listen carefully you will find that all of these stories have similar underlying themes which tell us about ourselves—our place in the universe, our relationships with others, and our inner experience. That these stories are told by people all over the world shows us that inside we are not so different after all. We are connected to one another and our differences are unique and interesting expressions of a single people."

*   *   *

STEVENS, Janet 1953-

■ Personal

Born January 17, 1953, in Dallas, TX; daughter of Jack (a naval officer) and Frances Stevens; married Ted Habermann (a research scientist); children: Lindsey Habermann, Blake Habermann. *Education:* University of Colorado, B.F.A., 1975. *Hobbies and other interests:* Mountain biking, camping, hiking, and skiing.

JANET STEVENS

■ Addresses

Home and office—3835 Spring Valley Rd., Boulder, CO 80304.

■ Career

Children's book illustrator, 1979—. Has worked in advertising, textile design, and architectural illustration.

■ Awards, Honors

Parents Choice Award, 1987, and National Council for Social Studies-Children's Book Council Notable Children's Trade Book in the Field of Social Studies citation, both for *The Three Billy Goats Gruff;* Caldecott Honor citation, and Notable Children's Books citation, both American Library Association, both 1996, Parents' Choice Honor Award, and American Bookseller Association "Pick of the Lists" citation, all for *Tops and Bottoms;* Stevens's books have been made Junior Literary Guild and International Reading Association Children's Choice selections, and have received several state children's choice book awards.

■ Writings

(Self-illustrated) *From Pictures to Words: A Book about Making a Book,* Holiday House, 1995.

RETELLER; SELF-ILLUSTRATED

Animal Fair, Holiday House, 1981.
Hans Christian Andersen, *The Princess and the Pea,* Holiday House, 1982.

Aesop, *The Tortoise and the Hare,* Holiday House, 1984.

Hans Christian Andersen, *The Emperor's New Clothes,* Holiday House, 1985.

The House That Jack Built: A Mother Goose Nursery Rhyme, Holiday House, 1985.

Goldilocks and the Three Bears, Holiday House, 1986.

Aesop, *The Town Mouse and the Country Mouse,* Holiday House, 1987.

The Three Billy Goats Gruff, Harcourt, 1987.

Hans Christian Andersen, *It's Perfectly True,* Holiday House, 1988.

Aesop, *Androcles and the Lion,* Holiday House, 1989.

How the Manx Cat Lost Its Tail, Harcourt, 1990.

Jakob Ludwig and Wilhelm Karl Grimm, *The Bremen Town Musicians,* Holiday House, 1992.

Coyote Steals the Blanket: An Ute Tale, Holiday House, 1993.

Tops and Bottoms, Harcourt, 1995.

Old Bag of Bones: A Coyote Tale, Holiday House, 1996.

ILLUSTRATOR

Myra Cohen Livingston, editor, *Callooh! Callay! Holiday Poems for Young Readers,* Atheneum, 1978.

Marjorie Sharmat, *Twitchell the Wishful,* Holiday House, 1981.

Marjorie Sharmat, *Lucretia the Unbearable,* Holiday House, 1981.

Ida Lutrell, *Not Like That, Armadillo,* Harcourt, 1982.

Steven Kroll, *The Big Bunny and the Easter Eggs,* Holiday House, 1982.

Edward Lear, *The Owl and the Pussycat,* Holiday House, 1983.

Marjorie Sharmat, *Sasha the Silly,* Holiday House, 1984.

Sheila Turnage, *Trout the Magnificent,* Harcourt, 1984.

Arnold Adolf, *The Cabbages Are Chasing the Rabbits,* Harcourt, 1985.

Paul Levitt and others, *The Weighty Word Book,* Bookmakers Guild/University of Colorado Foundation (Longmont, CO), 1985.

Steven Kroll, *The Big Bunny and the Magic Show,* Holiday House, 1986.

Squire D. Rushnell, *Little David's Adventures,* edited by Barbara Shook Hazen, Word (Waco, TX), 1986.

Eric Kimmel, reteller, *Anansi and the Moss-Covered Rock,* Holiday House, 1988.

Edward Lear, *The Quangle Wangle's Hat,* Harcourt, 1988.

Brent Ashabranner, *I'm in the Zoo, Too,* Dutton, 1989.

Barbara Shook Hazen, *Wally, the Worry-Warthog,* Clarion, 1990.

Eric Kimmel, *Nanny Goat and the Seven Little Kids,* Holiday House, 1990.

Polly Robertus, *The Dog Who Had Kittens,* Holiday House, 1991.

Eric Kimmel, reteller, *Anansi Goes Fishing,* Holiday House, 1992.

Margery Cuyler, *Barry Bear and the Bad Guys,* Houghton, 1993.

Eric Kimmel, reteller, *Anansi and the Talking Melon,* Holiday House, 1995.

Kathryn Lasky, *The Gates of the Wind,* Harcourt, 1995.

Anne Miranda, *To Market,* Harcourt, 1997.

■ Adaptations

The Tortoise and the Hare was narrated by Gilda Radner and televised on *Reading Rainbow,* Public Broadcast System, 1985.

■ Work in Progress

Anansi and the Magic Hoe.

■ Sidelights

What do Anansi the spider, Goldilocks, and the Quangle Wangle all have in common? They're all well-loved storybook characters who have been brought to new life through the talent of children's book illustrator and writer Janet Stevens. Using artistic mediums such as pastel crayon, pencil, pen and ink, and watercolor, Stevens is especially noted for her humorous illustrations that feature likeable animals. Her work as an illustrator has been described by *Booklist* reviewer Denise M. Wilms as "strong, showing a sense of movement, composition, and drama similar to that found in [noted illustrator Paul] Galdone's most successful works."

Stevens was born in 1953, in Dallas, Texas. Because her father, a career naval officer, moved about the country a great deal because of his job, Stevens was raised in Virginia, Rhode Island, Florida, and Hawaii. After graduating from high school, she earned a degree in fine arts from the University of Colorado, graduating in 1975. Involved since then in such creative endeavors as advertising, textile design, and illustrations for architects, Stevens is fortunate to have translated her early love of drawing into a career that has filled her life.

Stevens illustrated her first children's book, an anthology called *Callooh! Callay! Holiday Poems for Young Readers,* in 1978, after being inspired by a workshop she attended led by fellow illustrator and writer Tomie dePaola. "He encouraged me to give children's books a try," Stevens recalled. DePaola also gave Stevens her first break into publishing by showing her work to an editor at a New York publishing company, Holiday House. The editor liked Stevens's work so much that she offered her a contract. *Animal Fair* followed in 1981, a traditional nursery song that Stevens both illustrated and adapted as a read-aloud picture book. The book received good grades from critics: Michele Slung, for instance, commented in the *New York Times Book Review* that the illustrations display "such an array of inventiveness" that the reader might believe they "somehow have a life of their own."

Numerous other retellings would follow, including such classic children's stories as *The Princess and the Pea, The Emperor's New Clothes*—where Stevens casts a rotund porker in the starring role—and *Goldilocks and the Three Bears.* Her imaginative retelling of *The Bremen Town Musicians,* originally written by one of

Mule Deer was grazing nearby.
"Hey, Mule Deer," Coyote called out. "Can you help me?
A killer rock is trying to crush me, and I'm weak from all
this running. You're so strong, you could stop that rock
with your powerful antlers."
"I am strong, Coyote," Mule Deer agreed, puffing out his
mighty chest. "I will help you."

A trickster receives poetic justice in Stevens's retelling of an old Ute tale. (From *Coyote Steals the Blanket,* written and illustrated by Janet Stevens.)

the Brothers Grimm, has been particularly praised as a book worthy of a prominent spot during storytime. Using watercolor and pastel on textured rice paper, Stevens tells of the adventures of the four old animals who set out together for the city of Bremen in hopes of becoming musicians. "That Stevens can pull off chaos without clutter is a real tribute to her powers of composition and design," noted Betsy Hearne in *Bulletin of the Center for Children's Books.*

In *How the Manx Cat Lost Its Tail,* published in 1990, Stevens is truly in her animal element. Her story presents the explanation for an entire breed of tailless felines by showing Noah slamming the door on his favorite pet just as the cat scurries into the Ark at the last minute—the Manx cat's bad timing costs it one of its nine lives in addition to a tail. Hearne of the *Bulletin of the Center for Children's Books* praised the "rollicking details" of the artist's double-page spreads, while Kathy Piehl commented in *School Library Journal* that Stevens's watercolors "create dramatic tension" by contrasting the coming rainstorm with "the anxious and skittish expressions of the animals."

Similarly, in *Coyote Steals the Blanket,* Stevens introduces readers to the folklore of the Ute Indians with her characteristic action-filled and animal-packed illustrations. "I go where I want, I do what I want, and I take

what I want," announces the defiant Coyote, and his daredevil attitude ends up getting him into trouble. "A scruffier, more scraggly Coyote would be hard to find," noted Janice Del Negro in *Booklist,* praising *Coyote Steals the Blanket* as useful for "reading aloud, reading alone, and storytelling." A *Kirkus Reviews* critic likewise hailed Stevens's "briskly informal, well-honed telling" and found her illustrations create "an outstanding setting for a lively, sagacious, well-sourced tale."

Several fables by Aesop, including *The Town Mouse and the Country Mouse, Androcles and the Lion,* and *The Tortoise and the Hare,* have also been brought to new life through Stevens's colorful artwork and updated adaptation. Despite the criticism from some reviewers that Aesop's classic stories contained a compactness and simplicity that could not be improved upon in their appeal to children, Stevens's *The Tortoise and the Hare* would be honored by being showcased on Public Broadcasting's popular *Reading Rainbow* television series. In addition to providing both text and pictures to old tales, Stevens has also illustrated several stories by other authors, from Edward Lear's classic nineteenth-century rhymes *The Owl and the Pussycat* and *The Quangle Wangle's Hat* to Eric Kimmel's retellings of the African Anansi the Spider trickster tales and Arnold Adoff's humorous 1985 work *The Cabbages Are Chasing the Rabbits.*

Another trickster tale is the focus of Stevens's 1995 picture book *Tops and Bottoms,* which was awarded a Caldecott Honor citation. A clever Hare, noting that the rich but lazy Bear sleeps through the growing season, offers to work Bear's land in exchange for half of the crops—and Bear can even choose which half, tops or bottoms. When Bear chooses tops, Hare outwits his landlord by planting carrots and beets; when the Bear then selects bottoms, Hare raises lettuce and celery. "Stevens retells the story with vigor and humor," Susan Dove Lempke noted in *Bulletin of the Center for Children's Books,* "but the artwork is the real star." The critic added that the vertical, top-to-bottom positioning of the illustrations creates "an ingenious twist." *Horn Book* contributor Ellen Fader similarly praised the artist's "bold, well-composed watercolor, pencil, and gesso illustrations," and concluded that "the story contains enough sly humor and reassuring predictability to captivate listeners."

Stevens uses the technique of *anthropomorphism*—endowing animals with human characteristics—in approaching her work as an illustrator. In 1995's *From Pictures to Words: A Book about Making a Book,* she even uses animal characters to describe how she comes up with the idea for each new story. In fact, "Stevens barely has time to introduce herself before the text is taken over by a cast of imaginary animals clad in colorful clothing," according to Joy Fleishhacker in *School Library Journal.* "We need to be in a book," her animal characters demand of the illustrator at the start of her day in the studio. "We want something exciting to do. We need places to go, people to meet. We're like actors without a stage, burgers without buns, aliens

Bear stared at his pile. "But, Hare, all the best parts are in your half!"

"You chose the tops, Bear," Hare said.

"Now, Hare, you've tricked me. You plant this field again—and this season I want the bottoms!"

Hare agreed. "It's a done deal, Bear."

Tops & Bottoms, Stevens's self-illustrated adaptation of Bear's foolish deal with clever Hare, was named a Caldecott honor book in 1996.

without spaceships!" Faced with pitiful entreaties such as these, Stevens launches into a step-by-step guide to the way a children's picture book is constructed—setting, plot, cast of characters, and the development of a problem and solution that comprise the basics of dramatic tension. She portrays the creative task of bookmaking in a way that inspires young writers, and concludes by encouraging them to try their hand at the process as well. "I hope I always have the opportunity to create books for children," Stevens said, "so that my animal characters will have homes."

"I have always been interested in art and have studied and practiced for many years," the talented illustrator explained. "I am often asked how I learned to draw so well. My answer is lots and lots of practice!" Stevens lives and works in Colorado with her husband and children, Lindsey and Blake. "My books have changed since the birth of my two children," she told *SATA*. "Lindsey and Blake are good critics and help me make decisions about my books. It is important for me to remember that these books are for children. My own kids help me keep that in perspective.

"Each book is an opportunity and a challenge. A new book offers me a chance to expand and try something new. The process is both difficult and exciting—sometimes a struggle, sometimes fun. Most important is to create books that children want to read. This is the real joy of bookmaking."

■ Works Cited

Review of *Coyote Steals the Blanket, Kirkus Reviews,* April 15, 1993, p. 537.
Del Negro, Janice, review of *Coyote Steals the Blanket, Booklist,* April 1, 1993, p. 1428.
Fader, Ellen, review of *Tops and Bottoms, Horn Book,* May, 1995, p. 337.
Fleishhacker, Joy, review of *From Pictures to Words: A Book about Making a Book, School Library Journal,* July, 1995, p. 75.
Hearne, Betsy, review of *How the Manx Cat Lost Its Tail, Bulletin of the Center for Children's Books,* October, 1990, p. 47.
Hearne, Betsy, review of *The Bremen Town Musicians, Bulletin of the Center for Children's Books,* November, 1992, p. 73.
Lempke, Susan Dove, review of *Tops and Bottoms, Bulletin of the Center for Children's Books,* April, 1995, p. 287.
Piehl, Kathy, review of *How the Manx Cat Lost Its Tail, School Library Journal,* May, 1990, p. 101.
Slung, Michele, review of *Animal Fair, New York Times Book Review,* April 26, 1981, p. 66.
Stevens, Janet, *Coyote Steals the Blanket: An Ute Tale,* Holiday House, 1993.
Stevens, Janet, *From Pictures to Words: A Book about Making a Book,* Holiday House, 1995.
Wilms, Denise M., review of *The Tortoise and the Hare, Booklist,* October 1, 1984, p. 251.

■ For More Information See

BOOKS

Sharron L. McElmeel, *An Author a Month (for Dimes),* Vol. 3, Teacher Ideas Press (Englewood, CO), 1993.

PERIODICALS

Booklist, October 15, 1985, p. 341; May 1, 1987, p. 1371; November 1, 1989, p. 559; February 15, 1994, p. 1086; March 15, 1995, p. 1329; April 15, 1995, p. 1504.
Bulletin of the Center for Children's Books, May, 1981, p. 181.
Horn Book, July-August, 1996, p. 473.
Publishers Weekly, September 26, 1986, p. 78; November 2, 1992, p. 70.
School Library Journal, May, 1995, p. 103.

* * *

STOEKE, Janet Morgan 1957-

■ Personal

Born April 30, 1957, in Pittsfield, MA; daughter of Julius Paul (a mechanical engineer) and Carolyn S. (an artist) Stoeke; married Barrett L. Brooks (a marine botanist), July 21, 1990; children: Harrison and Colin (twins). *Education:* Colgate University, B.A., 1979; George Washington University, M.F.A., 1987.

■ Career

Author and illustrator. *Member:* Washington Children's Book Guild.

■ Awards, Honors

Dutton Picture Book Competition award, 1988, for *Minerva Louise;* Parents' Choice Silver Award, and American Library Association Notable Book citation, both 1994, both for *A Hat for Minerva Louise.*

■ Writings

SELF-ILLUSTRATED

Minerva Louise, Dutton, 1988.
Lawrence, Dutton, 1990.
A Hat for Minerva Louise, Dutton, 1994.
Minerva Louise at School, Dutton, 1996.

ILLUSTRATOR

Katie Evans, *Hunky Dory Ate It,* Dutton, 1991.
Katie Evans, *Hunky Dory Found It,* Dutton, 1994.

■ Work in Progress

On the Day We Were Born, a picture book.

■ Sidelights

Janet Morgan Stoeke has received high praise for her brightly colored, simple storybook illustrations, which

JANET MORGAN STOEKE

critics have found cheerfully silly. Stoeke regularly features endearing characters in appealing scenarios in her drawings; as the illustrator for Katie Evans's books about Hunky Dory, a mischievous dog who gets into everything, Stoeke's work has been singled out for the visual humor it added to Evans's silly rhyming tales. Stoeke is also the author of several self-illustrated picture books featuring Minerva Louise, a hen whose cheerful optimism and inquiring spirit is never daunted by her many mistakes. "At the merest stroke of her pen," stated a *Publishers Weekly* reviewer, "Stoeke invests her poultry protagonist with an abundance of character."

Stoeke's first attempt at writing and illustrating a children's book was *Minerva Louise,* a gentle story about a hen that won a picture book competition in 1988. After Minerva Louise succumbs to temptation and ventures into a house with red curtains, she turns everything topsy turvy, making a nest in the fireplace logs and befriending a rubber duck and a tabby cat she mistakes for a cow. A *Publishers Weekly* writer called this "a lighthearted story that will tickle the funny bone of the youngest child," and praised the brightly colored, simple drawings that accompany Stoeke's charming story. In another award-winning effort, *A Hat for Minerva Louise,* Stoeke's hen wants to play outside on a cold winter day and goes in search of clothes to keep her

warm. As in the earlier story, critics noted that much of the book's humor lies in Stoeke's depiction of what a *Kirkus Reviews* critic called Minerva's "comically bland certitude," as she mistakes a hose for a scarf and ends up proudly wearing a mitten for a hat, with the other mitten on her tail. "Stoeke's second book about that intrepid screwball, Minerva Louise, is a rare find: a picture book exactly on target for preschoolers that sacrifices none of the essential elements of plot, character, and humor," enthused *Horn Book* contributor Martha V. Parravano.

Stoeke has also garnered praise for the uncluttered, brightly colored illustrations she has created for the books of other authors. As the illustrator of *Hunky Dory Ate It* and *Hunky Dory Found It,* Stoeke's efforts were particularly well received. Critics found her depiction of an eager young puppy who eats everything in sight and gets a stomach ache, and who sneaks off with "lost" socks and other items, both endearing and amusing. "People enjoy hearing that I used my family and friends as models throughout," Stoeke told *SATA.* "I didn't have a dog; sketches for Hunky Dory were already started when my husband and I got a puppy. He grew up to look a lot like Hunky Dory and was a terrific model!"

Stoeke didn't plan to become a writer and illustrator; it sort of came upon her by accident. "I have had a number of other careers which came to me after some serious effort. But happily for me, this children's bookmaking one came along unforeseen, nearly out of the blue. I have been a gymnastics instructor, bookstore clerk, waitress, museum docent, and advertising designer. Throughout all of these jobs I painted, and felt that being a painter was the most important part of me. I still feel the need to paint, and sometimes call myself a painter, but the children's book creator title suits me best of all those I've so far tried out.

"In the middle of completing my master's thesis, and while working full time at my most serious job (ad designer), a small article about a contest came across my desk. A contest for a picture book. I thought about all of the time I'd spent in that bookstore, working primarily with children's books. I had developed a lot of uppity opinions during that time. Most of them revolved around how I might have better accomplished what others had tried to do. The contest was closing in two weeks. I decided to try it.

"My main objectives were to avoid the pitfalls that glared out at me from books at the store. Don't write down to children, be didactic, gimmicky, trite, or the least bit imitative of a previously successful illustrator/ author. All this, and be funny and original. I found it was extremely difficult to stick to the standards by which I had judged others.

"But my submission, *Minerva Louise,* won first prize! I would get a nice check, but not only that, a publishing contract! It was the start of a new, ever-surprising, and probably endless education, and a very happy change of direction for me.

Hunky Dory ate it.

The irrepressible dog in Katie Evans's story for young children takes the cake in more ways than one. (From *Hunky Dory Ate It*, illustrated by Janet Morgan Stoeke.)

"*A Hat for Minerva Louise* took a long time to come to me. I tried and tried to make Minerva Louise come to life again. Somehow she'd change or repeat herself too much when I worked at it. Then, when I looked the other way, and concentrated on something else—it fell into place, like a gift. The three books in between, not to mention the pregnancy and care of *twins,* really did take my mind off of the struggle. When I relaxed, there she was."

■ Works Cited

Review of *A Hat for Minerva Louise, Kirkus Reviews,* September 15, 1994, p. 1283.
Review of *A Hat for Minerva Louise, Publishers Weekly,* August 1, 1994, p. 77.
Review of *Minerva Louise, Publishers Weekly,* February 12, 1988, p. 82.
Parravano, Martha V., review of *A Hat for Minerva Louise, Horn Book,* January, 1995, pp. 55-56.

■ For More Information See

PERIODICALS

Booklist, February 1, 1992, p. 1039; January 15, 1994, pp. 935-36.
Bulletin of the Center for Children's Books, September, 1996, pp. 32-33.
New York Times Book Review, May 22, 1988, p. 30.
Publishers Weekly, November 22, 1991, p. 55.
School Library Journal, March, 1992, p. 214; February, 1994, p. 83; August, 1996, pp. 130-31.

SUN, Chyng Feng 1959-

■ Personal

Born January 14, 1959, in Taiwan, Republic of China; daughter of Parng Sun and Wen-shin Wei. *Education:* National Taiwan University, B.A., 1981; Syracuse University, M.S., 1982; Simmons College, M.A., 1990.

■ Addresses

Home—15 Paul Gore St., Apt. 2, Jamaica Plain, MA 02130. *Office*—Family, Friends and Community, c/o Judge Baker Children's Center, 295 Longwood Ave., Boston, MA 02115.

■ Career

Min-sheng Daily Newspaper, Taipei, Taiwan, reporter, 1984-89; Family, Friends and Community, Boston, MA, associate director. Linking Publishing Co., part-time editor, 1984-89.

■ Awards, Honors

Gold Medal, China Times Literature Contest, 1986; Silver Medal, Shin-Yi Picture Book Contest, 1988; Golden Cauldron Honor Book, National Educational Department, 1989; Gold Medal, Chinese Children's Literature Association Annual Contest, 1989.

■ Writings

FOR CHILDREN

Two Together, pictures by Robin Kramer, Houghton, 1991.

Square Beak, illustrated by Chih-sien Chen, Houghton, 1993.

On a White Pebble Hill, illustrated by Chih-sien Chen, Houghton, 1994.

Mama Bear, illustrated by Lolly Robinson, Houghton, 1994.

Cat and Cat-face, illustrated by Lesley Liu, Houghton, 1996.

Contributor of "The Strange Thing" to *Cricket,* 1990.

UNTRANSLATED WORKS

Bao-Bao in America, Linking Publishing, 1986.
The Magic Jar, Shin-Yi Preschool Foundation, 1988.
The Diary of an E.T., Kuo Yu Publishing, 1988.
Leaves-birds, Shin-Yi Preschool Foundation, 1988.
Cooking Something Up: How to Teach Children Creative Writing, East Publishing, 1988, Guan-Shi Publishing, 1994.
Little Red, Linking Publishing, 1989.

OTHER

Story, Story (video), Silver Burdett Ginn, 1991.
Bird Seeds Planting Birds?, Crown Publishing, 1995.
(With composer Miguel Picker) *Don Gato* (children's ballet), produced in Boston, 1995.

Translator into Chinese of Leo Lionni's *Frederick, Alexander and the Wind-up Mouse,* and *Matthew's Dream;* William Steig's *Doctor De Soto;* and David Macaulay's *Black and White.*

■ Adaptations

Don Gato was filmed by WGBH-TV, Boston, 1996.

Faced with the choice of fame or happiness, an artistic chicken opts for freedom to be herself in Chyng Feng Sun's *Square Beak,* a modern fable illustrated by Chih-sien Chen.

■ Sidelights

Chyng Feng Sun told *SATA:* "Being a children's book author, the question I am most often asked is 'Do you like children?' or 'Do you have children?' I always remembered Leo Lionni's answer that except for his own grandchildren, he wouldn't say that he liked children in general. Why don't people ask adult writers if they like adults? There are so many different kinds of people and some of them are inevitably obnoxious or unlikable. Children come in a million different varieties, too.

"It's not a conscious decision for me to write for children particularly. Except for some requests from editors who provided specific guidelines, I usually don't have an audience in mind who would govern me as to what or how to write. The stories are children's stories because they are similar to what most people define as children's stories. Maybe children and I happen to share the same interests. It always amazes me that children laugh or shed tears for the same reasons I do, when I see how they understand humor and when they actually behave or respond like my characters.

"Most of my stories are fantasies or fables and some of the themes are autobiographical. The most challenging and exciting part of writing fables is figuring out an analogy which is self-contained and engaging and also matches the message I want to convey. Through more than fifteen years of writing stories, I found out that egg seems to be a significant and powerful image in my subconscious. There were three times that it was writing stories related to eggs that dissolved my writer's block. *Square Beak* was the first one."

In *Square Beak* the title character is an outsider among the other chicks because of her square beak. After finding a hole in the barnyard fence, though, Square Beak finds happiness as she roams the lands around her home. These wanderings result in exotic dreams that enable Square Beak to lay beautiful eggs. This ability gains her some respect with the other animals, who convince Square Beak to represent them in an egg-laying contest. One of the conditions of the contest is being cooped up in a pen, though, which hinders Square Beak's creative process so much that she is unable to produce any of the eggs. In the end she returns to her travels and dreams and the resulting happiness brings back her artistic eggs. *Square Beak* is an "unusual and entertaining fable about the joys and challenges of being different," describes Julie Corsaro in *Booklist,* adding that it is "as different from the pack as its endearing protagonist."

Like her creative character Square Beak, Sun finds herself in different situations that influence what she writes about and the amount of time it takes her to produce a story. "Another question that I've often been asked was how long it took me to write a story," she explained to *SATA.* "This varies too. Some souls of stories have been carried in the back of my mind for several years but haven't found the right bodies yet. But

Mei-Mei strives to earn money to buy her and her mother an expensive Christmas present, but falls short and learns an important lesson in the process. (From *Mama Bear*, written by Chyng Feng Sun and illustrated by Lolly Robinson.)

some were quick. I was approached by a Chinese publisher who asked me to write a story about imagination for three- or four-year-olds. I thought about the environment for that age and felt the kitchen or the dining room might evoke a familiar, secure, and warm feeling. I looked at the salt shaker on the dining table in my kitchen/dining room/living room and got the idea: how to transform the ordinary into an adventure. I created *On a White Pebble Hill*, a little girl's day-dream journey on her dining table."

This daydream starts with Mimi playing on a hill covered with white pebbles and follows her as she climbs into a big green bush to view the landscape, gets a ride from a bird, swims through a lake filled with water snakes, and then climbs to the top of a great mountain. As the mountain begins to shake and Mimi fears the approach of a giant, she comes out of her daydream to find herself at the dinner table with her family. The entire adventure was created from the very plate of food sitting before her: mashed potatoes made up the hill with white pebbles, broccoli was the green bush, noodles were the water snakes, and the great mountain was really roast chicken. "Mimi has had a thrilling adventure in a strange and interesting land without having moved a single muscle," observes Marigny Dupuy in the *New York Times Book Review*. Dupuy goes on to conclude that "Sun captures beautifully and in simple

language the rush and freedom of a child's imagination at play."

Imaginative thinking is also important for young Mei-Mei in Sun's 1994 story *Mama Bear*. Seeing a huge teddy bear in a store window, Mei-Mei is told by her mother that they cannot afford it, but must instead fix the heater in their home. Unable to convince her mother that the bear can keep them warm instead, Mei-Mei and her mother begin to save their money. Trying to fill the jar faster, Mei-Mei even holds a cookie sale with the almond cookies she gets from the restaurant where her mother works. In the end, however, there is not enough to buy the bear, but Mei-Mei's mother cheers her up by pointing out that she is big and warm and soft, causing Mei-Mei to declare her "mama bear."

Mama Bear contains a theme that Sun herself finds puzzling, which is why she incorporated it into a story. She related to *SATA:* "If one wants something very much, works very hard towards the goal but still can't get it, what should one do? Could one actually gain something important in the process? *Mama Bear* explores this question. In my writing class, my fellow students called me heartless not to give the protagonist the teddy bear she worked so hard to buy. Some little readers told me frankly that they liked the book except the ending and demanded that Mei-Mei, the heroine, get the teddy bear. Interesting enough, while reading, the readers are actually experiencing the theme: they want Mei-Mei to have the bear but she can't."

In addition to writing about situations that pose interesting questions, Sun also draws on experiences from her personal life and cultural background to find inspiration for her writings. "Some of my books are published both in Chinese and English," she pointed out to *SATA.* "While I am doing the translation either from English to Chinese or vice versa, the differences between Chinese and North Americans in culture and language become so crystal clear. It also makes me more aware of who I am. The experiences of living in two very different worlds enrich my personal life as well as my writing."

■ **Works Cited**

Corsaro, Julie, review of *Square Beak, Booklist,* April 1, 1993, p. 1441.

Dupuy, Marigny, review of *On a White Pebble Hill, New York Times Book Review,* July 31, 1994, p. 20.

■ **For More Information See**

PERIODICALS

Booklist, September 1, 1994, p. 55.

Bulletin of the Center for Children's Books, March, 1994, p. 235; October, 1994, p. 68.

Publishers Weekly, March 1, 1993, p. 56; January 17, 1994, p. 430; August 22, 1994, p. 55.

School Library Journal, June, 1993, p. 90; June, 1994, p. 113; November 1994, p. 91.*

T

TERADA, Alice M. 1928-

■ Personal

Born November 13, 1928, in Hilo, HI; daughter of David M. (an auto mechanic) and Mitsuko (a homemaker; maiden name, Sekido) Marutani; married Harry T. Terada (an optometrist), August 25, 1951; children: Suzanne T., Keith Y., Lance S. *Education:* Case Western Reserve University, B.S., 1953; University of Hawaii, M.Ed., 1971. *Politics:* Democrat. *Religion:* Episcopalian. *Hobbies and other interests:* Art history, antiques (porcelains), and yoga.

■ Addresses

Home—One Keahole Place, #3313, Honolulu, HI 96825; and 5383 Manauwea St., Honolulu, HI 96821. *Office*—P.O. Box 24105, Honolulu, HI 96824-1054.

■ Career

Worked as a registered nurse in Cleveland, OH, Los Angeles, CA, and Honolulu, HI, 1952-55; employed as a teacher and reading specialist, Honolulu, 1962-82; freelance writer, Honolulu, 1983—. *Member:* International Reading Association, Zonta Club International, American Association of University Women, Zonta Club of Honolulu.

■ Writings

Under the Starfruit Tree: Folktales from Vietnam, illustrated by Janet Larsen, The University of Hawaii Press, 1989.
The Magic Crocodile and Other Folktales from Indonesia, illustrated by Charlene K. Smoyer, The University of Hawaii Press, 1994.

■ Work in Progress

"The Ghost of a Hawaiian Summer," "A Timeless Jungle," "Ngerchokl, River of Youth," "Story from Banda." Research on the history of the Dutch in

ALICE M. TERADA

Indonesia; Papua New Guinea; Shinto myths; Bataks of Sumatra.

■ Sidelights

"'Why did you write about Vietnam/Indonesia?' This is the most frequently asked question whenever I appear at book-signings," Alice M. Terada told *SATA.* "Let me answer that for those who'd like to ask but, for practical reasons, can't.

"I grew up on the island of Hawaii. My hometown, I believed at the time, received more rain than any other spot in the whole United States except for Seattle and Mt. Waialeale on Kauai. Reading was a rainy-day activity, accessible, acceptable, and encouraged within my home. It meant passage to different cultures around the world, vicarious living in snow, in desert sand, in African savanna, in almost every place but where I lived.

"My chief source of books was the Public Library. Its rules were explicit: the borrower must be at least in grade three; no more than six books could be taken out at a time on one card; two weeks was the maximum borrowing period. All six books I borrowed, read, and returned within a week, except for those days when— you guessed it—it rained. Six books, an open umbrella, and four long blocks to walk proved to be a test of balance and endurance. When I couldn't return my books, I took to reading *The Book of Knowledge* (Grolier) from my bookshelf.

"I discovered folktales. They told me more than any other available source how different people lived, their beliefs, and their practices. People from the tribes of Papua New Guinea to the hamlets of England and the villages of China taught and perpetuated acceptable behavior and values by suggesting standards through stories that leaned heavily on traditions and cultural practices. Their stories and rituals reflected a uniform concern with death and the hereafter. I learned through them that, no matter where they came from or what they looked like, people were concerned about pretty much the same things: creation, death, concept of a higher being, how to live this life.

"In 1986 I sat in a journalism class across the table from a gentleman whose ethnic identity escaped me. When I later learned he was Vietnamese, my curiosity was aroused. Questions which had nagged me in the '70s came back full force. What were these people like? I went to various libraries for information and sources about the people—and their folklore. My new friend expanded my understanding of the Vietnamese folktales we shared. This was the beginning of my first collection, *Under the Starfruit Tree: Folktales from Vietnam.*

"In researching one of the tales, I read that a princess from the country known as Vietnam today married a raja from Java. Again, led by curiosity to the history of Indonesia and folk practices and tales, [plus] a trip to Indonesia, and my second book resulted: *The Magic Crocodile and Other Folktales from Indonesia.*

"The more I wrote, the more I noticed a developing cycle of reading and writing in my work habits. Marked by an indulgence in satisfying a hunger almost physical in urgency, the initial phase was one of absorption. I sat and read to the exclusion of almost every other activity. I read anything I could get my hands on, good and bad—poetry, formulaic romances, mysteries, magazines, and books such as the Bible, Koran, and the translated version of Kojiki.

"After a brief period of lolling in gluttony, I start to weed out the badly written and concentrate on the more unusual. One day, amidst this orgy of reading, I am satiated. The books I had been devouring are quickly reduced to three: fiction, nonfiction, and a poetry book. I am ready to write, and these three books sustain me through the writing phase.

"I have purposely spent much time retelling folktales because they introduce and explain a nation of people different from the reader and yet similar in so many other ways. I expect to continue retelling folktales, but in between these tales, I have returned to writing contemporary fiction."

■ For More Information See

PERIODICALS

Booklist, December 15, 1989, p. 836.
Book Report, May, 1991, p. 58.
Parabola, August, 1995, p. 118.
Publishers Weekly, November 24, 1989, p. 71.
School Library Journal, December, 1994, p. 129.
West Coast Review Bulletin, April, 1990, p. 30.

*   *   *

THOMAS, Jane Resh 1936-

■ Personal

Born August 15, 1936, in Kalamazoo, MI; daughter of Reed Beneval (a salesman) and Thelma (a teacher; maiden name, Scott) Resh; married Richard Thomas (a copywriter), November 13, 1961; children: Jason. *Education:* Bronson School of Nursing, R.N., 1957; attended Michigan State University, 1959-60; University of Minnesota, B.A. (summa cum laude), 1967, M.A., 1971.

■ Addresses

Home—3121 44th Ave. S., Minneapolis, MN 55406.

■ Career

Worked as registered nurse, 1957-60; University of Minnesota at Minneapolis, instructor in English composition, 1967-80; freelance writer, 1972—; writing instructor for Split Rock Arts Program, The Loft, and private workshops, 1974—; freelance editor of children's books, 1988-95; lecturer throughout the country to children, teachers, and librarians about reading and writing children's literature. *Member:* Phi Beta Kappa.

■ Awards, Honors

Parent's Choice Award for fiction, for *Courage at Indian Deep;* American Booksellers Pick of the Lists citations, for *Wheels* and *Fox in a Trap;* Joan Fassler Award, 1989, American Library Association Notable Book citation, and Best of the Best for Children citation, all for *Saying Good-bye to Grandma;* British Children's Book Award Runner-up, for *The Princess in the Pigpen;*

JANE RESH THOMAS

Consortium of Latin American Studies Programs' America's Children's and Young Adult Book Award—Commended List, 1994, for *Lights on the River.*

■ Writings

JUVENILE FICTION

Elizabeth Catches a Fish, illustrated by Joseph Duffy, Seabury, 1977.

The Comeback Dog, illustrated by Troy Howell, Clarion, 1981.

Courage at Indian Deep, Clarion, 1984.

Wheels, illustrated by Emily McCully, Clarion, 1986.

Fox in a Trap, illustrated by Troy Howell, Clarion, 1987.

Saying Good-bye to Grandma, illustrated by Marcia Sewall, Clarion, 1988.

The Princess in the Pigpen, Clarion, 1989.

Lights on the River, illustrated by Michael Dooling, Hyperion, 1994.

Daddy Doesn't Have to Be a Giant Anymore, illustrated by Marcia Sewall, Clarion, 1996.

Scaredy Dog (chapter book), illustrated by Marilyn Mets, Hyperion, 1996.

Behind the Mask: The Life of Elizabeth I, Clarion, 1996, also published as *Elizabeth the Great: Queen of the Golden Age,* Houghton Mifflin, 1996.

OTHER

Book critic for the *Minneapolis Star Tribune* and the Cleveland *Plain Dealer,* 1972—. Contributor of articles and reviews to periodicals, including *Horn Book* and *New York Times Book Review.*

■ Work in Progress

Potluck Supper Fourth of July, illustrated by Raul Colon, for Hyperion; *Maggie's Eyes,* a picture book, for Hyperion; *Hunting for Bears,* a picture book, for Scholastic; *The Snoop,* a chapter book, for Kingfisher.

■ Sidelights

The children's books of Jane Resh Thomas are touched by the author's own life experiences, attitudes, and emotions. Both a dog from Thomas's childhood and one from her son's went into the making of *The Comeback Dog.* The Mexican migrant farm workers in *Lights on the River* were a familiar sight during Thomas's childhood on a Michigan farm. And though she did not realize it at the time, Thomas was writing about herself and her own difficult experiences when she told the story of Elizabeth in *The Princess in the Pigpen.* "The most surprising thing I have learned about writing fiction is the extent and subtlety of its connections to an author's own life," Thomas told *SATA.* "Fiction writers 'make up' their stories, but not out of thin air. Even Rumpelstiltskin couldn't make something out of nothing, but spun gold from the common straw at his feet. And it is the common straw of everyday experience from which fiction writers spin their stories—the people and places they've known, their own unique perspectives and attitudes."

The majority of Thomas's childhood was spent in Kalamazoo, Michigan, on her grandparent's peach orchard and tree nursery farm near Lake Michigan, and at a cottage on Big Cedar Lake. Nature and exploring were common activities for Thomas, as was fishing with her father, who taught her the names of many of the natural elements around them. "When we were at home in Kalamazoo, my favorite place was the Washington Square Library, with its stone entryway, its fireplace and leaded windows, and what seemed like miles of books," Thomas once described for *SATA.* And busy as Thomas's mother was raising four children with only financial support from her husband, she always found time to read to them. "I learned to love literature at her side," continued Thomas. "My family were uncommunicative people, and I relied on books, as I did on nature, not only to entertain but to sustain myself."

Desiring to be a writer since the age of seven, Thomas was at first discouraged by the responses of adults to the things she wrote. Overcoming this, she has since written a number of children's books depicting sensitively drawn characters and accurately describing their experiences and emotions. The first, *Elizabeth Catches a Fish,* describes the seven-year-old title character's birthday present of a fishing rod and equipment as well as the excitement leading up to her first fishing trip with her father. Barbara Karlin stated in *New York Times Book Review* that *Elizabeth Catches a Fish* is written "with vivid clarity and precision."

This same accuracy is found in the 1981 story *The Comeback Dog,* in which nine-year-old Daniel must deal with the recent death of his beloved dog Captain. Finding another dog near death at the side of the road, Daniel reluctantly brings it home and nurses it back to health. But Lady does not respond to his affections as Captain did, and when Daniel lets her off her leash she runs away. Reappearing a few weeks later and once again in need of Daniel's help, Lady slowly gains back her master's affections. A *Kirkus Reviews* contributor asserted that "once again ... Thomas invests a young-ish child ... with real and satisfying skills, and writes a graceful, evocative prose." And Celia H. Morris concluded in *Horn Book* that *The Comeback Dog* is an "exceptionally gentle, poignant story."

Fox in a Trap, the sequel to *The Comeback Dog,* finds Daniel a bit older and more interested in the exciting life of his Uncle Pete, a sportsman and writer, than what he perceives to be his family's boring life on their farm. Upset that his father thinks he will dislike trapping small game, Daniel convinces his parents to allow Uncle Pete to teach him the trade and help set up a trapline. In the end, though, Daniel finds himself unable to kill the animals he catches and decides he is actually much more like his parents than he thought. In *School Library Journal,* Charlene J. Lenzen praised "Thomas's sound knowledge of farm life" and "her emotionally charged writing style." A *Booklist* reviewer similarly related that in *Fox in a Trap* Thomas "carefully manipulates the characters' changing emotions with believability."

Sensitivity and believable emotions merge again to create Thomas's 1988 realistic story *Saying Good-bye to Grandma.* Told through the eyes of seven-year-old Suzie, the book begins with a two-day journey to Grandpa's lakeside home for her grandmother's funeral. Once there, both the joys of being together as a family and the sorrows of the occasion intermingle as Suzie plays with her cousins and listens to her grandpa crying in the night. At first afraid that the funeral will take her grandma away forever, Suzie is comforted by her parents and able to participate in the ritual of saying good-bye. In the end she leaves her grandpa's house looking forward to visiting next summer and learning to fish and cook.

"The purpose of this slim, quiet picture book is to prepare young children for the experience of a close relative's funeral," as Anne Tyler described it in the *New York Times Book Review.* Pointing out the effec-tiveness of using Suzie as the narrator, Tyler added: "The tone is understated—not so much grief-stricken as stunned and uncertain, which seems exactly the emotion you'd expect from a child in these circumstances." Patricia Pearl similarly praised the first-person narra-tive in *School Library Journal,* stating that this book was an "exceptionally sensible and sensitive examination of a young girl's feelings about the death and funeral of her grandmother."

A departure from the realistic themes of her other books, Thomas's *The Princess in the Pigpen* introduces elements of fantasy. The daughter of a duke in the year 1600, nine-year-old Elizabeth and her mother are sick in bed when a sliver of sunlight in the young girl's room magically transports her ahead in time to a Black Hawk, Iowa, farm in 1988. Taken in by the McCormick family, Elizabeth sees a doctor for her fever and is cured, all the while struggling to understand the new world in which she finds herself. Only the McCormicks' daughter Anne believes Elizabeth's story of her true identity, and in the end helps her return to her mother with a cure for her illness. "The book's real drama lies in the many revelations Elizabeth finds in what we would call ordinary American society," remarked Patricia T. O'Conner in the *New York Times Book Review.* "Through her we learn that the things we take for granted—from female doctors to refrigerated food—are miracles indeed." A *Kirkus Reviews* contributor asserted that "Thomas develops her story with logic and gentle, compassionate humor," concluding that *The Princess in the Pigpen* is "an excellent venture into new territory by a fine author."

Back on more familiar ground, Thomas describes the life of a Mexican migrant farm worker family in *Lights on the River.* As the family travels from job to job in the old station wagon that is their home, young Teresa keeps memories of her real home in Mexico alive in her mind at all times. She longs for the happiness of her last Christmas dinner there, as well as the custom of floating

Thomas's 1987 story *Fox in a Trap* tells of Daniel's moral dilemma when Uncle Pete takes him trapping and he finds a fox's severed paw. (Illustration by Troy Howell.)

Seven-year-old Suzie's curiosity and fears are assuaged when she attends her first funeral in Thomas's *Saying Good-bye to Grandma*. (Illustration by Marcia Sewall.)

candles down the river past other villages. As her family's situation continues to worsen, it is just such a candle given to Teresa by her grandmother that provides the memories of home needed to help the family through their rough times. "There's nothing heroic or sentimental about this poverty," stated Hazel Rochman in *Booklist*. Christine Heppermann, writing in *Five Owls*, also praised the realism of *Lights on the River*, maintaining: "Expressed in terms children will understand, this just indictment of the deplorable conditions migrant workers in the U.S. endure also eloquently attests to the importance of family and connectedness."

Connections to her own family as well as all the other events that have shaped her life are the sparks that generate Thomas's stories and make them so realistic. "I have always recommended that the adult writers I teach write what haunts them, drawing on the satisfactions and troubles that they remember in their hearts and bellies," she continued for *SATA*. "To do so is a dangerous thing, however, for writers who explore the unlit closets of their minds are always finding out things they didn't want to know."

■ Works Cited

Review of *The Comeback Dog, Kirkus Reviews,* June 15, 1981, p. 741.

Review of *Fox in a Trap, Booklist,* April 1, 1987, p. 1210.

Heppermann, Christine, review of *Lights on the River, Five Owls,* December, 1994, pp. 37-38.

Karlin, Barbara, review of *Elizabeth Catches a Fish, New York Times Book Review,* May 1, 1977, p. 47.

Lenzen, Charlene J., review of *Fox in a Trap, School Library Journal,* June-July, 1987, p. 102.

Morris, Celia H., review of *The Comeback Dog, Horn Book,* August, 1981, p. 427.

O'Conner, Patricia T., review of *The Princess in the Pigpen, New York Times Book Review,* April 22, 1990, p. 39.

Pearl, Patricia, review of *Saying Good-bye to Grandma, School Library Journal,* February, 1989, p. 76.

Review of *The Princess in the Pigpen, Kirkus Reviews,* October 15, 1989, p. 1537.

Rochman, Hazel, review of *Lights on the River, Booklist,* August, 1994, p. 2053.

Tyler, Anne, "In the Midst of Life," *New York Times Book Review,* November 13, 1988, p. 48.

■ For More Information See

PERIODICALS

Booklist, November 1, 1986, p. 415.

Bulletin of the Center for Children's Books, November, 1977, p. 55; April 1, 1987, p. 1210; October, 1989, pp. 46-47.

Horn Book, August, 1977, p. 436.

Kirkus Reviews, April 15, 1987, p. 645; August 1, 1988, p. 1158; September 15, 1994, p. 1284.

New York Times Book Review, May 10, 1981, pp. 38-39.

Publishers Weekly, October 31, 1986, pp. 65-66; July 1, 1996, p. 60.

School Library Journal, December, 1986, p. 96.*

*   *   *

THOMASMA, Kenneth R. 1930-

■ Personal

Born September 2, 1930, in Grand Rapids, MI; son of Peter (a factory worker) and Freda (a homemaker; maiden name, Jones) Thomasma; married Barbara Veurink (a teacher), June 16, 1955; children: Daniel. *Education:* Calvin College, A.B., 1953; University of Michigan, M.A., 1958. *Politics:* Independent. *Religion:* Protestant.

■ Addresses

Home—1170 Grand View, Jackson, WY 83001. *Office*—P.O. Box 2863, Jackson, WY 83001.

KENNETH R. THOMASMA

■ **Career**

Grand Rapids Public Schools, Grand Rapids, MI, teacher administrator, 1953-77; Teton County Public Schools, Jackson, WY, teacher, 1977-87. *Military service:* U.S. Navy, 1950-51, attained rank of seaman.

■ **Writings**

Naya Nuki: Girl Who Ran, illustrated by Eunice Hundley, Baker Book House, 1983, reprinted as *Naya Nuki: Shoshoni Girl Who Ran* ("American Indian Children" series), 1992.

Soun Tetoken: Nez Perce Boy, illustrated by Eunice Hundley, Baker Book House, 1984, reprinted as *Soun Tetoken: Nez Perce Boy Tames a Stallion* ("American Indian Children" series), 1989.

Om-kas-toe of the Blackfeet, illustrated by Cathlene Poindexter and Jack Brouwer, Baker Book House, 1986, reprinted as *Om-kas-toe: Blackfeet Twin Captures an Elkdog* ("American Indian Children" series), 1992.

Kunu: Escape on the Missouri, illustrated by Craig Fleuter, Grandview Publishing, 1989, reprinted as *Kunu: Winnebago Boy Escapes,* ("American Indian Children" series), Baker Book House, 1992.

Pathki Nana: Kooentai Girl, illustrated by Jack Brouwer, Grandview Publishing, 1991, reprinted as *Pathki Nana: Kooentai Girl Solves a Mystery,* Baker Book House, 1991.

Moho Wat: A Sheepeater Boy Attempts a Rescue ("Amazing Indian Children" series), illustrated by Jack Brouwer, Baker Book House, 1994.

Amee-nah: Zuni Boy Runs the Race of His Life, illustrated by Jack Brouwer, Baker Book House, 1995.

■ **Work in Progress**

Research on the truth about Sacagawea of the Lewis and Clark Expedition.

■ **Sidelights**

"Besides writing books for children, I have worked for eight years trying to help children and teachers become better at the skill of writing," Kenneth R. Thomasma told *SATA.* "I have traveled coast to coast doing storytelling and in-depth writing workshops for one hundred students per day. I have developed the most effective way to teach spelling that can be used by teachers. Inventive spelling is the enemy. My method of spelling instruction does not cost a cent. The high-impact writing workshops teach writing, spelling, reading, and thinking. They really produce results."

*   *   *

TICHNOR, Richard 1959-

■ **Personal**

Born May 26, 1959, in Concord, MA; son of Robert and Betsy (Lentz) Tichnor. *Education:* University of New Mexico, B.A., 1983; attended Boston Architectural Center, 1984-87, American College in Paris, 1986, and Master of Architecture program at University of California at Berkeley, 1988-90.

■ **Addresses**

Home—P.O. Box 590, Tahoe City, CA 96145.

■ **Career**

Architect, writer, and illustrator.

■ **Writings**

(With Jenny Smith; and illustrator) *A Spark in the Dark* (for children), Dawn Publications, 1994.

■ **Adaptations**

Michael Pinder (from the band *Moody Blues*) included *A Spark in the Dark* in his recording *A Planet with One Mind—Stories from around the World for the Child within Us All* (compact disc and audio cassette), which is a collection of creation myths with narration and music by Pinder and illustrations by Tichnor, One Step Records, 1995. This work won the Benjamin Franklin Award silver medal for children's audio, 1996.

■ Work in Progress

Two books to join with *A Spark in the Dark* in a picture-book trilogy: *The Little Blue Ball,* a work "inspired by the second half of many creation stories," in which "the point of view shifts away from the source and the unfolding of creation" to that which has been created; and *Tumble and Play,* a book "based on the mythic motif of the 'hero's journey,'" in which "the point of view is that of the individual looking within." All three stories in the trilogy will be included in Michael Pinder's series of recordings, *A Planet with One Mind, A People with One Heart,* and *An Earth with One Spirit.*

■ Sidelights

For information on Tichnor's work, see entry on Jenny Smith in this volume.

* * *

TRAVERS, P(amela) L(yndon) 1899-1996

OBITUARY NOTICE—See index for *SATA* sketch: Born Helen Lyndon Goff, August 9, 1899; died April 23, 1996, in London. Shakespearean actress, journalist, poet, and author. The creator of the immensely popular *Mary Poppins* series, Travers began writing in her native Australia at age seven. In the 1920s, while still in her teens, she toured with a Shakespearean company, but soon took a job as a journalist, moved to England, and began writing poetry for the *Irish Statesman* under the mentoring of poets George Russell (known as A. E.) and William Butler Yeats. Always enthralled by fantasy, Travers felt an affinity for children, and once explained to a journalist, quoted in *Something About the Author,* that she wrote books featuring young people who "know more than grown-ups do." Her 1934 fiction, *Mary Poppins,* about a magical, no-nonsense governess, was published to overwhelming critical and popular success, and became the basis for an Academy Award winning film by Walt Disney in 1964. Travers penned several other books in the Mary Poppins series, including *Mary Poppins Comes Back, Mary Poppins Opens the Door, Mary Poppins in the Park, Mary Poppins A to Z, Mary Poppins in Cherry Tree Lane,* and 1989's *Mary Poppins and the House Next Door.* A recognized scholar of folktales, mythology, fairy tales, and legends, Travers was a long-time contributor to *Parabola,* a magazine specializing in world mythology. She published several books on the subject, both fiction and non-fiction. Among her notable books in this genre are: *In Search of the Hero: The Continuing Relevance of Myth and Fairy Tale,* based on a 1970 college lecture; *Friend Monkey,* a novel based on Hindu mythology; *Two Pairs of Shoes,* a collection of folktales; and 1989's *What the Bee Knows: Reflections on Myth, Symbol, and Story,* a collection of essays and stories which some reviewers claim is as close to an autobiography as Travers ever wrote.

OBITUARIES AND OTHER SOURCES:

BOOKS

Twentieth-Century Children's Writers, 4th edition, St. James Press, 1995.

PERIODICALS

Chicago Tribune, April 25, 1996, p. 11.
Horn Book, September-October, 1996, pp. 640-44.
Los Angeles Times, April 25, 1996, p. A20.
New York Times, April 25, 1996, p. B14.
Times (London), April 24, 1996, p. 21.

* * *

TYLER, Anne 1941-

■ Personal

Born October 25, 1941, in Minneapolis, MN; daughter of Lloyd Parry (a chemist) and Phyllis (a social worker; maiden name, Mahon) Tyler; married Taghi Mohammed Modarressi (a psychiatrist and writer), May 3, 1963; children: Tezh, Mitra (daughters). *Education:* Duke University, B.A., 1961; graduate study at Columbia University, 1961-62. *Religion:* Quaker.

■ Addresses

Home—222 Tunbridge Rd., Baltimore, MD 21212. *Agent*—Timothy Seldes, Russell & Volkening, 50 West 29th St. #7-E, New York, NY 10001.

■ Career

Writer. Duke University Library, Durham, NC, Russian bibliographer, 1962-63; McGill University Law Library, Montreal, Quebec, Canada, assistant to the librarian, 1964-65. *Member:* PEN, American Academy and Institute of Arts and Letters, Authors Guild, Phi Beta Kappa.

■ Awards, Honors

Mademoiselle award for writing, 1966; Award for Literature, American Academy and Institute of Arts and Letters, 1977; National Book Critics Circle fiction award nomination, 1980, Janet Heidinger Kafka prize, 1981, and American Book Award nomination in paperback fiction, 1982, all for *Morgan's Passing;* National Book Critics Circle fiction award nomination, 1982, and American Book Award nomination in fiction, PEN/ Faulkner Award for fiction, and Pulitzer Prize nomination for fiction, all 1983, all for *Dinner at the Homesick Restaurant;* National Book Critics Circle Award for fiction and Pulitzer Prize nomination for fiction, both 1985, both for *The Accidental Tourist;* Pulitzer Prize for fiction, and National Book Award nomination for fiction, both 1989, both for *Breathing Lessons.*

ANNE TYLER

■ Writings

FOR CHILDREN

Tumble Tower, illustrated by daughter, Mitra Modarressi, Orchard Books, 1993.

ADULT NOVELS

If Morning Ever Comes, Knopf, 1964.
The Tin Can Tree, Knopf, 1965.
A Slipping-Down Life, Knopf, 1970.
The Clock Winder, Knopf, 1972.
Celestial Navigation, Knopf, 1974.
Searching for Caleb, Knopf, 1976.
Earthly Possessions, Knopf, 1977.
Morgan's Passing, Knopf, 1980.
Dinner at the Homesick Restaurant, Knopf, 1982.
The Accidental Tourist, Knopf, 1985.
Breathing Lessons, Knopf, 1988.
Saint Maybe, Knopf, 1991.
Ladder of Years, Knopf, 1995.

OTHER

(Editor with Shannon Ravenel, and author of introduction) *Best American Short Stories 1983,* Houghton, 1983.
(Editor with Shannon Ravenel) *Best of a Decade: From Ten Years of New Stories from the South,* Algonquin Books, 1996.

Contributor of short stories to *Saturday Evening Post, New Yorker, Seventeen, Critic, Antioch Review,* and *Southern Review.* Contributor of reviews to *New York Times Book Review.*

■ Adaptations

The Accidental Tourist, starring Kathleen Turner and William Hurt, was released by Warner Brothers in 1988; *Breathing Lessons* was released as a television film by CBS-TV in 1994, starring James Garner and Joanne Woodward; several of Tyler's books, including *The Clock Winder, Morgan's Passing, The Accidental Tourist, Breathing Lessons,* and *Saint Maybe,* are available on audio tape.

■ Sidelights

During a period of more than thirty years, Anne Tyler's body of work has garnered increased respect and recognition from critics. *Dinner at the Homesick Restaurant, Breathing Lessons,* and *The Accidental Tourist* have all received a number of literary awards, and the latter book was made into a critically-acclaimed film. Several of her books have been best-sellers, finding a wide audience that includes young adults. (*A Slipping-Down Life,* for instance, was marketed as a young adult novel when it first appeared in 1970; the novel focuses on a teenager struggling with her identity who carves the name of a rock star onto her forehead.) Tyler, who has also penned a picture book for children, sees her work as "populating a town," as she told Marguerite Michaels in an interview for the *New York Times Book Review.* "Pretty soon it's going to be just full of lots of people I've made up. None of the people I write about are people I know. That would be no fun. And it would be very boring to write about me. Even if I led an exciting life, why live it again on paper?"

Born in Minnesota, Tyler lived with her family in various Quaker communes throughout the Midwest and South before they settled in the mountains of North Carolina for five years. "There was nothing very unusual about my family life," the author told Sarah English in *Dictionary of Literary Biography Yearbook,* "but I did spend much of my older childhood and adolescence as a semi-outsider—a Northerner, commune-reared, looking wistfully at large Southern families around me." She attended high school in Raleigh and at sixteen entered Duke University, where she fell under the influence of Reynolds Price, then a promising young novelist who had attended her high school. It was Price who encouraged the young Russian major to pursue her writing, and she did—but it remained a secondary pursuit until 1967, the year she and her husband settled in Baltimore.

Most of Tyler's novels have used the Baltimore area for their settings, but they are not specifically Southern novels, according to critics such as Katha Pollitt. "They are Southern in their sure sense of family and place," the critic writes in the *New York Times Book Review,* "but [they] lack the taste for violence and the Gothic that often characterizes self-consciously Southern litera-

In Tyler's first book for children, **Princess Molly the Messy** proves to her ultra-tidy royal family that her disorganized lifestyle has its advantages. (From *Tumble Tower*, illustrated by Mitra Modarressi.)

ture.... The current school of feminist-influenced novels seems to have passed her by completely: her women are strong, often stronger than the men in their lives, but solidly grounded in traditional roles." These characters are the sort of people that one might meet in everyday life. They grapple with recognizable issues of contemporary life such as childhood, marriage, parenthood, career, and religion. Critic Caren J. Town notes in *Dictionary of Literary Biography* that "Tyler's popularity rests in part on the apparent ordinariness of her subjects: the power of family, the struggle for personal growth, the accumulation of possessions, and the influence of religion. Yet this ordinariness is not simplicity: she treats each common situation with wry humor and fills each plot with eccentric characters and unconventional developments."

One of her most popular works, *The Accidental Tourist,* for instance, contains characters whose quirks distinguish their otherwise ordinary and passive lives. The novel examines the life of Macon Leary, a travel writer who puts together guidebooks for reluctant travelers who must do so for business or personal reasons. Macon is a cautious, methodical sort of man who separated from his wife after their twelve-year-old son was murdered. He retreats to live with his sister and two brothers, who also view interaction with the outside world with reluctance. Only after becoming involved with Muriel, an animated, vivacious animal trainer, does Macon begin to emerge from his "accidental tourist cocoon," as Tracy Chevalier remarks in *Contemporary Novelists,* "and finally he has to choose between old ways and new." Rejuvenated by the passion and exuberance that Muriel injects into his life, Macon charts a new course for himself. The novel received the National Book Critics Circle Award for fiction in 1985, and in 1988 a film version was released which received a number of Oscar nominations.

Although she is best known as a novelist, Tyler has also branched out into children's books with *Tumble Tower,* which features illustrations by her daughter, Mitra Modarressi. This 1993 picture book is "a kid-pleasing story about Princess Molly the Messy and her royal family of neatnicks," according to *Christian Science Monitor* contributor Karen Williams. Unlike her obsessed parents and siblings, including Prince Thomas the Tidy, Molly lives a comfortably unkempt life in her messy tower room. When a flood forces her family upstairs, they discover enough spare clothes, leftover food, and books to occupy the time until the water recedes. "The moral of Tyler's tale," declares Suzanne Curley in the *Los Angeles Times Book Review,* "is that a princess unfazed by half-eaten candy bars left under her chair cushions, kittens nesting among fluffy slippers on the closet floor or a bed 'all lumpy and knobby with half-finished books' probably has her priorities straight, and may have much to teach about the way clutter often goes hand-in-hand with coziness." A *Kirkus Reviews* critic similarly praises Tyler's "gently subversive fable" for presenting "a child's-eye view of glorious muss in a witty economical narrative." "The story is humorous, compact, and well paced," Judy Constantinides concludes in *School Library Journal,* adding that "this is a winning first children's book."

Although she has won both popular and critical acclaim, Tyler prefers to remain out of the public eye, foregoing interviews and offers to teach in order to spend time writing and with her family. As she told English, "my main reason for doing little in public is that it's not what I'm good at—but yes, it also protects my working time. As I get older, I've learned to say 'no' more and more—and I get happier and happier."

■ Works Cited

Chevalier, Tracy, "Anne Tyler," *Contemporary Novelists,* 5th edition, St. James Press, 1991, pp. 891-93.

Constantinides, Judy, review of *Tumble Tower, School Library Journal,* September, 1993, pp. 220-21.

Curley, Suzanne, "Clutter and Coziness," *Los Angeles Times Book Review,* September 5, 1993, p. 9.

English, Sarah, "Anne Tyler," *Dictionary of Literary Biography Yearbook: 1982,* Gale, 1982, pp. 187-94.

Michaels, Marguerite, "Anne Tyler, Writer 8:05 to 3:30," *New York Times Book Review,* May 8, 1977, pp. 42-43.

Pollitt, Katha, review of *Searching for Caleb, New York Times Book Review,* January 18, 1976, p. 22.

Town, Caren J., "Anne Tyler," *Dictionary of Literary Biography,* Volume 143: *American Novelists Since World War II, Third Series,* Gale, 1994, pp. 232-49.

Review of *Tumble Tower, Kirkus Reviews,* July 15, 1993, p. 943.

Williams, Karen, review of *Tumble Tower, Christian Science Monitor,* December 17, 1993, p. 12.

■ For More Information See

BOOKS

Authors and Artists for Young Adults, Volume 18, Gale, 1996.

Bestsellers 89, Issue 1, Gale, 1989.

Contemporary Literary Criticism, Gale, Volume 7, 1977, Volume 11, 1979, Volume 18, 1981, Volume 28, 1984, Volume 44, 1987.

Croft, Robert William, *Anne Tyler: A Bio-bibliography,* Greenwood Press, 1995.

Dictionary of Literary Biography, Gale, Volume 6: *American Novelists since World War II, Second Series,* 1980.

Evans, Elizabeth, *Anne Tyler,* Twayne, 1993.

Petry, Alice Hall, *Understanding Anne Tyler,* University of South Carolina Press, 1990.

Petry, Alice Hall, editor, *Critical Essays on Anne Tyler,* Hall, 1992.

Quiello, Rose, *Breakdowns and Breakthoughts: The Figure of the Hysteric in Contemporary Novels by Women,* Peter Lang, 1993.

Salwak, Dale, editor, *Anne Tyler as Novelist,* University of Iowa Press, 1994.

Stephens, C. Ralph, editor, *The Fiction of Anne Tyler,* University Press of Mississippi, 1990.

Sternburg, Janet, editor, *The Writer on Her Work,* Norton, 1980.

PERIODICALS

Chicago Tribune Book World, March 23, 1980; March 21, 1982; July 20, 1986.

Christian Science Monitor, September 25, 1991, p. 13; May 18, 1995, p. 13.

Commonweal, November 8, 1991, pp. 656-58; June 16, 1995, pp. 21-22.

Detroit News, April 6, 1980; April 18, 1982.

Globe and Mail (Toronto), September 21, 1985; October 8, 1988.

London Review of Books, March 12, 1992, pp. 23-24.

Los Angeles Times, March 30, 1982; September 14, 1983.

Los Angeles Times Book Review, March 30, 1980; September 15, 1985; September 11, 1988; May 7, 1995, p. 3.

Ms., August, 1977.

National Review, June 26, 1995, pp. 59-60.

New Republic, May 13, 1972; May 28, 1977; March 22, 1980.

New Statesman, April 4, 1975; December 5, 1980.

Newsweek, April 5, 1982; September 9, 1985.

New Yorker, March 29, 1976; June 6, 1977; June 23, 1980; April 5, 1982; May 8, 1995, pp. 89-90.

New York Review of Books, April 3, 1980; January 16, 1992, pp. 53-55.

New York Times, May 3, 1977; March 17, 1980; March 22, 1982; September 30, 1983; September 3, 1988; April 27, 1995, p. B2.

New York Times Book Review, November 22, 1964; November 21, 1965; March 15, 1970; May 21, 1972; April 28, 1974; March 14, 1982; September 8, 1985; August 25, 1991, pp. 1, 26; May 7, 1995, p. 12.

Saturday Review, December 26, 1964; November 20, 1965; June 17, 1972; March 6, 1976; September 4, 1976; March 15, 1980.

Time, May 9, 1977; March 17, 1980; April 5, 1982; September 16, 1985.

Times (London), January 12, 1989.

Times Literary Supplement, July 15, 1965; May 23, 1975; December 9, 1977; October 31, 1980; October 29, 1982; October 4, 1985; January 20, 1989.

Tribune Books (Chicago), August 28, 1988.

Washington Post Book World, March 16, 1980; April 4, 1982; September 4, 1988.

V–W

V

See CHEKHOV, Anton (Pavlovich)

*   *   *

WEBER, Ken(neth J.) 1940-

■ Personal

Last name is pronounced Wee-ber; born July 10, 1940, in Neustadt, Ontario, Canada; son of Milton J. (a merchant) and Viola (a homemaker; maiden name, Greib) Weber; married Rita Harcourt, June 26, 1965 (divorced January 1, 1978); married Cecile King (a teacher), December 24, 1979; children: Mary Pat, Michael, Sean, Stephen. *Education:* University of Toronto, B.A., 1963; University of Guelph, M.S., 1975. *Politics:* "Not if I can help it!"

■ Addresses

Home—R.R. #1, Bolton, Ontario, Canada L7E 5R7.
Agent—Stoddart Publications, 34 Lesmill Rd., Toronto, Ontario, Canada M3B 2T6.

■ Career

W. A. Porter High School, Scarborough, Ontario, teacher of special English, 1963-69; University of Toronto, Toronto, Ontario, assistant professor, 1969-75, associate professor of English, 1975-77, professor of special education, 1977-96.

■ Writings

Truth and Fantasy, Methuen, 1970.
Prose of Relevance, two volumes, Methuen, 1971.
(With Allan E. Eagle) *Selling,* McGraw, 1971.
Yes They Can, Methuen, 1974.
Thinklab, Science Research Associates, 1974.
Thinklab II, Science Research Associates, 1976.
Read and Think, two volumes, Methuen, 1977.
Yes They Can! A Practical Guide for Teaching the Adolescent Slow Learner, Methuen, 1978.

KEN WEBER

Insight: A Practical Approach to Language Arts, Books 1 and 2, Methuen, 1980.
The Teacher Is the Key: A Practical Guide for Teachers of Adolescents with Learning Difficulties, Methuen, 1982.
(With Doris Cowan) *Canadians All 4,* Methuen, 1983.
(Editor) *The Globe Modern Dictionary,* Globe, 1984.
(Editor) *The Puffin Canadian Beginner's Dictionary,* Penguin, 1984.

Mental Gymnastics for Adults: Quintessential Quizzes, Puzzles, Mindbenders, and Other Trivia, Methuen, 1984.

(Editor with Alvin Granowsky) *Fearon New School Dictionary,* D.S. Lake Publishers, 1987.

Five Minute Mysteries, Running Press, 1988.

More Five Minute Mysteries, Running Press, 1991.

KIDZ Five Minute Mysteries, Running Press, 1994.

Further Five Minute Mysteries, Running Press, 1994.

Five Minute Trivia: Did the Corinthians Ever Write Back?, Stoddart Publications, 1995.

More KIDZ Five Minute Mysteries, Running Press, 1996.

Even More Five Minute Mysteries, Running Press, 1996.

Five Minutes Mysteries have been translated into fourteen languages.

■ Sidelights

Ken Weber has stated: "The majority of my work has been for education, and most of that for, and on the subject of, 'slower' learners. I call them slower, not slow, since I'm convinced they are capable of more than they, and the rest of the world, believe. Most of the work has been directed to improving their thinking skills, since it is not their supposed lack of intelligence that causes their trouble, but rather their inefficient thinking styles."

*   *   *

WILLIAMS, Garth (Montgomery) 1912-1996

OBITUARY NOTICE—See index for *SATA* sketch: Born April 16, 1912, in New York, NY; died of pneumonia, May 8, 1996, in Marfil, Guanajuato, Mexico. Illustrator and author. Williams gained prominence as the illustrator of nearly one hundred children's books, including E. B. White's *Charlotte's Web.* Williams spent his childhood in England, where he took up sculpting and eventually founded the Luton Art School near London in 1935. During World War II, he served with the British Red Cross Civilian Defense and St. John's Ambulance Organization as an ambulance dispatcher; he was wounded during an air raid in London. After the war, he returned to the United States and began work as an artist for the *New Yorker.* In 1945, he teamed with E. B. White to illustrate White's children's book, *Stuart Little.* From that time on, Williams illustrated many juvenile classics. Damon Runyon's *In Our Time,* Eva LeGallienne's *Flossie and Bossie,* and the *Little House* series by Laura Ingalls Wilder are just a few of his credits. He wrote several books himself, including *The Adventures of Benjamin Pink, The Rabbits' Wedding, The Chicken Book: A Traditional Rhyme,* and *Self Portrait: Garth Williams.*

OBITUARIES AND OTHER SOURCES:

BOOKS

Something about the Author Autobiography Series, Vol. 7, Gale Research, 1989.

PERIODICALS

Los Angeles Times, May 12, 1996, p. A24.
New York Times, May 10, 1996, p. A31.
Times (London), May 13, 1996, p. 21.
Washington Post, May 11, 1996, p. C5.

*   *   *

WILSON, Darryl B(abe) 1939-

■ Personal

Born November 21, 1939, in Fall River Mills, CA; son of Herman Ira Wilson and Laura (Larillard) Carmony; married Donna Lee Griffith (divorced); companion of Danell Rene Garcia (deceased); children: seven sons, including Rodney Williams; (with Griffith) Sonny, Lance Erik, Cory; (with Garcia) Thedoro and Seterro (twins). *Education:* University of California, Davis, B.A., 1992; University of Arizona, M.A., 1994, Ph.D. program, 1995—. *Religion:* "Traditional Iss/Aw'te."

■ Addresses

Home and office—249 East Drachman, Tucson, AZ 85705.

■ Career

Writer. Affiliated with the American Indian Language Development Institute, University of Arizona, Tucson, AZ, 1994—. Lawrence Intermediate School, Yaqui Reservation, Tucson, teacher, 1995. *Military service:*

DARRYL B. WILSON

U.S. Marine Corps, 1957-61, nuclear warhead assembly and field artillery fire direction control.

■ Awards, Honors

Recipient of grants from the Fund for Folk Culture, 1993, and SEVA, 1993; Ford Fellowship, 1994.

■ Writings

Wellen Auf Dem Meer Der Zeit (title means "Waves upon the Ocean of Time"), [France], 1974.
(Coeditor) *Dear Christopher* (a collection of letters addressed to Columbus), Riverside Press, 1993.
The Sound of Rattles and Clappers (six articles), University of Arizona Press, 1993.
Wilma Mankiller, Principal Chief of the Cherokee Nation, Modern Curriculum Press, 1995.
(With Lois Hogle) *Voices from the Earth* (anthology of Native American interviews), University of Texas Press, 1997.

Also author of essays, book reviews, and academic articles published in journals, including *American Indian Quarterly* and *Anthropology and Humanity Journal.* Contributor of short stories to anthologies, including *Earth Song, Sky Spirits,* Doubleday, 1993, *Coming to Light,* Random House, 1994, *Native American Oral Traditions, Collaboration and Interpretation,* Utah State University Press, and Smithsonian's *The California Reader.*

■ Work in Progress

Haya'wa Atwam (title means "Porcupine Valley"); *Yoken'aswi Yusji* (title means "Necklace of Animal Hearts"); *500 Years Dwelling Among Savages.*

■ Sidelights

The son of A'juma'wi and Atsuge'wi Indians, Darryl B. Wilson began his formal education in a one-room school house, yet learned many fundamental lessons elsewhere—in the mountains of Northern California, in the United States Marine Corps, and at the first United Nations Conference on Human Environment. Wilson has shared these lessons in scholarly articles, poems, short stories, and books. Wilson, who is working on a Ph.D. at the University of Arizona, explained to *SATA:* "As a child I traveled, hunted, fished, and walked in nature with my father, Herman Ira Wilson. Those were the moments of my happiness. Daddy worked in a meat packing plant at Fall River Mills, California, and drove an old delivery truck we called 'The Gray Ghost.' And Daddy loved my mother deeply, singing to her often while delivering: 'You are my sunshine, my only sunshine ... so please don't take my sunshine away.'"

"We are original native people, our 'wa'tu' (spiritual umbilical cord) connecting us with the landscape from the moment human life was permitted to exist upon earth. Our homeland is in the northeastern corner of California, from Ako-Yet (Mt. Shasta) and Wai'ko'qu

(Mt. Lassen) east to Watak'josi (the Warner Mountains stretching between California and Oregon), a land area of 3,386,110 acres that we, as a nation, have been struggling to regain from the U.S. government for over one hundred years.

"One day when I just finished the first grade, Daddy was laid off from work, and we had to move onto my grandmother's allotment close to Lake Britton near Jema'wehleo' Tiwiji (Burney Falls). That summer Daddy and I went to 'the old home place' and fixed it up for the rest of the family—my mom, and my four sisters and four brothers.

"Life was exciting then. In beauty and solitude we hunted, fished, and planted a garden while fixing up the little house, making it into a home. Mom stayed over the mountains in the Fall River Valley with the other kids until the place was livable. I did not learn much in school; instead, I learned from nature and from Daddy.

"Hunting and fishing became a major part of my life, and at that time I knew I was going to grow up to be the best hunter and fisherman in the whole world—never working for somebody else, never getting laid off. Finally, we were all together as a family—we children going back to school and learning as best we could."

Then, a "spirit-shattering event" occurred—Wilson's mother and baby brother were killed when a lumber truck smashed into the family's truck. Wilson continued, "Soon Daddy drank wine and was out of control of both his and our lives. The state took us away from him and placed us in foster homes, separating the boys from the girls. They were usually white Anglo-Saxon Protestant homes. We were compelled to go to church, to Sunday school, to church camp, and to Wednesday night fellowship. My sisters became strangers."

Wilson, troubled by the life he was forced to live, refused to conform, and felt that he was "nil'ladu'wi (wandering and wondering)." When he entered high school, he fared poorly and received many failing grades. Yet two people helped him transform his life through writing. After his first year of high school, Wilson spent the summer helping at a boys' camp. His employer, Mr. Lowrey, encouraged him to finish a long-overdue assignment over the summer.

When school resumed the following fall, Wilson's English teacher, Mr. Grossen, accepted the resulting paper about his mother's death. After reading it, Mr. Grossen surprised Wilson by telling him: "There is a story in here. It is difficult for me to follow because of the mistakes ... but ... there are a lot of people who would like to know what you are struggling to say." Along with this encouragement, Mr. Grossen gave Wilson a dictionary and grammar book to study for his career. "My career!" related Wilson. "Nobody ever told me that I was going to have a career.... I studied harder and with more conviction."

Throughout his life, because or in spite of its many adventures and tragedies—including the death of Danell Rene Garcia, the mother of his twin sons, Seterro and Thedoro, who was also killed in an automobile accident—Wilson has insisted on educating himself. He eventually received his high school diploma, going on to earn a bachelor's degree from the University of California, Davis, and a master's degree from the University of Arizona. "Somehow it seems important that I accomplish a Ph.D.," he continued. "And the thing that keeps urging me along this precipitous academic trail is the thought of my father. He always wanted an artist in the family. He said he wanted 'a good drawer.' I cannot draw pictures with a brush or pencil and pen, so I attempt to create pictures with words.

"Looking back there are mountains that I have climbed and chasms that I have spanned, alone. Looking forward there is the endless horizon yet to be challenged. Daddy might be proud of some of my life, some of my academic achievements, and the manner in which I have walked into life certain that the outcome would be favorable. He would, I think, forgive some of my weaknesses, and certainly understand my wounding—the spirit-shattering, emotion-deflating, thought-silencing effect of having love, then losing it in a single moment in eternal tragedy.

"When I am particularly lonely, I go to the mountains and sit under the blanket of silence listening to the messages that move upon the wind. Often I hear Mom and Dad talking and laughing. It is so good. My spirit searches for them in the shade of the forest and just beyond the rocks and the thicket in the sunshine. Early in the morning their foot prints in the dew lead me to the sunrise, then cease with the warmth. Somehow I gather myself together, take a deep breath, look all around, then begin another day of challenges."

* * *

WOOLMAN, Steven 1969-

■ Personal

Born August 31, 1969, in Adelaide, South Australia; son of Dean (an aeroplane detailer) and Judith (a homemaker; maiden name, Robertson) Woolman. *Education:* University of South Australia, Bachelor of Graphic Design, 1990. *Politics:* None. *Religion:* None.

■ Career

ERA Publications, Adelaide, South Australia, production staff member, 1990—.

■ Awards, Honors

Picture Book of the Year citation, 1995, for *The Watertower,* and Notable Book selections, 1995, for *Peter and the Polar Bear,* and 1996, for *The Lighthouse,* all from the Australian Children's Book Council.

STEVEN WOOLMAN

■ Illustrator

PUBLISHED BY ERA PUBLICATIONS

Janeen Brian and Gwen Pascoe, *There Was a Big Fish,* 1992.
Rodney Martin, *Wise and Wacky Works by Anonymous,* 1993.
Kath Lock and Francis Kelly, *Kuan Yin,* 1994.
Elizabeth Best, *Peter and the Polar Bear,* 1994.
Gary Crew, *The Watertower,* 1994.
Dyan Blacklock, *The Lighthouse,* 1995.
Gary Crew, *Caleb,* 1996.
Tagged, 1997.

■ Sidelights

"I've always been interested in the macabre and been attracted to tales of horror and the supernatural," illustrator Steven Woolman told *SATA.* "My teen years were filled with images from horror and black and white B-grade science fiction movies, TV shows and comics, and this has had a lasting influence on my work and the way I visualize stories. Looking back, I think the attraction to horror was not so much the thrill of being scared, but more the visual style with which these stories were told. Films such as *The Shining* and *Invasion of the Body Snatchers* (even schlock-horror splatter movies like *Evil Dead*) excited me through their use of closeups and strange angles, weird lighting, and cutaways. I find now when I begin illustrating manuscripts that my first step is to play out the action in my mind as though it were a movie, and the cinematic influence usually remains in the finished product. *The Watertower* was my first macabre book, and since it was aimed at an older audience I felt licensed to try a more sophisticated visual style and design. With its surreal photorealism, black borders, and wide-screen presentation, the book is very much a homage to those movies I watched in my teens. *Caleb,* the follow-up, also uses some of the same devices, with its unnatural viewpoints and manipulation of shadow and light.

"This is not to say all my work is horror-based and dark. I am after all a children's book illustrator and a large body of my work is humorous in nature and aimed at a younger age group. Books such as *Peter and the Polar Bear* and *The Lighthouse* are both complete diversions from my books for older readers, and I enjoyed the challenge of creating them just as much. In the future I hope to illustrate my own stories and continue developing my skills in different media."

Z

GORDON ZIMA

ZIMA, Gordon 1920-

■ Personal

Born June 20, 1920, in Mason City, IA; son of Albert G. (a metallurgist) and Agnes E. (a homemaker) Zima; married Phyllis M. Zima (a homemaker), July 10, 1942; children: Marguerite, Antonia, Paula. *Education:* Stanford University, B.A., 1942; California Institute of Technology, M.S., 1952, Ph.D., 1956. *Politics:* "Middle

of roader." *Religion:* Protestant. *Hobbies and other interests:* Painting, photography, fly fishing, archery.

■ Addresses

Home—2256 Humboldt St., Los Osos, CA 93402.

■ Career

Has worked primarily in defense laboratories in California and Washington state as a materials specialist for advanced power-plant systems, including rockets and underwater missiles, and nuclear power plants and weapons. *Military service:* U.S. Air Force, 1942-45, Western Pacific Theater; attained rank of first lieutenant. *Member:* Phi Lambda Upsilon (honorary chemical society), Sigma Xi (honorary research society).

■ Writings

Sun Birds and Evergreens: The Nuk-Chuk Stories, illustrated by daughter, Paula J. Zima, Winston-Derek, 1995.

■ Work in Progress

Adult novels: *Partly Extracurricular, The Ivan Spruce,* and *They Called Him ... HANNIBAL,* an historical adult novel about Carthaginian enigmas.

■ Sidelights

Gordon Zima told *SATA:* "Life in an earlier Southern California, and undergraduate work at Stanford, are good memories. Following World War II service, I blundered into an engineering situation at the Jet Propulsion Laboratory in Pasadena, where I picked up the impetus to enter the Ph.D. meat-grinder at Cal Tech.

"Following a career as a research engineer, largely in defense laboratories, I hope that non-technical writing will continue to look like a good energy outlet.

"In the latter respect, I have hopes for *Sun Birds and Evergreens,* a novel about the adventures of young Indians in the Pacific Northwest that I've posed between adult-young adult readers and a younger complement of listeners and sometime readers. The adult novel entries in progress include *Partly Extracurricular,* a fiction of an engineer's life; *The Ivan Spruce,* a story about fascinations of the *perestroika* that reach from the Yellowstone to below the Caucasus; and a historical novel about Hannibal."

* * *

ZUBROWSKI, Bernard 1939-
(Bernie Zubrowski)

■ Personal

Born February 22, 1939, in Baltimore, MD; son of Anthony and Catherine Zubrowski. *Education:* Loyola College, Baltimore, MD, B.S., 1962; Boston College, M.S.T., 1967. *Hobbies and other interests:* Sculpture.

■ Addresses

Home—48 Warren St., Littleton, MA 04160. *Office*—Education Development Center, 55 Chapel St., Newton, MA 02158.

■ Career

U.S. Peace Corps, Bangladesh, elementary school English and science teacher, 1962-64; Education Development Center, Newton, MA, Peace Corps teacher trainer, 1966-67; African Primary Science program, Kenya, East Africa, designer and developer of curriculum guides, 1967-69; Children's Museum, Boston, MA, senior science developer, 1969-93; UNHCR Refugee Camp, Galang, Indonesia, curriculum developer, 1983; independent consultant, Paris, France, 1983; Exploratorium, San Francisco, CA, artist-in-residence, 1990; Education Development Center, Newton, project director, 1993—. *Exhibitions:* Children's Museum exhibits include *Water,* 1977-79, *Tools,* 1979-81, *Bubbles,* 1981—, *Raceways,* 1982—, *Water Lifting Machines,* 1984, *Tops and Yo-Yos,* 1988, *Salad Dressing Physics,* 1988—, and *Waves and Vibrations,* 1991—. Sculptures include *Ghost of Amelia Earhart,* Exploratorium, 1989-92, *Liquid Light,* Austin Children's Museum, 1993, and *Nested Circles,* Austin Children's Museum, 1993.

■ Awards, Honors

Best Children's Books of 1979 Honorable Mention, New York Academy of Sciences, 1980, for *Bubbles: A Children's Museum Activity Book;* Best Children's Science Book Award, New York Academy of Sciences, 1982, for *Messing around with Water Pumps and Siphons;* Commonwealth Award, Interpretative Scientist Category, 1995.

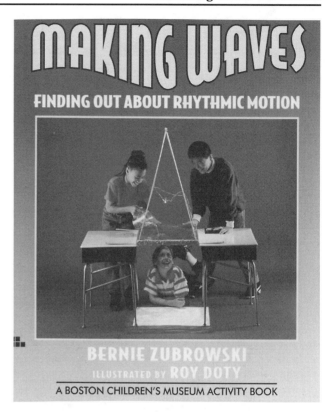

Bernard Zubrowski has developed hands-on exhibits for the Children's Museum in Boston that whet children's curiosity and teach scientific principles like this lesson on rhythmic motion.

■ Writings

CHILDREN'S BOOKS; UNDER NAME BERNIE ZUBROWSKI

Bubbles: A Children's Museum Activity Book, illustrated by Joan Drescher, Little, Brown, 1979.
Milk Carton Blocks: A Children's Museum Activity Book, illustrated by Otto Coontz, Little, Brown, 1979.
Ball-Point Pens: A Children's Museum Activity Book, illustrated by Linda Bourke, Little, Brown, 1979.
Messing around with Baking Chemistry, illustrated by Signe Hanson, Little, Brown, 1981.
Messing around with Water Pumps and Siphons, illustrated by Steve Lindblom, Little, Brown, 1981.
Messing around with Drinking Straw Construction, illustrated by Stefanie Fleischer, Little, Brown, 1981.
Raceways: Having Fun with Balls and Tracks, illustrated by Roy Doty, Morrow, 1985.
Wheels at Work: Building and Experimenting with Models of Machines, illustrated by Roy Doty, Morrow, 1986.
Clocks: Building and Experimenting with Model Timepieces, illustrated by Roy Doty, Morrow, 1988.
Tops: Building and Experimenting with Spinning Toys, illustrated by Roy Doty, Morrow, 1989.
Balloons: Building and Experimenting with Inflatable Toys, illustrated by Roy Doty, Morrow, 1990.

Blinkers and Buzzers: Building and Experimenting with Electricity and Magnetism, illustrated by Roy Doty, Morrow, 1991.

Mirrors: Finding Out about the Properties of Light, illustrated by Roy Doty, Morrow, 1992.

Mobiles: Building and Experimenting with Balancing Toys, illustrated by Roy Doty, Morrow, 1993.

Structures, Cuisenaire Co. of America, 1993.

Inks, Food Colors, and Papers, Cuisenaire Co. of America, 1993.

Tops and Yo-Yos, Cuisenaire Co. of America, 1994.

Making Waves: Finding Out about Rhythmic Motion, illustrated by Roy Doty, Morrow, 1994.

Ice Cream Making and Cake Baking, Cuisenaire Co. of America, 1994.

Shadow Play: Making Pictures with Light and Lenses, illustrated by Roy Doty, Morrow, 1995.

OTHER

Also author of African Primary Science Program Teacher's Guides, including *Construction with Grass, Making Paints, Colors, Liquids, Papers, Inks and Papers,* and *Tools Sink and Float.* Contributor of articles to periodicals, including *Technology Review, Journal of Research in Science Teaching, Day Care and Early Childhood Education,* and *School Science and Math.*

■ Work in Progress

Learning to See, a video case study project to be published and distributed by Heinemann.

■ Sidelights

Bernard Zubrowski's educational science books enable children to perform their own experiments and activities while learning about the properties and functions of the subject of their experiments. While emphasizing the fun aspects of bubble-making in *Bubbles: A Children's Museum Activity Book,* Zubrowski also challenges his readers to think about how the bubbles are formed and the mathematical relationships they demonstrate. Cake ingredients and what they actually do are examined in *Messing around with Baking Chemistry,* several wheel machines are built and the principles of physics used to make them are described in *Wheels at Work: Building and Experimenting with Models of Machines,* and the creation of waves demonstrates rhythmatic motion in nature in *Making Waves: Finding out about Rhythmic Motion.*

In the majority of his books, Zubrowski provides an easily attainable list of materials for the activities, gives a step-by-step explanation for the construction of models and the actual conduction of the experiments, and also explains related scientific principles and properties. "Explicit instructions, experiments that evoke curiosity for further investigation, and a sense of play mark these two Children's Museum Activity Books," asserts Marybeth Franz in a *School Library Journal* review of *Bubbles* and *Ball-Point Pens: A Children's Museum Activity Book.* Karen M. Klockner, writing in *Horn Book,* similarly states: "In each book the text integrates

questions with discussion and provides experiments which will help the reader learn answers as well as questions of his own." Zubrowski's books, concludes a *Bulletin of the Center for Children's Books* reviewer, "are evidence of the excellent results when subject knowledge is paired with experience in working with children who are doing experiments."

"Over the past twenty-five years I have been working with children in a variety of educational settings," Zubrowski told *SATA.* "I have introduced to them and encouraged them to explore many kinds of interesting phenomena or assisted them in the construction of models of simple technologies. They have always reacted very positively and enthusiastically to these materials. It is my long-held view that children are not provided enough opportunities to activate their native curiosity and develop the skills and intellectual abilities for making sense of the world. Teachers in the formal education system certainly do not carry out many 'hands-on' activities and there aren't many parents that encourage this at home.

"Science activity books are one means for promoting and providing directions for this to happen. However, too many of them are superficial in their exposure to phenomena and in their explanations. Many of them are a collection of activities where there is something different on every page. The readers are not encouraged to carry out extended exploration, and attempt to know a phenomena in an deeper way. What I have tried to do over the past twenty years is to write activity books and science curriculum for elementary and middle school which show how this can be done. I try to balance engaging materials in the form of games and interesting explorations with careful scientific explanations. When certain kinds of phenomena are presented in an interesting manner and sequenced in a thoughtful way, children will continue to explore for weeks. All of the activities that I describe in my books were tried out in classrooms and museum programs a number of times before I decided on their suitability for publication. It is my hope that children will try out these activities at home under the supervision of parents, and that teachers will find them a useful supplementary resource in their teaching."

■ Works Cited

Franz, Marybeth, review of *Bubbles: A Children's Museum Activity Book* and *Ball-Point Pens: A Children's Museum Activity Book, School Library Journal,* November, 1979, p. 83.

Klockner, Karen M., review of *Ball-Point Pens, Bubbles,* and *Milk Carton Blocks: A Children's Museum Activity Book, Horn Book,* October, 1979, p. 553.

Review of *Messing around with Water Pumps and Siphons, Bulletin of the Center for Children's Books,* June, 1982.

■ For More Information See

PERIODICALS

Booklist, March 1, 1982, p. 901; July, 1992, p. 1936; July, 1994, p. 1942.
Bulletin of the Center for Children's Books, October, 1990, p. 50.
Kirkus Reviews, November 15, 1979, p. 1330; December 1, 1986, p. 1802.

School Library Journal, February, 1987, pp. 86-87; August, 1994, p. 167.*

*　　*　　*

ZUBROWSKI, Bernie
See ZUBROWSKI, Bernard